TRYING TO HA

MAGGIE JONES is a freelan̲... graduated from Exeter Uni̲...̲ BSc in Biological Sciences. She then worked for five years at the Family Planning Association in their Press and Publications Department, where she wrote reports and edited the quarterly journal *Family Planning Today*. From her work with the FPA she gained considerable knowledge about the problems of infertility. She has also written articles which have appeared in such newspapers and magazines as *The Guardian, World Health, Doctor* and *The Sunday Times*. She is currently editing a series of practical guides for the National Council for Voluntary Organizations. She is married, and lives in London.

Overcoming Common Problems Series

Overcoming Common Problems Series

Overcoming Common Problems

TRYING TO HAVE A BABY?

Overcoming infertility and child loss

Maggie Jones

Recommended by
The Family Planning Association

SHELDON PRESS
LONDON

First published in Great Britain in 1984 by
Sheldon Press, SPCK, Marylebone Road, London NW1 4DU

Thanks are due to George Weidenfeld and Nicolson Ltd. for
permission to quote an extract from *Portrait of a Marriage* by
Nigel Nicolson.

British Library Cataloguing in Publication Data

Jones, Maggie
Trying to have a baby?—Overcoming common problems
1. Infertility—Treatment
I. Title II. Series
616.6'9206 RC889

ISBN 0–85969–440–2
ISBN 0–85969–441–0 Pbk

Typeset by Inforum Ltd, Portsmouth
Printed in Great Britain by
Richard Clay (The Chaucer Press) Ltd
Bungay, Suffolk

Contents

Introduction

Having a baby is one of the most commonplace and yet most extraordinary of human experiences. It is something expected of almost all of us. Mothers say to their daughters: 'When you get married and have children . . .', children play 'mothers and fathers', people save up old clothes, toys, prams for their children and grandchildren. When young people enter sexual relationships or marry, they assume that it is all too easy to have a baby, automatically start using contraception, and probably spend a lot of time worrying that they might be pregnant. The possibility that they might find it difficult or impossible to have children hardly ever occurs to them.

Yet about one in ten couples are 'infertile' according to the medical definition of the word. 'Infertility' is usually defined as the inability of a couple to conceive a child after a year of regular sexual intercourse — that is, at least two or three times a week at around the most fertile time in a woman's monthly cycle or throughout the month. As many as one in six couples will approach their doctor because they are worried about not having conceived.

For many of these couples, their infertility will prove temporary. To begin with, there may not even be a medical problem. Many perfectly fertile men and women have to wait a year or two before a baby is conceived. In other cases, diagnosis of the problem can lead to treatment with quite high rates of success, especially as more is known about the causes of infertility and better techniques for cure are developed.

Another aspect of infertility concerns people who can conceive, but do not carry the baby to term. In fact, a miscarriage is a very common event and affects something like one in seven pregnancies. Many women have one miscarriage and then go on to have the family they want. Even women who suffer several miscarriages, with all the pain and grief that this entails, are likely to have children in the end.

Infertility — and child loss — is one of the most traumatic experiences that people have to face in their lives. It is very difficult to remain calm and optimistic as the hope of having a child seems to fade further and further into the future and the loss presses in all around. Yet for most people, there is hope; and even if it becomes clear that there is none, it is not the end of a fulfilling life.

Women today who are ready to have children, who make the 'decision' to become pregnant, are often very impatient. The Family Planning Association gets calls almost every day from worried men and women, who often say something like: 'I came off the Pill three months ago, and I still haven't got pregnant. Do you think I am infertile?' Or 'We've been trying to conceive for six months. My wife and I are desperate. Is there anywhere where we can go to get help?'

The truth is that getting pregnant can often take a long time. The *average* time is about six months. That means that, on average, for every fertile woman who gets pregnant in the first month of trying, another woman will wait a year. This does not necessarily mean that the first woman is any more fertile than the second; it is just a question of luck.

This may sound very strange; but it is true. It is all explained by the laws of chance. The chain of events which lead up to a successful pregnancy are extremely complex, and in fact even if both the man and woman are quite fertile and make love at the right time in the woman's cycle, there is only about a twenty per cent chance that she will get pregnant.

Studies of women who have been given artificial insemination by donor (AID) — fertile women who have been inseminated at the right time with healthy, active sperm — indeed confirm that about twenty per cent (one in five) of women will get pregnant every month. So if you start off with 100 women, twenty will get pregnant the first month. That leaves eighty, of whom twenty per cent — sixteen women — will get pregnant the second month. That leaves sixty-four, of whom twenty per cent — thirteen women — will get pregnant in the third month. By the sixth month, there will be twenty-six women left, of whom six will get pregnant — again twenty per cent. By the end of the first year, there will still be just under ten per cent of the original 100 women who are not pregnant, even though they may be quite fertile.

The best way to make sense of this is to imagine that you are playing a game of 'Monopoly' and have been sent to jail. In order to get out of jail, you have to throw a 'double' to get out free — the chances of throwing a double are one in six. Everyone will remember the lucky person who gets out at the first throw; equally everyone will remember being stuck there turn after turn without throwing the lucky combination. No one is suggesting that there is anything wrong with the thrower — it is just the laws of chance in operation. So, hard as it is to believe, no one should be seriously worried about their failure to conceive till *at least* a year or eighteen months have passed.

The effect of age on fertility

Age does have an effect on fertility. Women are most fertile in their twenties; by the age of thirty-five there begins to be a substantial drop in fertility. Fertility in women comes to a sudden end at the menopause, which usually occurs somewhere between the ages of forty-five and fifty-five.

Men are more fortunate; male fertility does seem to show a slight decline over the age of forty, but it continues to fall only very slowly, and many men are still fertile well into their sixties and seventies. So, the women who postpone childbearing into their thirties may take a little longer to get pregnant than younger ones; but, unfairly, men need not begin to worry about their age until much later.

Is infertility on the increase?

Some people have said that infertility is on the increase; this is unlikely to be so. But the truth is that attitudes towards planning families have changed, and the problem of infertility is recognized much more than in the past. Two or three generations ago people got married without knowing very much about family planning and sooner or later a baby happened to turn up — or sometimes it didn't. People talked about such things much less, and were more cautious in seeking medical help — which in any case had less to offer then. Today, with the development of effective contraception and the emphasis on family planning, couples tend to decide exactly when they want their children and expect it to happen straightaway. People are much more open about discussing family planning and having children and are more likely to know about what happened to their friends and family, how long it took other people to get pregnant, and so on.

The myth of the easiness of getting pregnant is one that persists, because of, or in spite of, this. People hear all the time of friends getting pregnant while using contraceptives, of people having unplanned children, and literature is full of heroines who get pregnant the very first time they have sexual intercourse, like Tess of the D'Urbervilles. Even real-life heroines like the Princess of Wales get pregnant within a couple of months of marriage.

Kate, a woman in her early thirties, who had fitted in studying for her postgraduate degree with bringing up her first small baby, recalls with a smile:

I remember we decided a three-year gap between our two children was an ideal. That fitted in very well for me too, as far as my studies were concerned; it meant I would have my second baby as soon as I finished my course. So, when Sarah was a little over two years old, I put away my cap and expected to get pregnant. Nothing happened. Six months later, when I was starting to get quite worried, success! I missed my period and was pregnant. But to my horror, at about ten weeks pregnant I started to bleed and went on to have a miscarriage. I was told to wait six months before trying again, which I did; by that time of course a whole year had gone by. I had finished my course and had nothing to do but wait around to get pregnant, as there didn't seem to be any point in getting a job. For the second time I put away my cap and waited. Again, nothing happened. I became absolutely obsessive about it, crying

4

every time my period started, and getting more and more worried about the growing gap between Sarah and this new baby. I became impossible to live with, started to get obsessive about making love at the right time in the month, thought that I would never get pregnant again. Finally my husband sat down with me and told me he couldn't cope. I had one lovely daughter, a loving husband and a nice home, and every qualification for a good job and interesting life, and it wasn't as if I'd been told I was infertile, and here I was sitting around at home and crying and feeling I was wasting my life. That made me think, and I decided to get myself some part-time work and forget about having a baby every month. Three months later I missed my period, and as soon as I got that positive pregnancy test I felt quite ashamed of myself and couldn't imagine what I had been making such a fuss about.

It is often women who have had a career and been used to making decisions about their lives who feel most anxious when they don't conceive right away. They have had control over everything else, and been taught with contraception that fertility too can be controlled. To discover that it is out of your hands can be an alarming experience.

Another factor which has influenced attitudes to fertility is the shortage of children for adoption. Adoption figures for the year 1982 in England and Wales show that only about 2500 babies under the age of two were adopted – nowhere near enough to match the tens of thousands of infertile couples. For most couples only those willing to adopt an older or handicapped child are likely to have success.

This all puts much more pressure on infertile couples today. In the past, a couple who failed to conceive within three or four years could usually go ahead and adopt small babies with comparatively little trouble. One woman, who had one daughter in the 1950s and was then told she would be unable to have any more, remembers quite clearly the day the adoption agency rang up. 'They asked me whether I wanted a girl or a boy. When I said a boy, they then asked: "do you want him to have dark or red hair?" ' And that was how she chose her son.

It was the passing of the Abortion Act in Britain in 1967, followed by similar legislation in other countries, which led to the sharp decline in the numbers of children for adoption. Many people who have difficulty in conceiving or who have lost a baby feel considerable bitterness about abortion. This is understandable, but perhaps unfair, as the availability of safe, legal abortion has undoubtedly prevented a great sum of human misery, both for women who would have been forced to bear a child against their will and for children who would grow up unloved and unwanted. But unquestionably, the effect of legal abortion has been to make fewer children available for adoption, and to increase the pressure on men and women to have their own child.

Can contraception cause infertility?

Many people are concerned, if they fail to conceive rapidly, that long-term use of modern contraceptives such as the Pill or IUD (intra-uterine contraceptive device) could affect their fertility. Women who have had an induced abortion in the past sometimes worry whether this would have any effect on their future fertility.

In the overwhelming majority of cases, contraceptive methods do not affect a woman's fertility. However, some women find when they stop taking the Pill that their periods take a long time to return to normal, and may go for many months without a period at all. This condition is called post-Pill amenorrhoea. In almost all cases a woman's fertility will return to what it was before taking the Pill within a maximum of two years, and usually sooner than this.

Sometimes a woman may have had irregular periods, or not have been ovulating when she went on the Pill. The Pill, which induces a period-like bleed every month, can then mask the problem for years until the woman decides she wants to start a family. If she is then discovered to have a fertility problem, she may blame the Pill for having caused it.

In recent years it has been found that the intra-uterine device, or IUD, is linked to the increased danger of a woman contracting pelvic inflammatory disease, or PID. This is an infection of the womb and Fallopian tubes which, if untreated, can lead to infertility. For this reason doctors are increasingly reluctant to fit IUDs to women who have not had any children.

A past abortion should not affect a woman's future fertility. There is a very small chance – about five per cent – that during the abortion an infection is introduced into the womb, and this might lead to future infertility *in some cases*. However, the risk of this occurring is just as great during a spontaneous abortion, or miscarriage, or during childbirth. In the past, when women were driven to back-street abortions and had the operation carried out in insanitary conditions, the numbers of women who suffered from infections and subsequent infertility were much greater than today.

Why children?

One of the questions that couples who are desperate to have a baby will come up against again and again is, 'Why do you want children?'

It is a question that is asked by doctors at fertility clinics, by adoption agencies, by counsellors, by friends who do not have or do not want children, and often by the couple themselves.

It is almost impossible to say why you want children. There are so many reasons — and many of them, put into black and white, seem selfish or unreal. You want a child because you feel lonely or unfulfilled without one. You want a child to carry on your name, to inherit part of yourself and carry it into the future, to provide a bridge into the world which is to come. You want a child to complete the home and family, to provide fun and companionship. You want a child as the product of your relationship with your husband or wife, a living symbol of your love and closeness to one another.

But there is also a desire which goes much deeper than this, especially for the woman. She may desire the whole experience of pregnancy, birth, breast-feeding, motherhood — she may feel that she has not lived her life fully as a woman without these experiences. And then there is the simple, sensual joy of holding a new baby in your arms and providing it with the one thing it most needs and desires — love. Writer Adrienne Rich, mother of three sons, recalls in her book on motherhood, *Of Woman Born*, her meeting with a friend and new-born baby in the street which awoke in her 'a passionate longing to have, once again, such a small, new being clasped against my body'. She writes: 'How quickly one forgets the pure pleasure of having this new creature, immaculate, perfect'.

In a world which becomes increasingly materialistic and concerned with objects and technology rather than people, the experience of parenthood gives us a chance to discover a deeper, richer kind of life. Few mothers or fathers — today happily often present at the birth — can recall the moments of their children's births without referring to the process as miraculous, astounding. Yet ask a handful of people about having children and a large proportion of them will say, 'Oh, goodness, don't! All those dirty nappies, sleepless nights, the loss of freedom!' As a society we tend to disparage children, see motherhood as being a rather boring task, needing few skills, driving mothers to despair and depression ('She's stuck at home all day with the children'). These negative attitudes tend to make us undervalue the joys of parenthood and underestimate the terrible loss and tragedy of infertility when it occurs.

This book hopes to bring home the suffering faced by those who experience infertility or child loss, but also to provide reassurance and hope. The loss of a child is usually finally swallowed up by the joy of a new birth. Much infertility can now be cured by medical science. And even where all fails, many childless couples find a way to lead a rich and fulfilling life.

1

The Causes and Cures of Infertility

When people understand the delicate and complicated structure and function of the male and female reproductive systems, and what is necessary to lead to a normal pregnancy, the reaction is often surprise that people manage to get pregnant so easily, not that they should find it difficult.

What needs to happen for a couple to conceive is, briefly, this:

The man produces enough healthy, active sperm. The sperm must be deposited into the vagina, near the entrance to the womb (cervix) and swim up through the mucus produced by the cervix (cervical mucus) through the womb and into the Fallopian tubes. The woman must have produced a healthy egg, which is released by the ovary and swept up into the Fallopian tubes by the finger-like projections at the end of the tubes (fimbriae). The egg is fertilized in the Fallopian tubes, and since it may live for as little as twelve to twenty-four hours, and since the sperm live only one to three days, the couple must have made love at the right time in the month for the egg to be waiting in the tube. The fertilized egg must then move down the Fallopian tube and into the womb, aided by the hair-like cilia which line the tube, where it must implant into the lining of the womb (endometrium) and continue to grow. The body in the ovary from which the egg was released, the corpus luteum, must produce enough of the hormone progesterone to sustain the pregnancy till the end of three months, when the placenta takes over. The womb must be structurally sound and capable of expansion and the cervix strong enough to hold the baby in until it is ready to be born and natural labour begins.

It only takes something to go wrong at any stage and the chance of a pregnancy is lost for at least that cycle. This partly

Fig. 1 Female Sexual Organs

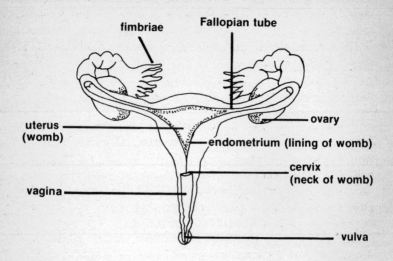

Fig. 2 Male Sexual Organs

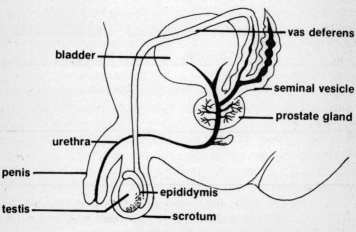

explains why it can take so long for even a perfectly fertile couple to succeed in starting a pregnancy. However, at each stage there may be a more serious, underlying problem — the result is infertility.

The diagrams on page 10 show the male and female reproductive systems.

Hormonal problems

One of the major causes of infertility in women is a hormonal problem. Unless the complex hormonal cycles which govern a woman's menstrual cycle are exactly right, the chances are she will not ovulate and therefore cannot conceive.

The woman's menstrual cycle is under the control of the pituitary gland in the brain. The pituitary itself is under the control of another gland, the hypothalamus.

The pituitary produces a hormone, FSH (follicle-stimulating hormone), which controls the production of the hormone oestrogen by the ovary. It also prepares one of the follicles inside the ovary to release its egg. Oestrogen is also responsible for causing the lining of the womb to thicken, ready to receive a fertilized egg. Finally, a second pituitary hormone called LH (luteinizing hormone) is necessary to cause the ovary to release its egg.

After the egg is released, the corpus luteum begins to shrink and the levels of oestrogen and progesterone decrease. The lining of the womb then disintegrates, and menstrual bleeding is the result.

The drop in levels of oestrogen and progesterone in their turn stimulate the pituitary to produce more FSH, and the cycle begins again.

If the egg is fertilized, however, the corpus luteum continues to produce oestrogen and progesterone until the placenta attaching the foetus to the wall of the womb is mature enough to produce the necessary hormones itself.

Lack of ovulation, then, is caused by inadequate pituitary hormones, or by poor timing in their release. Many women who do not ovulate or ovulate irregularly will already be aware of the fact that they have irregular or light periods, or even no periods at all. Some women, however, do bleed, and bleed heavily, without ovulating regularly.

Since the pituitary is ultimately controlled by the hypothalamus, anything which affects the hypothalamus can affect the pituitary. The hypothalamus is a very sensitive gland, and can be affected by severe emotional as well as physical stresses in a woman's life. Many women will be aware that the stress of travel, severe worry, or the excitement of being in love, can delay her period or even cause her to miss one. This is because the hypothalamus has stopped or delayed the pituitary in producing its hormones. Severe weight loss, as in the condition of anorexia nervosa where teenage girls refuse to eat, can also stop the production of necessary hormones; so can severe obesity or excessive physical activity. Sometimes — quite rarely — the Pill will stop the hypothalamus from working for months after its use has been discontinued.

It can be that the stress and worry of being infertile, or wondering if you are infertile, can also affect the hypothalamus. Some women who have had perfectly regular periods suddenly find, especially if they start to have to take their temperature daily to fill in the fertility clinic's temperature charts, that their periods go completely haywire. Severe depression can also affect the functioning of the hypothalamus and stop ovulation.

Fertility drugs
However, for many of the women who never or seldom ovulate there is now a cure through the use of one of the so-called 'fertility drugs'. There are two main kinds: those which prod the pituitary into producing FSH and LH on time, and those which replace FSH and LH if this approach fails.

Clomiphene (brand name Clomid) is an artificial drug which triggers FSH and LH release in the pituitary. It has been in use now for many years and seems to induce ovulation in about eighty per cent of women treated (although not all these will succeed in getting pregnant). Clomiphene is usually given on the fifth day of a woman's menstrual cycle and is taken for five days to induce ovulation. Sometimes a combination of clomiphene and human chorionic gonadotrophin (HCG) at day fourteen will induce women to ovulate who would not do so on clomiphene alone. Clomiphene also seems to help women with a progesterone deficiency.

The other fertility drugs are HMG (human menopausal gonadotrophin) (brand name Pergonal) and HCG. The first is a hormonal extract similar to LH from the urine of pregnant women. About ninety per cent of women will ovulate under this treatment, though again not all will conceive and some who do will go on to have miscarriages. It is the use of these drugs which causes most of the multiple pregnancies which hit the news from time to time. About twenty to thirty per cent of pregnancies resulting from this treatment will be twins — or more.

Pergonal works by preparing the follicles which release the egg to ripen; a separate injection of HCG is needed at the appropriate time to stimulate ovulation. One of the problems with taking Pergonal is that it is such a potent drug that the ovaries may become overstimulated. This means that its dosage must be monitored almost daily by measuring the level of oestrogen in the blood or urine. Many women who have had to take Pergonal recall the visits to the clinic with large bottles of urine which they have had to collect and transport — quite a feat for a working woman. A small percentage (one to three per cent) of women will develop hyperstimulated ovaries and have to go into hospital for a few days until their ovaries reduce in size.

A new development which may provide an alternative to Pergonal and help overcome some of these problems is a 'pump' which, attached to the woman's body, delivers small, even doses of hormone through a fine needle and reduces the risks of overstimulation. However, having to carry the pump day and night and having the needle repositioned regularly also has its disadvantages.

For those who will not ovulate on any of these drugs, there is some hope with a drug called bromocriptine. This seems to work in women who have a high level of a hormone called prolactin in their bloodstreams, which is normally only produced in any quantity during breast-feeding. Bromocriptine acts by stopping the pituitary from producing prolactin, and FSH can then be released as usual. Ovulation is normally induced in about ninety-five per cent of women with this problem.

One reason why conception does not always occur when clomiphene has induced ovulation is that clomiphene seems to prevent the cervical mucus from becoming more fluid so that the sperm can swim through it into the womb. This problem can sometimes be overcome by giving oestrogen as well in the few days before ovulation.

Some infertile women have a rare condition called polycystic ovaries, where the ovaries produce many small cysts instead of releasing eggs and may become enlarged. This is probably caused by a hormonal imbalance. The condition can be dealt with either by treatment with Clomid or Pergonal, or sometimes by removing a small wedge-shaped section of the ovary. This surgical treatment seems to make the ovaries respond by releasing eggs, but it only has a temporary effect and is clearly less desirable than using hormone treatments.

Surgical problems

The second major cause of infertility in the woman are scars caused by past illnesses or surgery, or structural abnormalities.

It is quite well known that one of the unfortunate consequences of untreated venereal disease, especially gonorrhoea, is infertility, as the infection spreads into the womb and up the Fallopian tubes. The problem with gonorrhoea is that many women — as many as eighty per cent — never have any severe symptoms with it. In most of these the infection will remain localized, and the body's natural defences may kill off the organism. In other cases, the disease may invade and damage the Fallopian tubes before symptoms such as abdominal pain and an increased vaginal discharge drive a woman to seek medical treatment. The increased incidence of gonorrhoea over the past years will inevitably have increased infertility from this cause.

Other infections than gonorrhoea can cause tubal scarring and blockage. Pelvic inflammatory disease (PID), if untreated, can lead to infertility. PID can start after infection with VD, after an induced abortion or a miscarriage, or after childbirth, or after a woman has had surgery in the pelvic region. As with gonorrhoea, once the infection has cleared up there may be scarring which blocks the tubes or makes them unable to function properly, and the result is infertility. Other infections — sexually transmitted or otherwise — which can affect fertility are chlamydia and mycoplasmas.

A further cause of problems with the tubes is previous abdominal surgery, in which there was bleeding into the abdominal cavity. Bleeding or trauma to the tissues may result in the formation of scar tissue or adhesions, which may then fix the tubes, ovaries or womb into an unnatural position, making conception difficult or impossible. One leading microsurgeon, who has specialized in repairing damaged Fallopian tubes, has criticized surgeons for not taking enough care when performing surgery in the abdominal region. Of 108 women with tubal damage referred to the Hammersmith hospital over a three-month period, seventy-three per cent had had previous pelvic surgery.

Another disease which can lead to infertility is endometriosis. This condition, which may affect as many as five to ten per cent of women at some stage in their reproductive lives, is caused by patches of the tissue which lines the womb, the endometrium, becoming deposited outside the womb. This tissue behaves just like the womb lining, and thickens and bleeds regularly with the menstrual cycle. Scar tissue is then formed, and this may block the ends of the Fallopian tubes, or adhesions may form which prevent the tube from being close enough to the ovary to pick up the egg and waft it down towards the womb.

Endometriosis can be treated by a number of drugs: birth control Pills or progesterone, or a drug called Danazol, which blocks production of the two pituitary hormones. The idea behind these treatments is to switch off the menstrual cycle, which will stop the patches of endometriosis growing and bleeding; after several months the endometrial patches will have faded away. The remains of endometrial tissue and any scar tissue which has formed can be removed by careful surgery. If the endometriosis is very severe, surgery may be necessary as a first step.

Other physical problems which affect fertility are the presence of fibroids in the womb, which can be removed by surgery, or malformations of the womb, such as the presence of a dividing wall or septum, which again can often be corrected by surgery.

Today, increasing skill in carrying out delicate surgery to correct these kinds of infertility gives women a better chance of achieving a pregnancy than ever before. In particular, the techniques of microsurgery, where very fine instruments are used and the operation carried out with the aid of a microscope, can help many women with blocked Fallopian tubes. The success rate of surgery varies widely according to the extent and location of damage; it may be as high as seventy per cent or as low as five per cent in some cases.

It is much simpler and more effective to treat a small damaged portion of the main body of the tube than it is to reconstruct the delicate fimbriae at the far end of the tube.

Ectopic pregnancy

A particularly tragic cause of infertility is a tubal or ectopic pregnancy. This means that when the egg is fertilized in the Fallopian tube it remains there, instead of moving down into the womb, and as it grows it swells and may finally burst through the Fallopian tube, causing considerable damage.

An ectopic pregnancy is thus both the loss of one pregnancy and a possible barrier to further conception. Often, the function of the tube in which the pregnancy occurred is permanently damaged. However, if there is much bleeding into the abdominal cavity, there is the risk of adhesions on the other tube and ovary as well. It is estimated that about fifty per cent of women who have an ectopic pregnancy will never conceive again.

Often the ectopic pregnancy was caused by there being some

existing damage to the tube, which prevented the egg from passing down the tube in the normal way. It is also a risk where there has been some tubal surgery, as the fine hair-like cilia inside the tube which move the egg along may not function although the tube itself is intact.

An ectopic pregnancy is usually very painful and can even be life-threatening. Any pain in the abdominal region or bleeding during early pregnancy should be immediately reported to a doctor. If the ectopic pregnancy is diagnosed before it has burst the tube, the pregnancy can be removed surgically, and this is both less dangerous for the woman and also gives a greater possibility of successful reconstruction of the damaged tube.

'Test-tube' babies

If surgery is unsuccessful, there is new hope for women with blocked or damaged tubes through *in vitro* fertilization, more commonly known as the 'test-tube baby' technique. Here all that is necessary is for the woman to have healthy, functioning ovaries, and a healthy womb. What happens is that through a minor operation a number of mature eggs are removed from the surface of the ovaries. The eggs are then fertilized by the man's sperm in the laboratory — this is the 'test-tube' part of the procedure. The eggs are watched through a microscope to make sure that they are dividing normally, and after a few days one or more fertilized eggs, or embryos, are inserted into the womb. It is usual to introduce two to four embryos as they seem to help one another 'take' — usually only one survives but most parents-to-be are quite happy with the idea of twins! It then remains to monitor the woman carefully to see whether the embryo has implanted and whether the pregnancy is proceeding normally.

Although the technique sounds very simple, in reality it is very complicated and much is still not understood. Many embryos fail to implant, and sometimes there are hormonal problems too which seem to prevent the continuation of the pregnancy. While it does present hope to many women in the future, at the moment the chances for any one woman undertaking the procedure are quite poor. At the only NHS 'test-tube baby' clinic the success rate is less than ten per cent. Better success rates — up to thirty per cent — are claimed at private clinics, but each attempt costs the couple around £1000.

Infertility and the man

In about forty per cent of infertile couples, the problem will be found to lie with the man. Unfortunately, not as much is known about the causes of male infertility as with the female, and the hopes for a cure are therefore less high. Despite the popular misapprehension, most male infertility has *nothing whatever* to do with a man's virility and sexual prowess.

The male reproductive system is under the same kind of control as the female's, and the same hormones from the hypothalamus and the pituitary play a part. The main difference is that sperm production goes on continuously, without anything approaching the woman's monthly cycle. The sperm are produced inside the testes in long convoluted tubes called the seminiferous tubules. These eventually lead through a series of ducts into an area called the epididymis, where sperm are stored. The testes not only produce sperm, but also the male hormone testosterone, which is responsible for all the man's secondary sexual characteristics — his hair growth, muscular body, deep voice, etc. Testosterone is also necessary for the production of healthy sperm.

When sperm have been produced inside the testis, they pass through into the epididymis where they mature further and become motile (capable of swimming). From the epididymis, the sperm travel through a long tube called the vas deferens. At the top of the vas deferens are a series of glands — the seminal vesicles, the prostate gland, and Cowper's gland — which together produce the fluid (semen) which is ejaculated at orgasm during sexual intercourse.

The whole process of sperm manufacture takes about three months, during most of which the sperm are maturing in the epididymis. When they are mature, they are temporarily stored at the top of the vas deferens. When a man becomes sexually excited and he has an erection, the vas deferens pumps up more sperm, and the sperm mix with the glandular secretions to form the semen. At orgasm, the entrance to the bladder is blocked by a muscular reflex, and the semen is ejaculated through the penis.

What can go wrong
One of the simplest causes of male infertility is simply too much heat! It has long been known that if the testes are too hot sperm production falls. That is why the scrotum hangs outside the abdominal cavity, where it remains 2 to 3°C cooler than the rest of the body. Undescended testes, which remain in the abdominal cavity instead of descending into the scrotal sac in the first years of a boy's life, result in complete infertility if not corrected. Recent fashions for tight-fitting underwear and trousers all overheat the testicles and can lead to a drop in sperm production which could make all the difference to a man's ability to fertilize his partner. Too hot a working environment — as with a lorry-driver sitting all day in a hot cab — or too many hot baths can also lower a man's fertility.

Feverish illness can temporarily depress sperm production, and as it takes three months for the sperm to be produced the effect is only noticeable three months after the illness. Some drugs, and severe stress, can also decrease sperm production.

However, the *main* reason for male infertility is a low sperm count. There is very rarely no sperm at all, but often the sperm are too few in number, are abnormal, or incapable of swimming rapidly. Although in some cases there is some obvious cause for the problem — such as a previous infection, adult mumps with inflammation of the testicles, undescended testes in childhood — in many cases no obvious cause can be found.

Infections such as gonorrhoea may cause scarring of the vas deferens, especially where it joins the epididymis, causing a complete blockage to sperm. This problem can be treated surgically, but unfortunately with disappointing results. One reason for a poor success rate may be that antibodies to sperm are formed, either as a result of the infection itself or because the sperm, which cannot be ejaculated, are reabsorbed by the body and give rise to antibody production. This is one reason why vasectomy reversals, even if successful surgically, do not always result in successful pregnancies.

Infection of the glands, such as the prostate, may also result in subsequent infertility.

Antibodies to sperm produced by the man himself are thought to be responsible for infertility in a proportion of men attending infertility clinics. Until recently there was little that could be done, but several techniques are now being tried out. These include separating sperm from the antibodies by spinning the semen very rapidly in a centrifuge, and then using artificial insemination; and using immunosuppressive drugs.

About thirty per cent of male infertility problems are thought to be due to the presence of a varicocele — a varicose vein around the top of the testis. This condition is also found in some fertile men, and it is not known exactly why a varicocele can cause infertility. One theory is that increased blood flow through the distended vein may cause a temperature rise in the testes which affects sperm production.

Varicocele is one of the few causes of male infertility for which there is a good chance of cure. A simple operation to tie off the vein results in an improvement of sperm quantity and quality in about two-thirds of cases, and thus increases the chance of conception.

Some low sperm counts, however, occur in otherwise perfectly healthy men, without any obvious cause to explain it away. It has often been thought that hormonal problems similar to those resulting in anovulation in women might be the cause, so a variety of drugs used successfully on women — clomiphene, HMG and HCG — have been tried on men. Individual doctors claim some success with these treatments, but results are not conclusive. Another therapy which was tried is testosterone rebound, where doses of testosterone were given to depress sperm production, and its withdrawal was supposed to stimulate new sperm production to greater levels than before treatment. Again, results have been inconclusive, and some experts believe that all these treatments are mere guesswork — they may work in some instances without knowing why, but more often they are no more effective than no treatment at all. Some men, however, will be willing to try anything — and even if treatment fails, they may comfort themselves by knowing they are helping with research.·

One treatment which may offer hope to the man who has a low sperm count is that of the 'split-ejaculate' technique. The idea behind this is that the first part of a man's semen is the richest in sperm. If the first part of several ejaculations are pooled together, and then stored, and the semen then introduced into the woman by artificial insemination, the woman should have a greater chance of conceiving. However, in some men with low sperm counts there are too many abnormal or immature sperm present for this technique to be any help.

Artificial insemination by donor (AID)

Because medical knowledge and treatment of male infertility is so poor, the main hope for a couple where the man is discovered to have the fertility problem is artificial insemination by donor — AID.

AID means simply that semen donated by an anonymous donor is introduced into the woman's vagina. Donors are carefully screened by the doctors concerned to make sure that there are no genetic problems which might affect a child, and are young, intelligent, healthy and psychologically well-balanced — in fact a great many of them are medical students. There will be some attempt to match the donor with the husband for such characteristics as hair and eye colour, height and blood group, so that the child might bear a similar appearance to the man who will bring it up as his own.

The woman receiving AID will have to go to the clinic at the most fertile time in her cycle to be inseminated. If her periods are irregular, she may be given ovulation-inducing drugs so that the doctors will be able to predict the best time to do the insemination. The semen is introduced into the vagina with a tube and deposited near the cervix, and the woman is usually advised to lie on her back for about half-an-hour to allow the sperm to swim through into her womb. Sometimes the insemination is done twice at around the time of ovulation to increase the chance of conception.

Rates of conception with AID are about the same as with ordinary sexual intercourse. This means that you may get pregnant straightaway, or may have to wait several months. Once you have conceived, the pregnancy will be no different from any other pregnancy.

AID is a subject surrounded by a certain amount of secrecy and hypocrisy. First, it is not easily available through the NHS and there are often long waiting lists, so many people have to go to private clinics who offer the service. Secondly, an AID child is technically not a legitimate child; the father is supposed to formally adopt the baby after its birth. In practice, few people want to go through all this rigmarole and simply register the baby as their own. At the time of writing a commission is sitting to discuss the legal questions surrounding AID, and this is one area where there may be a change.

Settling for AID is not a simple matter and there are many questions to be asked and answered by the couple themselves. Some of these will be discussed in Chapter 2.

Infertility and the couple

Sometimes infertility is caused not by a problem in either one or other partner, but by a joint problem in that particular couple. Problems of compatibility may be responsible for infertility in a surprising number of cases.

The woman's vagina is in many ways a hostile environment for the man's sperm. It is normally more acid than sperm like, although the sperm are protected from this by the alkalinity of the semen itself. The sperm have to be able to swim quite rapidly through the woman's cervical mucus, which becomes thin and fluid around the time of ovulation to facilitate their progress, and into the womb if they are to be able to fertilize the egg.

Sometimes, however, the sperm do not survive very well in the woman's cervical mucus. This may be because the cervical mucus does not change sufficiently around ovulation to let the sperm through. When in its usual, tacky form, the cervical mucus forms a sort of 'plug' which helps prevent bacteria and other unwanted organisms from entering the womb. It also acts as an effective barrier to sperm. This problem can often be helped by giving the woman oestrogens to take before the time of ovulation.

Sometimes the woman's vagina can be too acid for the sperm to survive well in it. This may be the effect of low-grade infection in the vagina — which should of course be treated — or the result of the woman's own body chemistry. This problem can be overcome by the woman having an alkaline douche shortly before having intercourse.

Another cause of infertility is when the woman produces antibodies to the man's sperm. These antibodies may be present in the cervical mucus, and effectively kill off any sperm before they are able to swim through into the womb. The outlook may sound hopeless, but in fact if the man wears a condom during intercourse for six to nine months, the woman will not be exposed to sperm and will cease producing antibodies. When she starts having sex again, there is a good chance she will get pregnant before the antibodies build up to harmful levels again.

Fertility tests

Investigations into what is wrong with a couple who fail to conceive are carried out at a special fertility clinic to which couples will usually be referred by their doctor. On first going to the clinic, the man and woman will be seen together.

Examination of the male and female sexual organs
At the first appointment, the doctor will examine both the male and female reproductive organs. For the man, this simply involves inspecting the testicles (for varicocele or any other abnormality). For the woman, it means a pelvic examination. The doctor will insert a speculum (a surgical instrument) so that he or she can view the vagina and the cervix, and may take swabs for testing if a vaginal infection is suspected. A cervical smear may also be taken.

The doctor will then insert one or two fingers into the vagina and press on the outside of the abdomen with the other. This may well show up any problems like scarring from previous infections, fibroids, ovarian cysts, and other problems.

The doctor will probably take the opportunity when he examines you alone to ask about any relevant details which one partner might like to conceal from the other, such as a past episode of venereal disease, a past pregnancy, and so on, which might give clues as to the fertility problem. The man might wish his partner not to know that he had had a past affair and made someone pregnant, and the woman might prefer that he does not know she once had an abortion.

At the first interview the doctor will inevitably ask personal questions about your sex life, such as how often you have intercourse, and so on. It is best to be honest, even if you feel that everyone else must have sex six times a week and you only do it once or twice. The doctor may suggest changing your pattern of sexual intercourse, and this can be one of the most difficult problems faced by infertile couples, as can be seen in Chapter 2.

Normally, when they have registered and made the appointment, the woman will be issued with temperature charts and the man with a plastic jar in which to produce a semen specimen. By the time the couple go to see the specialist, there should be some results for him or her to assess.

Temperature charts

The basal body temperature chart is a very useful tool for both the fertility specialist and the woman who has difficulty in conceiving because it shows whether or not she is ovulating without having to carry out any complicated medical tests. What you have to do is take your temperature every morning the moment you wake up, before you sit up, get out of bed, drink a cup of tea or start talking. Your basal body temperature is the temperature of your body at *complete rest*.

At the time of ovulation there is a small but distinct rise in the body's temperature. This is because production of the hormone progesterone, which occurs immediately after ovulation, slightly increases the body's temperature at rest.

The increase in temperature is only a small one—between 0.4 to 1.0 degrees F or 0.2 to 0.5 degrees C. Nevertheless it is a significant one. After ovulation, the body temperature stays elevated until just before menstruation begins, when it drops back to the lower temperature. Textbook diagrams of the normal basal body temperature chart look like Fig. 3 (page 26).

However, in reality the picture is likely to be much less straightforward, and some temperature charts need professional interpretation. Fig. 4 shows one example (page 27).

The temperature chart can also show if you are not ovulating, in which case there is no rise in temperature (Fig. 5, page 28). It can also show that, although you are ovulating, progesterone levels do not remain high enough for a pregnancy to establish itself—this is known as a short luteal phase. It can also be the first sign that you are pregnant if you do succeed in conceiving; the temperature will rise and stay at the same high level for well over the fourteen to sixteen days after ovulation, when a period normally begins (Fig. 6, page 29).

Most doctors want you to go on doing the temperature charts while you are having fertility investigations as they help with some of the tests which have to be carried out at a certain time in the menstrual cycle. At the very least you need to do them for three months to show that the one chart in which you did or did not ovulate was not simply a fluke.

The sperm count

Similarly, the sperm count is a simple test which will tell the specialist much of what he or she wants to know about a man's fertility. He simply has to produce a specimen of semen by masturbation after two or three days' abstinence and take it immediately to the laboratory where it can be tested. If the couple do not live too far from the clinic, this can be done in the privacy and comfort of home. It is important to deliver the sample within two or three hours, as otherwise sperm will begin to die and a false result may be obtained.

There is some debate as to what is a 'normal' level of sperm in

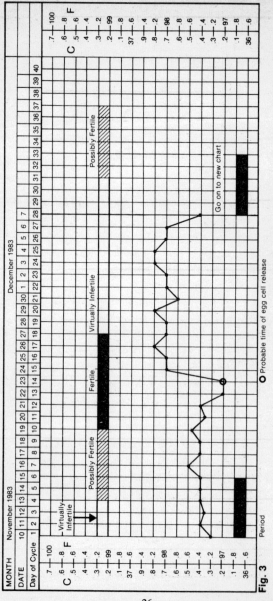

Fig. 3

○ Probable time of egg cell release

THE CAUSES AND CURES OF INFERTILITY

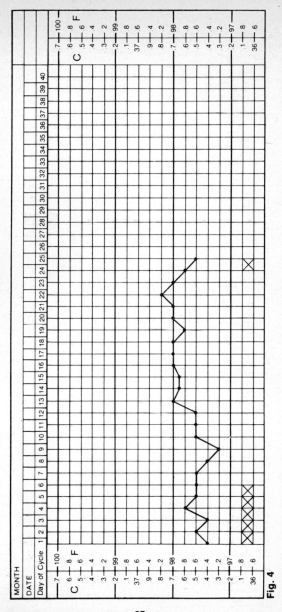

Fig. 4

27

TRYING TO HAVE A BABY?

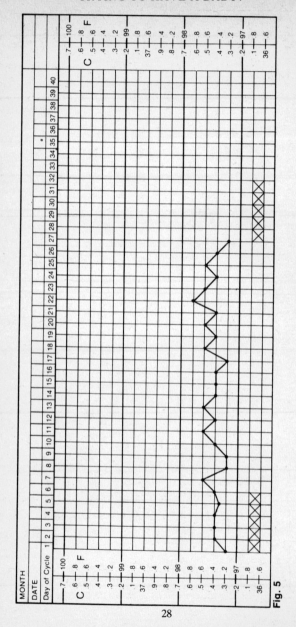

Fig. 5

28

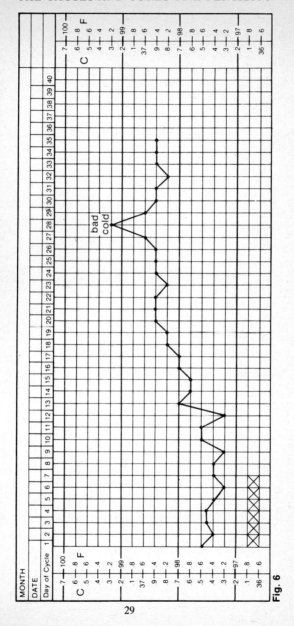

Fig. 6

29

the semen. Most men produce an average of two to six millilitres (ml) of semen (about a teaspoonful) and these should contain at least twenty million sperm per millilitre to be normal, or at least to be considered capable of fertilizing the egg. If there are over fifty million per millilitre, sperm number should certainly present no problem.

Numbers are not all that is important, however. At least fifty to sixty per cent of the sperm should be motile for conception to be easy. Further, at least sixty per cent of sperm should be normal in appearance — if a large number are abnormal, these will not be able to fertilize the egg and the chances of conception are therefore much poorer.

The post-coital test
The post-coital test is another simple and valuable procedure. When your period starts you are asked to ring in to the clinic to make an appointment for the most fertile time in your cycle — you will have to help estimate this by reference to your temperature charts. You will then be asked to make love, either the night before or the morning before the test, and then the woman has to go in to the clinic. The doctor will remove some of the cervical mucus with a tube inserted through a speculum and placed under a slide for examination under a microscope. If you ask, you may be allowed to look for yourself.

The post-coital test shows how many sperm there are and how well they are swimming through the cervical mucus. This will depend on the sperm count, the quality of the cervical mucus, and whether there are antibodies against sperm which are preventing them surviving well in the mucus. If the test is not very good, you will probably be asked to repeat it in the next cycle; you may have two or three such tests. It is not always easy to get the timing right, and it is important to be sure that any one result is not a fluke. If it looks as if there is a compatibility problem, other tests of sperm and cervical mucus can be done.

Progesterone peak
Another test for ovulation which can be done is to take a blood test

at the point in a woman's cycle when the amount of progesterone is at its peak — in a 28-day cycle this is around day twenty-four. If there is a high level of progesterone in the bloodstream, this is a good indication that you have ovulated.

Endometrial biopsy

Another test to establish ovulation is to take an endometrial biopsy. This means that a small part of the lining of the womb is removed under a general anaesthetic, and the tissue examined to see whether the lining of the womb has gone through the usual changes under the influence of progesterone after ovulation. If both the temperature charts and blood test show that you are ovulating, it may be an unnecessary procedure. Because it is usually done under a general anaesthetic, it is often combined with another procedure such as laparoscopy (see below).

Tubal insufflation test (Rubin's test)

In this test carbon dioxide gas is blown through the womb and tubes and the gas pressure is measured. If you have no blockages, the gas should pass through freely and you will feel a pain in the shoulders afterwards caused by gas in the abdominal cavity. The gas is absorbed harmlessly by the body very quickly. It was thought that this test could help to clear any small blockage or adhesion in the tubes, but it is not clear that this really is so.

Hysterosalpingogram

This test — an X-ray of the womb and tubes — is carried out by injecting a small quantity of dye into the womb and tubes and taking an X-ray. If there is a blockage in either tube, this can be clearly pinpointed. If there is no blockage, the dye will pass through the tubes and into the abdominal cavity where it is absorbed. Most women will have cramping, like a bad period pain, with this test. Sometimes one or other or even both tubes will go into spasm during this test, and appear to be blocked when they are not. Giving a muscle relaxant may help overcome this problem.

Laparoscopy

Laparoscopy is carried out under a general anaesthetic. A small incision is made into the abdominal cavity at the navel and a small instrument like a miniature periscope passed through so that the internal organs can be viewed. This will allow the extent of blockage or scarring of the tube, and any adhesions, to be seen clearly. It will also allow the doctor to see any abnormalities of the ovaries.

If all these tests were carried out rapidly in quick succession, they could probably all be carried out within a few months. Since they have to be undertaken at different times in the menstrual cycle, it would be difficult to complete them before this. In practice, they are usually spread out over a much longer period, often over a year or more. This is partly because doctors hope that a woman might get pregnant before they get on to the more complicated and invasive tests, involving general anaesthetic and therefore some small risk to the patient. However, it does mean that a couple may have no real answer to the cause of their infertility for a long time, which can increase the anxiety and trauma that they face.

2

Reactions to Infertility

The realization that you may have a fertility problem is something that comes gradually to most couples. But at every stage, as you do not conceive and the possibility of having a child seems further and further away, there is a sense of loss and grief. Sometimes the knowledge may come suddenly — when a test at the clinic reveals that you have blocked tubes, or when you have a low sperm count — and then the impact of this news can be overwhelming. For others, there may just be a gradual realization over months or years that conception is very unlikely to occur.

Many infertile people — or those with a fertility problem — suffer from the same grief that you would suffer if you were bereaved; the sense of loss and the intensity of it can be just as great as the loss of a child who has lived. Yet there is a difference. The first difference is that, when a person dies, there is no hope of their coming back to life; with infertility, there is often, at least for a long time, hope that a child will come. This complicates the process of grief. Secondly, with infertility, the grief has no object; there is no child, no person, no photographs, no memories to think of and to mourn. Peter and Diane Houghton, who are childless and formed the National Association for the Childless in Britain, have called the kind of grief experienced by childless couples 'unfocused grief', because it cannot be focused on any one person or event.

The emotions which many people feel at the slow revelation of their infertility are well summed up in these two accounts:

I had always assumed that one day I would marry and have children; it never really occurred to me that there would be anything else. I was one of three sisters, and we had a close, happy family, and I suppose that's what I wanted for myself.

After John and I had been married two years, we started to think about having a baby. I came off the Pill and we looked forward to having the baby with joy and excitement. I remember that it really gave us both a kick when we made love, knowing that another life might come from it. It made it seem somehow more real.

After six months I hadn't conceived, and I began to get a little worried. My mother had always got pregnant straightaway, in fact the problem for her seemed to have been stopping getting pregnant, and my younger sister was always cheerfully told she was a 'mistake'. I talked to my mother and she said not to worry, lots of people took a long time, her sister had to wait two years and a baby turned up all right.

So we went on till the end of the year, and Christmas came and went, and I still wasn't pregnant. It's funny how family occasions like Christmas seem to make it all much worse. I had been getting more and more reluctant to have sex, just didn't see the point I suppose, and finally John and I had an enormous row about it. I suppose it was a good thing, a lot came out and we finally admitted to one another how angry and how frightened about it we both were. We agreed I would go and see my doctor and ask to go to see a fertility specialist.

I went to see her, and she was very reassuring, and said she'd get me on the waiting list though we might have to wait a few months. She said we shouldn't worry since a year wasn't a very long time, but since I was in my late twenties there was no reason to waste time. That made me feel a lot better, as if we were finally doing something about it, and I was quietly confident that I would get pregnant anyway before we had to go to the clinic.

We got our appointment and then they asked us to start the temperature charts. That was when the trouble all began. I knew roughly what they were supposed to do, and that my temperature was supposed to go up, and it didn't. I got hysterical about it, and John kept saying I was silly and that he was sure it *was* going up, but neither of us could be sure.

When we got to the clinic we were both in a state of terrible nerves. The specialist, instead of giving us the results of the sperm test and looking at the temperature charts, asked us detailed personal histories and explained things to us, which neither of us were able to take in. Then when he gave the sperm count result and said it was 'normal', and looked at the temperature charts and said that I 'seemed to be ovulating' I was too relieved to take in most of the other things he said.

We were told when was the best time to make love, and told when to make the next appointment, and that was that. We both went home in a state of optimism and hoped that no other tests would be necessary.

But we still didn't conceive. The temperature charts started to dominate our sex life, and we had endless rows because John was too tired just on the night when I had worked out we had the best chance, or had to go away on business just at the most fertile time in my cycle. Every month seemed incredibly important. And then the tests at the clinic somehow didn't seem very conclusive. They said my cervical mucus wasn't very good, and they suggested a douche before intercourse, which of course made our sex life even less spontaneous. The investigations proved nothing major was the matter, but still I didn't conceive.

At that point I began to get terribly depressed and angry about our childlessness. Every time I went out in the street I saw pregnant women — I had never noticed them before. Children in prams and small screaming toddlers suddenly changed from being a noisy nuisance to being the thing I wanted most in the world. I saw a baby once in the post office with an enormous red birthmark on her face, and I was overcome with a sense of how much I would have loved that baby had it been mine, despite its disfigurement. When people talked about how handicapped babies would be better left to die, I was shocked at their callousness, and thought that they just didn't understand how much a baby could be loved and wanted.

The worst thing was the jealousy I felt. I was jealous of everyone who had a baby, and the closer they were to me the more jealous I was. John's sister rang up one day to say she was pregnant and I felt that I could have stabbed her with rage. I refused to go and see her all the time she was pregnant, and when we were sent an invitation to the christening I tore it into little pieces and hid it in the bin so that John wouldn't see it and expect me to go.

The clinic tried me on oestrogen pills before ovulation to help 'improve' my cervical mucus. By now I didn't expect anything to happen, and I was shocked when, three months later, my period failed to turn up as usual. I even thought, oh, that really is the end, even my periods have packed up now. When I had the test result and it was positive I can't tell you how I felt. I rang John and he left the office at once and we went for a long walk and just couldn't believe it was true.

Everybody else was pregnant — except me!

Some basic facts of life you do not — or at least *I* did not — question. I assumed that I would marry, that I would have children, that we would live happily ever after. Is that a conditioned reflex or a naive response to life? Anyway, item one was accomplished — I married at the good age of twenty-five and moved to an old house which we decorated and did the usual newly-married things.

I stopped taking the Pill and we planned a baby quickly, as I was then twenty-six or twenty-seven and Jim was well over thirty. But as I stopped taking the Pill, so did my periods stop. It didn't bother me that much as I assumed I had become pregnant — I waited a while and then had a pregnancy test. Horror! It was negative. This was the first of many such tests, all negative. With each test there was at least a week's delay to get the result, and the doctor said, 'We'll try again then!' With each week I would develop false hopes, even imagining the symptoms of feeling sick in the morning and not being able to wear some clothes as I imagined my waistline was larger. Several times I had to ring up from school to hear the bad news and go back to a classroom to look after other people's children. This caused me real distress and obviously affected my teaching ability.

The next stage was to be booked into the infertility clinic. Although the doctors view this positively it has in fact a very negative effect on the couple — at least it did with us — it is admitting to the problem. Also the treatments all take so long — the reproductive cycle lasts one month and the treatments all seem to need testing over months. All the doctors start with the simplest diagnosis and treatment — let's give you more of the hormone and boost your fertility. If that fails more investigations are carried out.

As each stage progresses hopes begin to fade. Each couple of months you meet the same people at the clinic — perhaps one has been successful. Every visit produces new hopes — but you reflect how long this has been going on. By this time all your friends have had Baby One and many are on Baby Two. Some will know why you have not produced, others will assume that you are an independent female with no intention of having a baby — their attitude hurts as it is so far from the truth.

My own story has a happy ending. I conceived my first child after hormone treatment; the second was more hard work but, with a bigger gap than I intended, Rupert arrived. Number three arrived without any help at all, which finally made me wonder, is it psychological? Perhaps emotional traumas do affect the hormonal system.

I would conclude by saying: approach any childless couple with care. Is it through choice or not? And also, any woman who eventually gets pregnant after this battle is going to be very tense during the pregnancy, and will perhaps need help in adjusting to the baby when it arrives.

The above quotes are absolutely typical reactions of infertile couples. First, there is the gradual realization that infertility may be a problem. Secondly, there is the search for treatment and the inevitable ups and downs that this involves. Third, there is a disruption of the couple's sex life, both due to demands set by treatment and by a loss of confidence in the couple's sexuality. Fourth, there are all the emotions that go with the inability to have a child — anger, jealousy, depression.

Reactions to infertility treatment

Going to an infertility clinic for the first time can be a very stressful and difficult occasion. The couple have admitted, probably for the first time, that they have a fertility problem to the outside world. 'When I first went to the clinic I burst into tears. It was the same building I had gone to to get family planning, and now I was there because there was something wrong with me.' The couple may find the discussion about their sex life and past history a difficult and humiliating one. 'It sounded awful saying that we only made love twice a week. I was sure that everyone else was doing it all the time.'

Sometimes the doctors seem to be lacking in tact and understanding.

He had me flat on my back and was screwing the ghastly speculum open inside me. Then he poked around taking smear tests and so on, and I found it excruciatingly uncomfortable. He kept telling me to relax, and then he asked me — still in that position — whether I enjoyed intercourse with my husband, because I seemed so tense. I mean, as if you could possibly compare having a speculum put in you by a doctor in cold blood with making love to your husband.

The staff are not always very good at putting across bad news at the clinic. They may try to fudge around as much as possible — 'Well, your sperm count does seem to be a little bit low' — or not give realistic expectations to the couple. On the other hand, the whole procedure can be very reassuring.

I had become convinced that it might be Michael's fault, and that was really worrying him too, I know. When we went to the clinic they were terribly reassuring, and they said his sperm count was fine, and I was ovulating, and we were young and there was lots of hope for us. We went away feeling terribly relieved and our sex life got much better after that. In fact I got pregnant only two months later, before I'd gone back for any more tests.

38

Many women — who have to undergo the bulk of the tests — find the seemingly endless round of tests profoundly depressing.

> Each time I would get incredibly worked up and nervous, thinking, well what if this is it and they find the problem, half hoping that they would so I would know what was wrong with me, and half dreading it in case there'd be no cure. Some of the tests were quite unpleasant and I did get angry that it was me who had to go through it all and spend all those hours in waiting rooms and seeing doctors, and not my husband.

At the end of the tests and treatment, there may still be no hope.

> They finally said that there was nothing more that they could do for us. It was a relief, in a way, because we just had to start thinking about our lives in a different way. But I also felt cheated that they had given us hope in the first place. I thought, there must be some reward for all we've been through — the humiliation and the anxiety and all those awful tests. At the beginning I don't think I even 100 per cent wanted a baby — I just thought we might as well find out what was wrong. At the end of it, having a baby seemed the least reward we could have got.

Sometimes the couple themselves will call a halt to the treatment.

> I had had one ectopic pregnancy, so I knew I only had one tube. When they did a laparoscopy to see what else was wrong they said both tubes were damaged, but they could do surgery on one. It was possible that it might work, there was about a ten to fifteen per cent chance. I just said, 'Forget it, I couldn't bear to go through all that and get my hopes up and then find out I was still in the same boat. I would rather know where I was and look into adoption.'

One of the first things that the majority of couples say when an infertility problem is suspected or diagnosed is that their spontaneous enjoyment of sex suffers. First, sex becomes geared to 'success' or 'failure'. Some couples will be told to make love at a certain time in the month, aided by their interpretations of their temperature charts. Many couples actually get this wrong — they think they must make love exactly when their temperature goes up, showing that they have ovulated — in fact, the best time for conception is in the few days *prior* to ovulation, *before* the temperature goes up. Men with a sperm count which is on the low side may be told to 'save up' the semen for a few days before having intercourse at the appropriate time. In other cases, women may be advised to douche before intercourse, or the couple may be asked to use an insemination cap to increase chances of conception, and the couple may be told that the best chance of conception occurs in the classic 'missionary' sexual position, with the man on top and the woman underneath. They may also be told that the woman should stay lying on her back for about half an hour after intercourse to minimize the chances of semen and precious sperm spilling out of her vagina after intercourse.

It is not surprising that under these conditions a couple's sex life suffers. Indeed, some doctors are now becoming aware that this kind of advice may be the couple's own worst enemy, as sex will rapidly become less frequent and tension between the couple, stress and anxiety, may increase, making conception less likely. Probably the best advice a couple can be given is to make love every other day or so during the woman's most fertile week, and do what they like the rest of the time.

I remember sex became an absolute torture for both of us while we were trying to get pregnant. I lost all interest in sex really, except that I knew we had to make love or I wouldn't get pregnant. So around the right time in the month I would have to pretend to feel sexy and of course we both knew I was only pretending, and we would duly get on with it. But sometimes I really felt too tired, and too dreadful, and then nothing would happen, and I would lie awake at night secretly fuming about it. The initiative always came from me at that time; I suppose he didn't feel any more interested in sex than I did. It was a dreadful time.

Sometimes he would deliberately stay out late to avoid the issue and sometimes he would just say he was feeling ill. I was afraid to push him about it because I thought, the next thing is he will become impotent and then I never will get pregnant!

I felt like some kind of stud. Either I got her pregnant, or it wasn't any good. Love, tenderness, excitement, none of those things seemed to count for anything any more. If she didn't conceive I felt useless.

When an infertility problem is diagnosed, such as blocked tubes or a very low sperm count, the problems with sex may last for a long time afterwards. The couple will grieve the loss of their fertility, and their self-image will inevitably be very dented.

The pressure that is put on a couple through the tests they have and the pressure to 'perform' or 'succeed' in the sexual relationship can put terrible demands on other aspects of a couple's relationship. In the first place, one or other of the couple may be more keen on parenthood than the other. They may become obsessive about having a child, while their partner is much happier to let things take their course and 'see what happens'. These kinds of differences can lead to real problems in a relationship.

We split up because of it. We were always rowing. He used to deliberately work late and say he was too tired for sex just when he knew I wanted it. He was very reluctant to go to the fertility clinic, and finally he did do a sperm test and that was all right, and then he didn't want any more to do with it. I suppose he just didn't really want to be a parent that much, he was into his job and having a good time and he could see that things would be very different if we had a baby.

We didn't split up because we came to hate one another, or anything like that. It was tragic, really. I think we both felt it very hard, and bit by bit we just stopped really sleeping with one another. The whole thing had become empty, meaningless. In the end I met someone else, an older man who had had children and was separated from his wife, who had run off and left the children in his custody. It was just too good to be true, to move into a family with children and become a stepmother to them, so

I went. In the end David married someone else and had children. But I still care about him, we're still in touch.

Often, of course, the opposite happens, and a couple are brought even closer together by their inability to have children. 'We didn't have all the distractions most people have, with their families, and children, and never being alone, so we were able to give much more to one another. It also helped us realize how precious we were to each other.'

One thing which almost all couples who can't conceive will be told, by doctors and friends alike, is to 'relax'. This implies that the woman especially, who is the usual target of this advice, is stopping herself from conceiving through worry. This may be true to some extent — emotional disturbance can cause a woman to stop ovulating, as seen in Chapter 1 — but probably it is not a significant factor for most couples. After all, thousands of women spend a great deal of time worrying that they might get pregnant — and no one is suggesting that this stops them conceiving.

> The trouble is that you do become obsessive. All the women I know who had trouble getting pregnant, and one or two who had miscarriages, got obsessed with the idea of having a baby. I, and they, would think about nothing else. All around, people would be saying, 'Oh relax! It'll happen when you're not thinking about it — a watched pot never boils', and that sort of thing. Of course in a way they may be right, although I don't think I was any more relaxed than usual when I finally conceived.

> I found all the advice to 'relax' absolutely infuriating. I couldn't just forget about it, as they seemed to imply, so of course it made me worse. And then I thought, it's your own fault, you are stopping yourself from conceiving, and that made it all worse because I blamed myself even more than before.

Whether there is a real psychological dimension to infertility or not is not really known. It is often raised to explain cases of 'unexplained fertility', where no medical cause can be found. Psychologists suggest that women may be immature, have

42

deep-seated fears of motherhood, be rejecting their femininity, and so on. However, there is no evidence that this is true. Further, these kinds of arguments always seem to be used about women, not men; when no medical cause is found, doctors seldom suggest that the husband may have deep-seated fears of fatherhood, and he is seldom urged to 'relax'. It is assumed that as his sperm count is high enough, there is no further problem.

However, women themselves often subscribe to what may be a myth about their blocking pregnancy.

> I tried for two years to conceive and I was going mental. Finally my husband suggested a long holiday in Italy and off we went. I was so happy, seeing all these places I had always wanted to see, and eating good food and drinking wine, and we both enjoyed sex in a way we hadn't for a long time. I forgot all about getting pregnant, and of course I found that I was pregnant as soon as I got back.

Cause or coincidence? It is hard to say. Even more surprising is this story:

> I had my first baby when I was twenty. We planned to have a second a couple of years later, but nothing happened. I had some tests, but they didn't say conclusively that anything was wrong, so we just went on trying. It became an obsession with me really, for years, sometimes I felt it worse than others. Then, I remember about ten years later, something finally went 'ping' in me. I said, we'll never have another, we're lucky that we've got our son, so let's forget it. I went upstairs and turned out the cupboard in the attic, and threw out all the things — pram, nappies, cot, baby clothes — which I'd been hoarding all these years for my second baby. I felt as if a weight had been lifted off my mind. And then, a few months later, I was pregnant, and went on to have my little daughter.

Another common story is the couple who find the wife is pregnant as soon as they have adopted a baby — something which obviously was more common in the past than it is now. Probably a lot of couples were persuaded into adopting a baby because they thought it would help them conceive themselves — probably not the best of reasons to bring a child into your home. However, some surveys have shown that about the same number of women who adopt babies conceive as those who don't — about five per cent of all infertile couples. Where treatment has failed and all seems hopeless, a small number of couples will eventually have their own child without doing anything further to bring this about.

This is one of the most difficult problems faced by infertile couples — the fact that hope is seldom entirely dead.

> People were always trotting out to me stories of people who had finally conceived after years and years of waiting. 'Oh, so-and-so, down the road, she had to wait six years and then she had this beautiful baby boy.' Or, 'What about this test-tube baby thing, can't you try that?' They are always trying to give you hope when you know you should give up. I used to cling to every story I ever heard about people having babies against innumerable odds, as I wanted so much to believe there was hope. It made adjusting to the whole problem so much harder.

Sharing the problem of infertility with other people can be problematic. Relatives, especially parents who want grandchildren, may be so upset by the idea that their son or daughter is infertile that they do not want to talk about it, or cannot accept the news. Friends may not sympathize, and often infertility is not understood. If a couple just say that they cannot have a baby, it will usually be assumed that it is the woman's fault. She may find it hard to put up with this if in fact her partner has the problem, but it does seem even more difficult for men than for women to accept and talk about infertility. Through ignorance, many people assume that an infertile man must be lacking in virility too; hurtful remarks may be made by friends or colleagues in the office. Although it almost always helps to share a problem, many men may find it easier and better for them to keep quiet about the issue, except with the very few who understand.

If the couple remain childless, their problems seem to extend forwards forever into the future. There are few outlets in our society for the expression of love and affection except within the family. People who are childless cannot express the kind of love which they received from their parents and wish to pass on to their children. If they came from an unhappy family, they never have the chance to heal those wounds by creating a loving family atmosphere for their children, and living through the new experience.

People who are childless often feel they have to invest all their love in one person, their spouse, and that this increases their dependence on them to frightening levels. 'I often think, suppose he dies, and there are no children. There will be nothing of him left for me, and there will be no children through whom I can live in the future.' While some childless couples do have more and closer friendships than their friends with families, many find that as their friends have children and get involved in family life they become estranged. You have none of the same interests — stages of child development, schools, holidays for children, children's illnesses and so on. 'I found seeing my best friend became a terrible bore. I would go to see her, and she would spend an hour talking about her child, and I would spend an hour talking about my job, and then we would part, and neither of us had really listened to a thing that the other was saying.'

People who are childless and decide to concentrate on other areas of pleasure or fulfilment, such as a career, travel, sport, or hobby, are often accused by people who may not know about their infertility of being materialistic, workaholic, ambitious and self-seeking. Childlessness is often seen to be people's fault in some way, even if they may have spent years striving for a child through a whole series of medical operations or treatment. Perhaps because of society's often unfeeling or hostile attitudes, many childless people become depressed and angry.

I completely withdrew from people as my infertility problem proved more and more serious. Every time one of my friends became pregnant, it was like a knife in the ribs for me. I became sick with rage and wanted nothing more to do with them, and of course the friendships couldn't last. Then I turned my anger against my husband, and pleaded with him to divorce me, to find someone else who could give him a child, and then it would be all over. Finally, I turned my anger against myself and contemplated suicide, making constant threats which people soon ignored but which at the same time frightened me, because at the time I really did think there was a good chance I might do it someday, in a particularly dark moment of depression. But in the end, I don't know how, I came through. Finally I can contemplate a life without children.

Secondary infertility, or so-called 'second child' infertility, is when a woman is unable to conceive although she has done so successfully in the past. Often this may occur because of damage or infection following childbirth.

The desire for a second child is often as strong as it is for the first. Many parents have very strong views about their children not being only children, and friends and relatives may constantly ask the parents why they are not having another child. Some parents feel that they do not get enough sympathy as they may be told that they are lucky to have the one child.

We had our first child, a boy, easily enough, and it never occurred to us that there could be any problem. When he was about two, we decided to try for another—I very much wanted a girl. In fact I used to say that I would have at least three or four children in order to have a daughter among them!

But I didn't conceive and didn't conceive. Nearly two years went by before we finally decided to seek help — it still didn't occur to me that anything serious could be wrong. After a number of tests which showed that I was ovulating and there was nothing wrong with my husband, I went into hospital to have a laparoscopy. They said afterwards that there had been damage, probably caused in childbirth, and that I had a number of adhesions which were holding down the tubes. They said that they could operate, and there was quite a high chance of success.

AID as a solution

If the infertility problem is insoluble, there is the possibility of adoption (see Chapter 6). However, if it is the man who is infertile, there is another possibility —artificial insemination by donor, or AID (see also Chapter 1).

In the past, before AID was available, there is little doubt that many wives of infertile men went out and had a discreet extra-marital affair in order to conceive. Sometimes they would do this to spare the man's feelings, as he would think he had succeeded in having a child after all, although often the man must have guessed. In some relationships there is no doubt that a man would even countenance his wife having an affair so that she should not be denied the chance of having the child she so much wants.

AID removes many of the emotional barriers to this solution. It is approved by the medical profession, the woman does not have to be 'unfaithful' to her husband, and she can go back month after month for insemination if she does not conceive straightaway. However, there are some people who feel that AID can never be an answer. 'To have a child growing inside you is the most intimate experience I could ever imagine. Not to know who the father was — to have some unknown donor who might be anybody — would seem unreal, almost as bad as having a child as the result of a rape.'

Others feel that the experience is too clinical, that the doctors set too many arbitrary standards.

> When they interview you, they ask all sorts of questions about are you happily married, do you suffer from any diseases, how old are you, and so on. They turned one couple who were waiting with us down because they said the husband was too old. Nobody would ask you any questions like that if you went and had an affair or did something irresponsible like that, so why should they ask you with AID?

Indeed, the AID child starts off in life with all sorts of advantages denied to many 'naturally' conceived children. The donor will have been screened for any hereditary problems, the prospective

47

parents screened for any problems in their health or their relationship. It does appear that sometimes the medical profession take their sense of responsibility in creating a child too far.

Many couples fear the secrecy involved in AID. The child, because not legitimate, in fact has no legal claim to inherit from the father's side, unless he has gone through formal adoption procedures, which would make disclosure of the truth more likely. The husband is often anxious that his parents should not know that the child is genetically not 'his', in case they refuse to recognize it as their grandchild. They also fear the impact on the child if it is told the truth. Parents today are encouraged to tell adopted children their origins as early as possible, but the AID child is very seldom told. However, some children guess that there is some kind of secret surrounding their birth, and their fears or fantasies about this may be worse than their knowing the truth.

The need for secrecy is one of the most difficult problems admitted by couples having AID.

> Everyone told us that we mustn't tell the child for the child's own sake, and that meant keeping it a secret from everybody. As I had to go on having the AID treatment over a long time, this was very difficult for me, as there was no one I could share the problem with. I wish there were some kind of support group for people having AID, where they could share their feelings without having to worry about the truth getting out.

Being open about AID is a real alternative, although it can be very difficult to tell the truth. A young child cannot understand what AID is all about, and when he or she is told much later the news is likely to be more traumatic, as it is with telling an adopted child, especially during the difficult teenage years.

Often, however, the secrecy is to protect the husband, and keep friends, colleagues, and family from knowing he is infertile. The experience of AID couples who *have* been open about it is largely that family and friends *are* sympathetic and *do* understand. Both can provide valuable support, and will often share in the couple's joy at conception and after the birth.

A lot of controversy surrounds AID, a great deal of it around such issues as whether doctors should allow AID for single women or for lesbian couples. Another issue which will no doubt become increasingly controversial is the possibility of 'self-insemination'. It is in fact perfectly possible for a couple to carry out AID without the mediation of a doctor or clinic. All that is necessary is for the couple to ask a willing male friend to donate some sperm into an insemination cap (an ordinary contraceptive diaphragm will do). The woman then inserts this into her vagina straight away and the sperm will set off on their way.

Some couples may go to even further lengths along these lines. A story which appeared in the press in 1983 concerned a couple who were unable to have children because the wife was infertile. She had a sister to whom she was very close, who had two children and clearly enjoyed pregnancy and motherhood. This couple had obtained an insemination cap from a private clinic, ostensibly to help conception. The infertile woman's husband used this to inseminate his wife's sister, who conceived and gave birth to his child. She then handed the baby over soon after birth to her sister and the baby's father for them to bring up as their own. The whole family were very happy about this arrangement, though there were a great many people who saw fit to condemn it.

AID can be difficult to come to terms with because of deep insecurities which the father may feel about his sexuality and fertility. He may also fear that the child will look so unlike him that people will realize that the child couldn't be his and will therefore mock him. These fears are seldom founded on fact. To begin with, most families are astonishingly diverse, and with many AID children the grandparents will find some relative to whom the child bears a strong resemblance, whether it is blood related or not — 'Oh, he's just like Uncle Albert' or 'How funny, her hair's the same colour as my sister's was, isn't it funny how these things skip a generation'.

Secondly, there must be many children who are in fact not the biological children of their fathers, who never know and never realize. One survey of blood groups of married couples and their children carried out in England showed that in fact an astonishing thirty per cent of children *could not* be the biological children of their fathers! Yet, presumably in most cases neither they nor the fathers ever knew. Thirdly, many adopted children find that friends or acquaintances not in on the secret say 'Isn't she just like her mother!' though there is no blood relationship.

And finally, most children pick up and copy the mannerisms and behaviour patterns, and even facial expressions, of the parents who bring them up. They copy the voice and often use the parents as a model. These resemblances are often much more striking and immediate than actual physical ones.

Many AID fathers do fear, however, that if their marriages break up, their wives will use the fact that 'the child isn't really yours' to win custody and deny access to them. Sadly, this does sometimes happen when such marriages break up — but probably not more often than similarly destructive behaviour when the father *is* the biological father of the children. Some men, it is true, do find it difficult to adjust to the children as their own, so it is important that they raise any doubts about their feelings before going ahead with AID.

Taking the decision to have AID can be a hard step:

I was afraid that he wouldn't accept the child, that it would be as bad as if I had been unfaithful, that he might turn against me because of it. We talked it over and over, and he kept insisting it would be all right. In the end we went ahead. I conceived, the child grew, he saw it born, he was full of pride and joy. I could see that my doubts were really a lack of trust in me for him, and nothing to do with him at all.

I hated having AID. I found it sordid, the idea of someone else's sperm swimming inside me. I stuck it for three months, and I didn't conceive, and when I was supposed to go back for the fourth time I felt sick at the thought of it. We talked it all over and I said, 'It won't do, it's your child I want, not any old child. Let's forget it.' He was delighted and said he had secretly dreaded it. I'm glad that we got it out in the open because I'm sure it would have been a dreadful mistake and probably have split up our marriage, which is closer now than it's ever been.

Surrogate motherhood

Just as AID offers a way out for infertile couples where the man has the fertility problem, there is a potential answer where the infertile partner is the woman — surrogate motherhood. This means that the husband — usually through artificial insemination — fertilizes a woman who is prepared to carry the child and give it up at birth to the father and his wife (see page 49).

The issue of surrogate motherhood has been gathering importance, as an increasing number of people are resorting to it, especially in the United States. Any contract made between parties that a woman should bear a man's child and hand it over to him and his wife at birth is not legally valid in the United Kingdom; if anything goes wrong, such as a miscarriage, stillbirth or the birth of a handicapped child, the law cannot sort out the resulting tangle. Unscrupulous people have become involved in setting up organizations to help the surrogate mother and parents in working out these arrangements, and who take a financial cut.

Yet surrogate motherhood is in fact as old as civilization; it can even be said to have a Biblical precedent:

And when Rachel saw that she bare Jacob no children, Rachel envied her sister, and said unto Jacob, Give me children, or else I die . . .

And she said, Behold my maid Bilhah, go in unto her; and she shall bear upon my knees, that I may also have children by her. And she gave him Bilhah her handmaid to wife; and Jacob went in unto her.

And Bilhah conceived, and bare Jacob a son.

And Rachel said, God hath judged me, and hath also heard my voice, and hath given me a son; therefore called she his name Dan.

Genesis, 30, 1–6

The legal and ethical issues surrounding surrogate motherhood need to be sorted out, especially as science has made *in vitro* (test-tube) fertilization possible. This technique opens up a new possibility; that a woman who has functioning ovaries, but cannot carry the baby in her womb, could have her eggs fertilized *in vitro* and the embryo could then be introduced into the womb of a surrogate mother. The surrogate mother would hand over the baby at birth to the 'real' or genetic mother of the baby.

There are obviously cases where the surrogate mother — perhaps a friend or relative of the infertile woman — undertakes this in a genuine spirit of responsibility and altruism, and this can be the answer to an infertile couple's prayers. However, wherever the question of paying the surrogate mother arises, there must be doubts about the ethics of the procedure. What if the surrogate mother, not really caring about her baby, drinks or smokes throughout the pregnancy? What if the baby is unhealthy or handicapped? What if the surrogate mother has a miscarriage or the baby is born dead — will she still get paid? What if she or the would-be parents change their minds? All these questions are more than theory — they have already occurred more than once in the United States where surrogate motherhood is on the increase.

3

Losing a Baby: Miscarriage and Stillbirth

This chapter discusses in detail what happens when a woman actually loses her baby through either miscarriage or stillbirth, and what can be done to help.

Miscarriage

A miscarriage is the premature delivery of a foetus before it is capable of surviving on its own. Most miscarriages in fact occur very early in pregnancy, during the first three months; some occur so early that the woman may not even know that she is pregnant. But as modern pregnancy testing can show a woman that she is pregnant so much earlier, most women are already looking forward to a baby when they have a miscarriage, and the event is a great shock and disappointment.

How common are miscarriages? The usual figures quoted are that about one in five or one in seven *recognized* pregnancies end in miscarriage. If miscarriages of pregnancies which occurred so early that the mother was not aware of them were also included the figure might be as high as one in two. Indeed, miscarriage is such a common occurrence that some doctors refer to it as a 'normal variation of the pregnancy process'. This may be true; but it does not help the woman who has lost her baby adjust to her grief and disappointment.

There does seem to be a slightly greater chance of a woman miscarrying as she gets older — just as there is a greater chance of her having an abnormal baby. There also seems to be a slightly greater chance of a first pregnancy ending in miscarriage than for subsequent ones. But having one miscarriage does not mean that there is any greater risk of having a second one. After two miscarriages, the chance does go up from about one in five to one in three; after three subsequent miscarriages the chances are about fifty-fifty that the pregnancy will go to term. But the great majority of women who have miscarriages will go on to have a healthy baby in the end.

Medically, a distinction is usually made between miscarriages which occur up to, and after, thirteen weeks, as they usually have different causes. The great majority — eighty-five per cent — of miscarriages occur before the end of the twelfth week of pregnancy.

What happens when you have a miscarriage?
The first sign of a miscarriage during the first three months of pregnancy is usually a small amount of bleeding, like the start of a period. This spotting may go on for several days, and may cease — in which case the pregnancy will continue as normal — or it may progress, become heavier, or there may be period-like pains or severe cramping. If a woman has some bleeding this is called a threatened miscarriage or a *threatened abortion* (the medical profession refer to both miscarriages and induced abortions as 'abortions', a practice which may distress many women who might feel they are being accused of not wanting the baby). If a miscarriage threatens there is usually a fifty–fifty chance of things working out all right. If the bleeding becomes very severe or if severe cramping occurs, this is usually an *inevitable abortion* — either the foetus is dead or the cervix (entrance to the womb) is open and nothing can save the pregnancy.

Sometimes a miscarriage occurs after the first three months of pregnancy, and may be very sudden, without the warning bleeding and without much pain.

One woman related her experience like this:

I was very happy about being pregnant and looking forward to my baby—already wondering whether it would be a boy or a girl and daydreaming about what to call him or her and what he or she would look like. At about twelve weeks — in fact exactly when my period would have been due — we went out to a concert in the evening. I had been feeling tired and didn't really want to go, but it seemed silly to make a fuss. At the end of the evening when I went to the loo there was a tiny bit of bleeding — like the beginning of a period. I felt very panicky, but when I rang up a friend who had had children she reassured me and said that some women did have a little bleeding at the time of their period and not to worry, but to stay in bed for twenty-four hours.

I stayed in bed and the bleeding seemed to stop, but every time I got up there would be a little bit more. My doctor said I must rest in bed and not do anything, which I did, but as the week wore on I began to feel more and more depressed and anxious. On the fifth day I had a terrible backache, which I didn't think much of, because I thought it was from lying awkwardly in bed trying to read — but actually I think it was like the beginning of labour. After that I began to have terrible cramps and they took me into hospital — I had a real labour which went on all night and was agony, and made me realise why they give you breathing exercises in antenatal classes, because I simply couldn't breathe properly, the pain was so awful. In the morning I passed a lot of blood and they told me I had only partially miscarried and I would have a D and C that evening to remove what was left. I felt absolutely terrible and quite bereft, but at least the pain was over.

A miscarriage — even at so early a stage — may be comparatively quick and painless or it may involve a long labour, as in this woman's case. Some doctors may give pain-killing injections or even an epidural as in childbirth, but others may leave the woman very much to herself. A D and C (dilatation and curettage, or scraping of the womb) is usually given to make sure that nothing is left behind which could lead to an infection and damage the woman's future fertility.

Another woman's experience of a later miscarriage was rather different:

It was all so sudden. One day I was four months pregnant, looking forward to the birth of our baby. Then that evening I

55

had some cramps and pain. I rang the doctors' emergency number and was told to stay in bed and rest. I did manage to sleep — when I woke up I felt all right and thought everything would be fine. But when I got up the waters burst; I ran to the bathroom and suddenly the foetus came out, a tiny little baby, with the umbilical cord and everything. I screamed for my husband who rang for the ambulance and I just lay on the floor, with a blanket wrapped over me and towels because I was bleeding, until the ambulance came and they took care of everything.

What causes a miscarriage?

When a woman has had a miscarriage, her first question will almost always be: but what *caused* it? Being told that it happens in one in five pregnancies doesn't really help someone accept why it happened in her case.

The truth is that in many cases, doctors do not actually know. This is partly because, since miscarriages are so frequent and most women will have another, successful pregnancy soon after, doctors do not investigate until a woman has had two or even three miscarriages. If a woman has had miscarriages at different times in pregnancy, it is referred to as *recurrent abortion* and is usually the result of extreme bad luck. If the miscarriages occur at the same time in pregnancy and with the same symptoms, this is known as *habitual abortion* and can usually be traced to the same medical cause. However, increasing knowledge about the early stages of pregnancy and some studies which have been carried out do shed some light on the question.

Most miscarriages seem to be caused by once-only accidents. The processes of fertilization, early growth and development, the implantation of the egg into the lining of the womb and the establishment of the right hormonal environment for the foetus to continue development are all very complex and delicate processes, and it is not perhaps so very surprising that sometimes an error occurs.

Studies which examine spontaneously aborted foetuses show that in about fifty per cent there is some kind of chromosomal

56

abnormality. Other abnormalities, such as those with spina bifida, often cause the baby to be miscarried too.

Most of these would prevent the baby from being able to live at all, but it is also thought that spontaneous miscarriages prevent many more babies with recognized abnormalities such as Down's syndrome from ever being born. The fact that over half of miscarried foetuses are abnormal has considerable influence over the treatment—or lack of treatment—that is given to women who threaten to miscarry — no one wants to continue a pregnancy which would result in the birth of a severely abnormal baby.

Women who miscarry may hear the term 'blighted egg' or 'blighted ovum' used to explain what went wrong. This means that either the egg or the sperm which were fertilized was abnormal, so that the fertilized egg failed to develop in the normal way. This will usually result in an early miscarriage.

Some men and women have a genetic abnormality which is passed on to all pregnancies, since it is present in all their eggs or all their sperm. However, these are comparatively rare, and even so, it does not mean that a couple will never be able to have children; some foetuses will still be able to develop normally.

Another reason for miscarriage may be hormonal problems. This is actually much rarer than may once have been thought, as nowadays doctors tend to think that a decrease in levels of the hormone progesterone, which is necessary to sustain a pregnancy, is a symptom and not a cause of failed pregnancy. However, illnesses such as over-functioning or under-functioning of the thyroid or adrenal glands, or diabetes, can affect a pregnancy — and some women may have a progesterone deficiency which is not enough to prevent pregnancy but just severe enough to allow a miscarriage to occur. This can usually be established by taking blood samples and screening these for levels of hormone throughout the woman's monthly cycle.

Many miscarriages do appear to occur around the three-month mark. This is a very delicate time in pregnancy, when the womb suddenly starts to expand rapidly as the foetus begins to grow apace, and when the task of maintaining hormone levels switches from the corpus luteum in the ovary to the placenta itself. If something is not quite right at this point the placenta can become detached from the wall of the womb or the hormone level can fall too low and the pregnancy will be rejected.

Another explanation for miscarriage, especially in a first pregnancy, is that the womb may resist the process of sudden expansion, or simply fail to grow quickly enough to accommodate the growing foetus, so that it 'kicks back', expelling the pregnancy. In a small number of cases some physical abnormality in the womb such as fibroids or an extra 'partition' (or septum) in the womb may prevent a pregnancy from growing any further.

After thirteen weeks, miscarriages are usually caused by problems either in the attachment of the placenta to the uterus, or by what is known as an 'incompetent cervix'. The muscles around the entrance to the womb are very strong, and need to be so if they are to hold the growing weight of the foetus and the sac of water enclosing it. If the cervix is weak — usually through having been stretched too much in an earlier pregnancy, or during an induced abortion or an operation such as a D and C — the cervix may dilate too soon in the pregnancy and cause the bag of waters and the foetus to pass out.

Preventing miscarriages

Most women want to know the cause of a miscarriage for one main reason: they want to know how to prevent it happening again.

Unfortunately, there has been very little progress in understanding what can be done to prevent miscarriages, except for a number of specific reasons. Fibroids can be removed from the womb, and if there is an abnormality in the structure of the womb that can be operated on. If the woman has an incompetent cervix, this can be treated by stitching the muscles around the cervix so that it cannot expand — this is usually done after the first three months of pregnancy — and these stitches are then removed a week or two before the baby is due.

If miscarriage threatens, there is usually only one course of action recommended by doctors — bed-rest. Some doctors will recommend that the woman lies down all the time, only getting up to go to the toilet; others that she should simply take things very easy. There is some medical reason why this is advised: if the placenta is becoming detached, rest may help it to attach more firmly again. But usually bed-rest is seen only as a way of relieving the woman's anxiety while the outcome is awaited, and so that she cannot blame herself for the miscarriage if it finally occurs. Perhaps the main reason why doctors recommend bed-rest is that 'it certainly can't do any harm'.

Attitudes to the treatment of miscarriage have changed quite a lot in recent years; ten to fifteen years ago injections of the natural hormone progesterone seem to have been given almost as a matter of course to women facing the threat of a second or third miscarriage. Earlier, some women were given synthetic hormones, but these were stopped when risks to the baby's health were discovered. No one seems to know how helpful these hormone injections are in preventing a miscarriage, and many doctors do not want to give them at all—they say they may not help prevent a miscarriage, and if they did, they might either cause abnormalities in the foetus or result in the birth of an abnormal baby which should really have been miscarried. However, hormone injections are still given, especially for women who have had multiple miscarriages, and some women are sure they would never have had a baby without them:

> I had two miscarriages, one on top of the other. When I was pregnant for the third time, I went into hospital to rest, and they gave me hormones from about the seventh week to the thirteenth. They explained that there might be a very small risk of it causing some kind of abnormality, but I was so desperate, I said I'd take the risk. I did threaten to lose that baby too — I had some light bleeding — but then I went on to have my daughter without further trouble. She's five now, and she's quite perfect.

Another change of opinion over the past decade or two has been over whether a woman's activity can have any effect on the outcome of pregnancy. Grantly Dick Read, in his original *Childbirth without Fear*, states that women should 'take care' in early pregnancy, particularly at the times when the woman's period would have been due — when miscarriages are most likely to occur. He believed that sexual intercourse in the early months, especially when the woman's womb contracts strongly with orgasm, can undoubtedly trigger a miscarriage.

Yet contemporary books challenge this notion; the popular view is that nothing bad can come out of sexual intercourse. Women are told to have sex as often and as vigorously as they like until the later months of pregnancy—and even then orgasm can be beneficial by starting the childbirth process if a baby is slightly overdue. The modern view is that a miscarriage will happen whatever you do. The same arguments apply over any kind of activity — running, cycling, swimming, playing tennis or other sports.

However, this does not fit in with the fact that women threatening to miscarry are told to rest in bed and not to make love — and that women with a history of miscarriage are often advised to be a little more cautious and are sometimes advised not to make love during pregnancy until after the time that the miscarriage previously occurred.

A study of women, some of whom had planned and some unplanned pregnancies, shows that about twelve per cent of women who had wanted, planned pregnancies had a miscarriage. Those who got pregnant by accident — all were still using a contraceptive method—had twice as many miscarriages. Women who got pregnant with an IUD in place are a special case, as there is a very high rate of miscarriage for IUD pregnancies — sixty per cent. Why were the unplanned pregnancies more likely to miscarry?

The man who did this study, Professor Martin Vessey, says that no further research has been done on this question although the figures are 'highly significant'. His explanation for the difference in miscarriage rates was that there may have been some kind of 'interference' with the pregnancy among women who did not really want a baby — not obvious interference such as trying to obtain an abortion, as women were offered this choice, but a kind of 'neglect' of the pregnancy, perhaps smoking, drinking or strenuous activity. He also pointed out that if the thirty per cent of pregnancies which were artificially aborted had continued the rate of spontaneous miscarriage would almost certainly have been even higher in the unplanned group — over twice that found among women with wanted, planned pregnancies.

'A link between a woman's behaviour in pregnancy and her likelihood of miscarrying is particularly likely because there is a clear difference in miscarriage rates for three groups of women: those who had a planned pregnancy, those whose pregnancy was unplanned but a spacing failure, and those who definitely had not wanted a child then, but perhaps continued with the pregnancy because they had moral objections to induced abortion'.

Can psychological problems cause a miscarriage?
Some psychiatrists have argued that miscarriage can be caused by an unconscious deep-seated rejection of the father of the baby, or the baby itself, or a deep-seated fear of motherhood. However, there seems to be no real evidence for this view, only isolated case histories. Moreover, the fact that this view has been often voiced may be the cause of some doctors feeling that induced abortion and miscarriage are 'really the same thing' — a view which has no foundation and which can only lead to unsympathetic treatment of the woman who loses her baby.

Others have felt that anxiety might be a cause, or the stress caused by work, by conflict with the husband or father of the child or with other family members. One study of 'habitual aborters' by a doctor, Michel Wolfromm, showed that three times as many women receiving psychotherapy during a subsequent pregnancy gave birth to babies compared with a control group. But this is the only evidence which seems to exist on this subject.

In conclusion, it seems that the majority of miscarriages do have a medical cause, whether this is easily established or not. At least half of all miscarriages clearly cannot — and should not — be prevented as they would result in the birth of a handicapped baby. However, to ensure the greatest possible chance of avoiding an unnecessary miscarriage, it does seem sensible to give up drinking, smoking and strenuous activity in the first months of pregnancy; and if you have had previous miscarriages, to rest as much as possible, and avoid sexual intercourse until one or two weeks after the stage of pregnancy in which the miscarriage occurred.

Stillbirth

It is probably true that the later in pregnancy a miscarriage occurs, the greater is a woman's distress. Even greater is the grief if the baby dies at birth or soon afterwards.

Stillbirths and early infant deaths are now comparatively rare, thanks to medical science. However, this does now mean that no mother coming to the end of her pregnancy today really considers the death of her baby as a possibility. The rarity of stillbirth means that a woman whose baby dies will be even more shocked and more isolated than women in the past.

In Britain about one in fifty births results in a stillborn baby or a baby which does not survive beyond the first week of life. The risk still depends a great deal on the mother's general health and nutrition before and during pregnancy and the quality of medical care. Death at birth or in the first week of life is between three and four times greater in women from the lowest social class as compared with women from the highest. The risk of loss is five to ten times higher in women who have no antenatal care and the risk also increases with age.

The risks are also greater for a woman who has twins. There are more complications of pregnancy with twins, and babies are usually of a lower birth weight — often one baby being much smaller than its twin. The commonest cause of loss with twins is premature birth, with the second twin to be born usually at greater risk. With triplets the risk of stillbirth is double that for twins.

Stillbirth is a terrible and traumatic experience; two women give their different experiences:

> I was expecting twins, which I had known for some months — this wasn't too much of a shock, as I knew that having twins did run in the family. I became increasingly excited as I looked

forward to the birth, and we made all the preparations, buying two of everything, and I took every care with visiting the antenatal clinic and doing my exercises. I was told that there was a slightly greater risk of something going wrong with twins, so I am sure that the hospital did take extra care at this stage.

A few days before the due date, I went to bed early, and felt the babies — or a baby, anyway — moving as usual. In the night my waters broke, and to my shock were discoloured. My husband immediately rang the hospital and ran me over in the car — both of us were very anxious, but trying to keep calm and hopeful. I didn't really believe that anything dreadful could happen. The consultant who I had been seeing of course wasn't there at this hour of the morning, and there was a lot of fussing around and waiting while it seemed everyone wondered what to do.

About five hours after we arrived at the hospital we were told that the situation was very worrying and that it would be best to do a Caesarean. Both the twins were dead. They were identical, which means that they shared the same placenta, and sometimes this means one twin may get less nourishment and grow more slowly than the other, and I was told that one of the babies might have died and that this then damaged the other. I don't think I really took it in, what with the after-effects of the anaesthetic and everything, but by the time the consultant came round in the morning I felt absolutely in despair. He told me that the operation should have been done as soon as I came in, but that even then probably they wouldn't have saved even one baby. But he looked very apologetic, and I had the feeling that perhaps one baby could have been saved. The cause of death on the certificate was simply 'foetal stress'. It took me a long time getting over it; they gave me an injection to stop the milk coming but I left hospital feeling terrible, swollen, torn apart, and nothing to show for it.

The first sign that anything was wrong was at five months, when I didn't feel the baby move as expected. I mentioned this at the antenatal clinic but the doctor was not concerned. After a month more I was very worried, but the doctor said the baby was small for the delivery dates, did an ultrasound scan, and decided that I must have got my dates wrong and that the baby was a month younger than I thought it was. This relieved me, but still as the pregnancy progressed I didn't grow as much as I felt I should and the baby seemed very inactive.

Finally, the doctor agreed that something must be wrong, and there were more hospital visits and tests, and second opinions, but no one seemed to have anything conclusive to say. I was desperately worried all this time, yet still hoped that all would be well.

Then I went into labour early. It seemed that the baby, who was still very small, was in the breech position and a Caesarean was decided on. I was unconscious when the baby was born — I think they put me out deliberately — and when I woke up the first thing I said was, 'Where is my baby? Is it all right?'

My husband and a nurse tried to explain that the baby was severely deformed and had been born dead, but at first I couldn't take it in. My husband was wonderful. He had had the courage to see the baby and he told me it was quite all right to look at it — her face was beautiful, and seemed quite perfect, although there were a number of external and internal abnormalities.

I was told that it was a chromosomal defect and was very unlikely to happen again, when I had another baby. But I couldn't think of the future at all, only about the terrible loss, and I didn't even have the consolation of being able to wish that this baby had lived.

What causes a stillbirth?
Stillbirths include both those babies who die during the process of being delivered, and those who die in the womb before labour begins. In up to half of all foetal deaths, the cause of death is never determined; on the death certificate it is often given as 'foetal stress'. Lack of oxygen to the baby, known as 'anoxia', is often given as a cause, although there are a number of reasons why this

should occur — the umbilical cord may have been compressed before or during delivery, or may wrap itself around the baby's neck.

A baby which is more than two weeks overdue may be deprived of necessary nourishment from the placenta, which is why most hospitals and doctors will press the mother to have the labour induced if it is two weeks past the baby's due date. Toxaemia (a metabolic disturbance) or high blood pressure in the mother can affect the proper flow of nourishment to the foetus.

In other cases, the placenta may separate from the wall of the womb too soon — this is called *abruptio placentae*, and causes the death of about 1 in 1000 babies. This may happen due to high blood pressure, or during a difficult labour, or sometimes because the baby has been moved if it was in the breech position — but often no reason can be given.

Some babies may die literally from the stress of being born — they may have a mini-heart attack. The premature baby is particularly at risk, and the commonest cause of death for premature babies is difficulty in breathing — the 'respiratory distress' syndrome. Premature babies are also more vulnerable to death from infections.

Another major cause of death at or soon after birth is congenital abnormalities. Some of these will be so severe that the baby cannot survive at all outside the womb, but in some cases the doctors and parents may have to make the traumatic decision of trying to decide whether to operate to give some chance that the baby may live, or whether to allow it to die in as much peace and dignity as possible.

In rare cases, mismanagement of labour may be responsible for the death of a baby.

Preventing stillbirths
Although many stillbirths are unforeseen disasters which cannot be prevented, there are some things within the mother's control. The first is good nutrition; this will help ensure the adequate growth and development of the foetus and the placenta. The intake of the right vitamins before and during pregnancy can help

prevent some congenital abnormalities such as spina bifida. Cutting back on drinking and giving up smoking will help avoid low birth-weight babies.

Attending antenatal classes will help doctors trace problems with a pregnancy and take preventive action, and also ensure that the mother is in the best physical and mental condition to enter labour.

The prevention of deaths from congenital deformities can be brought about by screening by amniocentesis, where some of the fluid in the womb is drawn out through a fine needle. This test is usually done only in higher risk mothers because there is a small chance that it will precipitate a miscarriage. If an abnormality is found, the mother can choose to have the pregnancy terminated, but this will have to be done at sixteen to twenty weeks, as the test cannot be carried out earlier, so it can be as traumatic as the death of a full-term baby.

New technology childbirth has helped prevent many deaths at birth, with monitoring of the foetal heart and rapid intervention if there are any signs of distress. But high technology birth has had its casualties too — reliance by nursing staff on machines which did not work has led to some deaths, and many women have rejected using epidural anaesthetics which cut off sensation below the waist and inhibit the mother from helping in the baby's birth; this can lead to more forceps deliveries or Caesareans. On the whole, however, medical technology — and especially intensive care for premature babies — has helped reduce the loss of newborn babies.

4

Reactions to Child Loss

Vita Sackville-West, in a letter to her husband Harold Nicolson after the death of their second, stillborn son, wrote:

> Harold, I am sad. I have been thinking of that white velvet coffin with that little still thing inside. He was going to be a birthday-present to you next Sunday. Oh darling, I feel it is too cruel. I can't help minding, and I always shall. I mind more when I see Ben, how sweet and sturdy he is, and the other would have been just the same. I mind his being dead because he is a person. It is silly to mind so much. I can't bear to think of people with two children. Oh Harold darling, why did he die? Why, why, why did he?
>
> *Portrait of a Marriage*, Nigel Nicolson, Weidenfeld and Nicolson (1973)

People's grief at the loss of a baby, whether through miscarriage or stillbirth, can be almost intolerable. The later the loss occurs, the greater the grief is likely to be, although it is always dangerous to compare or assess the depth of grief. The loss *can* be as great at three months' pregnancy, or at five months, after it has 'quickened', as it is shortly before birth, or at birth, or in the days after birth. It can be doubly hard to bear if it has taken a long time to get pregnant, or if there has been an infertility problem, as people all around will say, 'There will be other babies', without knowing the struggle that has gone into producing this one.

Almost everyone who has lost a baby will go through all the classic phases of grief, which can take many months or even years. First there is disbelief, denial: 'It can't be happening. Tell me it isn't true.' Then there is anger: 'Why me, why not someone else?' 'Why did they let her die?' 'How could God let this happen?' Then

67

there is a period of grief and mourning, and finally there is acceptance.

With the loss of a baby, though, the grief is not so simple as when an adult or an older person dies. First, there is no preparation through a phase of illness or suffering. Second, the parents and relatives are prepared for the joy of a birth and may in a few moments be expected to respond to the reality of death. Third, the loss of a child after its initial impact is also complicated by the fact that the grief and loss can be offset by the hope of another child, which may prevent the parents' grief from ever running its course. Fourth, people do not know how to react very well to the death of a baby and may find it hard to share the parents' grief. And lastly, the baby which died was never really known by the parents as a reality, though they will already have loved it. They will have created a fantasy of a future which then has to be unpicked, piece by piece.

Many parents feel guilt about the loss of their child and wonder whether they have in some way caused it. This is particularly common when the mother or father have had some ambivalent feelings about having the baby and then feel they have somehow caused the death. Another problem with parents of stillborn children is that they tend to fantasize about and glorify the child, which becomes a kind of paragon. Later on, if they have other children, they may find the real child's personality does not match up to their image of the lost child's, and they may blame the child for it.

The grief felt for the loss of a baby, a baby which may well have never been seen or known, can be particularly traumatic. Some parents say that it is as if in some way the child represents the future; when the child dies it is as if the whole future has died with it. The death of a baby is an inversion of the natural order of things, and as such is profoundly disturbing. We expect that our parents will die before us, but not our children. Often there is no cause given for a baby's death, which makes the loss more frightening. Many people who are religious find it very hard to accept that a child, which has never lived or done any wrong, should be so cruelly destroyed.

Outsiders find it hard to accept the reality of the parents' loss.

They keep wanting to comfort you by saying, 'Never mind, you can have another, you'll be back in a year with another baby.' But I didn't want another baby, I wanted *this* baby! It was the insensitivity, the stupidity of it. If a woman lost her husband, they wouldn't say, 'Oh, never mind, you'll soon find another one', would they? Although he died, he was unique, my baby. If I have another one it won't be the same, it won't be Peter, so why should they not accept my grief?

People just don't know what to say. They ask, in the street, if they've seen you looking pregnant, 'Oh, what did you have?' and you say, 'A dead baby', and they just say 'Oh' and start talking about something else, or rush off suddenly. Sometimes I don't know what to say either. They ask, 'Are you a mother?' 'Do you have children?' And I don't know what I should say. 'Yes, I am a mother, I had a baby, I went through all that, but it died.' And then they can't talk about it. It's a strange state to be in; to be both a mother and not a mother.

They make all sorts of assumptions about what will happen to you. One doctor said to me after my miscarriage: 'Well, at least you won't have to go through all those infertility tests.' But then I didn't conceive again, and eighteen months later I was there signing up at the infertility clinic for all those tests. I wanted to ring her up and scream at her down the phone, and say, how dared she say that to me and give me false hope? What did *she* know about it?

They say stupid things like, 'Never mind it's all for the best', or 'You wouldn't have wanted that handicapped baby to live'. That is not the point. I wanted to have, I expected to have, a live, healthy, un-handicapped baby, and that is what I have lost. In a way it makes it even worse for me that I can't even wish that this baby had lived.

People very seldom give a couple enough time to mourn for their baby; they assume it will all be forgotten in a couple of months and that the couple will soon be looking forward to having another baby. In fact, people who have had a stillbirth, or who have had a miscarriage, should wait some time before attempting pregnancy again so that they can work through their grief to the full. If a woman conceives too soon after a stillbirth she may find that her grief has not worked itself out and that she simply puts it to one side while she is pregnant again. Then, when the new baby arrives, she may find she is grieving for the loss of the first baby at the same time she is loving and accepting a new life. The same sort of thing may happen even after a miscarriage.

> I lost my first baby after the third month of pregnancy. The fear of not having another baby and the grief of losing that one became completely mixed up inside me. I tried frantically to get pregnant again, to replace that lost baby as soon as possible, but to no avail. I wished that instead of the hospital saying, 'Don't worry about it, you'll soon have another one,' they had said: 'Don't feel that you have to conceive again as soon as possible. Get over the loss of this one before you think about another.' As it was I didn't know what I was doing, really, and I still believe that I could never have conceived while I was so preoccupied with loss and death.

Fathers even more than mothers are prevented from living out their grief to the full. It is always assumed that the mother is the worst affected by the loss of a child; this is often true, but not always. The father is always prevailed upon to help the mother, to be her support, and because of this is allowed very little room for grief himself. He may want to share his grief with her, but find that in the end it is he who has to support and contain her grief. When a baby dies soon after birth, it is often the father who is more involved, because while the mother is recovering from the delivery he is the one who attends the intensive care unit and may become more closely bonded to the baby.

> In a way my husband suffered more than I did, though he wouldn't show it in the way that I did. He was with our baby and saw her die. She was a perfect baby, two months premature, and she succumbed to some kind of infection. He went all quiet

about it and would never talk about it to anyone, but often at the time I would see him crying, and I know he still feels it to this day.

If people find it hard to accept the grief parents feel when their baby dies at birth, this is even more true for a miscarriage. The woman may be expected to be upset and disappointed for a while, but then is soon encouraged to 'start another one'. This is usually far from the reality of the parents' reaction. A miscarriage, especially if it occurs later in pregnancy, is a real bereavement. Further, many women find that their depression and loss *increases* in the months after the miscarriage, and can be especially acute around the time when the baby was expected to be born.

About five or six months after the miscarriage, I had this extraordinary, vivid dream. I was going into the hospital, nine months pregnant, and everyone was wishing me luck — my mother, my husband, my stepdaughter were waving to me. Then I was walking along this long hospital corridor, and I looked down at my stomach and — to my horror — it was flat, there was no baby. I was overcome with panic — how would I tell everybody? — and also loss — I had been expecting to hold my baby in my arms in a few hours time. I remember clearly the absolute horror of it, and I woke up out of sleep with tears running down my face. When I got up in the morning I went and checked in my diary. It was almost exactly the day when the baby was due to be born, although I hadn't consciously been aware of that at the time.

I felt as if the pregnancy continued somehow in my mind for the rest of the nine months. It was only when the due date was passed that I began to think about having another baby and began to put the loss of this one behind me.

With almost every woman who has lost her baby, there is the anxiety: will I ever have another? Except in a very few cases, where an infection following or complication of pregnancy may lead to an infertility problem, the couple will in time have another baby. But it may take years, and be a hard journey.

My son David died in hospital on the fourth day after his birth. He had suffered from lack of oxygen and was in distress during labour — this wasn't picked up by the midwives. It was obvious there was something wrong as soon as he was born and he was taken to the special care unit. There was some confusion over what different doctors said about whether he would live or not, and I found that hard, as I didn't know whether there was hope; meanwhile I was in the normal ward with mothers and babies. I wasn't there when they disconnected the life support system and let him die — there was no point in doing anything. If I had been more involved by and helped by them I would have chosen to be with him and to have held him when he died.

David's father and I rowed endlessly after that, as I was obsessed with the need to have another baby, while his reaction was never to have a child again. After a year we split up. I mourned very fully for David which was important, but I still found it difficult when one friend after another became pregnant, and I wasn't. It was more than four years later that I finally conceived, with a man who understood my point of view, and so I finally have a daughter.

Until quite recently, women who lost their babies at birth were not encouraged to see or mourn them. Now it is becoming clearer that parents should be able to see and hold their dead child, to acknowledge it as a real person, to make it easier for them to accept the loss. This may be particularly important where the child has died because of some congenital abnormality. If the parents do not see the child they may imagine that the child's deformities were far worse than they really were. Even if the sight of the child is very distressing, many doctors now believe that no deformity can be as bad as the parents' worst imaginings.

They gave us the baby to hold and the nurse said she'd leave us for a few minutes, to ring for her if we wanted anything. So we had a little while by ourselves to say goodbye to our baby. I'm so glad they let us do that. It made it much easier afterwards, to have something to remember and to share.

If possible, the parents may like a photograph of the baby to keep and remember. 'I found that I just couldn't remember what she looked like, and though I tried and tried, it was all a blur. I wish I had had a photograph so that I would know.' Keeping the idea of the lost baby as a real baby, and not just a fantasy, is very important. Sometimes the hospital will take a photograph to keep on file, and the parents can ask for it whenever they want, as they may change their minds later.

Sue, whose baby died in the womb before the birth, was afraid at first to see her baby because neither she nor her husband had seen a dead person before, and didn't know what to expect.

> I was afraid that the body might have deteriorated or that we would see something horrible, but they said, 'We're sure you'd like to see the baby', so I nodded. We had given her a name, Amy Margaret. So they brought her to me, wrapped in a hideous orange hospital blanket. I didn't look too closely — I saw one eye was closed and one was open, a beautiful deep blue colour. I was frightened to look too closely in case we saw anything wrong — but the short glimpse we had of her confirmed what we wanted to see — that she was a very pretty, *normal* baby. They said I could go and see her again, and I lay there thinking, yes, I could, I could get up and go and look at her — it must have been going through my head for hours. But in the end I didn't go.

With a late miscarriage, mothers are also sometimes 'allowed' to see the baby.

> It was a third pregnancy, so no one was very sympathetic — they said I was lucky to have the two boys. But this baby — I miscarried at five months — was a girl, and I saw her. She was beautiful. I don't know whether it was better or worse for me really, seeing her, as I'm haunted by that image, but I'm still glad that I did.

After a baby has died, there are some practical things that need to be done. The death — and birth — need to be registered; for a stillborn baby, you have to register his or her birth in a special stillborn register. You can ask if you want to give the baby a name, which will help you feel that he or she did exist as a real person. You will be given a copy of the stillbirth registration certificate and a certificate for the burial of the child. If the baby died after the actual birth, you have separate birth and death certificates.

Hospitals usually arrange for cremation or burial free of charge. Many parents are too distressed at the time to think about a funeral, and go along with these arrangements, but may afterwards be upset because the baby was buried with others and is in an unmarked grave. Parents often find that if they do organize a funeral and have a marked grave they have given the baby's existence and death a proper recognition, and this helps them to mourn the baby properly, and not feel that the whole thing has been swept under the carpet. In the past, many parents of stillborn children had the baby whisked away at birth, never had a chance to see it, never knew what happened to the body, and were issued with a death certificate which just said 'baby girl' or 'baby boy'. No wonder they found it hard to accept the death.

Grief after a bereavement may take many years to run its course. Often parents who lost their baby, either through stillbirth or a miscarriage, are not given time to grieve. The Stillbirth and Neonatal Death Society (also known as SANDS) found that on the whole mothers of stillborn babies were given about six weeks to grieve and fathers about two weeks! After this time, people will start telling them to 'pull themselves together' and to forget about it. This cannot be done in so short a time.

One mother of a stillborn baby put the process of mourning very eloquently:

> At first you think about it all the time, there isn't a single waking moment when you don't think about it. Then, after some time has gone by, you'll be doing something, and you'll suddenly think to yourself, goodness, I haven't thought about the baby for five minutes! And eventually, you may be able to forget about it for half an hour, or an hour, or a morning, and then the worst is over. But it may be years — it may be never — that you never think of that baby once in a whole day.

It is not only the death of the baby that you mourn, but all the things it might have been.

> You think, it would have been six months old now, it would have been sitting up and playing. Or it would have been a year, it would have been walking now. Or, if I'd had that baby, she'd have been going to school, or growing up, or getting married. All those future experiences to which you had looked forward during the pregnancy have been wiped out for ever.

As well as grief, most mothers who have lost their babies feel tremendous anger and jealousy. These feelings can be aimed at almost everyone — everyone who doesn't understand, everyone who has a baby.

> The only people I could really talk to after I lost the baby were people who had been through the same experience. I remember I went out to lunch with a colleague of mine who I remembered had once said to me that her first baby had died. I told her what I felt, and she said, 'Oh, I *do* understand — I felt all the same things when my own baby died.' And then we talked about it, all the things I'd never dared tell anyone else — the anger, the jealousy, the fears I'd never have another, and she had felt exactly the same. I remember we were still there talking about it all till four o'clock. After I went home I felt much better, that what I felt was normal and didn't mean I was going mad.

Many women have a poor self-image after losing a baby. It may mean their confidence in themselves as a woman — their ability to have a child — is shattered for a while: 'I felt ugly, abnormal'. To add to this, the feelings of jealousy for other women may add to their guilt and make things worse. Often the jealousy is directed against one person, who becomes a kind of symbol:

> There was someone in the office opposite me who got pregnant at about the same time I did. After I miscarried I went back to work and there she was, getting fatter and fatter. I hated her, I considered leaving the job because of her, but I was scared I wouldn't get another job, and anyway I'd lose out on maternity

leave if I got pregnant again. So I had to stick it. When she left and they gave her a farewell party and gave her lots of presents for the baby, no one gave a thought to what I might have been feeling. I hated her so much I wished her baby would die or something, I was longing to hear that it had died or was deformed, and I hated myself for thinking such a terrible thing.

Women should be reassured that such reactions are normal — the Stillbirth and Neonatal Death Society says that about two-thirds of women in a survey who had lost a baby have such fantasies. Fathers may be equally affected by the loss of a baby, but do not seem to respond so often with the same jealousy. They may find it difficult to understand their partner's reaction, and this can also lead to an increase in the mother's guilt and self-doubt.

As with infertility, a couple's sex life may become disturbed after the loss of a baby. At first, both may be grieving, and will not want to make love. After a stillbirth, it may take some time before the woman is comfortable enough to resume sexual activity. But even after she is physically ready, it may take some time longer for emotional wounds to heal. The woman, in particular, may find sex deeply upsetting after a miscarriage or stillbirth: 'I felt that my insides belonged to my baby and I didn't want anything else in there.' The release of emotion that comes with making love — usually the release of joy — can for a long time be instead the release of pain and grief.

Every time we made love I burst into tears, I couldn't help myself. It always made me think of the dead baby and how I could never cry enough for it. He was very good about it, and comforted me while I cried, and sometimes he would cry too. In a way it didn't matter, because we were still close.

Sometimes the bereaved parent seeks sex frantically as a form of comfort or consolation, or to create a 'replacement baby'. If both partners feel that they don't want sex, or both seek comfort through sex, this can be all right; but sometimes one will have one response while the other has the opposite. This can be very difficult to manage, as both will feel that they are wounding or being wounded by the other.

I just had to make love to him because I had to have another baby. But he didn't want me to get pregnant again, he said he couldn't bear to see me go through all that again, I must have time to recover. I knew he was right really, but deep inside I had this feeling, I must have another baby, I must have another baby or I'll die.

Sometimes doctors can make it worse with an inappropriate remark:

They told me to go and have another baby as quickly as possible. I thought they meant medically I must do this, or I might not stand a chance. So we both forced ourselves to try for a baby, even though I was really thinking, I don't want this other baby, I want the little girl I lost.

One woman, after a stillbirth, said that she couldn't feel herself as attractive or sexually desirable after she lost her baby, until she had an affair.

I had to do it, not to hurt my husband or anything, but because this man found me sexy and attractive and he didn't know about the stillbirth. When I went to bed with my husband, the dead child was always between us, but with him I could forget it all and feel human again. We soon drifted apart — it was only a physical thing — and I found my attitude to my husband had changed as well. A year later we decided to try again, and now I have a little girl.

After I had the miscarriage, I had fantasies of going off with other men, of moving house, of running away. I thought, I can't bear to go through the same experience again, to have a repetition of the miscarriage. Somehow I got it into my head that if I made love somewhere else, if we lived in another country, if someone else was the father, it would all be different, and I wouldn't lose the second baby.

If there are other children in the family when there is a stillbirth or miscarriage there is the problem of what to tell them. It is best to tell the truth, making it clear that just because the other baby died, nothing is going to happen to them. If parents don't make this clear, or explain the baby's loss away with euphemisms, the children may not understand and be very afraid. They will be upset enough by the parents' grief, and may also feel some guilt — the older child might not have liked the idea of another baby and have wished it away, and feel that somehow he or she has achieved this.

Children who are told: 'God decided to take away our little baby' may imagine that God will decide to take them away too. A child told: 'It was such a pity your mother lost that baby' thought that the mother had literally lost it somewhere, and was afraid she might lose him too.

Parents who have told their child or children that another baby is on the way, may not know how to explain a miscarriage. They may not say anything, hoping the child will not realize, but he or she is bound to wonder what has happened. The child who has been prepared for 'another brother or sister to play with' may be angry when this brother or sister does not appear, as promised. Again, it is best to tell the truth in the most sensitive way possible.

After a miscarriage or stillbirth you will inevitably feel anxious about a subsequent pregnancy, expecting the same thing to happen again. The past experience will obviously colour events in the future. Many women who have lost a baby try to protect themselves in the next pregnancy by not allowing themselves to become too excited, too hopeful:

In my second pregnancy I refused to think of what to call the baby, didn't want any prams or cots in the house till after it was born safely, refused to enter into all the thoughts I'd had before, like, 'I wonder what he or she will look like?' and imagining the baby's birth, and coming home from the hospital, and the christening, and showing him to all my friends. I was a bit withdrawn, and didn't want to talk about it to anyone else. I was afraid that if I did it might all go wrong again.

After my miscarriage I refused to take the next pregnancy seriously, even though I was very sick and throwing up all over the place, and was sure that it would all be over by three months. When I went along to my first antenatal appointment, I still hadn't really accepted it, emotionally. They said they would do an ultrasound scan, and when they did, they let me see the screen and I could actually see my baby, a four-month foetus. I could hardly believe it was true and I wept and wept all the way home, I was so overcome and excited.

Every pregnancy is different, and because something has gone wrong in one, it does not mean that it will go wrong in the next. All parents who have lost a baby feel considerable anxiety in the next pregnancy; this is normal. They will need a lot of support during this time; organizations like SANDS can help. Nonetheless, it is important to try to keep as calm and optimistic as possible, even if things look as if they're going against you.

I had two miscarriages before — both times I started spotting blood at eight weeks, and went on to lose them. With the third, at eight weeks I spotted again, and I was in despair. I thought, here we go again, it's exactly the same pattern. But that time the bleeding stopped, and I went on to have a healthy baby.

For many women who have a stillborn baby the knowledge of death comes before the birth begins. Probably more than half of stillbirths are intra-uterine deaths, so the mother is often aware that her baby has died while she is still carrying it.

I had had a threatened miscarriage at three months, so after that I took great care with the pregnancy. My husband ran me into work so that I wouldn't have to brave the rush hour tube and I made sure I had a lot of rest.

At about seven months, I noticed one day that I hadn't felt the baby move. I mentioned this to one or two people who said, 'Oh, don't worry, I expect it's just having a rest.' But I didn't feel it move on the second day either and on the third day I rang my doctor's surgery, and told them I hadn't felt the baby move for three days. They said: 'Try not to worry, but can you come down here straightaway and we'll get the doctor to look at you.' So then I really did panic, and rushed straight down to the surgery, and they fitted me in to see my doctor right away. She examined me and listened for the foetal heartbeat, and then she said, 'I think we'd better go down to the hospital and get them to have a look.' She was very calm and reassuring in her manner, but she took me out of the surgery and ran me to the hospital in her car, and I thought, you don't just walk out of your surgery dropping everything unless something is really wrong. So by then I already really knew the worst, although I was still trying to hope. But when we got to the hospital all my worst fears were confirmed.

Obstetricians are reluctant to induce labour because there are risks to the mother in induction when the baby is dead, although new techniques mean this practice is changing. Doctors also do not like to perform a Caesarean because that may affect future births. So some women have to go on carrying the dead baby, sometimes for as long as several weeks until labour starts or finally a Caesarean has to be carried out.

A dead baby feels different inside you to a live one. Not only does it not move, but it lies differently; the sensation is very difficult to explain. I think very few doctors understand the horror for a mother of being a walking coffin, of going around each day knowing if you go out that people are going to say, 'When's the baby due?' and feeling all the time a terrible suspension of your grief because you do not dare to feel it, do not dare in case you go mad.

When mothers know that the baby had already died, it frequently means a long and painful labour, knowing that the result is all for nothing. Parents in this situation often are not able to grieve at first, for their first feeling after the labour is over is relief that the ordeal is finished. Some people who have been told that their baby is dead and they must go home to wait for labour to begin, and have to wait a long time, may get stuck in the phase of suspending their grief and never really come to terms with the dead baby.

The great majority of women who lose a baby, through miscarriage, stillbirth, or early infant death, go on to conceive again and have as many children as they want. But the sadness and grief, though they will fade in time, are always there, and no subsequent pregnancy ever entirely wipes out the loss. As Sue and Roger, whose baby died before the birth, said: 'We feel *robbed*.

That was our first baby, and she was dead. Even if we have another baby — and I'm sure we *will* have another baby — it will never be my firstborn. That experience has been taken away from us for ever.'

5

The Problem of Waiting

In our society we are conditioned to expect instant satisfaction. The example of advertising, the higher standards of living which enable us to buy more and more material things, extended credit facilities which enable us to buy today what we would otherwise have to save for tomorrow, all change and condition our approach to life. So, when the majority of people decide they would like to start a family, they expect that this will happen straightaway. The idea that they might have to wait a year or two or more, or that something might go wrong, is pushed to the back of people's minds.

Of course, the majority probably do conceive fairly quickly — within six months — and go on to have a normal pregnancy and birth. But when this does not happen, we are not prepared. We did not expect to have to wait. When things go wrong, there seems to be no way that we can deal with it. Couples feel abnormal, are grief-stricken, obsessed. Where do they turn for help?

Almost all couples with an infertility problem, or who have lost a baby through a miscarriage or stillbirth, admit that waiting is an extra dimension to the problem. Waiting for test results, waiting for a cause to be found, waiting all the time to conceive. Waiting for the recommended time to pass between losing one baby and trying for another, waiting for the grief to subside, waiting to become a parent. Few people bear up well to all the stresses involved in this process of waiting. And even when you do conceive, the waiting goes on; waiting for the nausea and risk of miscarriage of the first three months of pregnancy to be over, waiting for the birth, waiting to see if the baby will be all right.

Our society views waiting as a purely passive activity, something that we all grumble and groan at from day to day.

Waiting at bus stops, we glance at our watches, fret as minute by minute passes, thinking how late we are going to be. At hospital appointments we hang around in corridors, grumbling and groaning, trying to concentrate on a book or magazine. We feel that our precious time is being wasted, and this feeling of waste makes us angry and resentful. Anger and resentment increase the stress that we feel.

One of the reasons why trying to conceive is such a difficult process for the woman to remain objective about is that the experience is such a physical one. In the days before a period is due, she will find herself tuning in to all the sensations in her body — are her breasts larger than usual, is there a vague ache in her abdomen, is her period about to start, or is she pregnant this time? On the day it is due, or if it is late, all these feelings are magnified; then, if her period starts, it may only be with a little spotting and she may continue to hope that perhaps this isn't the beginning of a proper period, but just the light spotting some pregnant women experience at the time their periods are due. Then, when the period starts properly, there is disappointment or even despair.

It can be very difficult to explain to any man how powerful these experiences are. The fact that the menstrual cycle is linked to very real emotional changes in the woman doesn't make it easier for her to ignore it — her emotions will intensify the physical symptoms. Women who want to become pregnant become more focused on their bodies than usual and will often wish so much to be pregnant that they will perceive the symptoms they look for. And, in fact, the symptoms of early pregnancy are identical with those of the pre-menstrual syndrome, so it is hardly surprising that this happens so often.

While I was trying to conceive, I saw every period I had as the loss of another baby. Each time my period came, I cried and cried inconsolably. I tried very hard not to get into such a state about it, I deliberately stopped myself counting the days to when the next period was due, but I still couldn't help getting so depressed. But I had always suffered from pre-menstrual tension, so I suppose the wanting to conceive just added to the usual stress and tension I used to feel every month.

Many women are surprised by the force of their desire to have children once they have trouble conceiving or have lost a baby. It seems strange that having children, something once thought about only theoretically and usually as somewhere in the future, suddenly becomes an immediate, pressing need. As the mother of two children, whose first two pregnancies ended in miscarriages, said: 'It's as if some sleeping part of a woman has been awoken, and once it's awake, it can't be put back to sleep again.'

The experience of being pregnant, or of wanting to be pregnant — the experience of thinking you might be pregnant while you wait for your period to start or not — changes your image of yourself as a woman and the way you view other women and children. When you go out and see a mother with a small child, that child seems very real and significant to you; you find yourself wondering what it will be like when you have a child that age, how it would behave, what it would look like. You become aware of pregnant women when you never noticed them before. You become aware of babies and children everywhere. When someone talks about a friend or relative having a baby, you feel immediately interested and involved. These feelings stay with you and often intensify when the child you want and expect is denied you.

Along with the problem of waiting, for those who fear they are infertile, or who have lost a baby, come the inevitable feelings of jealousy and being left out. Everyone else seems to be pregnant or having children, the whole world seems geared around the family and children, and they are caught on the outside. These feelings — which must be acknowledged and given vent to, otherwise they will build up and get worse — lead to more anger and resentment, till there seems no way out. Finally the couple may feel so bitter that they even begin to lose sympathy for themselves, feeling that they are horrid people, have brought it all on themselves, and so on.

But there is a way out of it; the vicious circle can be broken. As one woman explained:

I lost my first baby, and eighteen months later I still hadn't conceived again. I could think of nothing else but my grief and anger. We went to some friends for dinner, and they had invited another couple, who had a little six-month-old daughter. There was a lot of fuss over this baby, but I ignored her and the mother and talked to the other people. Inside, I felt a lot of jealousy and anger.

When dinner was ready they took the baby upstairs and she wouldn't settle and kept on crying. The mother came down and we all sat down to dinner, and that baby went on and on crying throughout the entire meal — not loudly enough to upset the others, but enough to go right through me. I thought, what did they want a baby for if they can just leave it to cry like that for hours? Part of me wanted to go up and see to it myself, but I just didn't dare, I didn't trust myself.

Of course the dinner ended with a terrible row, supposedly about politics, though it was really my anger about the baby. It ended with my shouting at my friend and stomping out of the house, and afterwards my husband and I were both very upset about it. I told my mother about it, and what I had felt, and then she said something that was terribly wise. She said, 'But why did you harden your heart against that baby? Why didn't you ask if you could hold it, could take an interest in it? You would have felt so much better if you had. You could have told the mother what had happened to you, and I'm sure she would have had a lot of sympathy.' I thought about that a lot afterwards, and those words, 'Why did you harden your heart?' really spoke to me. It was true — that was what I was doing, I was allowing myself, almost deliberately, to sink deeper and deeper into unhappiness and bitterness.

There is a difference between acknowledging the inevitable feelings of grief, anger, and jealousy which you will feel after losing a baby and allowing yourself to be swept up by these feelings completely. We do not know how great an impact a person's state of mind has on their fertility, and while it is futile to ask people to 'relax', a tense, negative, bitter state of mind does not help at all. The links between the mind and body are very close, and anger, especially when it is turned inwards to become depression and self-destructive thoughts and acts, *may* be an enemy to conception.

Often when a person experiences a profound grief, one of the protective mechanisms which the mind adopts is to deny hope, to assume the loss is a permanent one, to be convinced that you will never get over it. So the woman who has lost her baby says: 'I will never have another one', or even, 'I don't want another one'. This is done to protect her from suffering a second loss. Similarly, anxiety can be seen as a defence — 'If I worry about it enough it won't happen'. But these protective defences, if clung to for too long after the grief has been experienced, can become the sufferer's worst enemy. Anxiety and the denial of hope bog the woman down into a depression which may make it very difficult for her to achieve the goal she so much wants.

It would be much more constructive, if feelings of anxiety seem to overwhelm you, to try to think positively. Instead of saying, 'If I worry enough it won't happen', try saying, 'If I'm optimistic enough it won't happen'. Try to replace the negative charm with a positive one (because all these reactions are really left-overs from a child's 'magical' way of thinking). Rather than saying, 'We will never have any children', the childless couple should try to think, 'We will have children if we want them enough, somehow or other', as long as there is a real hope.

A certain level of stress and anxiety does seem to cause a delay in conceiving, though obviously not always so. A number of surveys have shown recently that a large number of people attending infertility clinics are teachers or others from high-stress jobs. Actresses also seem to suffer a higher-than-usual rate of infertility and miscarriage. However, it may be that these women take longer to conceive not just because they have demanding jobs but because they are older — and age does have an effect on fertility. However changing your life-style to a more relaxed one may help. Learning to relax is a great benefit — try attending yoga or relaxation classes. These should be seen not so much as something which will help you conceive, to be rejected with anger if they don't, but a way of coping with the stresses you will inevitably be feeling.

Using the time in which you are 'waiting' for some positive use is another good way to alleviate stress. If you recall times when you have been waiting, in a railway station, in an airport, waiting for exam results, waiting for someone to arrive after a long journey— the worst is when you have nothing to do *but* wait. If you can find some absorbing task to occupy you in the meantime, the time will seem to have passed much more quickly. The same thing applies to waiting to have a baby. Take up some activity which you've always meant to get on with — a course of study at evening classes, for instance, or painting, or a sport, or learning a language, or anything about which you've often said, 'I wish I could do such-and-such'. Or use the time to do something which would be quite impossible if you had a small baby—an adventurous holiday which you had wanted to take, a visit to a country you always wanted to see. You can justify the expense by working out how much it would have cost you to have a baby, especially if the woman would have given up work. Then, when you look back over that time, instead of seeing it as a complete blank in which you were simply waiting, you can see it as a time in which you did something really interesting and worthwhile.

One of the problems frequently voiced by people who have not conceived or who have lost a baby is that it tends to alienate them from their friends and sometimes their family too, as people do not seem to understand the problem and they may all be wrapped up with their own family lives and children. It can be difficult in these circumstances to make new friends, especially if you are feeling depressed and anxious. In fact, there are a number of organizations for people who are childless, or who have suffered a miscarriage and stillbirth, which often have informal meetings and which put people in touch with others who have a similar problem. These organizations (listed on page 113) can provide a wonderful opportunity not only to talk about and share the problems you are feeling, and to know you are not alone, but also to make new friends. Such groups can open up a new horizon for people suffering from the loneliness of childlessness and can also help in finding positive solutions.

Another possibility is volunteering. One woman, who had had a stillbirth and whose husband was then killed in a car accident, was determined to do voluntary work with young children. She was interested in helping with mentally handicapped children, and felt that being able to give love and assistance to these children she would be helping to heal the wounds of her own loss. This can be a very difficult step to take, and other people are not always as sympathetic as you might expect — as so often happens with the childless, their motives are viewed with some concern. People will wonder whether you are quite 'stable', whether you might not run off with one of the children in your care!

Another childless couple, considering adopting a handicapped child, decided to do voluntary work with mentally handicapped babies to see whether they could in fact cope with the problem. They found that the rewards of helping a handicapped child reach its full potential far exceeded any of the doubts that they had had in being able to cope with it.

> People's expectations are that a handicapped baby will be a 'cabbage' when it grows up. The truth is that many mentally handicapped children are abandoned by their parents, either literally or emotionally, and are never encouraged or stimulated to learn. In a warm and stimulating environment, many handicapped babies can learn to achieve a surprising amount.

Some people find that individual counselling can be very helpful. Many couples find that being unable to have a child changes the way they look at their whole lives, which may seem suddenly to become purposeless. They may find that the crisis of childlessness brings many other areas of conflict and uncertainty into the fore.

> I began to wonder whether what I had always thought as a teenager was true; that it was only women who did not have children who became writers or artists or achieved great things. All the historical women I admired had been childless. I thought yet again, if I have children will all my creativity go into that instead of into writing? Am I unconsciously stopping myself from having a child?

At the very least, counselling can help you put some of the 'waiting' time to good use and can help you to express some of your grief, anger and guilt without being judged for it. 'I found that I could tell her *everything* I felt, without having to cover up anything. For example, I couldn't tell my husband that I had fantasies about leaving him because he had a fertility problem, because I knew I wouldn't leave him, so it would only torture him unnecessarily; but it was such a relief to be able to get it off my chest.' One woman whose baby had died soon after birth became involved in co-counselling, where one person 'counsels' the other over some problem, listening and offering sympathy, and then roles are reversed, with the second person counselling the first. This was an enormous help to her in the years that followed before her second baby was born.

Other organizations exist, such as The Compassionate Friends, who help parents who have lost children, at whatever age. What people suffering through a crisis like infertility or the loss of a child need most is to talk and share their experiences with someone who understands — and the only people who can really understand are those who have been through the experience themselves. People who do not understand are tempted to try to console, with platitudes such as 'It is all for the best', and 'You'll have a baby soon, you know'. But people in this situation cannot be consoled in this way. It is better just to listen and say nothing than try to help with well-meaning but ill-judged words of wisdom, as any bereaved parent knows.

The period of waiting is often made worse by the fact that the childless couple are often dealing with grief — the grief of a miscarriage, a stillbirth or discovering that there is some kind of fertility problem. Often the people around them do not understand the best ways of coping with that grief. They may try to help, but end up making the couple feel worse:

After our baby died I was still in hospital. My mother went round to the house and cleared everything to do with the baby out of the room — the cot, the pram, the baby clothes, the toys, the mobile we'd hung on the ceiling. I know she was trying to help, but when I got home I was devastated, as if they'd wiped out every trace of the baby as if he'd never existed.

They told me I had blocked tubes and they could operate with a fifty–fifty chance of success. I felt absolutely numb. Nobody seemed to understand, they all said, 'Oh, I'm sure it'll be all right', and left it at that. I was completely unable to think of anything positive at all. All I could think was, there really was something wrong with me, there's a fifty per cent chance I'll never have children. Nobody I talked to understood — they said, 'Well, now they know what's wrong they can put it right, can't they?' as if I should be glad and not devastated by the news.

Grief, for the loss of a baby or the loss of fertility, can often best be helped by concrete symbols. One couple made up a book in memory of their stillborn daughter, with photographs, all the letters from friends and relatives in sympathy at their loss, dried flowers from the funeral, a favourite poem, the cutting from the announcement in the paper. Making the book and being able to look at it made the loss more real and more accepted. Another woman, told she was infertile, made a corner of the garden — at the suggestion of a counsellor — as a special place where she would plant things and watch them grow, a sort of fertility ritual of her own.

Many friends and relatives keep their children away from a bereaved or childless couple, thinking that seeing children will make it worse for them. For a time this may be true, but in the end it may hurt the couple more than anything else; not only are they deprived of their own children, but also from enjoying other people's. It is a very difficult position to be in, but friends should remain open and sensitive:

After I had the miscarriage, I was invited to my cousin's baby's christening, who was conceived at about the same time. I couldn't bear to go, so we made an excuse. Then, for months afterwards, they didn't ring us up or ask us round, and I became quite hurt. We finally rang up and suggested going over — they asked us to go in the evening 'when the baby was in bed'. Finally we went and I felt very awkward — the baby cried and then I asked if I could go up and see it. My cousin was surprised and said 'yes', so I did. It *was* very painful seeing the baby, who was beautiful, but not nearly as painful as the feelings of isolation, of feeling a kind of social leper whenever babies were mentioned.

We need advice and guidance often on how best to cope with these circumstances. Organizations like the National Association for the Childless or the Stillbirth and Neonatal Death Society can help:

After our baby died I rang them and they were marvellous. The woman I spoke to, who had had a stillbirth herself, knew exactly what to say. It wasn't just giving sympathy; there was a lot of practical advice as well. She said: 'Have you got a room all full of the baby's things?' and I said yes. She said I should go and clear it out myself, painful though it was, not leave the door locked for weeks avoiding it. Then she asked me if I had a friend with a small baby, and I said I did; she told me to go and see them as soon as I could, and look after the baby, hold it, even be alone with it for a while; it would help me to see things more clearly. She was absolutely right — we went and looked after this friend's baby for an evening and it grizzled, and we worried, and it was a great relief to leave and go back to be by ourselves. It did help prevent me from seeing motherhood as a wonderful fantasy.

Some practical ways to cope with infertility or the loss of a baby

If you have difficulty in conceiving:

Don't worry straightaway; you may get pregnant sooner than you think. But once the worry has reached a certain point, *do* seek medical help. If there is a medical problem, the sooner it is dealt with the better; if there is not, your mind will be put at rest.

Do involve yourself as much as possible in the infertility investigations. Ask as many questions as you like — it is *always* a good idea to take with you a piece of paper with the questions on it you want to ask so that you don't come out having forgotten to ask the one thing you really wanted to know. Make the doctor repeat or explain more clearly to you anything you don't understand.

Don't bottle your fears up — do tell people you have a problem, even if it seems an admission of failure. But be selective whom you tell — it won't help to tell everybody you meet, or to tell people who are unlikely to be sympathetic; people who are spending all their time trying to avoid unwanted pregnancies or who say that they never want children are unlikely to be able to give you the support you need.

If you have lost a baby:

If it was a stillbirth, and you had a room at home all ready for the baby, *do* clear it out straightaway, and do it yourself, perhaps with the help of a friend or relative. Don't lock the door and leave the room to become a mausoleum, which you dread entering more and more with each day and week that passes. Give the baby's things away or store them up for a future baby. Hard though it may seem, it is better to do these things yourself than hand it over to someone else — it will help in the process of grieving.

Do go out and face the world as soon as possible. Get a friend to warn people what has happened, so that you don't have to explain things over and over again to everybody and you don't have to face too many ill-informed remarks. Don't stay at home and shut yourself up for too long — it will be harder to get back into your life the longer you leave it.

Do allow yourself to mourn. Act out some kind of ritual if you feel it will help; hold a funeral or memorial service, keep mementoes of that baby's brief existence, allow yourself to cry and express your feelings. This is as important for the father as for the mother.

Do try to go and see people who have small children as soon as you can — even look after one for an evening if possible. This will help prevent you from making too much of a fantasy out of your lost baby, and remind you that there is a difficult side to parenthood too. It will also help you not to shut yourself off from babies and small children.

In both cases:

Don't harden your heart against friends who have children or children themselves. Feelings of grief and jealousy are normal, but try not to encourage your bitterness. Try to take an interest in children and enjoy their company — this may seem hard at first but will help you in the end.

Do try not to become obsessive, hard though this is to do. Learn what circumstances make your depressions worse and learn how to short-circuit them by acting quickly — by going out, by involving yourself in something creative, by talking to someone who understands.

Do go for professional counselling if you feel it would help. You can ask your doctor or ring a local advice centre or even ask some organization like the Samaritans. Having an hour a week set aside to talk exclusively about that problem without feeling you are a drag on your friends, or meeting to talk to people with similar problems, can be very valuable.

Do try to do something really significant in your life which you couldn't have done if you'd had a baby. Go on holiday somewhere you've always wanted to go, or enrol in a course of study, or look for a better job. Then, when you look back, you will see that something positive came out of the experience, it was not just a waste of time.

6

Adoption and Fostering

Almost every couple who have failed to conceive after a certain length of time think to themselves: 'Why don't we adopt?' Adoption can seem the perfect answer to infertility, and until the past ten years or so this was often the case. However, the numbers of children available for adoption has now shrunk to far fewer than the numbers of couples wanting to adopt. In 1982, 10,240 children were adopted in England and Wales. However, over half of these were adoptions where one or both of the adopting couple was a natural parent. This is happening increasingly as divorce rates rise, and a step-parent wants to formally adopt the child for whom he or she is caring.

Of the remaining 4500 children adopted, only just over 2500 were of babies under the age of two. Since most people who want to adopt want small babies, this does not offer much help to the tens of thousands of infertile couples.

Thinking about adoption is not easy. Many parents may think about adopting in the heat of the moment, while they are still suffering from the grief and distress of finding out they will probably be unable to have children of their own. They have had little time to weigh up their real feelings about both childlessness and adoption. It is better to give some time to let your grief subside and make some practical decisions about your life and how much you really want to adopt. This process may well be magnified when you come to look into adoption possibilities.

My husband and I both thought about adoption. At first I said, 'Yes, yes, let's adopt, I don't care even if it's a handicapped baby as long as I have a child.' But after I had calmed down a bit and we began to look into the reality of it, I began to feel that it wasn't just any baby I wanted, it was *our* baby. There was a small chance that treatment might in the end help us and our first tentative enquiries to adoption agencies were so off-putting that we decided to let it drop.

Adoption seemed impossible, but the more I thought about a life without children, the more terrifying it seemed to me. I had never been really interested in jobs I'd done, had always seen them as 'filling in', and looking after children was what I wanted. So we decided, we'll adopt, even if its older or problem kids, I don't care, I really want to be at home and have kids in the house even though they wear me out with their problems.

Because of the scarcity of children for adoption, most agencies set fairly strict criteria for couples seeking to adopt. After all, they have the interests of the child at heart and, since they can pick and choose, they want to find what seems to them the most suitable couple for a particular child. Many agencies have so many couples on their lists that they have to close their books from time to time, and may be unable to say when they will re-open them. For all these reasons, applying to adoption agencies can be a most frustrating and upsetting experience.

I decided to see what happened, so finally I picked up the phone and rang one agency which didn't seem to have too many restrictions. The woman who answered the phone said, 'Can I help you?' and I said, 'Yes, I'm interested in adopting.' Then she said, straightaway before I could go any further, rather rudely, 'You realize there aren't any white babies for adoption'. And I said, 'Yes, I do know that, we're not particularly interested in a white baby'. So then she said, 'Well, we prefer black babies to go to black parents, you know', and I said, 'Oh.' There was a pause, and then she asked some questions, such as how old was I, how old was my husband. When I said I was thirty and he was forty-five, there was another long pause, and then she said, 'Would we be prepared to adopt an older or handicapped baby?' And I said, 'Yes, I thought we might, I'd like to look into it.' So then she suggested we wrote in and went along to one of their regular information meetings, where they got a number of interested couples together and give them more information. I put the phone down and burst into tears, she seemed so rude and so unconcerned with what I might be feeling. But then, I suppose they get dozens of calls like that every day.

Many couples interested in adopting say that they feel they are being considered guilty of ulterior motives when they want to adopt a child. They often feel that they are being asked all kinds of irrelevant questions, that details of their life-style, income, marital happiness and even their sex life are dragged out in the open to uncaring ears. They are often asked why they want children — a question most people, whether they have children or not, find hard to answer. 'I just couldn't think of a "proper" reason. Because I was afraid of being lonely? Because I wanted to kiss some little baby fingers and toes? Because I love playing games with children? Because I love to watch them learn and grow? Which of those answers — if any — would be acceptable to them?'

Many see their contacts with the adoption agencies as a whole series of obstacles designed to put them off.

They are very off-putting when you first ring up. They put you off even further when you go to their information meetings. They go on putting you off and putting you off till you've almost given up — and many people do give up. I'm not saying that they're unkind, and perhaps it's a good idea really — to screen out all those who aren't really set on it. But I don't know whether the ones who stick it all out are necessarily those who would make the best parents.

Most agencies set restrictions on age – anyone over the age of thirty-five would be very lucky to be considered as a parent for all but an older (and possibly teenage) child, or a child with a handicap. The idea behind this is that the child has already lost one set of parents, so the agency would like the adopting parents to be young and healthy. Large age gaps between the spouses are also not usually accepted. Divorced couples who have remarried may face difficulties, though less so than before, and the childless are not considered ideal for some children. Many agencies prefer older children with special needs to be adopted into families where there are existing children or the parents have experience of bringing up children.

Despite all this, there are many children needing homes and families who no one wants to adopt. These may be older, of mixed race, handicapped, or brothers and sisters who want to be adopted together. All these children have special problems and needs, and the would-be adopters should be aware of these and not just adopt them because it seems to be their only way to have a child. Older children who have come from very unhappy homes or have lived in residential care may find it very hard to settle into life in an ordinary family much as they might want it. Insecure children often do everything they can to test the strength and affection of their new family, and the new parents may find this more than they can take.

White families who adopt black children may find themselves victims of prejudice, as their children do, and suffer with them. They may also find that they are unable to relate to the child's attempts later on to uncover his or her culture and roots; research has shown that black children in white families tend to be brought up as white, and this may cause identity conflicts later on. For all these children, the couple who have had experience of parenting may be much more able to cope with extra needs and demands, so are often preferred by adoption agencies. It seems the infertile couple cannot win!

Recent changes in the law in Britain have also made adoption more difficult. It is now possible for all adopted children to trace their natural parents after they reach the age of eighteen, and have access to their birth and adoption records. This may have further put off people thinking of giving up their children for adoption, as they may fear the effects of being traced in the future. Secondly, private adoptions were made illegal in Britain from February 1982 unless the proposed adopter is a relative of the adopted child. All other adoptions must go through recognized agencies — this is to ensure that prospective parents have been properly screened and that legal requirements have been met. This now makes it impossible, however, for someone to legally adopt a baby which she knows of through a friend, clergyman, doctor or relative, or to make special arrangements with an abortion agency when a mother is refused abortion because her pregnancy is too far advanced. Many such adoptions have been successful in the past, but as pressures from couples wanting to adopt increase, so does the likelihood of money exchanging hands in such arrangements. More and more couples unsuccessful in adopting through the usual channels say that they would be willing to 'buy' a baby. The new law intends above all to protect the interests of the child.

Many people look abroad for possibilities to adopt a baby, especially when they see publicity for some Hollywood personalities who have adopted Vietnamese or Korean babies. Unfortunately, this is very difficult in Britain for a number of reasons. First, there is no agency which deals with the adoption of babies from abroad in Britain; this is not the case in all countries, and the United States and Sweden do have such agencies. Secondly, many Third World countries are increasingly reluctant to allow their babies to go abroad for adoption, even if they cannot be properly cared for in that country. Some nations have passed laws making it very difficult for foreigners to adopt — for example, Indonesia insists that a foreign couple should have lived in the country for seven years before they are able to apply to adopt a child. Other countries have such mountains of red tape that all but the most determined couple would be put off. Even if this hurdle is overcome, there may be difficulties of convincing the authorities at home to recognize the adoption and allow the child into the country. You usually have two choices — either to go through official channels, accepting a long wait and complicated paperwork, or turn up at the airport with your child and hope some official will take pity on you and let you in. Because of the tightening of immigration laws in Western countries in recent years, it is becoming increasingly difficult to bring a foreign — and especially black — baby into the country.

These laws do not seem to make sense when you consider the number of ill-fed, unwanted, poorly cared-for children in the Third World, and the numbers of families in the West who would love to have the opportunity to bring them up. But a lot of prejudice remains about this issue, and Third World countries who are recovering their sense of cultural identity and pride may see this export of unwanted babies as a further aspect of colonialism. They would argue that people in rich countries should give money to enable the children to grow up with their own family and their own culture in their own country, rather than taking them abroad to ease the heartache of infertile Western couples.

However, the couple who really want to adopt should not be put off too early in the process — someone has to succeed, and it may be you. Further, as you look into the various possibilities and are presented with individual children to consider, you may find your heart is won by a child whose description, in cold blood, might not have sounded quite what you would have wanted to take on.

Sometimes adoption can be easier than anticipated. To counteract all the stories of heartache and disappointment involved in considering adoption, here is at least one happy outcome:

We had had many years of infertility problems, and finally had to accept that it was most unlikely that we would have a child born to us. So we applied to the Church of England Adoption Society in 1979. We had an interview—they told us how difficult it was to adopt a child and said we were a bit old—thirty-five and forty at the time. They were pleasant, but off-putting. They told us about the children who wait — older and handicapped children — we thought about one or two, but in the end we decided that what we wanted was an oriental baby (I am part oriental). We also went to see someone in London to find out about going abroad and trying to bring a baby home. They told us how difficult it was, and we weren't willing to take the risk.

The adoption officer came to see us two or three times — looked around our home and asked questions. I must say that she was a very nice person, very thorough in her questions, and very considerate. I remember many of the searching questions she asked us, such as, 'Is there anything you would do in bringing up a child which would be different from the way you were brought up?' and I remember she stressed that we must *always* tell the truth to the child about its origins, and not pretend that he or she was an orphan.

This process must have taken about six months. Then very soon after her last visit — two months or so — we were given details of a little boy of eight or nine, half Chinese, very intelligent, with a photo and details of what he liked doing, his background and so on. But there had been social problems in his family, and I did want a baby. It was an agony, living with the image of this child for a whole week, opening your heart to him and really considering it. In the end we said no, which wasn't easy.

A couple of months later, we were told that there was a little oriental baby in London, nearly three months old. We were sent a photograph and told her background. We were quite happy about all the information we received, and went to see the baby.

The foster mum let us in, and proudly showed us the baby, now about four months old. She loved this child, and was nearly in tears, expecting us I think to say 'yes' or 'no' on the spot — but we had already decided we mustn't rush into a decision. After all, we had had years of infertility problems of different kinds, and this was an enormous change, and very, very sudden. So we went back and talked about it, but as soon as we did, we knew that if we didn't want this child, then we didn't want to adopt. So we said 'Yes'.

There was about a month's wait before the papers were sorted out and then it was all a mad rush. We had to buy everything for the baby and get a room ready, and then we went to stay with the foster mother for two days. She was very kind and showed us how to do everything, bottles and nappies and so on — I was completely unused to young babies. Then we went for a walk and the foster mother put the baby in my arms and said she must go off and do something — when she came back to her flat we were getting on peacefully together.

We took her home the following day with the presents which were given to her at Christmas by the foster mother's children. I sat in the back of the car with her and we both sang songs very loudly for her. When we got home she wouldn't take the bottle for some time, but she ate normally and didn't cry — I'm sure that she registered the change.

She is a very placid, happy child. She prefers to weigh up anything new, and is very logical in her responses to people. She is very sensible emotionally, she takes time to trust, but she had many dear friends who she does love and trust and I pray that the future will be a happy one for her.

People have said to us how kind it is for us to have adopted a child — quite the reverse — we are grateful to her for being with us and loving us.

If you are successful in being accepted as a suitable couple to adopt, however, the process is only just beginning. First, you must look after the child for a probationary period before it can become a legal member of your family through the granting of an adoption order by the courts. During this probationary period, prospective parents have no legal rights. The child still belongs to the natural parents, who have to agree to the adoption order being made in the vast majority of cases. The natural parents can at any time decide that they do not want the child adopted, or that they wish to look after it themselves. Even if the child is in the care of a local authority, the natural parents still have certain rights.

You have to care for the child for at least three months — not including the first six weeks of a baby's life — and you also have to give the local authority three months' notice that you have in your care a child whom you intend to adopt. You then may have to wait some time for the court hearing, so the whole process can take many months.

During the probationary period a social worker will visit your home to make further enquiries. This can be nerve-racking for the prospective parents who can feel that they are being examined and fear that they are not the perfect parents they are expected to be. Just as many parents who have just given birth to a child may feel depressed and unable to cope in the first few weeks their small baby is at home in their care, the couple looking after a baby they hope to adopt can be going through teething troubles. The social worker will not be trying to catch you out, but to offer advice and help, and will keep in touch till the adoption takes place.

The adoption agency worker will also keep in close touch with you, and some agencies have discussion groups for new parents which can be very helpful. The purpose of the probationary period is to make sure that you, the child, and any other children, can settle down to a happy life together. If you find that you have real doubts about whether this child is the right one for you, or you the right family for them, do raise this now, as it would be much better for the child if the agency found alternative parents.

Adoption is finally legalized by the magistrates' or county court; the adoption agency will help with the procedure and a solicitor is not normally needed. Cases are heard privately and the proceedings are short and simple. From the moment the adoption order is granted, the child becomes one of your own children in law, inherits from you and your family, and the natural parents have no further rights over it. You are issued with a copy of the entry in the Adoption Register to replace the original birth certificate, although the child will be able to have access to these records after reaching the age of eighteen.

The question of whether and how to tell children that they are adopted can present problems for parents, not dissimilar to the dilemma faced by parents of AID children. In the past, when the children adopted were of the same race as their adoptive parents, many parents did not tell. Now, however, adoption agencies believe very strongly that children should always be told, preferably as young as possible, and that they should always be told the truth about their own background. In fact, many children would guess the truth anyway — they may notice that when other mothers discuss how difficult the birth of their children was, or talk about breast-feeding or how they felt when they were pregnant, their own mothers remain silent. They may realize that they look physically different from their parents and wonder whether they were in fact adopted, and this uncertainty may be far more distressing than the truth.

Nowadays, more children adopted by white parents are black or of mixed race, and so could not be the natural children of the parents. Others may have been adopted old enough to have distinct memories of their life before they came to their new family. In all these cases, telling the child is a necessity right from the beginning. Most people now think that this is the best way to tell any adopted child — to mention it in a matter of fact way from the beginning and answer the child's questions appropriately as its understanding grows.

Fostering

Couples who are not considered suitable by adoption agencies, perhaps because they are too old, may think of fostering as an alternative. However, adoption and fostering are very different. When you foster a child, you know that he or she may only be with you for a limited period. You will have to stay in touch closely with the social services, and sometimes with the natural parents, and any decisions that are made about the future of the child will not be made by you alone. You may have to face periods of considerable disruption if the natural parents decide they want the child returned to them, but cannot cope and the child is returned to you again in a disturbed state. Sometimes agreement will be reached that it is destructive for the child to be in touch with the natural parents, but often the parents will want to visit and keep in touch. Sometimes, the fostering couple and the child's parents can form a happy relationship, though mostly the fostering couple view the natural parents' visits with a certain amount of nervousness and distrust. While these visits can seem to upset the child in the short term, studies show that the long-term emotional development of the child is best when the natural parents do visit and show an interest in their child's welfare.

There are three main types of fostering: short-stay, where the couple look after children for a matter of weeks, usually during parental illness or some other family crisis; medium-term, when the hope may be to return the child to his or her natural parents or to a suitable home for adoption; and long-term fostering which aims to create a stable, secure home for the child when, for some reason, adoption is not possible. The majority of couples who foster in fact have the child or children with them for a number of years. When a couple foster in the long term, they usually build permanent links with the child, who will return to visit them after leaving home, and this is what most foster families would hope for. It is quite wrong, however, for couples to foster only in the hope that they will eventually be able to adopt the child. Parents who undertake fostering with this hope are likely to end up in considerable distress.

> There was a family in the road that put me off the idea of fostering for ever. They were looking after these Indian twins, beautiful children, whom they adored. These children's mother was completely incapable of looking after them, so they hoped that in time they would be able to adopt. But the mother was against adoption. She would from time to time insist that she could cope and make improvements in her life, and then she would have the twins back for a while. It never lasted long, the children were miserable and neglected, and then they would be taken back into care and end up back with the foster parents again. As this went on, the children became more insecure, and the foster parents finally broke down and said they couldn't cope any more, either they adopted them or that was it, and so the children were taken away and put in a home. I will never forget that woman crying after they had gone, it broke my heart.

Fostering probably works best where the couple are happy to foster, and if adoption is possible at the end this is an extra bonus, not something they have been desperately hoping for all along. For this reason the most successful foster parents often have, or have had, children of their own, so that they are not investing all their energies and emotions in the one child.

Many childless couples who do decide to foster find that sharing part of their lives with the children who come to live with them provides much pleasure, as well as inevitable difficulties too. It allows them to share in the joys and heartaches of parenthood, as well as providing a much needed home for society's unlucky children.

7

Adapting to Childlessness

For some of those who have infertility problems, there will be no 'happy ending'. Medical science will not be able to help them — or they may not be able to afford private treatment which might bring about a cure. They may be too old to be considered good candidates for adoption, and they may not be prepared to adopt someone else's older, problem or handicapped child. They may have to resign themselves to not having children.

Yet when a couple accept their childlessness and accept that hope is gone, they may surprisingly enough feel happier than they have felt for a long time. All the doubts, worries, uncertainties and fears, and desperate clinging to straws of hope are over, and the couple can start anew. The moment of acceptance itself can be painful — possibly the most painful experience of a person's life — but as soon as it is over, and the grief has been expressed and washed away, being childless will never seem quite so bad again. Often the fear of pain is worse than the pain itself — equally the fear of childlessness is usually worse than a couple's actual experience of life without children.

After the stress of many years wondering whether they would have a child or not, a couple can adjust to a different way of life, and take the decisions they may have been putting off for years; to move to a bigger house or not, to change jobs, for the woman to take up a new career.

All those years I had never dared change my job, because I kept thinking, what if I got pregnant and then couldn't get maternity leave, and what's the point in starting a new job when I might get pregnant in a few months. I also couldn't bear to leave the people who helped support me through that time for a new set of faces, where I'd have to start all over again. But finally having a child began to seem so unlikely that I decided I couldn't go on planning my life around that possibility — if it did happen, it would be such a miracle that all the other things didn't matter. So I looked around and got a new, much more challenging job. It was a very good and positive step for me.

Inevitably, infertility will have had its effect on the couple's relationship and especially their sexual relationship. When they finally accept their infertility, it may be possible to get back to the kind of relationship they shared before they ever started thinking about having children. Many couples say that they can only get back to a happy sex life after discovering they are infertile by somehow breaking the link between sex and the possibility of conception. Some people do it by using contraception, to prevent their being able to say to themselves, 'Perhaps this time, by some miracle . . .' others by using variations of sex which do not involve the penetration and ejaculation associated with years of trying hopelessly to conceive.

> For years our sex life was completely messed up by trying to conceive. Then when we were beginning to realize that I never would, we both went through a phase when we didn't want to make love at all. Finally, I made the decision to start using contraception again, at least for a while — it meant that we both knew I couldn't get pregnant, and it helped us to see things as they had once been, when we were first in love with one another and didn't want a baby, and things started to get much better then. But it took a very long time.

Other pressures are removed from the couple too:

> All that time we had been taking so much care that we wouldn't do anything that might interfere with the chances of conception. I took lots of vitamin pills to make sure that I wasn't lacking any vital element, and neither of us drank — I had given up smoking too. If I did conceive, then we were going to have the perfect baby. But once we realized we weren't going to make it, I just chucked away the vitamins and we bought a couple of bottles of good wine and we got *drunk*, and then we staggered off to bed,

just like we used to in the old days. It was a wonderful moment of liberation.

Sometimes an event will intervene that makes childlessness seem less important, such as a serious illness or accident:

We hadn't really thought about making the decision to have children in a very conscious way, as we both enjoyed our work, but as time went by and I didn't get pregnant, I began to wonder and then to worry. Philip hadn't been feeling very well, and had been having some tests, and then the doctors told us, 'It's a form of cancer, we can treat it but it means he'll be infertile. What do you want us to do?' And all I could say was, 'Forget about being fertile, just do whatever you can'. During the time that followed, all I could think was, please let him live, please let him get better — which after a long illness he did. I suppose I do feel some regret that we never had children, but nothing like the joy I feel that we still have one another.

People usually think of childless couples as being lonely, self-contained and even aloof. But in fact many childless couples do form close friendships either with other couples like themselves or with those who have children. They may also form close links with friends' children and other young people.

My best friend said she would make me her daughter's godmother. I thought that was pretty poor compensation for having one of my own, but now I'm not so sure. Sarah, my god-daughter, called me her favourite aunt, and sometimes she came to stay with me by herself, and we had a great deal of fun. Now she's grown up and got a job and flat in London she still writes and rings me up from time to time, and we go on shopping expeditions together. Some people bring up their children and then once they are grown up only see them once a year. I never had a child of my own, but Sarah and I are still close friends and we often visit one another.

We always had students staying in the two rooms at the top of our house. It meant there were always young people around, and sometimes we would form quite a friendship with them, and they would keep in touch and come and visit us sometimes. It made a lot of difference to us.

Some childless couples may find, especially at first, that they have to isolate themselves from children or from families with children because the pain is too great. Sometimes this is the best way of self-preservation, but usually it is just a phase. Certainly the period when all your friends seem to be engrossed in young children and you have none may be very difficult. But eventually children grow up, they become independent and you may not seem too different from your friends. Children, too, can be a problem to their parents; they may develop some illness or disability, or may not get on with their parents when they get older.

I remember how jealous I was for years of my friend who had children. But then her daughter married a man she hated and they moved to the North and she hardly ever sees them. And her son became an alcoholic. I sat with her through all the tears she shed for those children and I thought, perhaps it was better not to have them than to lavish so much love through all those years and still end up with nothing.

Many people want children because they see them as a relationship that will be lifelong, and closer than most friendships are. In our culture, this is probably less and less the case; children do not feel they have to care for elderly relatives in the way that they used to, and more and more families live at great distances from one another. Children are not necessarily the security in old age or the continuation of the family line which they were once thought to be, though these things still matter:

I know it is ridiculous, but I used to think, if I don't have a daughter, who will I pass on my mother's jewellery to? What will happen to all those things that I've bought and cherished over the years? That's a minor point, I know, in comparison to other things, but I do think about it from time to time.

108

It often helps infertile couples to examine all the reasons why they want to have children. Sometimes this process can help them see that a lot of the reasons are not very good ones. No one can finally say why they want children; but not being able to think of a good reason doesn't really make the loss any easier if you can't have them. However, some couples do find, once they have 'forgotten' about the problem, that a lot of their distress was caused by all the pressures on them — the medical tests, families waiting for the 'good news', friends all having babies. Some couples may find that, after all, having children is *not* the most important life-event for them, and then begin to reorganize their lives accordingly.

Some childless people — women in particular — may find that although they may not have their own children, they do want and need contact with other people's children. There are ways to do this — child-minding, baby-sitting, volunteering to work with young children, teaching. Many childless couples are able to form satisfying and lasting relationships with some of the children they have cared for. Our society, however, mainly organized as it is around the 'nuclear' family, does not make this easy for many people; it is possible to live in a city street for years without really getting to know any of your neighbours, unless you have children who will make friends with one another and run in and out of one another's houses. Schools, playgroups, school rounds and childhood crises are all good ways of forming links with the people around you — one reason why many childless couples fear that they will be lonely.

Sometimes it helps to change the emphasis from 'childless' — implying a lack — to 'childfree', implying a gain. More and more couples today are calling themselves 'childfree' — deciding that with the uncertain future of this world and the population explosion there are few reasons to bring another child into being. Many more women, now that the benefits of higher education and a career are more readily available to them, decide that their work is more important than a family. At first there may seem little in common between someone who decides not to have children and someone who has struggled desperately for years trying to have a baby — but as the pain of infertility fades, many similarities may emerge. Both may have suffered the misunderstandings of friends, the pressures of family, and the pain of not having young people around — a pain which may be no less real because it was consciously chosen.

> At first I didn't really trust talking to Jenny about my feelings because I knew she had chosen *not* to have children. But one day I was talking to her in her kitchen after having dinner there and she said that sometimes she regretted not having children. She said that she had had an abortion a long time ago, before she was married; she had married very late, when she was nearly forty, and was too worried about the risk of a handicapped baby and becoming a mother so late in life to give it a try. She said that she sometimes wept about the baby she might have had, and that she often thought about it when she felt low and depressed — but then she said that she supposed that if she went back over her life and lived it again she'd make the same decisions and be happy with them, and that there were lots of advantages in not having children. After that I found I could talk to her about our problems, and she was very sympathetic, and we became great friends.

When you still want a child, it may seem insensitive to talk about the pleasures and advantages of childfree living — but some people do have to live without children, and those who have learned to make the most of their misfortune can be a great help to others in the same situation. Again, joining a group like the National Association for the Childless can provide enormous support and help; people in the Association who have accepted their childlessness come together to help one another lead a full life without children.

Some childless couples will point to the advantages of more money, time and freedom than other couples; of being able to travel more, have better holidays, buy a better house, have a wealthier life-style. These are all material things, and people on the outside may be envious and imply that the childless couple, quite unfairly, are selfish and meterialistic — but there are other, non-material advantages too. The childless couple have more time and emotional energy to devote to one another, and more time together to help their relationship to grow and to deepen.

Many conventional marriages reach a crisis point when the children grow up and leave home, and the husband and wife suddenly find themselves confronting one another as strangers, having neglected their relationship throughout years of family life and the demands and crises caused by children. This cannot happen with childless couples — and in fact, statistics show that the divorce rate is significantly lower among couples with no children. These marriages are often happier and more enduring.

There is another positive thing that can come out of childlessness. We tend to think of resignation, or acceptance, as a passive, negative act. If we say that people have 'resigned themselves to childlessness' this conjures up the image of a weary couple, carrying their burden sadly and reluctantly with them for ever. In reality, resignation can be a very brave, a very positive act. The musician and philosopher Albert Schweitzer writes very profoundly in his book, *My Life and Thought*, on the meaning of true resignation, which he sees as a way to inner freedom. It means accepting everything that is hard in your life in such a way as not to resent it, but to use it in such a way that you can become a deeper, more compassionate and thinking person.

One woman explains very well the feeling of release and freedom that comes when you really accept, or resign yourself:

I remember walking up the hill — it was a bright day in early summer — after having the final results of the tests and thinking, that's it, I shall never have children. The thought gave me a lot of pain, but as soon as I had thought it, I had the sensation of a huge weight being lifted off my shoulders. I no longer had to go on thinking, if, when, somehow, if only . . . it was all suddenly settled. I walked past the children's playground on the corner of the street and two small boys were playing on the swings. I stood and watched them for a while, and again, I was no longer thinking, if only, perhaps one day, and feeling that familiar stab of jealousy; instead I was standing in the warm sunlight and listening to their high, clear voices with something approaching joy. Suddenly I felt completely washed clean, and at peace —

111

and freer than I had ever felt in my whole life.

People who are childless, whether through infertility or the loss of a child, have suffered in a way in which the majority of people do not suffer, and in a way which we do not expect to suffer in our protected society. This will enable many to extend a kind of sympathy and understanding to other people who are in difficulties or suffering from the loss of someone they love, and share their pain with them. This is a great gift, and the source of many rewarding relationships and friendships in life. It also gives a point and purpose in life of equal or even greater value to that of bearing and bringing up children.

Useful Addresses

British Pregnancy Advisory Service
Austy Manor, Wooten Wawen, Solihull, West Midlands
Tel: (05642) 3225

BPAS provides counselling and infertility services for couples who find difficulty in obtaining the help they need through the National Health Service. They provide a full infertility investigation, AIH and AID, vasectomy and sterilization reversals, laparoscopy and tubal repair if necessary. A leaflet with more details and fees is available on request.

Child
'Farthings', Pawlett, Near Bridgwater, Somerset
Tel: 0278–683595

Provides information for those who are not able to conceive. A newsletter and fact sheets are available. A 24-hour information service is available on the above number.

The Compassionate Friends
Gill Hodder, 5 Lower Clifton Hill, Clifton, Bristol BS8 1BT
Tel: Bristol (0272) 292778

Helps bereaved parents through meetings and home visits. A free leaflet, 'No Death So Sad' is also available.

CRUSE (National Organization for the Widowed and their Children)
Cruse House, 126 Sheen Road, Richmond, Surrey TW9 1UR
Tel: 01–940 4818/9047

As well as advising and helping widows, Cruse offers advice and support to parents of a stillborn child. There are seventy local branches.

Family Planning Association
27–35 Mortimer Street, London W1N 7RJ
Tel: 01–636 7866

As well as providing information on contraception and sexuality, the FPA will give advice and information on infertility.

TRYING TO HAVE A BABY?

The Miscarriage Association
'Dolphin Cottage', 4 Ashfield Terrace, Thorpe, Near Wakefield, West
Yorkshire WS3 3DD
Tel: Wakefield (0532) 828946

Provides support, help and information for women and their families who
have had, or are having, a miscarriage. It produces leaflets, pamphlets
and a newsletter and can also refer people to local groups.

National Association for the Childless
318 Summer Lane, Birmingham B19 3RL
Tel: 021–359 4887

Provides advice, information and support to childless couples — both
counselling for people with infertility problems and helping the childless
to find a fulfilled life-style. Members can be referred to local contacts,
many of whom run self-help groups. A newsletter and fact sheets on
childlessness are available.

National Childbirth Trust
9 Queensborough Terrace, Bayswater, London W2 3TB
Tel: 01–221 3833

As well as promoting education for parenthood and supporting choice in
childbirth, NCT's post-natal support group will provide information and
support for parents who have lost a baby.

National Marriage Guidance Council
Herbert Gray College, Little Church Street, Rugby, Warwicks CV21
3AP
Tel: Rugby (0788) 73241

Provides confidential counselling for couples with marriage or relationship problems, whatever the cause.

The Samaritans
St Stephens Church, Walbrook, London EC4
Tel: 01–626 9000

There is a branch in every major town.

The Samaritans will talk to anyone about any problem—you don't have to
be suicidal. They can also refer you to other organizations which may be
able to help more specifically with your problem.

USEFUL ADDRESSES

The Stillbirth and Neonatal Death Association (SANDS)
37 Christchurch Hill, London NW3 1LA
Tel: 01–794 4601

Offers information and support for parents who have been bereaved through a national network of parents.

OUTSIDE UK

Infertility
AUSTRALIA
The Australian Federation of Family Planning Associations
Level 4, 70 George Street, Sydney NSW 2000.
Tel: (02) 211 1944

CANADA
Planned Parenthood Federation of Canada (PPFC)
151 Slater Street, Suite 200, Ottawa, Ontario, K1P 5H3.
Tel: (613) 238 4474

NEW ZEALAND
The New Zealand Family Planning Association Inc.
PO Box 68200, Newton, 214 Karangahape Road, Auckland 1.
Tel: Newton 31 835

SOUTH AFRICA
Family Planning Association of South Africa
412 York House, 46 Kerk Street, Johannesburg 2001

All these organizations, while primarily concerned with contraception and sex education, will offer advice and information on infertility problems and know where you can be referred for help.

Adoption
AUSTRALIA
The law and practice on adoption vary from state to state. It is best to contact the state government department responsible for welfare services or children's welfare. Doctors and priests may also be able to advise on adoption.

CANADA

Most adoptions are arranged through the Department of Social Services in each province. There are also some private agencies, including:
Families for Children Inc.
10 Bowling Green, Point Clare, Quebec, Canada.

NEW ZEALAND

Director-General, Department of Social Welfare, Private Bag, Wellington, New Zealand.
Most adoptions in New Zealand are arranged through the Department of Social Welfare at the above address. This department would also be the contact point for welfare programmes for couples who are childless because of infertility.

Infertility Support Groups

CANADA
Infertility: Facts and feelings
Deborah Reesor, 10 South Street West, Dundas, Ontario L9H 4C1
Tel: (416) 628 8549

Index

HEALTHCARE FOR WOMEN

**A major new series
to give help, advice and comfort to
women on common emotional and
medical problems.**

Lifting the Curse
How to relieve painful periods
Beryl Kingston

0 85969 408 9   paper **£2.50**

Women and Depression
A practical self-help guide
Deidre Sanders

0 85969 418 6   cased **£6.95**
0 85969 419 4   paper **£2.50**

Women's Problems: An A–Z
Vernon Coleman

A comprehensive, easy-to-use reference book

0 85969 409 7   cased **£6.95**
0 85969 410 0   paper **£2.50**

Thrush
How it's caused and what to do with it
Caroline Clayton

0 85969 421 6   cased **£6.95**
0 85969 422 4   paper **£2.50**

Everything You Need to Know About the Pill
Wendy Cooper and Tom Smith

A complete up-to-date guide

0 85969 429 1   cased **£6.95**
0 85969 415 1   paper **£2.50**

Women and Tranquillizers
Celia Haddon

0 85969 420 8   cased **£6.95**
0 85969 414 3   paper **£2.50**

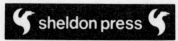

sheldon press

CW00972498

Poecilia reticulata (Veiltail Guppy)

Other titles of interest:

The Tropical Aquarium
Community Fishes
Coldwater Fishes
Marine Fishes
Maintaining a Healthy Aquarium
Garden Ponds
Aquarium Plants
Central American Cichlids
Fish Breeding
African and Asian Catfishes
Koi
Reptiles and Amphibians
Hamsters, Gerbils, Rats, Mice and Chinchillas
Rabbits and Guinea Pigs

A FISHKEEPER'S GUIDE TO
LIVEBEARING FISHES

Xiphophorus variatus (Variatus Platies)

Hemirhamphodon pogonognathus (One of the Toothed Halfbeaks)

A FISHKEEPER'S GUIDE TO

LIVEBEARING FISHES

A splendid introduction to the care and breeding of a wide range of these fascinating fishes

Peter W. Scott

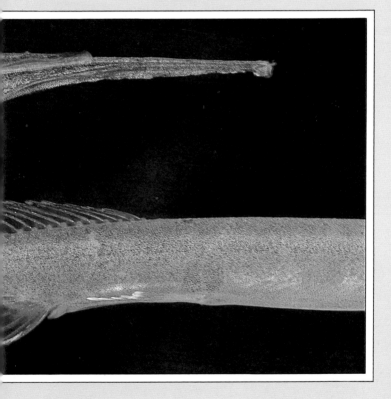

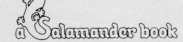

Published by Salamander Books Limited
LONDON • NEW YORK

A Salamander Book

ISBN 0 86101 281 X

Distributed in the UK by Hodder and Stoughton Services,
P.O. Box 6, Mill Road, Dunton Green, Sevenoaks, Kent TN13 2XX.

Priapella intermedia

Credits

Editor: Geoff Rogers   Design: Graeme Campbell
Colour reproductions:
Melbourne Graphics Ltd.
Filmset: SX Composing Ltd.
Printed in Belgium by Henri Proost & Cie, Turnhout.

Author

Peter W Scott MSc., BVSc., MRCVS, MIBiol is a veterinarian who qualified at
Liverpool University with a special interest in fish, reptiles and amphibians.
He has kept fish for over 20 years, and is a member of several fish societies.
As a member of the International Zoo Veterinary Group, a practice which
works solely with zoo and aquatic animals, he is widely involved with public
aquariums, fish farmers, retailers and wholesalers in Europe, the USA and
the Far East. He is also the Veterinary Advisor to Ornamental Fish
International (OFI). He is the author of four books and a contributor to several
others, and numerous articles on various aspects of fish health, on which he
has lectured in a number of countries.

Consultants

Dennis Barrett has kept tropical fish for over 20 years. For the past nine years he has
concentrated on livebearing fishes and widened his experience by making trips to
Mexico and Bogota. Since 1985, he has been Chairman of SLAG (Southern Livebearer
Aquatic Group – an international specialist organization) and he regularly advises on
the keeping and breeding of livebearers. **Jim Chambers** works in the Fish Section of
The British Museum (Natural History). In addition to his curatorial duties and related
research, he also advises aquarist societies on egglaying and livebearing toothcarps.

Contents

Introduction

A major part of the fascination of fishkeeping comes from being able to breed the fishes successfully in the aquarium. It takes enthusiasm and care to establish a tank in which the fishes feel sufficiently 'at home' to breed, and even more care to provide the right conditions for the offspring to survive. One livebearing fish above all others – the Guppy – parallels the popularity of the Goldfish, largely because it is so eager to breed in the home aquarium. Even beginners to the fishkeeping hobby can enjoy the beauty of these colourful fishes and feel a sense of satisfaction at the birth of live young in their own aquarium. And this is just one of many colourful and rewarding livebearing fishes – including Platies, Swordtails and Mollies – that are justifiably celebrated the world over in the aquarium hobby.

In Part One of this guide, breeding is given full weight, with practical advice being presented alongside revealing insights into

the biological processes at work. And a brief look at the genetics of livebearers shows how the potential variation in these fishes is being exploited by dedicated breeders. In the sections leading up to this vital subject area, Part One looks at livebearing in general (with an all-important explanation of the difference between livebearing and egglaying fishes), siting and stocking a community aquarium, how to create and maintain optimal water conditions (with particular emphasis on pH and salinity), arranging suitable lighting and heating, plants for the livebearer aquarium and advice on feeding and diets, including how to provide safe live/fresh foods.

Unfortunately, even the best laid plans of mice, men and fish-keepers can go astray, and diseases can occur. This is the subject of the closing section of Part One, with detailed advice being given on recognising and treating all the principal health problems liable to affect livebearers in the aquarium.

11

What are livebearers?

It is an interesting fact that in animals methods of reproduction are even more variable than the conventional differences in colour, shape and size. In broad terms we tend to think that the so-called lower orders of animals, such as reptiles, fishes and birds, are all egglayers and that all mammals are livebearing. But nature is full of surprises: there are three mammals which lay eggs (two species of echidna and the duckbilled platypus) and a great many examples of livebearers among the lower groups – including fishes.

In the majority of livebearing animals, the young are born well developed and able to make at least a reasonable attempt to escape and avoid danger. This is true of species as widely separated as the Black Molly and the giraffe, but is not the case with some of the higher mammals such as man and the rest of the primates.

Basic terminology
Before we look further at livebearing in fishes, we should clarify the basic terms used to describe breeding methods:

Oviparous – animals that lay eggs.
Ovoviviparous – animals that produce eggs and hold them within the body to hatch, making no contribution to their nutrition other than through the yolk in the egg.
Viviparous – animals that provide ongoing nutrition for the developing embryo, which may be achieved in a variety of ways.

Livebearing in fishes
Since time has taught them that their eggs and fry are tasty snacks for crustaceans and other fishes, some species of fish produce several million eggs at each spawning. The livebearers have a different system: internal fertilization and the development of the embryos inside the female's body to protect the young. This means they generally need to produce relatively small numbers of fry to ensure the survival of at least some offspring. Some marine

OVIPAROUS – Egglaying

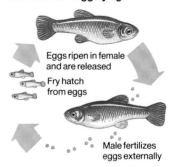

Eggs ripen in female and are released

Fry hatch from eggs

Male fertilizes eggs externally

OVOVIVIPAROUS – Livebearing

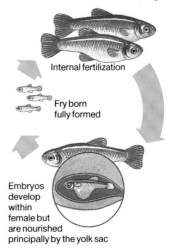

Internal fertilization

Fry born fully formed

Embryos develop within female but are nourished principally by the yolk sac

VIVIPAROUS – Livebearing

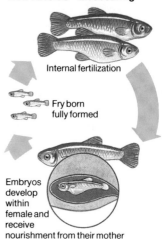

Internal fertilization

Fry born fully formed

Embryos develop within female and receive nourishment from their mother

species, including the Redfish (*Sebastes marinus*), have compromised and produce large numbers of very small, relatively undeveloped larval fish. This gives them a decent start in life but 'allows' that some will be eaten. In such cases, the female is simply acting as a brood chamber in which the eggs hatch, with no further contribution from her. Such females tend to remain in a better condition than those of other species that supply nutrients to the embryos until they are born.

Which fish are livebearers?

Less than three percent of the 18,000 or so species of bony fishes are livebearers, although arguably these include some of the most interesting types. This figure is strikingly different in the cartilaginous fishes (the sharks and rays, etc.), where over half are livebearing.

Livebearing is seen in fourteen families of living fish. There are a few families of marine fish that contain livebearers; these include some perch-like fish, such as the Clinidae (Clinids), and the Embiotocidae (Surfperch). In the Surfperch, the males and females are six months out of synchronization: the male develops seasonal modifications to his anal fin and fertilizes the female six months before the eggs are ready. A fairly well-known marine livebearer is the viviparous Blenny, one of the oddly shaped Eelpouts (*Zoarcidae*). Certain members of the Scorpaenidae (Scorpionfish) are also livebearers, including the Redfish previously mentioned. This family is distinguished by its huge broods of up to two million in some members. One member of the Scorpaenidae, *Helicolenus percoides*, hatches its eggs in a mass of jelly that dissolves in the water to release the yolk-sac fry.

Celebrated among livebearers are the Coelacanths (*Latimeria sp.*), which are familiarly known as 'Old Fourlegs' because of their odd leg-like fins. Until specimens were noted among the catches of East African coastal fishermen in 1938, this fish was thought to have become extinct about 360 million years ago. Since its initial rediscovery, a number of further specimens have been caught off the east coast of Africa. Fossil evidence which suggested that it was a livebearer was confirmed in 1975, when freshly caught female specimens were examined. It has not yet been possible to keep any alive for any length of time, but preserved specimens of this 'living fossil' can be seen in museums.

Most of the sharks, including the Sand Sharks, Threshers, Porbeagle, Mako and the Great White, are ovoviviparous. They have a gestation period of approximately nine months, although this may be much longer in a few cases. A number of sharks, including the Blue Shark, the Hammerheads and the oceanic Whitetip, are fully viviparous. Once again, the gestation period is about nine months. The usual number of pups born to sharks is five to fifteen, although a few species can produce up to 100. To complicate matters further, breeding methods can vary even within a genus: *Galeus melastoma*, for example, is an egglayer while *Galeus polli* gives birth to live young. Nurse sharks may be viviparous or ovoviviparous, depending on circumstances. The majority of Rays are ovoviviparous, all except the *Rajiidae*, which are egglayers. If a generalization is possible, it seems that egglaying is more common among sharks and rays that live near the bottom in shallow waters.

Livebearers for the aquarium

Fishkeepers choose livebearers for a number of reasons. Some simply want brightly coloured fishes which, given suitable conditions, are self-perpetuating in a community tank. The community may be a mixed one or may be based solely around the livebearers. Other fishkeepers prefer to keep the 'cultivated' varieties and pursue new colour variations or the perfection of particular patterns through breeding. Other enthusiasts keep the rarer varieties simply for their beauty and fascination. Probably more than any other small group of fishes, therefore, the livebearers truly cater for all tastes.

Aquarists are primarily involved with members of the following families (listed in the order we review them in Part Two):

Anablepidae
Hemirhamphidae
Goodeidae
Poeciliidae

The most common aquarium species are the attractive and colourful Guppies, Mollies, Platies and Swordtails. These are all members of the Poeciliidae which, along with the Anablepidae and Goodeidae, are referred to as the New World Cyprinodonts or Livebearing Toothcarps. The whole group originates in the fresh and brackish waters of Central and South America and some of the Caribbean Islands. The Hemirhamphidae, or Halfbeaks, are from a different continent, being fairly widespread in the streams and ponds of Southeast Asia and the Malay Peninsula.

Adaptibility of livebearers

Members of the Poeciliidae, particularly the Guppy (*Poecilia reticulata*) and The Western Mosquito Fish (*Gambusia affinis*), are now very widespread. They have been used for the biological control of mosquitos far beyond their origins in the New World. Brackish water and saltwater marshes are well known mosquito breeding grounds, and these fishes adapt to most waters with a minimum temperature of 15°C (59°F). They are capable of withstanding immediate transfer into half-strength sea water, for example. They have prodigious appetites for mosquito larvae; it is claimed that *Gambusia affinis* is able to eat its own weight of mosquito larvae in a day. In an attempt to control the reproduction of mosquitos, and thus prevent the spread of diseases that they transmit, these fishes have been

transported in plastic bags and dropped from low-flying aircraft into lakes, ponds and rivers throughout the tropics. These little fishes are said to have made a considerable contribution towards the building of the Panama Canal (between 1904 and 1914) by controlling the mosquitos that plagued the construction workers.

While this sounds like the perfect solution, it did cause some problems in practice. Because the livebearers are so adaptable, they had a considerable impact on the local mosquito-eating fishes. Not only did they eat their food, but worse, they ate the eggs and fry of the other fishes and generally took over the habitat.

Wild populations of Poeciliids have established themselves in warm waters wherever they have been introduced. In the often cold, wet North of England, for example, a disused section of canal has a thriving mixed livebearer population as the result of stock dumped there by a bankrupt aquarium shop. The fish have gone from strength to strength in the warm water effluent from a glass factory cooling system.

Colour and selective breeding

The basic natural colours of most of the livebearing species are variations on an olive-green background. They feature blues and blacks, often with an iridescence and lighter speckles to disrupt the shape. This coloration helps the fishes to escape predators, such as *Belonesox* (itself a livebearer), by blending in with their natural habitat, in which the light is broken up.

Generations of aquarists have separated the genes which govern this basic colour and 'reassembled' them to make some fabulous fishes. The male Guppy, (*Poecilia reticulata*) has been the subject of considerable attention in selective breeding, resulting in the wide range of colour and tail shape varieties now available. And the female Guppy has been transformed over a relatively short period from a rather drab fish into a very impressive looking fish in her own right.

Below: *The combined natural distribution of the Families Anablepidae, Goodeidae and Poeciliidae in the Americas.*

Below: *Examples of species in these Families. In terms of aquarium species, the Goodeidae and the Poeciliidae are the most important.*

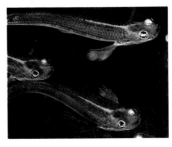

ANABLEPIDAE *Anableps anableps*

POECILIIDAE *Poecilia reticulata*

GOODEIDAE *Characodon lateralis*

Below: *The natural distribution of the Family Hemirhamphidae – the so-called Halfbeaks – that occupy the niches in Southeast Asia.*

Below: *Two subspecies of Nomorhamphus – a member of the Hemirhamphidae. Other Halfbeaks are shown on pages 64-65.*

Nomorhamphus liemi liemi

HEMIRHAMPHIDAE *Nomorhamphus liemi snijdersi*

15

Aquarium forms of the Guppy
(Not to scale)

Female, larger and less colourful than the males shown below.

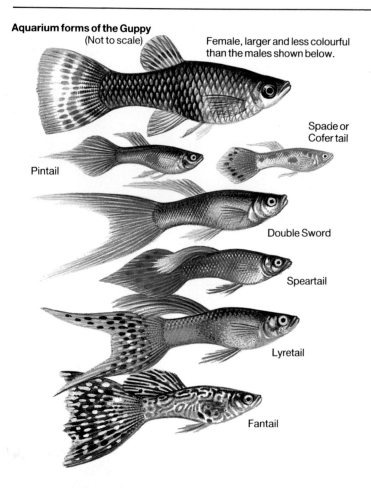

Spade or Cofer tail

Pintail

Double Sword

Speartail

Lyretail

Fantail

Above: *This panel shows a small selection of the many colour forms and tail shapes of the Guppy,* Poecilia reticulata. *It is the male fish that displays the brightest colours and the most flamboyant fins, but even the drab female has been 'enlivened' by selective breeding.*

The genus *Xiphophorus* (Platies and Swordtails) offers the best example of what is possible with years of selective breeding and meticulous attention to detail. The Platy was discovered in 1866 in Central America. The two original fishes sent to, and still held at, the British Museum (Natural History) were classified originally as *Platypoecilus maculatus* (hence their common name). Within a very short time of obtaining specimens of this fairly drab wild fish, aquarists used selective breeding methods to develop a kaleidoscope of colour varieties. They also soon found that the Platy would hybridize with the Swordtail and that this produced even more colour variations. Since many of these hybrids were fertile, the colours could be stabilized and a wide range of colour variants were created for the aquarium hobby.

A huge range of colour varieties and fin forms have been developed. Colours include green, red, and black, plus tuxedo and piebald patterns, and the particularly attractive pineapple. In addition, there are short-finned, high-fin and lyretail varieties. The lyretail Sword is almost impossible to breed naturally, as its anal fin is abnormally long and without the modifications to the tip which allow successful mating. Fortunately, lyretail females are normal and can be mated with short-finned males. This results in a 50:50 lyretail and short-finned batch of fry. (See also Breeding and genetics, pages 36-49.)

There are now about 300 varieties of *Xiphophorus* on the market, but there are even more in existence as breeders hold stocks of forms that have not yet become commercial or still have varieties that have long gone out of fashion.

For the general aquarist the *Xiphophorus helleri* and *X.maculatus* groups are the most

important. Commercially available Swordtails are usually hybrids of *X.helleri* with *X.maculatus* or *X.variatus*, but some varieties also have some contribution from *X.montezumae*. (See pages 104-113 in Part Two of the book.)

Other livebearers

There are many other species to choose from, generally with 'quieter' colours, but nonetheless special for reasons of their own. *Alfaro cultratus*, for instance, has a lovely delicate golden sheen and a slightly elongate body with a long 'knife-edged' anal fin. *Jenynsia lineata*, the One-sided Livebearer, is fascinating because of the problems encountered in making a pair – i.e. finding a right-handed female for a left-handed male, or vice-versa. (See pages 36-45 for further details on breeding livebearers.) The appeal of some of the smaller species may be scarcity or simply their delicacy or breeding habits. *Heterandria*, for example, produces very large fry for its size because of its remarkable production-line breeding method.

Left and below: *These photographs show how the Swordtail X.helleri has been developed into showy aquarium forms. The photograph at top left shows a natural looking form. Compare this to the 'Simpson' form shown at left, which has extended fins and a long flaring tail. This type reaches its most extreme in the High Fin Lyretail form below.*

Aquarium selection and compatibility

The aquarium size is not too critical for livebearing fishes, since they are generally small. If you wish to breed livebearers seriously, either the aquarium varieties or the more unusual species, you will need several small tanks rather than one or two large ones.

Ideal aquarium size
Aquariums with a water volume of 45-90 litres (10-20 gallons) are ideal for single species or variety breeding. (As a guide, a tank measuring 45x38x30cm / 18x15x12in holds approximately 45 litres and one measuring 60x45x38cm / 24x18x15in holds approximately 90 litres.) For the small species, even smaller tanks can be used. Having a number of small tanks is essential for breeding so that you can keep breeding pairs apart and separate the fry into males and females as soon as they can be sexed. This is necessary to avoid unwanted inbreeding. (See page 40.) It is particularly important with the Poeciliids, since a single mating is sufficient to produce perhaps six broods over as many months.

Communities fare better in larger aquariums in which a variety of habitats can be created to give shelter to young fishes. In addition, community tanks usually call for more fishes and a wide selection of fish species, which often means that the stocking level is higher than in the 'species' or 'variety' tank. As well as providing a greater surface area to support more fishes (see below), the greater water volume in larger tanks can provide a more stable environment by buffering chemical changes occurring in the aquarium over a period of time.

Stocking levels
The number of fishes that a tank will support depends on its surface area, not its volume. This is because the water/air surface acts as the 'lung' for the tank, allowing oxygen to enter the water and carbon dioxide and other wastes to disperse. Aeration helps in the process of gas exchange, not so much from the conspicuous bubbles than from the stirring activity that they produce at the surface. Because of this water

Tanks and stocking levels

Tank size (L × D × W)	Surface area	Volume of water
45×25×25cm (18×10×10in)	1125cm^2 (180in^2)	27 litres (6 gallons)
45×38×30cm (18×15×12in)	1350cm^2 (216in^2)	45 litres (10 gallons)
60×30×30cm (24×12×12in)	1800cm^2 (288in^2)	54 litres (12 gallons)
60×38×30cm (24×15×12in)	1800cm^2 (288in^2)	68 litres (15 gallons)
60×45×38cm (24×18×15in)	2280cm^2 (360in^2)	90 litres (20 gallons)
90×38×30cm (36×15×12in)	2700cm^2 (432in^2)	104 litres (23 gallons)
120×38×30cm (48×15×12in)	3600cm^2 (576in^2)	136 litres (30 gallons)

Above: *A community aquarium featuring Guppies and Swordtails. Plastic and real plants blend well.*

Below: *As this table shows, stocking levels depend on the water surface area rather than volume.*

Weight of water	Maximum fish capacity
27kg (60lb)	38cm (15in)
45kg (100lb)	45cm (18in)
54kg (120lb)	60cm (24in)
68kg (150lb)	60cm (24in)
90kg (200lb)	75cm (30in)
104kg (230lb)	90cm (36in)
136kg (300lb)	120cm (48in)

movement effect, submerged power filters are effective in maintaining adequate aeration. (See also page 25.) The standard guide for stocking rate is to allow 75cm^2 (12in^2) of surface area for every 2.5cm (1in) of fish body length (measured from the tip of the nose to the end of the body, excluding the tail – which is the 'standard length').

Siting the aquarium
The siting of the aquarium is very important. Direct sunlight will cause algal problems and, possibly, overheating. Keep the aquarium out of draughts, which may chill the water. Ideally, position the aquarium in such a way that the environment created inside it is under the full control of the filter, lights and heaters: these, in turn, are under the control of the aquarist. Bear in mind that the chosen site must have adequate access for maintenance or this will become a chore and may become neglected. Suitably positioned power points are important for the necessary equipment, as trailing wires are dangerous and unsightly.

Aquarium compatibility
Some species of livebearers seem to prefer to be alone while others

prefer company. Mixing genera of the smaller species seems to work well. For example, *Quintana atrizona* or *Priapella intermedia* mix well with *Heterandria formosa*. *Dermogenys* (Halfbeaks) also prefer the company of other species. On the other hand, a number of Goodeids, such as *Xenotoca eiseni* (the Red-tailed or Orange-tailed Goodeid), are reported to be fin nippers if kept with other fishes, yet they are fine on their own.

For the serious aquarist, the Goodeids are generally best kept in species tanks, as are most of the Poeciliids, particularly *Poecilia* and *Xiphophorus* sp. Otherwise, interspecies hybridization becomes a problem and pure lines are lost.

Community aquariums
As colourful additions to the community aquarium, livebearers are excellent value. They are active fishes that use the whole tank volume, and they will eat significant amounts of algae; (*Limia melanogaster* (Black-bellied Limia) is particularly renowned for this. They breed fairly readily if shelter is provided for the fry to hide in.

Three of the four most popular livebearers – Guppies, Platies and Swordtails – are easy going and cause little trouble. The fourth group, the Mollies, are temperamentally fine but they often do better in slightly saline water and prefer temperatures at the higher end of normal community tanks, preferably not below 25°C (77°F). All efforts to maintain good plant cover and to separate females into breeding traps or nursery tanks will be amply repaid with all these fishes, which will produce regular broods of brightly coloured fry.

The community aquarium is conventionally stocked with fishes living at different levels of the tank. Most of the livebearers fit into the group of midwater swimmers, although several are surface feeders. The common livebearers are often combined with 'easy' species in the mixed community tank. These include Zebra and Spotted Danios (*Brachydanio rerio*

and *B.nigrofasciatus*), Neon and Cardinal Tetras (*Paracheirodon innesi* and *P.axelrodi*), Bronze Corydoras (*Corydoras aeneus*), Harlequins (*Rasbora heteromorpha*), and Dwarf and Three-spot Gouramis (*Colisa lalia* and *Trichogaster trichopterus*).

A variety of fishes make suitable cohabitants for specialist livebearer community tanks. The hard, slightly saline water used by some aquarists suits such widely varied species as Bumblebee Gobies (*Brachygobius xanthozona*), Glassfish (*Chanda ranga*), Monos (*Monodactylus sebae*), and Rainbow Fish (*Melanotaenia spp.*). Cichlids such as Chromides (*Eutroplus*

maculatus) and Kribensis (*Pelvicachromis pulcher*) are also well suited to these conditions.

The continental-style paludarium tanks, which combine water with a planted airspace, are now becoming more widely available, and add a new dimension to keeping livebearers. The brightly coloured, more common forms of livebearers are ideal for these heavily planted displays, which can actually resemble a full section of riverbank. A paludarium is also perfect for the fascinating Archerfish (*Toxotes jaculator*), which also thrives in saline water.

Community tanks can be stocked with livebearers only, or unrelated

Above: *Platies share a well-planted community aquarium with similarly sized fishes, including elegant Glass Catfishes and Characins.*

species can be mixed to produce a very interesting and attractive tank. For example, the Goodeids *Ilyodon xantusi* and *Ameca splendens* could be mixed with others such as *Xenotoca eiseni* (although these can be fin nippers), and perhaps a quiet Poeciliid, such as *Heterandria*. There are a number of suitable combinations, but take care to mix only easily distinguishable species and those which are as unrelated as possible, otherwise hybridization may occur. (See also page 40.)

Water requirements and filtration

The correct water conditions for livebearers are probably the major point of argument among livebearer aquarists. Some enthusiasts prefer peat-stained acidic water similar to that suitable for Discus fishes (*Symphosodon* spp.), and Neon and Cardinal Tetras (*Paracheirodon innesi* and *P. axelrodi*). Others recommend hard alkaline water. In fact, neither group is entirely correct since the natural origins of the different fish species vary.

Natural water conditions

The rivers and mountain lakes on the western side of Central America are moderately hard and alkaline due to the limestone over which the water runs. Even so, some small streams are acidic due to the accumulation of humus from decaying plants, particularly in the dry season. Along the coastal region the water is well mineralized. Further into South America the waters become less mineralized and alkaline, and some forest streams are very acidic 'blackwater'.

In contrast to the Discus, which come from acidic blackwater jungle streams with very few aquatic plants, many livebearers tend to live in quiet, overgrown, shady, slow-moving waters. Generally, livebearers prefer more mature, moderately hard water with a good growth of algae and plants. This supplies their need for plant material as their basic diet. (See also page 32.) Some species, particularly the Poeciliids, live in lowland coastal regions and benefit from some salt in the water. All seem to prefer well-mineralized water rather than soft water. Members of the genus *Xiphophorus* (Swordtails and Platies) generally live further from the coast in the backwaters, which still tend to be well mineralized.

Right: *Using a paper strip indicator to record the pH value of aquarium water. After dipping it in the water, simply compare the strip to a printed chart and read off the pH value. Other tests involve adding liquid reagents to water samples or using an electronic pH meter.*

Aquarium water conditions

The most important water quality parameters for successful fishkeeping are:
  - pH value (degree of acidity or alkalinity)
  - hardness
  - salinity
  - organic waste
  - ammonia, nitrite and nitrate levels
  - temperature

Here we consider how the first three parameters are measured in the aquarium and what values suit livebearing fishes. Then we look at the role of filtration in 'cleaning' the water of organic waste and controlling the levels of ammonia, nitrite and nitrate in the aquarium. Temperature requirements are covered in the section on lighting and heating, on pages 28-29.

The pH value

The pH value of the water is a measure of its acidity (pH 1-7) or alkalinity (pH7-14); pH7 is regarded as neutral. The scale is actually a logarithmic one based inversely on the number of hydrogen ions in the water; the more hydrogen ions, the more acid the water and the lower the pH value.

Although there is considerable discussion about the preferences of livebearers, the majority seem to do best in water just on the alkaline side of neutral, approximately pH7.2-7.5, although some variation is acceptable. This optimum range equates very well with the pH value of most tapwater, although in some areas the water can be very acid or very alkaline and needs adjustment.

Above: *Playa Azul on the west coast of Mexico, the habitat of many livebearers, including* P. sphenops.

Left: Poecilia sphenops, *widely distributed in fresh and brackish waters from Venezuela to Texas.*

Chemical methods of measuring pH are used routinely in laboratories, and some very good kits involving adding colour-change reagents to a measured sample of tank water are now marketed specifically for the aquarist. An alternative is to use pH papers that register pH value by changing colour when dipped in a water sample. Several ranges of pH paper are available; 'wide range' ones provide an approximate idea of the pH value, then 'narrow range' papers can be used to determine it more accurately. Both types entail comparing the used paper with a standard colour guide. For fish dealers or enthusiasts with many aquariums who need to monitor water conditions regularly, the best method is to use an electronic pH meter. This simply involves dipping a probe into the aquarium water.

Water hardness

Water hardness is due to the presence of various dissolved ions in the water, particularly calcium (Ca^{++}), magnesium (Mg^{++}), bicarbonate (HCO_3^-), sulphate (SO_4^{--}), chloride (Cl^-), and nitrate (NO_3^-). These ions can be grouped according to the different types of hardness they produce:

Carbonate hardness (KH), also known as temporary hardness because it can be reduced by boiling, is caused by bicarbonates of (chiefly) calcium and magnesium.

Non-carbonate hardness, which is also known as total, general (GH) or permanent hardness, is caused principally by calcium sulphate, but also by magnesium, barium and strontium associated with sulphate, chloride and nitrate.

Water hardness can be expressed in various scales, including the American °hardness, English °Clark and the German °dH. How these scales relate to each other in terms of softness and hardness and to a scale based on milligrams of calcium carbonate ($CaCO_3$) per litre is shown in the table on page 24. This shows that the 'moderately hard' water preferred by many livebearers is calibrated as 12-18°dH or 200-300 mg/litre $CaCO_3$.

As with pH value, there are several ways of measuring water hardness, the most convenient being a test kit that involves counting the number of drops of a chemical needed to cause a colour change in a sample of water treated with an 'indicator' solution.

Water hardness in comparative terms			Specific gravity	Salinity
dH°	Mg/litre CaCO₃	Considered as	1.0000	1.1
			Fresh water 1.0001	1.2
3	0-50	Soft	1.0002	1.3
			1.0004	1.6
3-6	50-100	Moderately soft	1.0006	1.9
			1.0008	2.1
6-12	100-200	Slightly hard	1.0010	2.4
			1.005	7.6
12-18	200-300	Moderately hard	1.010	14.1
			1.015	20.6
18-25	300-450	Hard	Sea water 1.020	27.2
			1.025	33.7
Over 25	Over 450	Very hard	1.030	40.2

The most effective way of softening very hard tapwater to the desired level is simply to dilute it with soft water, such as rain water, or with pure deionized water. Domestic water softeners are not suitable because they simply replace the calcium with sodium and produce water that is too alkaline for aquarium use. Increasing the hardness of naturally soft water can involve filtering it through marble chips or dolomite, or adding chemicals such as monosodium dihydrogen phosphate in conjunction with bicarbonate.

It is important to consider water hardness and pH value together, since changing one parameter often affects the other. Soft water is usually acidic, for example, and hard water alkaline. The level of bicarbonates is also important because they act as a 'storage area' for carbon dioxide and help to stabilize the acidity/alkalinity balance of the aquarium water.

Salinity

Salinity is much discussed by keepers of livebearers. This is a measure of salt concentration and figures are usually quoted in grams of salt per litre of water. Sea water contains approximately 35gm/litre, and brackish water may be any mixture of sea water and fresh water. Salinity can be quoted in terms of specific gravity, which is the ratio of the density of the liquid compared to that of pure water.

Specific gravity is measured using a hydrometer, of which two types are available for aquarium use: the traditional floating type similar to that used in home brewing, and a 'swing-needle' unit. Measuring the specific gravity of the water using a hydrometer therefore also indicates its salinity.

The usual amount of salt added to livebearer tanks is really quite small, only about 0.5-1.0gm/litre (equivalent to 0.5-1.0 teaspoonful per gallon) which will give a hydrometer reading of around 1.0001.

When you are adding salt to a livebearer aquarium, bear in mind that the salt should also contribute some of the other minerals present in the fishes' natural habitat. Therefore, it is best to use sea salt or a commercial product specifically formulated for aquariums. Do not use ordinary table salt as some of the additives may harm the fishes.

The Mollies in particular seem to benefit from a certain amount of salt in their water, supposedly due to their origins in waters close to the coast. This is not essential, and with some care they can adjust to fresh water. However, since salt helps to fend off diseases – notably skin diseases – good aquarium hygiene is vital in totally fresh water.

Halfbeaks (Dermogenys sp.) also find salt beneficial, especially for breeding. The usual amount added is 0.5-1.5gm/litre (0.5-1.5 tspn per gallon). If much more than this is used, plant growth can be inhibited.

Many fish wholesalers and retailers keep newly arrived livebearers in brackish water. This is very important as it helps the fish to recover from the stress of transport, the water acting like a saline drip to a sick person. When buying livebearers, try to find out tactfully if they are in brackish water or whether they have been acclimatized to fresh water – it may make the difference between success and failure. There is nothing more disheartening than to take fish home to your own soft water tank, not realizing that the dealer had kept them in brackish water. There is no doubt that with some acclimatization most livebearers will adjust to such conditions, but a sudden transfer is often too much for them.

Filtration

Within the bounds of common sense, there is no such thing as over-filtration. Efficient filtration is vital in all aquariums but livebearers are particularly susceptible to bacterial skin infections caused by *Flexibacter columnaris* (see page 55) and, unless the water is well filtered, skin problems will occur.

Filtration is carried out by three main methods: mechanical, biological and chemical.

Mechanical filtration

The various means of mechanical filtration available range from simple corner box filters and the foam filters, both operated by air diffusers, to more sophisticated power filters of various sizes. All have their uses and their advocates. Generally, it is best to avoid too much disturbance with breeding fish or fry, particularly with the smaller species. In these cases, therefore, do not use the larger power filters.

In smaller breeding tanks or fry tanks, a foam filter mounted on the side of the tank does an excellent job. Combine this with regular vacuuming of the tank bottom using a simple siphon tube or one of the siphonic action gravel cleaners available. In larger 'species' or community tanks, use a small internal power filter, again combined with regular tank vacuuming. Livebearers from fast-flowing streams, such as *Alfaro*

Above: *An air-operated foam filter, which is ideal for tanks housing livebearers from 'quiet' waters or for use in fry-rearing tanks.*

cultratus and *Jenynsia*, need very clean water and will happily tolerate the water movement from power filters. On the other hand, species such as *Limia melanogaster* from slower moving waters can be disturbed by these filters and you will therefore need to rely more on frequent, large water changes. The gentle foam filters are fine for these quieter species. For the majority of livebearers, power filters that turn over the tank volume once an hour are probably sufficient.

Biological filtration

Biological filtration systems deal with the dissolved waste products of fish, primarily ammonia. In acidic conditions, ammonia (NH_3) is ionized to ammonium (NH_4^+), which is non-toxic. In alkaline water, however, it remains as toxic ammonia. At a low level this damages the gills and at a high level it causes brain damage and death.

In the bacterial activity common to all biological filtration systems, the ammonia is taken up by *Nitrosomonas* bacteria, which live in the water of all tanks, and is converted to nitrites (NO_2^-). Another group of bacteria, called *Nitrobacter*, which live attached to gravel and other surfaces, convert the nitrites to nitrates (NO_3^-). The dissolved nitrates are much less

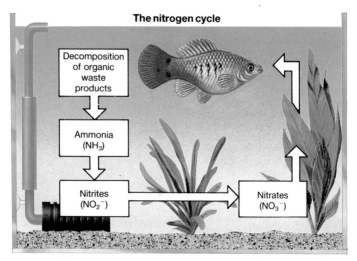

The nitrogen cycle

Decomposition of organic waste products

Ammonia (NH_3)

Nitrites (NO_2^-)

Nitrates (NO_3^-)

toxic for freshwater fish, although different types of fishes differ in their tolerance to nitrate levels. In combination with the phosphate in the faeces (waste from the vegetable components of the fishes' diet), the nitrates act as a plant fertilizer – just like the nitrate/phosphate fertilizers used by farmers to boost crop yields.

Because of the increased nitrate and phosphate levels, algal growth may be a problem if the aquarium is not well planted with mature, actively growing plants that will use up the ready supply of plant food. A certain amount of algal growth is not necessarily bad from the fishes' point of view, since most like to eat algae, but for the aquarist it impairs visibility and makes the tank look dirty and neglected.

The most effective way of controlling nitrate and phosphate levels is to make regular partial water changes. Removing approximately 25-30% of the aquarium water every fortnight is adequate. Do not wait until the algae have become a problem. Once they have become established it is too late to control their growth in this way. Replacing old plants with new young stock is another measure that will inhibit algae, because actively growing vigorous plants remove more nitrate and phosphate than do older plants in the aquarium.

Above: The principal stages in the nitrogen cycle, the natural process of bacterial decomposition of nitrogenous wastes. Biological filters encourage the growth of these bacteria to convert toxic ammonia to less harmful nitrates that, together with phosphates, act as a 'food' for growing plants.

All filters will have a degree of bacterial action if they are prevented from becoming clogged with solids, but undergravel filters are designed to operate biologically from the outset. The bacterial action is aerobic and thus the bacteria need to be supplied with oxygen to stay alive. If the filter is blocked they will die and may release toxins that can kill fishes.

Undergravel filters are designed to support a bed of gravel which provides a large surface area on which the bacteria can grow. Water is drawn evenly down through the gravel bed to the filter plate at the base of the tank. A minimum depth of 5cm (2in), using 5mm (3/16in) gravel, is needed above the filter plate; the ideal depth is about 7.5cm (3in). For the best effect the bed should be even; aquascaping tends to disturb the water flow and draw more water and solids into shallow gravel areas where the flow is greater. The increased flow of solids through a section of filter results in that section becoming blocked, killing the bacteria which then release toxins into the water.

To avoid the undergravel filter becoming blocked with solids, it is often better to run a small power filter or foam filter in the tank as well. A good alternative to the standard undergravel system is to use a reverse-flow undergravel filter with a foam prefilter. In this arrangement, the water first passes through the prefilter, which removes any solids, and is then pushed down and distributed by the filter plate under the whole gravel bed, through which it percolates upwards as it returns to the main part of the tank.

Unfortunately, undergravel filters can disturb plant growth because of the continual flow of water around their roots. The best plants for growing in tanks with undergravel filters are those which are already well rooted in small plastic pots.

Always take care that any medication added to an aquarium with biological filtration does not disturb the filter. Methylene blue and some antibiotics may cause serious problems in a long-established tanks with a heavy bacterial growth in the filter bed. The bacteria die and release poisons into the tank. This, linked with a failure in the nitrification process (as the cycle of bacterial action is called), can kill the fish. The deaths may occur a couple of weeks after treatment if the biological system fails to re-establish itself quickly enough.

Systems have been developed which are said to reduce the high nitrate levels which can build up in mature aquariums. These make use of anaerobic bacterial processes, i.e. those occurring in the absence of oxygen. The bacteria use nitrate as a source of oxygen to combine with the carbon present in waste matter and ultimately produce free nitrogen gas from the nitrate. This then simply diffuses out of the aquarium. These systems – one version of which is illustrated on this page – cannot be operated by air lift and so are simply placed in the tank beneath the gravel layer and operate on diffusion.

Nitrate reduction system

One box per 100 litres (22 gallons)

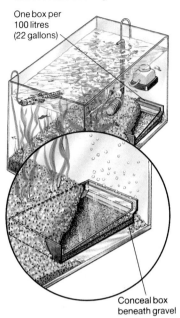

Conceal box beneath gravel

Above: *A system for reducing levels of nitrate in the aquarium. Anaerobic bacteria living within the material in the container convert nitrates to harmless nitrogen gas, which bubbles to the top and dissipates.*

Chemical filtration
Chemical filtration in freshwater aquariums is usually limited to the use of activated carbon. This adsorbs waste products on to its surface and is particularly useful for removing medications from the water after a course of treatment. (The term 'adsorb' indicates that the substance is taken up by the surface area of the medium, rather than being absorbed like a sponge.) Conversely, of course, be sure to remove activated carbon from filters before using any medication in the aquarium. (See also Health care, pages 50-59.) A white granular substance called zeolite can also be used to extract ammonia, although this should not be necessary in a stable, well-balanced tank. This is only possible if there is no salt in the water, since salt washes the ammonia out of the zeolite.

Lighting and heating

Because plants are important in the livebearer aquarium, it is essential to get the lighting right. From the aquarist's point of view it can make or break the display; a poorly illuminated tank looks dull while a well-lit tank can look fantastic.

Lighting a livebearer aquarium
Indirect daylight is ideal for plant growth, but since this cannot be regulated the aquarist must provide a suitable close substitute. A minimum of ten hours of light per day is needed for the plants. This also applies to the fishes, since their breeding behaviour partially depends on the number of hours of daylight. To mimic natural night a dark period should also be given; twelve hours of light and twelve hours of darkness is the simplest system to begin with. Plants will 'outgrow themselves' and die if subjected to an unnaturally constant light, and excess light will also encourage algae to grow. If there is a fair amount of natural light or room lighting, it may be necessary to reduce the intensity of the tank lighting to avoid encouraging excess algal growth.

In practice, the best lighting for livebearer aquariums is that from fluorescent lights. They are cheap and cool to run, although certain types can be initially expensive to buy. Tungsten spotlights can be used to great effect for highlights but, as they are difficult to house in narrow aquarium hoods, they are best for larger community tanks.

Many different 'colours' of fluorescent tubes are available for aquarium use. Those that concentrate on providing the red and blue emissions needed by plants generate a pinkish glow that creates a warm effect in the tank and enhances the red colours of the fishes. A minor disadvantage of these tubes, of which Grolux is the most common example, is their fairly low light emission. When using these relatively dim tubes it is particularly vital to prevent a layer of floating plants building up and starving the lower plants of light. To avoid this, prune the floating plants.

To supplement the light output from Grolux and similar tubes, consider adding one of the 'artificial daylight' tubes. These give a whiter and brighter full spectrum light

Recommended heating and lighting levels

Tank size (L×D×W)	Surface area	Volume of water	Weight of water
45×25×25cm (18×10×10in)	1125cm^2 (180in^2)	27 litres (6 gallons)	27kg (60lb)
45×38×30cm (18×15×12in)	1350cm^2 (216in^2)	45 litres (10 gallons)	45kg (100lb)
60×30×30cm (24×12×12in)	1800cm^2 (288in^2)	54 litres (12 gallons)	54kg (120lb)
60×38×30cm (24×15×12in)	1800cm^2 (288in^2)	68 litres (15 gallons)	68kg (150lb)
60×45×38cm (24×18×15in)	2280cm^2 (360in^2)	90 litres (20 gallons)	90kg (200lb)
90×38×30cm (36×15×12in)	2700cm^2 (432in^2)	104 litres (23 gallons)	104kg (230lb)
120×38×30cm (48×15×12in)	3600cm^2 (576in^2)	136 litres (30 gallons)	136kg (300lb)

Above: *A 60cm (24in) tank with the hood open to show a 45cm (18in) 15 watt Grolux fluorescent tube.*

output. Used on their own they may give too stark an effect in the aquarium – an effect perhaps more suited to the marine aquarium.

Whatever form of lighting you use, be sure to protect it from the effects of condensation. New aquarium hoods incorporate a transparent panel between the lights and the water surface. Alternatively, use a condensation tray or cover glass to prevent moisture reaching the electrics. Make a habit of regularly wiping down the cover glass to

ensure that as much light as possible reaches the tank.

Heating the tank

Individual species of livebearers have their own temperature preferences – and these are given in Part Two of the book – but most are happy in the 22-25°C (72-77°F) range. This is not difficult to achieve using standard heater/thermostats widely available at aquarium dealers. When choosing a heater, a basic guide is to allow 10 watts per 4.5 litres (1 gallon) of water for tanks up to 60cm (24in) long, and 6 watts per 4.5 litres (1 gallon) for tanks up to 120cm (48in) in length.

Maximum fish capacity	Heating required	Lighting required
38cm (15in)	100 watt	1×38cm (15in) Grolux 14 watt
45cm (18in)	100 watt	1×38cm (15in) Grolux 14 watt
60cm (24in)	150 watt	1×45cm (18in) Grolux 15 watt
60cm (24in)	150 watt	1×45cm (18in) Grolux 15 watt
75cm (30in)	200 watt	1×45cm (18in) Grolux 15 watt
90cm (36in)	1×100 watt 1×150 watt	1×75cm (30in) Grolux 25 watt
120cm (48in)	1×100 watt 1×200 watt	1×106cm (42in) Grolux 40 watt

Plants

In the wild, most livebearers live in densely planted pools, swimming among the shadows and roots of submerged plants. These provide security from the attentions of predators, such as birds and even from other livebearers, such as the carnivorous *Belonesox*. Here we review a selection of commonly available aquatic plants suitable for aquariums housing livebearers.

Plants for livebearer aquariums
Most plants are fairly happy in the moderately hard, mildly alkaline water of the livebearer aquarium. If the water is slightly saline to suit the more delicate Mollies or Halfbeaks, a number of plants can be acclimatized to living in brackish water. It takes just a few days of building up the salt level. Some browning of the leaves will occur, but the plants will settle down.

Vallisneria spiralis (Eel Grass or Straight Vallisneria) and *Vallisneria tortifolia* (Twisted Vallisneria) will provide good shelter in the aquarium. Both of these plants will acclimatize to saline conditions, although *Vallisneria* species in general do not like undergravel filtration and are best grown in pots if this system is in use. Planting several of these long-leaved varieties along the back and the rear corners of the tank creates a splendid display. When allowed to trail into the outlet of a filter uplift or power filter, they add a pleasing rippling motion to the background. They are easy to propagate because they put out abundant runners in ideal conditions. They relish minerals in the water, notably iron.

The fine feathery fronds of *Vesicularia dubyana* (Java Moss) make very good hiding places for fry. Water conditions must be good for this plant to thrive or it will become choked with algae. The plant looks lovely anchored to bogwood or rocks. It will even flourish floating free, although it must be prevented from swamping other plants. Because it will also grow out of water, it makes a good plant for the paludarium, disguising the water/land boundary.

Above: *A well-planted livebearer aquarium with (l to r)* Ludwigia, Cryptocoryne, Alternanthera *(red-leaved) and* Aponogeton *species.*

Below: *Sailfin Mollies obviously at home among the elegant fronds of* Vallisneria spiralis *(Eel Grass).*

Another bushy plant that is particularly good in the corners and as a background subject is *Synnema triflorum*, also known as *Hygrophila difformis* (Water Wisteria). Although this Asian plant is at its best in soft water, it will still succeed in moderately hard water and will adjust to slightly saline conditions if necessary. In common with most *Vallisneria* varieties, it is quite tall (up to 45cm/18in) and provides very good cover for young fishes. It is easy to propagate: almost all the cuttings will root readily in the aquarium gravel. Because it will put stems and leaves out of the water it, too, is ideal in the paludarium for 'softening' edges.

For filling space *Egeria densa* (formerly called *Elodea densa*) is an excellent choice. It thrives in almost any water conditions and is particularly suited to the hard, slightly alkaline water that most livebearers prefer. It is also useful for controlling algae because it absorbs a significant proportion of its nutrients directly from the water through its leaves. Its bushy growth

provides good shelter for fry. It needs plenty of light, so plant it in a clump away from the Water Wisteria and Java Moss. Propagate it by taking cuttings of the rapidly growing shoots.

Good feature plants suitable for aquascaping a livebearer aquarium include the Broad-leaf Amazon Swordplant (*Echinodorus paniculatus*). It is tolerant of a wide range of pH and hardness values and its distribution matches that of the Poeciliids. For a feature plant in livebearer aquariums to which salt has been added choose Java Fern (*Microsorium pteropus*), a brackish water plant widely distributed in Southeast Asia. Its hairlike roots anchor the rhizome to rocks or bogwood in the aquarium and it develops into a fine decorative subject that will flourish even at low lighting levels.

Many other plants can be incorporated into a livebearer aquarium and it is worthwhile asking for advice from a good dealer or one of the plant specialists who attend fish shows (covered on pages 48-9).

Feeding

Livebearers generally have fairly long intestines in relation to their body size. This suggests that they are basically omnivorous, tending towards vegetarianism, and there is no doubt that most benefit from the roughage in vegetable matter. The carnivorous Poeciliid, *Belonesox belizanus*, is a notable exception.

Aquarium foods

Most of the Poeciliids, and the Goodeids in particular, need plenty of greenfoods in the aquarium. Try to avoid feeding an excess of rich high-protein flakes and choose those formulated for vegetarians. As an alternative, garden peas, quickly cooked and mashed, are a good fresh greenfood, as is scalded or finely chopped lettuce. Mollies like to browse on algae growing on plants and rocks. Feeding a high-protein diet can encourage excess fat production because fish will convert excess protein into an 'energy store' of fat. This can cause some loss of breeding potential. In addition, a high-protein diet adds unnecessarily to the ammonia in the fishes' wastes, which the filtration system must cope with.

A variety of home-made foods are concocted by enthusiasts: liquidized spinach, with or without the addition of beef heart, or fresh in-shell prawns can be used as a base for adding various freeze-dried foods, such as bloodworm, shrimp, *Tubifex* or fish eggs. These freeze-dried foods transmit no disease and act as flavouring. To this mixture you can add a suitable amount of a proprietary powdered multivitamin preparation and then set it with gelatin or agar, which minimizes the risk of pollution. You can freeze the mixture in ice cube trays and take out a portion when necessary. Once it has thawed, cut off pieces to feed to the fishes.

Suitable livefoods

Live foods are important in the aquarium for providing trace elements and boosting vitamins, although it may be that the thrill of the chase is the major reason for enhancing the fishes' condition.

Daphnia are the most commonly used live food for livebearers. These 'water fleas' are about 93% water and only 3.5% protein, but they are relatively high in vitamins A and B_{12}. The major disadvantage of feeding *Daphnia* to fish is that they are of aquatic origin and so may introduce disease into the aquarium. Always try to be sure of the safety of your source. The same reasoning applies to *Tubifex* worms. Since these tiny red worms live in mud and sewage, they are best avoided as a food because of the risk of introducing disease into the aquarium.

Old sinks, small ponds and water butts can be useful for culturing live foods. Position a clean container filled with water in a well-lit position off the ground out of reach of frogs and other animals. To begin the cycle, encourage a good growth of algae by adding a little horse manure. This will support a *Daphnia* population; introduce a few carefully selected *Daphnia* or a culture from a safe source. During the summer the container will be used by gnats and midges for breeding; their larvae and bloodworms are good live food, especially for surface feeders. To make the container a decorative feature in the garden, you can add some aquatic plants, but be sure that they come from a reliable source.

A good way of collecting non-aquatic flying insects is to attach a piece of fine netting to the front of the car to trap the insects as you drive around. During the summer, sweeping a net through undergrowth will also produce a useful crop of insects. Another collection method is to lay a blanket on the ground under a bush and give the bush a good shake. The insects will fall on to the blanket and can be brushed into a jar. The Halfbeaks in particular rely on surface-living insects as a staple diet in the wild and most will take insects scattered

Right: *Guppies move in to feed from a cube of freeze-dried* Tubifex *worms stuck to the aquarium glass. Use these foods in a balanced diet that includes vegetable flakes.*

Right: Belonesox belizanus *about to consume a cichlid in the tank. It may be possible to persuade the fry of such carnivorous fishes to take suitable non-living meaty foods.*

Below: *A clean water butt in the garden is ideal for culturing various live foods for fishes, as shown here.*

Live foods in a water butt

Container Make sure that the water container is clean and out of reach of frogs and other animals. For decoration, add plants from a disease-free source.

Gnat larvae These hang at the water's surface and are thus an ideal food for surface-feeding fishes.

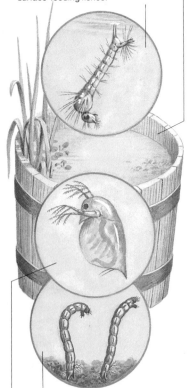

Bloodworms These swimming larval stages in the life cycle of midges form a nutritious food for livebearing fishes.

Water fleas These tiny swimming crustaceans (*Daphnia* sp.) will thrive in warm well-lit water. Introduce them from a safe source to avoid diseases.

on the water surface in the aquarium. Cultures of fruit flies (*Drosophila* sp.) are easy to buy through laboratory suppliers. The wingless form is very easy to maintain and provides a simple, relatively nutritious and safe live food for livebearers, especially for Halfbeaks.

Cultures of whiteworm (*Enchytraeus albidus*), grindalworms (*Enchytraeus buchholzi*) and microworms (*Panagrellus silusiae*) are not difficult to maintain in a ventilated container of moist peat with bread or cereal as food. They are very good live foods, with the major

advantage that they carry no fish diseases into the aquarium.

Feeding Belonesox
The Pike Livebearer (*Belonesox belizanus*) can be a problem to feed because in the wild it only eats live fish. In addition to being unpleasant and unacceptable to many people on the grounds of animal welfare, this can be dangerous because many fish purchased as live food are likely to transmit disease. The fry of *Belonesox* can often be coaxed on to a diet of surface-swimming insects and liquidized beef heart. Try grating a piece of frozen beef heart and dropping the finely ground

lean meat into the outlet stream of a power filter. The fry will often chase the moving pieces. Take care not to add too much beef heart as it can seriously pollute the tank. Siphon out any uneaten food as soon as possible to prevent this problem.

Feeding livebearer fry
In general, the fry of all species of livebearers will do better on higher protein foods than the adult fishes. The demands of growth call for this – hence their preference for live foods. It is only later as they become adult that the need for protein decreases. (See also Breeding and genetics, pages 44 and 45.)

Breeding and genetics

As we have seen on page 12, livebearing calls for a method by which the male can get the milt, containing the sperm, into the body of the female to achieve internal fertilization. Once fertilization has been achieved, the female must make provision for the developing embryo to receive nourishment. This is very important because, in evolving a system of livebearing, most fish have sacrificed the ability to produce large numbers of eggs in return for the alternative of giving fewer fry a better chance of life.

Internal fertilization

The problem of internal fertilization has been solved in different ways in the various families, generally through a modification of the anal fin to form the equivalent of a penis.

In Poeciliids the first few rays of the anal fin are modified to form a long pointed gonopodium. This can be swung forward, becoming grooved in the process, to allow the passage of packets of sperm, or spermozeugmata. In these packets all the sperm have their 'tails' embedded in a mucus core and their 'heads' face outwards. (In Goodeids, they are the other way round). One mating can result in up to 3000 of these packets being passed into the female. There the packets break up to release the sperm, some of which fertilize the ripe eggs, while the remainder are stored in the folds of the oviduct wall for fertilization of successive broods.

The Goodeids have modified the anal fin in a different way. The shorter leading rays are separated from the rest by a notch, and during mating this so-called spermatopodium cups the female's opening to allow the passage of sperm packets, which are literally shot at her.

In Jenynsia lineata (the One-sided Livebearer), the gonopodium bends to one side and the male can only mate with a female with a genital opening inclined to the opposite side. That is, a right-handed male mates with a left-handed female. The female has an enlarged scale which obscures the opening from one side or the other, and it is this that causes the left- or right-handedness.

Like Jenynsia lineata, Halfbeaks (Family Hemirhamphidae) are also 'one-sided', with the modified anal fin being referred to as the andropodium.

The Anablepids have a tubular, fleshy, penis-like organ, which is supported by curved anal fin rays.

Sustaining the embryo

Nutrition of the embryos as they develop inside the female is achieved in a variety of ways.

In most Poeciliids there is an abundance of yolk in the egg when it is fertilized and this feeds the growing fry within the female. In this arrangement, known as ovoviviparity, the female is really just protecting the young until they are born. In some Poeciliids, such as Heterandria, along with the Goodeids and Jenynsia, there is little yolk for the full growth of the embryo, and most sustenance is supplied by the female; this is true viviparity.

Viviparous livebearing fishes show a range of methods for supplying food to the developing embryo. Poeciliids and Anablepids, for example, use a process called follicular gestation. This means that the eggs are fertilized before being shed from the ovary, and after fertilization they remain in the follicle with the yolk sac acting as a type of placenta between embryo and mother. The Anablepid embryo (in the follicle) absorbs nutrients from the fluid around it by way of vascular bulbs over its belly sac.

In the Goodeids and Jenynsia, parental care begins with follicular gestation, but after a short time the developing embryo passes to a cavity within the ovary. In the Goodeids, trophotaeniae (literally 'feeding worms') develop. These are long processes that grow out of the anus of the embryo, and take nutrition directly from the mother via the wall of the ovary. Jenynsia solves the problem in a converse way: the wall of the ovary grows

Above: *A pair of* Belonesox
belizanus *about to mate. The
smaller male approaches the female
from below and to the side – his
gonopodium swung forward to
transfer packets of sperm.*

processes that insert into the gills
and mouth of the embryo.

Among the livebearing Halfbeaks,
Dermogenys use a similar system to
the Poeciliids but *Nomorhamphus*
more closely resembles the
Goodeids and *Jenynsia*.

Repeat brooding
Most livebearers maximize the
production of offspring in some
way. *Gambusia* spp. have a simple,
easily understood system: as one
brood is born the next batch of eggs

begins to ripen, ready for
fertilization. The other Poeciliids
speed up the process by ripening
the next batch of eggs during the
gestation of the current brood. In
this way, the eggs can be fertilized
directly after the young are born.

In certain species, particularly
Heterandria spp., there is an
amazing production-line system
called superfoetation. This means
that a female may have unfertilized
eggs developing at the same time as
embryos at various stages of
growth, from just fertilized to ready
for birth. By this method, a small
species such as *Heterandria*
manages to keep up production of
relatively large fry (up to a third of the
size of their mother) with minimal
demands on the female. In this way,

Below: *A pair of Sailfin Mollies,*
Poecilia velifera, *just after mating.
The gonopodium of the male is
visible in the forward position.*

Below: *Pairing in Poeciliid fishes.
The male rolls under the female,
swings the gonopodium forward
and flicks its tail to provide thrust.*

Ovary wall and tissue

 Ovarian cavity

 Follicle wall (granulosa)

Follicle wall with villi

 Follicle ruptured (ovulation) soon after fertilization

POECILIID – Ovoviviparous (Follicular gestation)

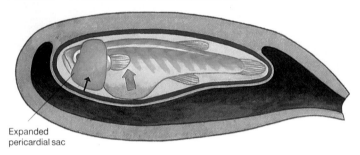

Expanded pericardial sac

Above: *The embryo is nourished mainly from yolk, plus some* *maternal contribution through the embryo's enlarged pericardial sac.*

POECILIID – Viviparous (Follicular gestation)

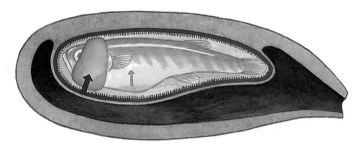

Above: *Here, the embryo has little yolk and receives nutrition from the* *mother through the modified follicle wall by way of the pericardial sac.*

POECILIID – Superfoetation in Heterandria

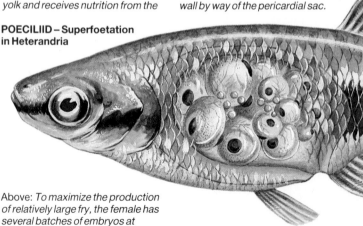

Above: *To maximize the production of relatively large fry, the female has several batches of embryos at different stages of development.*

Embryonic tissue

 Vascular bulbs

 Yolk

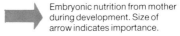 Embryonic nutrition from mother during development. Size of arrow indicates importance.

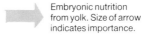 Embryonic nutrition from yolk. Size of arrow indicates importance.

ANABLEPID – Viviparous (Follicular gestation)

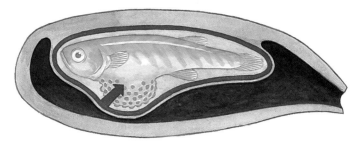

Above: *The embryo is nourished mainly through the expanded belly* *sac, the surface being covered with tiny knots of blood capillaries.*

GOODEID – Viviparous (Ovarian gestation)

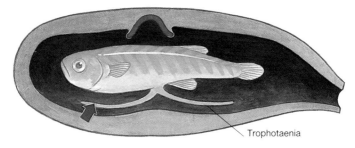

Trophotaenia

Above: *The embryo is nourished by ovary wall secretions, absorbed* *through trophotaeniae – temporary outgrowths from the anal area.*

JENYNSIA – Viviparous (Ovarian gestation)

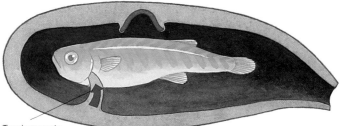

Trophonemata

In this form of ovarian gestation, the embryo is nourished through *trophonemata – processes that grow from the ovary wall into the gill.*

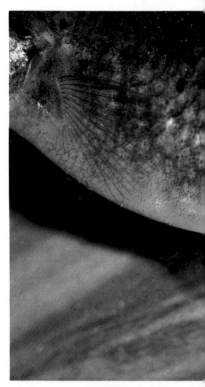

Right: Belonesox belizanus *giving birth. As in most Poeciliids, the embryos are held in the female's body and nourished from yolk sacs.*

a few large fry can be born every few days, whereas to produce more would mean reducing their numbers or individual size. Most other Poeciliids, such as Guppies and *Gambusia*, do this occasionally, as do the Halfbeaks; but it does not occur at all in the Goodeids or in *Jenynsia*.

The Poeciliids and Halfbeaks can store sperm, so that one mating can provide enough for brood production over a period of several months. *Dermogenys*, for example, can produce up to six broods from a single mating. This has drawbacks for the aquarist, since a mismating will result in continual production of unwanted fry for perhaps six to eight months. The Goodeids, however, cannot store sperm and therefore need to be mated for each brood. This makes selective breeding with them somewhat easier.

Hybridization
Hybridization is the bane of the serious breeder of livebearers. Generally, the members of a genus will hybridize and, frequently, so too will the members of families of livebearers. In other words, the various species of *Gambusia* will hybridize with each other, as will most species of *Poecilia*. The latter will also hybridize with the *Limias*. Mollies seem willing and able to breed with any of the other *Poecilia* species. Similarly, quite a few of the Goodeids will hybridize.

Some, but not all, of these hybrids are fertile, and so are capable of further hybridization. Hence the fantastic variation of commercially available forms, mostly produced by hybridization within the various *Xiphophorus* species and other Poeciliids. If you are serious about breeding livebearers be very careful

Right: *More fry emerge from the* female Belonesox, *which may drop 20-80 fry after a gestation period lasting between 30 and 50 days.*

Above: Belonesox fry at three days. At birth, they are 15mm (0.6in) long. Provide refuge amid plants for them to avoid their mother's attentions.

Below: *Four-week-old* Belonesox fry, already taking on the sleek shape of their parents. They become sexually mature at 6-9 months.

Above: A rearing tank of red Platies. Such a densely planted 'nursery tank' is an ideal environment in which to place the gravid (pregnant) female. Up to 100 fry may be born after a gestation period of about 34 days. Feed the fry on powdered dried foods and small brineshrimp.

about the species you put together and always record the results. Whenever possible, try to avoid mixing species which are closely related, otherwise pure species will be lost. This is an area where specialist societies can help, not only in maintaining stocks, but also by keeping careful records of which species hybridize.

Breeding livebearers

Although fishkeepers often consider that breeding livebearers is easy, dedicated enthusiasts must take more care when breeding livebearers than with many other species. With so many strains and colour variants within species, and a certain amount of hybridization between them, extreme vigilance is required in order to preserve strains and keep them breeding true. The parent stock must be selected and reared in the absence of other potential mates. A single 'misalliance' can affect the breeding programme for many months, since, as we have seen, the females of many livebearing fishes are able to store sperm from one mating and use it to fertilize successive batches of eggs as they ripen.

Telling the sexes apart

Most young livebearers look like females when they are born. This is because they are immature and the male's anal fin has not yet become modified. 'Puberty' happens to most males within the first couple of months, although in some Swordtails and Mollies it may not occur until they are nine to twelve months old. Sexing Guppies, is fairly straightforward and can be carried out when they are about three weeks old.

Female Platies are precocious and can be fertilized at about ten days old, although they rarely give birth before they are three months old. It is important to separate the fry from their parents if a breeding programme is being followed, otherwise adult males will fertilize the young females. Also remove males from the group of fry as soon as they can be identified, to prevent

them fertilizing their sisters. Failure to do this will result in unwanted repeat broods from the mismated females and a delay in the breeding programme.

In many livebearers, once females have become pregnant and developed a brood, the darkly pigmented peritoneum shows through the side of the abdominal wall on the side as the 'gravid spot'. Late in pregnancy in some species it is even possible to see the eyes of the fry through the mother's abdominal wall. Due to a combination of thicker muscles and strong colours, however, the gravid spot is less obvious in the Swordtails.

Seasonality of breeding

For the majority of livebearers in the aquarium there is no seasonality, although some of the larger Mollies have a period of rest during the winter. The major influence is probably the number of hours of daylight per day (the photoperiod), since the breeding cycle slows down as daylength shortens.

Because fish are ectothermic (cold blooded), all their bodily functions slow down as the temperature falls. Since this applies to breeding as well, the gestation period also lengthens in colder conditions. The interval between broods of Guppies, for example, lengthens from about 28 days at 27°C (80°F) to nearly 40 days at 20°C (68°F). Eventually, at about 15°C (59°F) the breeding cycle in most livebearers stops altogether. A long daylength is needed to keep the fishes breeding at these low temperatures.

Breeding traps

The need for some protection for the newborn fry of most species of livebearer is widely known. Many females will turn and eat the fry as they are born, and other fishes in the tank, including males and other females of the same species, will tag along waiting for dinner to be born.

The problem is how to provide the necessary protection. The act of netting and transferring a pregnant female to a commercially available small floating breeding trap is very stressful. In a breeding trap she is fully exposed, and even trying to give her security by putting plants in the trap only reduces the amount of space available.

One alternative is to make a more generous breeding trap from a suitable receptacle, such as a one-litre plastic ice-cream carton. To do this, clean the container thoroughly and then cut most of the bottom and sides away, leaving a 1cm (0.5in) rim around each edge. Cover the open panels with a layer of 0.5cm (0.25in) plastic netting and glue it in place with aquarium silicone sealant. Suspended in the tank, this trap is large enough to hold a little floating vegetation to give security both to the female while she is giving birth and to her brood immediately they are born. The mesh allows the young fishes to swim into the relative safety of the main tank.

It is essential that water circulates through a breeding trap to bring oxygen to the often over-excited female. Plants restrict the water flow, so compensate for this by placing an airstone underneath the breeding trap.

Natural nurseries
Since stress can result in still-birth, reabsorption of the embryos, or even the death of the female, setting up a so-called 'natural nursery' may be a better option than using a breeding trap. *Alfaro cultratus* and other shy, easily upset species definitely benefit from such an arrangement. The simplest way of setting up a natural nursery is to put the male and female into a well-planted tank and, when the birth is expected, screen off most of the tank with a plastic mesh, restricting the parents to the smaller well-planted end. Plants such as *Myriophyllum*, *Limnophila*, *Utricularia*, and *Riccia* are particularly good for providing 'immediate' shelter for the fry. In such a natural nursery the fry can reach shelter quickly and then make their way safely through the mesh to the screened section of the tank.

Many variations on this basic set-up are possible, including the use of two panels arranged across the tank with a small gap between as an 'escape route' for the fry.

Feeding fry
As we saw on page 35, fry tend to require a higher protein level than their parents, and so will consume large amounts of live food and commercial dried foods. They will eat small *Daphnia*, newly hatched brineshrimp and finely powdered dried foods for the first few weeks, moving on to finely chopped beef, prawns, scrambled egg, grindalworms and microworms, plus suitable flake foods.

Give them more than they actually need, otherwise some fry will rapidly get left behind by the bolder, more aggressive feeders. These stronger fry will look better and will therefore often be used as breeding stock in preference to their runty siblings. Over the course of many generations, this artificial selection leads to a change from the placid wild fish to an aggressive fin-nipping bully. The technique is well known in sport fish husbandry,

Above: *A breeding trap floating in a well-planted aquarium. The fry fall through small perforations into the safety of a separate compartment.*

Breeding trap

A foam filter will keep the water clean and provide a flow towards the 'safe end'.

Position glass panels in a 'V' arrangement about two-thirds along the length of the tank.

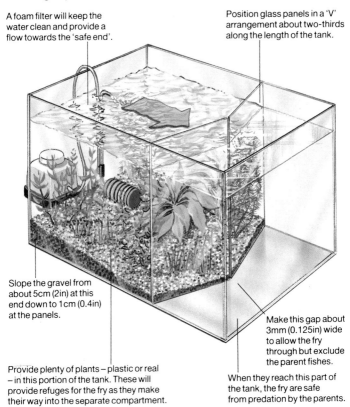

Slope the gravel from about 5cm (2in) at this end down to 1cm (0.4in) at the panels.

Make this gap about 3mm (0.125in) wide to allow the fry through but exclude the parent fishes.

Provide plenty of plants – plastic or real – in this portion of the tank. These will provide refuges for the fry as they make their way into the separate compartment.

When they reach this part of the tank, the fry are safe from predation by the parents.

Above: *This breeding trap is based on a tank measuring approximately 30x20cm (12x8in) and 23cm (9in) deep. The glass panels about 10cm (4in) wide are arranged to form a 'V' shape across the tank, with a gap between them just wide enough to allow the fry into a 'safe' zone.*

where aggressive fish are considered desirable as they will fight well on the fishing line.

Introducing excess food into the tank means that close attention to tank hygiene is called for. By concentrating on floating plants and long-leaved rooted varieties, the tank bottom should be fairly unobstructed and reasonably easy to clean every day with a siphonic action cleaning device. Use gentle foam filters all the time and clean the foam cartridges regularly. Failure to practise good hygiene will lead to water quality problems, bacterial infections and death of fry.

Mixed species rearing
Sometimes it is beneficial to mix species through the rearing stage. With Guppies in particular, a planned mating will often produce the desired result but, during the rearing period of the fry, brother/sister matings can occur which may result in deformities, poor colours and other unwanted effects of inbreeding. Some breeders therefore rear Swordtails or Speckled Mollies with the Guppies so that as they grow the Swordtails and Mollies become large enough to eat the unwanted second-generation Guppies.

Above: *A young pair of Swordtails* (Xiphophorus helleri), *the male below. 'Late developing' males and sex reversals occur in Swordtails.*

Sex reversal

Just when you think you have it all sorted out, things can become confusing later in the fishes' life. Some species produce early- or late-maturing males; the former look like females for quite some time before they 'change'.

Occasionally, true females suddenly begin to develop male characteristics, such as a gonopodium or a sword, but these sex-reversed fish are almost always sterile. This problem is most common in Swordtails, but it may happen in other livebearers, such as Mollies, Platies and Guppies. The phenomenon has been the subject of considerable interest, and it is thought that one reason might be

that the immature fishes have the potential to be either sex. It is suggested that in some fishes the ovaries grow more quickly than the testes to produce a female; in the remaining fishes the opposite occurs to produce males. As the females grow older, their ovaries cease producing hormones and the still undeveloped testes begin to produce hormones, causing the fish to develop certain male characteristics. It is still uncertain, although considered unlikely, whether males may become female.

Environmental factors can influence the initial 'decision' as to whether an individual fish becomes a male or a female. Low pH in the region of pH5-6 can cause more males to be produced, for example. Sex reversal has been seen in the wild with *Gambusia affinis*, and in at least one case it is believed to have been caused by pollution.

Genetics of livebearers

As in other creatures, the potential appearance of a livebearing fish is governed by its genes. These are not subject to normal outside influences, although certain rare chemicals and drugs, atomic radiation and X-rays can cause changes to the genetic make-up, or genotype. Normal environmental factors, such as diet, temperature, water quality etc., have no influence at all. Some of these factors can, however, alter the actual appearance of the fish (the so-called phenotype), but do not affect the genetic potential which it passes on to its offspring.

Genes are segments of chromosomes, which normally exist in pairs. The Guppy and Molly have 46 chromosomes in each cell, while the Platy and Swordtail have 48. Individuals usually receive one chromosome of each pair from each parent, there being two genes present for each character: one on each chromosome. These are referred to as alleles and they are not necessarily alike.

A particular allele is said to be 'dominant' if only one needs to be present in the pair for that allele to express itself. It is 'recessive' if both need to be the same before the alleles can express themselves. An individual is said to be homozygous when two alleles for a particular character are the same, i.e. it possesses two dominant or two recessive alleles, and heterozygous when one is dominant and one is recessive. To illustrate how the principle of dominance operates, the inheritance of gold skin colour in Guppies provides an example (see 'genetics cards' shown on page 49). The gene for skin colour in this case has two alleles:

G – grey (dominant)
g – gold (recessive)

Individuals may be

GG – grey (homozygous)
Gg – grey (heterozygous, with grey dominant over gold)
gg – gold (homozygous)

Different matings are possible:

GG with GG – this produces all grey fry (GG)
GG with Gg – this produces all grey fry (half of which are GG and half Gg)
Gg with Gg – this produces three grey fry (one GG and two Gg) for every one gold fry (gg)
gg with gg – this produces all gold fry (gg)

These ratios of offspring can be expected only when large numbers of fry are considered. With small numbers, the ratios often deviate from those predicted due to the laws of chance.

All kind of relationships can exist between genes and alleles, which modify the final appearance of an individual fish. Sometimes, one gene needs the presence of another to express itself fully. When that second gene is absent, the effects of the first may be limited. An example is the development of the swordtail in Guppies, which is recessive to the dominant roundtail allele. Even if both swordtail alleles are present (i.e. the fish is homozygous), a second gene is needed which simply causes the presence or absence of the sword. For the sword to be seen, the fish must be homozygously recessive for both genes.

Some characteristics are dependent on several genes all working together. The expression of that particular feature may then vary over a wide range depending on the several genetic influences at work.

Even the inheritance of sex is confused. Guppies and Platies are thought to have a similar sex-determination system to that of mammals: XX being female and XY being male. However, there is some transfer between chromosomes in Guppies, suggesting that X and Y are more similar than in mammals. The Platy is known to exist in races which are reversed in their sex chromosomes; this means that certain crosses of wild strains can only produce males, and others only females. In Swordtails the situation is even more unclear. The genes that control sex are not on the X and Y chromosomes. Instead, several chromosomes are involved and variations in degrees of 'maleness' can occur. All this has prompted scientists to experiment with these intriguing characteristics.

Exhibiting and specialist interests

As well as the intrinsic enjoyment and fascination that if offers, breeding livebearers can also be directed towards producing prize-winning fishes for shows and exhibitions. Many fish shows are held all over the world. Local societies may hold bowl shows, or there may be area shows between several local societies. Larger-scale open shows allow non-members to come along and compete. At the highest level are the large national open shows, often called exhibitions. The types of classes are similar at all but the local bowl shows. There are individual classes for specimen fish, fish pairs, breeders' teams (four to six fish from one spawning), and furnished aquariums. At exhibitions, the societies usually enter tableaux for competitive judging, and the dry goods companies and fish dealers bring the latest equipment and sample fishes to show aquarists.

Parents

Heterozygous Grey/Gold

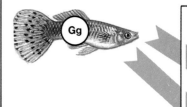

Right: *These overlapping 'genetic cards' show the result of pairing two Grey Guppies that each carry one dominant 'grey' gene and one recessive 'gold' gene. These factors become separated in the sex cells – sperm and eggs – and statistically recombine as shown. Only the double recessive Guppies – about 25% of the offspring – show the gold feature. In 50% of the offspring the gene for goldness is dominated by the grey gene.*

Below: *Tanks on display at an open fish show. Such shows include classes for all types of fishes.*

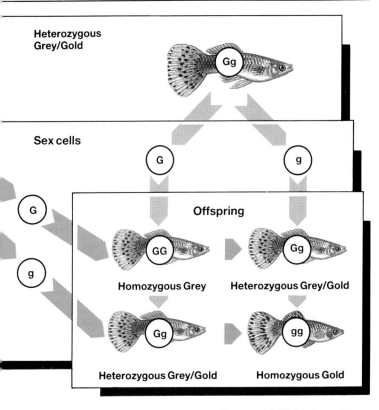

Heterozygous Grey/Gold

Gg

Sex cells

G

g

G

g

Offspring

GG
Homozygous Grey

Gg
Heterozygous Grey/Gold

Gg
Heterozygous Grey/Gold

gg
Homozygous Gold

Preparing fish for shows

It goes without saying that any fish to be shown should be in the best condition possible. It is sensible to isolate specimen fishes to avoid any damage from other fishes. Moving and catching the fish should be carried out very carefully: use a net to drive it into a clear plastic bag, which it will not see under water. This should be the routine for catching livebearers whenever possible because their skins are so easily damaged. Avoid taking heavily pregnant females, as this is unnecessarily stressful and may cause premature birth.

It is possible to condition show fish to the stresses of being peered at by the public, enabling them to be at their best on the day and to display their brightest colours. The simplest way of doing this is to put them in a show tank for an hour or so at home with plenty of people around to mimic show conditions.

Always exhibit fish in the water they are accustomed to at home. Take a supply of aquarium water with you and add a small amount of salt to the show tank. Try to set the show tank at a degree or so above normal tank temperature to bring out the fishes' colours. Another technique to bring out the colours of a male fish is to display a female on either side of the male being shown. Show rules generally require the tank bottom to be bare, but you can put black plastic underneath to make the tank a little more comforting for the fish and make the colours stand out. Be sure to obtain the show rules before entering.

The specialist societies are generally custodians of the standards for the various fish species. These standards are laid down in detail for each fish and are used by judges in their assessment; they will also look at the fishes' general condition and presentation.

Health care

Most of the diseases that affect livebearers are fairly easy to recognize. They are usually parasitic or bacterial in origin, and the signs are visible externally. In most cases, if the problem is diagnosed promptly and accurately, it can be treated quite successfully. However, there are some diseases of the internal organs which, like their human equivalents, can be very difficult to treat. Unfortunately, fish are very good at concealing the evidence of these diseases until it is too late for any treatment to be effective.

Once a problem has been identified, either remove the sick fish and treat it separately in a hospital tank or, if it is affected by a contagious disease, treat all the fish in the tank together.

Hospital tanks

With some diseases it is better to remove the fish to a hospital tank. In addition, isolation in a separate aquarium is always needed where the medication would disturb the function of the bacterial filter system. These substances include methylene blue, most antibacterial treatments and antibiotics. A tank used for treating fish should have:

Suitable heater and easily adjustable thermostat. A 'cocoon' of plastic mesh around the heater will prevent fish resting too close to the heating element.
Simple filtration by means of a box, foam or internal power filter. Filters should not contain activated carbon as this removes many medications from the water.
Adequate aeration since many treatments reduce the oxygen-carrying capacity of the water.
Dim light because some treatments are neutralized by light and others sensitize the fish to light, causing skin diseases.
Plastic plants to give a sense of security. Real plants may be killed by treatments.
Shelter, such as rocks or pots.
Suitable water, as similar as possible to water from the tank in which the fishes normally live.

Once a fish has been successfully treated, acclimatize it over a period of a few days by gradually replacing water in the hospital tank with tank water. Then return the fish to the main tank by driving it into a plastic bag, but *not* by netting it.

Humane disposal of sick fish

If it is necessary to dispose of a sick fish, be sure to do this painlessly. A suitable method is to drop the fish into water chilled with crushed ice. Alternatively, ask your veterinarian to administer a suitable anaesthetic.

Signs of illness

Before we look at some specific diseases and conditions that may afflict livebearers, here we review the general signs of illness that aquarium fishes may show:

Loss of appetite This is often the first sign of ill health, but in a well-populated tank it is easy to miss.
Listlessness Sick fishes may hang around looking rather dull. This also occurs fairly early in serious diseases and is easily missed because the fish may hide.
Rapid gill movements A fish with this symptom will often spend time near the surface of the water or close to pump outlets. It usually signifies a gill problem. If there is no obvious skin damage, it may be *Oodinium* (velvet disease) or a bacterial infection.
Change in colour Fish often become pale if acutely distressed or they may look pale as the result of excess mucus caused by parasites on the skin. In long-standing cases of stress they may become darker.
Change in shape All kinds of things can change the shape of a fish. Wasting and a hollow-bellied appearance may suggest tuberculosis, or a female that has simply worked hard producing fry. A swollen belly can be caused by pregnancy or dropsy. Odd bumps may be due to the presence of parasites in the tissues; this is more common in wild-caught specimens. Fin erosions also come under this heading, since they do cause a change in the fishes' appearance.

Above: *A sick Platy, hanging listlessly in the water and showing clear signs of weight loss.*

Flashing A fish may flick against hard objects, such as rocks, as if scratching or trying to dislodge parasites. It suggests slime disease, skin flukes, etc.

Abnormal posture Difficulty in maintaining balance or an abnormal posture suggest a serious parasitic or bacterial infection.

'Shimmying' This is a strange sideways undulating 'swimming on the spot'. It usually suggests chilling or reaction to a change in water conditions. It is also seen in livebearers infected with columnaris (caused by *Flexibacter columnaris*), and is especially common in the larger Sailfin Mollies.

Below: *If possible, treat ailing fishes in a separate 'hospital tank' set up along the lines shown here. It is easier to 'fine-tune' the conditions and to monitor the progress of fishes when treated in such a tank.*

Basic hospital tank

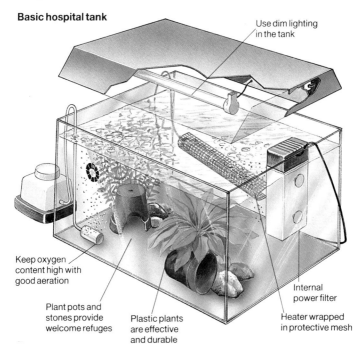

Use dim lighting in the tank

Keep oxygen content high with good aeration

Plant pots and stones provide welcome refuges

Plastic plants are effective and durable

Internal power filter

Heater wrapped in protective mesh

Skin diseases

Most of the parasitic infections of the skin produce common signs. Affected fishes are unsettled and they often try to scratch on rocks and the gravel bottom. (Do not mistake normal feeding behaviour for this). Their colours begin to look a little 'washed out' or grey and dull, due to the parasites causing irritation and the excessive production of mucus. The eyes are similarly affected and often appear slightly cloudy. If the fishes are left untreated, they will lose their appetite, their fins often begin to look ragged and frayed, and eventually inflammation (redness) and holes may appear. Afflicted fishes often die before this happens because of damage to the gills.

Bacterial diseases of the skin, such as columnaris, may appear as distinct white areas, sometimes with fine whitish filaments visible. In other fish there may be simply erosion of the skin in the form of fin rot or ulcers. In severely infected fish where the bacteria have caused septicaemia (blood poisoning), there may be skin wheals or ulcers, haemorrhages around the eyes, reddened fins, bulging eyes or the scales may stand out with dropsy (swelling of the abdomen).

Careless handling, particularly when combined with poor water conditions, often causes minor damage which permits bacterial infections – or even fungal infections – to establish themselves. Sometimes fluke infections can cause cataracts and the lens deep inside the eye becomes cloudy.

Gill diseases

The signs of gill disease are not always immediately obvious. Initially, the fish lose their appetite and they tend to remain near the surface of water and around the aeration stone or filter uplift, where dissolved oxygen levels are highest. The gill covers move more rapidly than normal and often you can see the gills inside, which may be swollen and greyer then normal due to the mucus caused by irritation. Sometimes it is possible to see light or dark marks in the gill; these are individual parasites. Or you may see large eroded areas where an infection caused by flukes has eaten away the tissues. If the fish is left untreated and survives for long enough, the gills begin to thicken in response to the chronic irritation (like a callous on the foot caused by a tight shoe). This slowly suffocates the fish, destroying its appetite until it eventually dies.

COMMON SKIN AND GILL DISEASES

Freshwater white spot (Ich)
(*Ichthyophthirius multifiliis*)
This is the most well-known fish disease of all; almost every aquarium has been infected at some time. The parasites are easily visible to the naked eye as white spots on the fish (up to 1mm/0.04in in diameter). Proprietary treatments usually aim to kill it before it forms a cyst, or when the cyst ruptures to release the free-swimming stages that infect other fishes. When the mature parasites 'punch' out of the skin they create large holes that can become secondarily infected by bacteria or fungus. Rapid gill movements are a warning that the gills are also badly affected.

Above: *White spot infection cycle.*
1 *Parasites beneath the skin* 2 *Mature parasites break through skin and form capsule* 3 *Free-swimming parasites can infect new hosts.*

Above: *A Red-tailed Goodeid* (Xenotoca eiseni) *with the clear symptoms of white spot (ich). This responds well to treatment.*

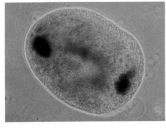

Above: *A single white spot parasite, showing the typical curved nucleus. Hair-like cilia propel the free-swimming stages in the water.*

Treatment: Use proprietary products in the tank and remove any activated carbon from the filter while they are being used.

Gill flukes (*Dactylogyrus*)
These are rarely visible to the naked eye, but can be seen with a good hand lens or microscope. They use their many-hooked 'foot' to wander around on the fishes' delicate gill membranes, browsing on the tissues. They produce signs typical of gill disease.

Treatment: Use proprietary treatments in the tank and formalin short-term baths. Use formalin (a solution of approximately 35% formaldehyde in water) at a dilution of 0.2ml formalin per litre of water (approximately 1ml per gallon). This can be used for a period of up to one hour, but stop treatment if the fish become distressed. The bath will kill the adult flukes, but tank treatments will have to be repeated as the fluke eggs, which drop to the tank bottom, are resistant until they hatch. Treatment of individual fish with short-term formalin baths needs to be carried out in conjunction with treatment in a hospital tank.

Remember that some eggs can lodge in the gills and be missed by treatment, only to fall out later and cause reinfection. Therefore it is vital to clean out the infected tank and all the equipment thoroughly before returning fishes to it.

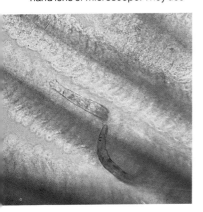

Left: *Two gill flukes* (Dactylogyrus *sp.) attached to the gill filaments. A heavy infestation causes swollen gills and increased respiration rate.*

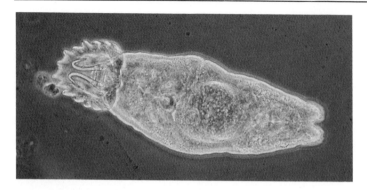

Above: *An individual skin fluke (Gyrodactylus sp.), which may be up to 0.8mm (0.03in) long. Clasping hooks anchor it to the skin.*

Skin flukes (*Gyrodactylus*)
These relatives of *Dactylogyrus* live on the skin. Being livebearing, they have a different life cycle and, rather like Russian dolls, each adult may contain several generations at various stages of maturity inside.

Treatment: Use proprietary treatments in the tank and separate short-term formalin baths. This is usually sufficient, since there is no resistant stage in the life cycle.

Below: *A Guppy with signs of slime disease. The fraying tail fin is the most obvious sign, although this could also result from bacterial rot.*

Slime diseases (*Chilodonella, Cyclochaeta* [*Trichodina*], and *Costia* [*Ichthyobodo*]). All three of these protozoan parasites will cause the symptoms described for skin parasites; the dulling of colours due to excessive mucus, fraying of the fins, weakness, gill damage and death if not treated promptly.

Treatment: It is best to treat early cases with proprietary medications for protozoal diseases by adding the treatment to the tank. *Chilodonella* is the most resistant to this approach and may need formalin treatment. This is best postponed with severely infected fish already weakened by gill damage. Dipping the fish briefly into a 3 percent salt bath will kill most of the parasites and lift some of the mucus off the gills. (Make up a 3 percent salt bath

using common salt at a concentration of 30gm per litre – approximately 27 teaspoonsful per gallon.) Use salt dips with care.

Velvet disease (*Oodinium limneticum*) This parasite is very tiny but can show up as a fine gold-dust on the skin. Its 'roots' penetrate the skin cells and it often attacks the gills, so signs of gill disease may be apparent first. It has a pigment in the cells, like plants, which can use light as an alternative source of energy.

Treatment: Use a proprietary treatment and remove any activated carbon from the filter during medication. It is often helpful to darken the tank during treatment to rob the parasites of light energy.

BACTERIAL INFECTIONS

Some internal bacterial fish diseases are treatable with proprietary preparations, such as nifurpirinol, or prescribed antibiotics. There are also a number of antibacterial preparations that are effective against superficial bacterial infections. Dirty conditions in the tank – from dead plants, faeces or uneaten food – encourage the growth of bacteria, so good hygiene is essential to avoid these problems occurring in the aquarium.

Finrot
Fin-nipping by other fish, or damage caused by careless netting or handling, especially when water conditions are marginal or poor, are major factors in the spread of finrot.

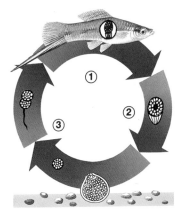

Above: *Velvet infection cycle.*
1 Fish hosts the parasites attached to the skin by 'roots'. 2 Mature parasites fall off and form cysts. 3 Swimming stages seek hosts.

However, a high bacterial level in a dirty tank may be sufficient on its own. A poor diet deficient in vitamins can also cause problems with heavily pigmented fishes such as Black Mollies.

Treatment: Carry out a general clean-up of the aquarium water. Proprietary cures will help to speed up recovery, but cannot overcome neglect by the fishkeeper.

Columnaris – 'Mouth fungus' (*Flexibacter columnaris*)
Livebearers are particularly susceptible to this. Black Mollies are especially prone to infections, which show up as white patches on the skin. Despite being widely, but incorrectly called 'mouth fungus', it is not caused by a fungus at all, but by a slime bacterium that links with others in the colony to form threads. True fungal threads are thicker, like cotton wool, while 'mouth fungus' is finer and shorter.

Treatment: Proprietary treatments in the tank are usually successful. Particularly stubborn cases can be

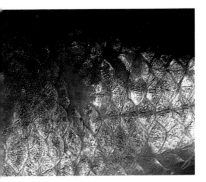

Left: *Signs of columnaris on the flank of a fish. The fungal-like threads are actually slime bacteria.*

treated with a range of antibiotics, but they must be administered in a separate treatment tank. Do not use a net to transfer the fish to a treatment tank, since any further damage will allow the bacteria to spread. Instead, use the net to drive an affected fish into a transparent plastic bag and then transfer it for treatment.

Septicaemia – blood poisoning

Bacteria can enter the blood vessels and circulate throughout the tissues, lodging in a variety of organs, including the heart, and causing inflammation and tissue damage – the typical signs of septicaemia, or blood poisoning. The tissue damage results in leakage of fluids into the abdomen, and this is seen as dropsy (see below). The skin and the base of the fins show clear signs of inflammation (reddening). Septicaemia may follow on from untreated skin infections, such as finrot, or may occur as the direct result of keeping stressed fishes in dirty conditions.

Treatment: You will probably require veterinary help. In the larger fishes, antibiotics may be given by injection; for smaller species, they are given via food or, as a last option, in the water. Once this problem has occurred, always try to identify and correct any potential triggering factors, such as poor water quality.

Dropsy

Medically, this means fluid in the abdomen, but in practice the term has been extended to include all diseases which make the abdomen swell abnormally. This makes sense, since it is often difficult to distinguish these diseases without a post-mortem examination. A swollen abdomen can develop slowly due to cancers in the internal organs, or as the result of large parasites, either lodging in or damaging the organs. In livebearers, peritonitis (infection of the peritoneum that lines the abdominal cavity) can also cause dropsy. These forms of dropsy are all relatively benign and do not spread, provided that the fish is removed from the tank when it becomes ill, i.e. before it initially develops the signs of dropsy.

There are other more acute malignant forms of dropsy in which the scales stand out due to the sudden stretching caused by excess fluid in the abdomen and under the skin.

Treatment: The only proprietary remedies likely to have any effect are those containing the antibacterial compound nifurpirinol,

Below: *A Platy with the protruding scales typical of dropsy, commonly caused by bacterial infection.*

Below: *Reddening beneath the skin on a Sailfin Molly – clear signs of septicaemia, or blood poisoning.*

Above: *A male Sailfin Molly with protruding eyes – so-called 'pop-eye' – caused by tuberculosis.*

since the commonest causes of this problem are bacterial septicaemias. Otherwise, treatment with suitable antibiotics on veterinary prescription is required for the affected fish and for other fishes that may have been in contact with it.

Draining off the fluid from acute cases is not recommended, as the fluid is full of protein and essential salts. In chronic cases, however, a veterinarian can drain it off under anaesthetic, although this is more likely to cause the fish to die from shock. Successful antibiotic treatment should cause the dropsy to regress.

Tuberculosis
(*Mycobacterium* spp.)
Affected fish usually feed normally, but continue to lose weight as the internal organs become progressively damaged. Some fish develop nodules under the skin, which eventually ulcerate; in others the nodules form behind the eye, causing 'pop-eye'.

The bacteria that cause the disease prefer lower temperatures than most human infections, but they will still occasionally produce disease in people. This usually takes the form of an infected nodule on the skin, but in rare cases it can cause internal infections. Treatment of human infections is difficult and, once tuberculosis is diagnosed in

the fishes, it is essential to take great care with hygiene when servicing the tank. Sensible precautions include washing your hands thoroughly after contact with the water and not using a siphon that might allow you to swallow any tank water during routine maintenance.

Treatment: This is very difficult and requires specialist veterinary advice and antibiotic treatment to stand any chance of success. Fish positively identified as suffering from tuberculosis rarely respond to treatment, but other fish that have been in contact with an affected fish should be treated via the water and the food. Remove these so-called 'in-contacts' to a hospital tank and strip, clean and disinfect the infected tank.

Infected fishes shed bacteria into the water in their faeces, and from ulcerated areas. Therefore, isolate them or dispose of them painlessly. Never allow infected fish to die in the tank as they will be cannibalized and so infect other fish.

FUNGUS

Saprolegnia
This is the most common fungus infection seen in aquarium fishes. It looks like tufts of dirty green cotton wool stuck to the fish, because algae grow on the fungus. Fungal infection is always secondary to another problem and may have the same causes as finrot, infection with white spot, skin or gill flukes, etc.

Above: *The fluffy growths of fungus* (Saprolegnia), *often a secondary infection of damaged or weak fish.*

Treatment: Transfer the fish to clean water and treat it with a proprietary broad-spectrum medication. It is also very important to identify the underlying cause of the fungal infection and remedy it.

PARASITIC WORMS

Above: *A microphotograph of the fungal threads of* Saprolegnia *that feed on dead and decaying tissues.*

Below: *A close up of the 'head' of a single* Camallanus *worm. The tiny jaws 'chew' the intestinal lining.*

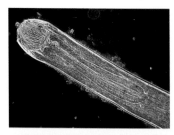

Camallanus
Livebearers seem to be particularly susceptible to infestation with this worm. These 8-10mm-long (0.3-0.4in), red bloodsucking worms have strong biting jaws with which they chew the lining of the intestine. They are often seen as a red 'paintbrush' protruding from the vent. Because they cause bleeding, they can produce anaemia and poor growth, leading to emaciation and ultimately death in heavy cases.

Below: *The typical 'red paintbrush' of* Camallanus *worms protruding from the vent of an infested fish.*

The worms are also livebearing, producing larval young that can be transmitted by live food, such as the tiny crustaceans *Cyclops* and *Asellus*. They may also be passed from fish to fish by cannibalism, or even directly through fish pecking at worms on infested individuals.

Treatment: Veterinary drugs, such as levamisole, are generally required, although feeding food soaked in the antibacterial compound phenoxyethanol is said to be successful.

NON-INFECTIOUS CONDITIONS

Cancer
Fish of the genus *Xiphophorus* have been studied by scientists looking at cancer. The pure species seem to be unusually resistant to tumour formation (cancer), but this resistance turns to susceptibility when the species are hybridized. The major form seen is a melanoma (a skin tumour consisting of melanin-pigmented cells) developing from the black spots on *X.maculatus* (Platy) which, when crossed with *X.helleri* (Swordtail), may sometimes become out of control and cause a fatal cancer in an individual fish. This is not infectious to any other fish in the aquarium. A similar problem may occur in *Limia vittata* (Cuban Limia), where the excess yellow which develops in the better show fish may be pre-cancerous, causing a so-called xanthoma (a yellow equivalent of a melanoma).

Siamese twins
This disorder, producing what is sometimes called a teratoma, is seen in all livebearing species, although some strains, particularly Guppies, seem very prone to producing these deformed offspring. Affected fishes may survive and mature into adults if the degree of deformity is not too severe.

Below: *The yellow patches on this splendid male Cuban Limia may be pre-cancerous forms of xanthomas.*

Above: *A Guppy with a teratoma – a birth defect of varying severity seen particularly in these livebearers.*

Species section

Many committed fishkeepers begin their life-long involvement with the aquarium hobby by setting up a community tank that invariably includes some of the 'easy' brightly coloured livebearing fishes. Later on, as interest grows into dedication, some fish-keepers specialize not only in livebearers but in one particular group or species, often the more obscure the better!

This part of the book satisfies both those aspirations, by including a wide selection of livebearing fishes, including both the popular Guppies, Mollies, Platies and Swordtails and also some of the less common 'enthusiasts' fishes. All are presented in A-Z order of scientific name in their respective Families and are described under a series of headings that examine their habitat, length, diet, features, care and breeding. The sizes given refer to the standard length, i.e. not including the tail, and where appropriate both male and female measurements are given. In most cases, the size is

quoted as an expected maximum in the aquarium. The gestation period and number of fry to be anticipated are also quoted as a range; these figures can vary so much in different water conditions, at different temperatures, from one individual fish to another, etc. that it is not possible to be dogmatic.

The dietary information given for each species forms an extension of the general advice given in Part One. Most livebearers will adapt to taking dried foods, but many relish algae and live foods – even other fish in the case of *Belonesox belizanus*. The advice given on care and breeding reflects the needs of each species in relation to its natural environment, i,e. whether it lives in static salty marshes or in fast-flowing mountain streams far from the coast. Combining the advice given in both parts of the book will enable even total newcomers to the delights of the aquarium hobby to try their hand at nurturing and breeding livebearing fishes.

Family: ANABLEPIDAE/Genus: ANABLEPS
These fascinating fishes from the brackish waters of Central and South America are highly specialized surface feeders. Their eyes are divided horizontally so that when swimming at the surface they can see clearly both above and below the water. An aquatic vivarium would be ideal for them.

Anableps anableps
Four-eyes

● **Habitat:** Slow moving brackish waters throughout southern Mexico and into the northern parts of South America.

● **Length:** Up to 30cm (12in) but 23-25cm (9-10in) is more typical.

● **Diet:** In the wild these fishes feed on insects landing on the water surface; in captivity, they will take most foods fairly greedily, although some individuals appear not to like fish. Flying insects caught using a net on the car bumper are useful, as are crickets, mussels and home-made meat-based foods.

● **Features:** *Anableps anableps* is unmistakable in appearance, with a long body – brownish with violet stripes on the sides – a flat head and large frog-like protruding eyes. The cornea, pupil and retina are divided horizontally by a layer of tissue which allows the fish to see both above and below the water level as it cruises at the surface. The males have a fleshy tubular penis-like organ supported by curved anal finrays. In common with *Jenynsia lineata*, these fishes are 'one-sided' (see text on opposite page).

● **Basic care and breeding:** This brackish species will live in full seawater. A specific gravity of 1.010 is suitable. They are good jumpers so be sure to provide a sturdy cover on the aquarium. This will also help to maintain the necessary high humidity. Also provide a large shallow water area and a gravel beach area to enable them to come out. The ideal temperature is in the region 24-28°C (75-82°F). Good filtration is essential in the aquarium to cope with the waste and uneaten food from these large fishes.

Populations seem to be heavily biased numerically towards females, so finding a male may not be easy. Anableps usually produce two small broods of between three and five fry per year; occasionally up to 20 may be seen. These measure about 3-5cm (1.2-2in) at birth.

Above: **Anableps anableps**
Protruding 'bifocal' eyes allow this fish to see above and below water.

Above: **Jenynsia lineata**
An elegant bottom-dwelling species
that will adapt to a wide range of
water conditions. Male at right.

Genus: JENYNSIA
Although only one species is known to aquarium hobbyists, members of the genus *Jenynsia* are distributed across South America south of the Amazon. Their distinctive feature in terms of reproductive biology is their curious trait of being 'one-sided' – as explained fully on page 36.

Jenynsia lineata
One-sided Livebearer
● **Habitat:** Two strains seem to exist: one lives in brackish pools and slow-flowing rivers in southern Brazil, Uruguay and northern Argentina; the other strain lives in high-salinity lagoons, where evaporation has raised the salinity to above that of sea water.
● **Length:** The sexes are very different in size; males reach 3-4cm (1.2-1.6in) and females 9-12cm (3.5-4.7in)
● **Diet:** Most aquarium foods.

● **Features:** A slender silvery grey body with fine black markings in lines along the sides; there may be an orange mark close to the anus of young virgin females.
● **Basic care and breeding:** These are slow-moving, bottom-dwelling fish. Older males and large females can be rather aggressive. Like the Anablepids, these are one-sided fishes; the male has a rather short gonopodium slightly curved at the tip and can only curve it one way. Similarly, females have a genital opening which is directed to one side. Therefore, a left-handed male can mate only with a right-handed female and vice-versa. A number need to be kept together to find 'matching pairs'.

Once a pairing is successful, broods of about 20-30 fry are seen at intervals of about 28-35 days. The fry are quite large and, like the Goodeids, will thrive on live foods, such as grindalworms and crushed snails, plus small pieces of ox-heart. The best temperature for ensuring successful breeding in the aquarium is in the region of 25°C (77°F).

Left: **Anableps anableps**
These fishes need a spacious tank
or vivarium with a shallow beach.

Family: HEMIRHAMPHIDAE

The Halfbeaks fill the type of niche in Southeast Asia occupied by the Poeciliidae in Central America. They are schooling fishes living in the surface layers of rivers and streams, in both fresh and brackish waters. The males have a well-formed andropodium developed from the anal fin, although it is less mobile than the gonopodium of the Poeciliidae and means that the fish must get closer when mating to ensure transfer of 'sperm packets'.

Dermogenys pusillus

Malayan Halfbeak; Wrestling Halfbeak
● **Habitat:** Fresh and brackish

water of streams and ponds in much of Southeast Asia.
● **Length:** Females up to 7cm (2.75in); males up to 5.5cm (2.2in).

Above: **Hemirhamphodon pogonognathus**
This Toothed Halfbeak from the forest streams of Singapore will thrive in the surface waters of a well-planted tank. This is a colourful male.

Above: **Nomorhamphus sp.**
These Beakless Halfbeaks have a relatively short extension of the lower jaw, which in males (here the upper fish) curves downwards.

Right: **Dermogenys pusillus**
This is the most commonly kept member of the Halfbeak Family. This is a fine female specimen.

● **Diet:** These fish need live food such as *Tubifex* worms fed via a floating worm feeder and floating insects; they are top feeders and cannot feed from the bottom. Flying insects caught with a hand net or using a net fixed on the car bumper are suitable.

● **Features:** Halfbeaks have a characteristically long pointed lower jaw which is fixed in position; the male's anal fin is modified and appears folded. Both sexes have a silvery blue iridescence.

● **Basic care and breeding:** Keep these interesting fish in a moderately planted tank of about 50-100 litres (11-22 gallons) at a temperature of about 26°C (79°F). Some floating plants are important. Cover the tank securely since halfbeaks live in the upper waters and are keen jumpers. As with other livebearers, use hard water in the aquarium, perhaps with some added salt – 0.5-1.5gm per litre (0.5-1.5 teaspoon per gallon) – particularly in softer waters. Proprietary buffers can be used to keep the pH above pH7.

For breeding, use a tank set up as described above and be sure to include some floating plants; these provide a refuge for the female to escape the over-enthusiastic attentions of the male.

The most suitable sex ratio is one male for two or three females. This avoids the fighting which often breaks out between males (hence 'wrestling') and prevents one female being too harassed by an overly attentive male. Pregnancy lasts between five and seven weeks, and 10-20 young are usually produced. These fishes are very cannibalistic, so if possible move pregnant females to a smaller but similar tank to give birth. Do this very carefully since the pregnant females – with a prominent gravid spot and bulky appearance – are prone to lose their broods. After the birth, move the female back to the main tank.

Raising the broods can be difficult at first; the fry feed on newly hatched brineshrimp, moving later on to the same food as the parents. The fry begin to develop the beak after about four to six weeks.

● **Other genera:** Another genus of interest in this Family is *Nomorhamphus*, the Beakless Halfbeaks of the Indonesian island of Sulawesi. They grow much larger than *Dermogenys* – to about 11cm (4.5in) – and although the lower jaw does have an extension, it tends to curl downward and in the males takes on the appearance of a pronounced goatee beard. They are good feeders, taking anything that moves, living or not. Breeding is difficult but along similar lines to *Dermogenys*.

The Toothed Halfbeaks, *Hemirhamphodon* species, are also worthy of mention. Like the other members of the Family, they come from Indonesia. *H.chrysopunctatus* from the soft acid, blackwaters of the Borneo jungle and *H.pogonognathus* from the forests near Singapore. They are larger than *Dermogenys*, although not as large as *Nomorhamphus*, and the andropodium is longer than in the other genera. General care of *H.pogonognathus* is similar to that of *Dermogenys* except that it is more strictly a surface feeder. The aquarium needs of the recently discovered *H.chrysopunctatus* are not yet fully understood. Never mix these genera of Halfbeaks since fighting will occur.

Family: GOODEIDAE
In overall shape the Goodeids are similar to the Platies, but with a somewhat deeper body and a very narrow caudal peduncle; the females have a well-rounded anal fin. All the species come from Mexico. Their distribution in the wild centres on the highland catchment area of the Rio Lerma, where the Family is represented in a variety of ecological niches, from pools to fast-flowing streams. Goodeids are fairly adaptable to temperature and are not too difficult to keep in the aquarium.

Because of the different system of embryo development in Goodeids, the fry are born significantly larger than those of other similarly sized livebearers. Often the trophotaenia, which act as a type of placenta, can be seen hanging from the rectum at birth. (See pages 36-49 for further details on breeding.)

Ameca splendens

Butterfly Goodeid
● **Habitat:** The Rio Ameca Basin in western Mexico.
● **Length:** The males are quite a bit smaller than females; 6.5cm (2.5in) as opposed to 9cm (3.5in).
● **Diet:** Typically vegetarian with a preference for such plants as *Synnema* (Water Wisteria) and *Ceratopteris* (Indian Fern). If the fish will accept it, offer them flaked diet with fresh green foods as supplements; this seems more acceptable to them if they are introduced to it as fry. Midge larvae may be eaten more avidly than *Daphnia* (water fleas).
● **Features:** The male is particularly attractive, with blue-green iridescent flanks and a yellow-orange underside. A black band

runs along the side and breaks up on the caudal peduncle. On the tail there is a definite vertical black band and a bright yellow one. The female is relatively drab, with less iridescence. These fishes will thrive in a wide range of temperatures – 18-30°C (65-86°F) – and water conditions in the aquarium.
● **Basic care and breeding:** Courtship is obvious, combining displays with mild aggression. After a successful mating, a brood takes six to eight weeks to develop into large well-developed fry, up to 1.5cm (0.6in) long at birth. The birth may take 10-60 minutes. Adults are not cannibalistic and so the urge to hide shown by most livebearer fry is not seen. The fry are ready to eat the same food as their parents from the very first day (see notes on diet).

Left: **Ameca splendens**
This male has the typical iridescent markings and yellow edging on the tail. A highly adaptable species that will breed readily in the aquarium.

towards each other in the tank.
● **Basic care and breeding:** The optimum temperature is 24°C (75°F). The water hardness is less important than pH, which should be 7.6-7.8. Salt is not absolutely necessary but is probably worthwhile in softer waters.

Broods of 10-20 fry about 6mm (0.25in) long are produced approximately every six weeks. Ideally, place the female in a trap in shallow water about seven days before she is due to give birth; this allows the fry to reach the surface to fill their swimbladders. First feeding with grindal- and microworms leads quite well on to commercial flaked foods. (See also pages 32-35.)
● **Other species:** *Characodon lateralis*, the Rainbow or Red Rainbow Goodeid, is fairly aggressive and consequently makes a poor community fish. They seem happier in a relatively overgrown, dark tank and when kept together in a large group. In this situation no one fish is vulnerable to a high level of victimization. Avoid trapping the females; they often drop the fry prematurely. Best results are usually achieved in well-planted 'species' tanks, when broods of up to 12 can be expected.

Characodon audax
Black Prince
● **Habitat:** Streams and ponds in western Mexico.
● **Length:** Males reach up to about 3cm (1.2in) and the females up to 5.5cm (2.2in) in length.
● **Diet:** As with all the Goodeids, some green food is well worthwhile, although flaked foods are a good basis for their day-to-day diet.
● **Features:** Males are greeny/gold mottled with grey, and have black fins. Females are a drab greeny/grey with two black spots on the caudal peduncle, a silvery belly, and a good strong gravid spot when they are due to give birth.

A generally peaceable species, although the males are fairly territorial and can be aggressive

Below: **Characodon audax**
A male specimen with the typical jet black fins. Males are territorial and will show aggression to one another.

Girardinichthys viviparus
Amarillo

● **Habitat:** Found only in a single, virtually stagnant pool in a Mexico City park. The water is very hard and alkaline (pH9), is green with algae and has occasionally been found frosted.

● **Length:** Males are 3.5cm (1.4in); females 6.5cm (2.5in).

● **Diet:** Their natural environment is rich in live food and captive diets need to mimic this; algae growing on plants, *Daphnia*, brineshrimp, grindal - and microworms are all suitable foods for this species.

● **Features:** Both sexes are basically grey with slight black barring and a black belly; the dorsal and anal fins of males are edged with black.

● **Basic care and breeding:** The Amarillo has so far been very difficult to maintain, needing hard mature water at a temperature of 21-23°C (70-73°F). They seem to be very delicate and particularly sensitive to netting. Therefore, drive them quietly into a cup or small plastic container for tank transfers.

It is best to establish new tanks with fry, since adults take less well to transfers. Use only light aeration or none at all and keep the lighting at low level. Excess aeration and bright light encourage too much algal growth and increased levels of waste products in the tank, which may account for the reports of fin rot in fry and death of adults. The best approach is to use a large aquarium – 120cm (48in) long – heavily planted and filled with well-matured water filtered through foam filters. Ideally, maintain a low stocking rate to parallel the natural situation as closely as possible, although this approach is not easy in small tanks.

Colony breeding in a well-planted aquarium seems best. Alternatively, move the female to a nursery tank about 10 days before she is due to give birth. Since this may prove rather stressful, it is best to leave her alone unless she is likely to be harassed. The gestation period is six to eight weeks. Remove the female after the babies are born to protect her from the males.

Above: **Girardinichthys viviparus**
This species needs mature water and a roomy 'natural' aquarium environment to thrive and breed.

Below: **Goodea atripinnis**
An attractively marked species that may prove aggressive in the aquarium. The male is at top.

Goodea atripinnis
Black-finned Goodea
- **Habitat:** Streams and lakes in the area of the Rio Lerma in western Mexico.
- **Length:** Males reach 8.5cm (3.3in); females 13cm (5in) or more.
- **Diet:** Members of this genus are filter feeders, eating plant and animal plankton, but in captivity they will eat a range of vegetable matter and some live foods.
- **Features:** Both sexes have a long, laterally compressed body, olive-green in colour tinged with pink and a slight bluish iridescence. The fins are yellowish but darken in colour in response to stress and moods. Females have a typically rounded anal fin.
- **Basic care and breeding:** This is a difficult fish to breed; best results are likely to be achieved in a nursery tank or a well-planted species tank at a temperature of 20-24°C (68-75°F). After a gestation period of six to eight weeks, the female produces about 20-40 young. Feed these on newly hatched brineshrimp and on 'green water' from a tank left out in the sun to develop an abundance of suspended algae. Certain commercially produced fine diets for fry are also acceptable.

Ilyodon xantusi

- **Habitat:** Fast-flowing streams among the highlands of the Pacific coast of Mexico.
- **Length:** The sexes are about the same size, quite large for Goodeids, at approximately 10cm (4in).
- **Diet:** These are very much algae eaters; a tank receiving direct sunlight or an excessive amount of artificial light and too little vegetation may look unsightly but it will suit these fishes perfectly.
- **Features:** The male is striking in appearance, with a blue iridescence and a golden belly. A diffuse black line runs along the flanks to a tail edged in black; a chequer-board black pattern covers the remainder of the body.
- **Basic care and breeding:** Keep these fishes in a well-lit tank with plenty of aeration and water movement caused by power filters. Provide rocks, bogwood and a few clumps of plants to give the fish some shelter and provide suitable surfaces for the growth of algae. Enriching the water with blackwater extract will further encourage the algal growth needed for success. After a gestation period of about 55 days, 20-35 fry are produced. At this point the trophotaenia (wormlike 'feeding extensions' explained on

Above: **Ilyodon xantusi**
A splendid male of this attractive species. Provide plenty of algae.

page 36) are still present, but these usually wither away within the first 24 hours after birth. The young feed well and become sexually mature at four to five months.

Below: **Skiffia bilineata**
A long-established aquarium species, previously Neotoca. *Female.*

Skiffia bilineata

Black-finned Goodeid

● **Habitat:** Rivers in volcanic areas of Central Mexico.

● **Length:** Males up to 3.5cm (1.4in); females 6cm (2.4in).

● **Diet:** Vegetable matter and some live food.

● **Features:** The sexes are similar. The dorsal fin starts halfway down the olive-grey body and, like many Goodeids, the belly is tinged yellow. Along the flanks is a narrow blue-green iridescent zone with a dark longitudinal line running from the snout to the caudal peduncle, where it is crossed by dark bars in males. Mature males develop black fins.

● **Basic care and breeding:** Best results will be obtained in a well-planted, large aquarium. Maintain the temperature at 22-25°C (72-77°F) and as near to pH7 as possible. The gestation period is six to eight weeks, and 5-40 young may be produced in a typical brood.

Xenotoca eiseni
Red-tailed Goodeid; Orange-tailed Goodeid
● **Habitat:** Streams in Mexico.
● **Length:** Male up to about 5cm (2in); females up to 7cm (2.75in).
● **Diet:** A wide range of foods, from dried foods to live and green foods; they will also browse on algae.
● **Features:** A deep stocky body with a narrow caudal peduncle. The front of the male fish has a bluish band and there is a bright orange band around the caudal peduncle; the tail is a yellow-orange in colour.
● **Basic care and breeding:** It is fairly tolerant to aquarium conditions, although it will thrive best in moderately hard water. It is a reasonably quiet fish, but can be a fin nipper in a community tank. Breeding traps are not needed since the fry are rarely bothered by the parent fishes. Providing plenty of food for the parents in a well-planted aquarium usually affords the fry sufficient protection. Generally broods contain between 20 and 60 good-sized fry.

Right: **Xenotoca eiseni**
A male specimen showing the typical orange coloration at the base of the tail. Hardy and adaptable.

Family: POECILIIDAE
This Family includes 26 genera and over 138 species, one species of which, *Tomeurus gracilis*, is not necessarily a livebearer. Officially it is an egglayer but on occasion under certain conditions becomes a livebearer! In this Family, the gonopodium is made up from the 3rd, 4th and 5th anal fin rays. *Poecilia* and *Xiphophorus* are the major genera and these are discussed in separate sections. First, we look at a range of other Poeciliid fishes.

Alfaro cultratus
*Knife Livebearer; Alfaro's
Livebearer*
● **Habitat:** Running streams in the
Atlantic coastal regions of the Central
American countries of Guatemala,
Costa Rica and Panama.

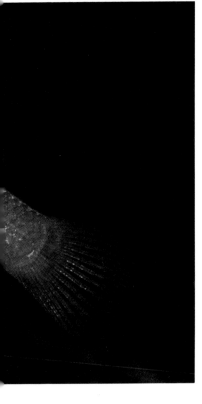

● **Length:** The male generally
reaches about 5cm (2in); the female
in the region of 6-8cm (2.4-3.2cm).
● **Diet:** It will accept flaked foods
readily, especially when tempted
with live foods. Being a surface
feeder, it will relish midge larvae.
● **Features:** The fish is very
slender, with the spine clearly
apparent through its translucent
body. The two rows of scales on the
lower edge of the caudal peduncle
give it a characteristic knife edge
appearance. The colour is a yellow-
green, pale on the belly and with a
greenish purple iridescence above
the anal fin.
● **Basic care and breeding:** This
shy but aggressive fish needs a
well-planted tank for shelter and
benefits from the movement
created by a small power filter.
Maintain the temperature at
25-28°C (77-82°F) for successful
breeding. After a gestation period of
between 28 and 32 days, a brood of
30-100 small fry is produced. If the
adults can be prevented from eating
the fry, they grow quite rapidly.
Although it is possible to trap the
female about 10 days before she is
due to give birth, this causes serious
stress to these nervous fishes.
Using a nursery tank or tank division
is preferable (see pages 43-45).

Left: **Alfaro cultratus**
*The characteristic 'blade-like' row
of scales along the rear lower edge
of the body are visible on this male.*

Belonesox belizanus

Pike Livebearer; Pike Top Minnow

● **Habitat:** Still waters, marshes and lakes along the Atlantic coast of Central America: Southern Mexico into Yucatan and Honduras.

● **Length:** This is the largest Poeciliid, the males up to 10cm (4in), and the females 18cm (7in).

● **Diet:** *Belonesox* is carnivorous, even on its own species. Females may eat small mates, so keep them alone except under supervision. They seem to need virtually all live food, including insects, earthworms and fish, although it may be possible to cajole them into taking flakes or home-made heart-based foods.

● **Features:** Greyish silver with tiny black dots in rows along the upper body and a black spot in the tail. A

Above: **Belonesox belizanus**
A female displays a wide-opening jaw, bristling with sharp teeth.

dark lateral line shows along the side of the fish depending on mood. The pointed snout and small sharp teeth of this sleek fish are instantly recognizable features.

Above: *The brownish grey waters of Rio Atoyac in Mexico, a typical habitat for* Belonesox belizanus.

● **Basic care and breeding:**
Naturally shy, the Pike Livebearer seeks out plant cover in which to lurk for its prey. Keep it in a tank on its own, therefore; a community aquarium would equate to a restaurant to such a fish and would not remain a community for long. Keep it in a large aquarium at a temperature of about 25-28°C (77-82°F), ideally with some salt in the water – 0.5-1.0gm per litre (0.5-1.0 teaspoon per gallon) – although this is not essential.

These fishes can be sexed at three to four months old, and become sexually mature at six to nine months. After a gestation period of 30-50 days, 20-80 fry 1.5cm (0.6in) long are produced. Feed the fry initially on *Cyclops* and day-old guppies, and give them immediate protection from their mother. Using a heavily planted nursery tank is the best strategy, since this gives the fry a chance to reach some shelter; remove the female from the nursery tank as soon as she has given birth.

Left: **Belonesox belizanus**
A superb pair of these streamlined voracious fishes. Female at top.

Right:
Brachyrhaphis rhabdophora
*A male, with the broad dorsal fin and
black gonopodium typical of its sex.*

Brachyrhaphis rhabdophora

- **Habitat:** Costa Rica, Atlantic and Pacific slopes of the central mountain ranges.
- **Length:** Males can be up to 4cm (1.6in); females 7cm (2.75in).
- **Diet:** Plenty of live foods, such as insects and grindalworms, with the addition of flaked food.
- **Features:** These fishes are a similar shape to Guppies but with a thicker caudal peduncle and smaller fins; males have a fan-like dorsal fin.
- **Basic care and breeding:** This is a hardy but rather aggressive fin-nipping fish, not ideally suited to a community aquarium. Keep known fin nippers and males separately, both from each other and from a community aquarium. For successful breeding, maintain the aquarium at 21-30°C (70-86°F). There is a gestation period of 28 days between broods of about 25 fry. Females are very quick to eat fry, but unfortunately these fishes are not good in breeding traps. The small broods mean that it can be difficult to detect any swelling and there is no gravid mark. Because of this, it is best to breed this species in

very heavily planted aquariums. The fry can be difficult to sex because the female has a black mark on her anal fin easily mistaken for the male's black gonopodium. They are fairly slow growing and take seven to nine months to reach maturity, although not full size.

Below: **Brachyrhaphis episcopi**
An attractive species from Panama that will thrive in the aquarium. This is a fine pair. Provide a separate nursery tank to rear the fry.

Brachyrhaphis episcopi
The Bishop
● **Habitat:** Still waters in coastal Panama.
● **Length:** The male is 3.5cm (1.4in) and the female 5cm (2in).
● **Diet:** Live foods: *Daphnia*, insects and grindalworms, etc., plus some flaked food.
● **Features:** Two long red lines with green between run from the flat head along both sides of the elongated body. The scales have a dark border, giving them a netlike pattern. The male has a sickle-shaped red anal fin.
● **Basic care and breeding:** For best breeding results provide a well-planted brackish water aquarium with a good growth of algae and maintain it at a temperature of 25-30°C (77-86°F). The broods of 6-20 fry need cover from their parents. A separate nursery tank is ideal since the fry are difficult to rear. Be sure to provide an excess of small brineshrimps and *Daphnia* to get them feeding without delay.

Gambusia affinis

Western Mosquito Fish; Silver Gambusia; Spotted Gambusia

● **Habitat:** The basins of the San Antonio and Guadalupe rivers in Texas. There are two local varieties or subspecies, *G.affinis affinis* (western form), and *G.affinis holbrooki* (eastern form).

● **Length:** The males grow to about 4cm (1.6in); the females up to approximately 6.5cm (2.6in).

● **Diet:** True to their name, these fishes love to eat surface-dwelling insects, particularly mosquito larvae in vast amounts. Fortunately, they will also take flake foods and vegetable matter.

● **Features:** They have a noticeably flat head, which confirms their surface-feeding habit. The female is a fairly dull olive-green with scattered black spots. The colour of the male is very variable, being basically yellowish with a pale belly and often with a lot of black markings, especially on the dorsal fin, tail and under the eyes.

● **Basic care and breeding:** These are fairly easy fishes to breed,

provided that the fry can escape the attentions of their hungry mother. A temperature of 20-22°C (68-72°F) is suitable, and salt can be added to the aquarium water (0.5-1.0gm per litre/0.5-1.0 teaspoon per gallon) *Gambusia* becomes sexually mature at just a couple of months old, probably because of pressure from predation, since they are very vulnerable living at the water surface. The gestation period is 30 days, the female producing 10-100 fry (average 23 fry). This species responds well to being placed in a

Above: **Gambusia affinis affinis**
A pair of these surface-dwelling fishes, the female noticeably larger.

trap for aquarium breeding.
    Although this species was the first livebearer available to the aquarium market, it is unsuitable for inclusion in community tanks because of its aggressive nature.

Below: **Gambusia affinis holbrooki**
Here, the male of the subspecies shows an abundance of black. Other specimens may be clear.

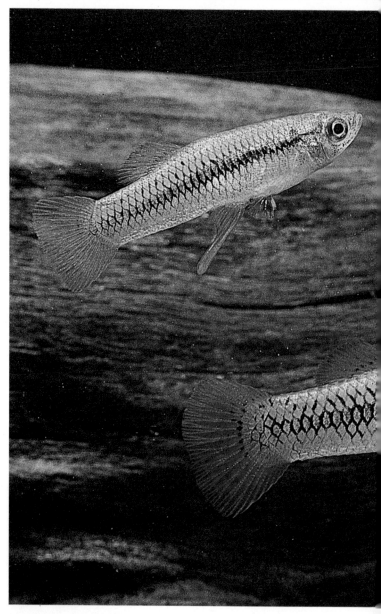

Gambusia marshi

● **Habitat:** Lives in large rivers of northeastern Mexico.

● **Length:** Males up to 3cm (1.2in); females up to about 5cm (2in).

● **Diet:** A simple, mixed diet of commercial flaked foods and some live foods is taken avidly.

● **Features:** A slim grey body with a black speckling above the lateral line. The adults develop a yellowish sheen, which is particularly prominent in the females. Some strains are darker and the sheen appears blue. The fins are rounded and may have a black edging. The

gonopodium is relatively long.
● **Basic care and breeding:** This species is fairly straightforward to maintain, preferring water at about 22-27°C (72-81°F). This is an active fish and, like many such active species, can be a fin nipper. Therefore, it is best to keep it in a

Above: **Gambusia marshi**
An active species that can prove to be a fin nipper in the aquarium.

species tank rather than in a community aquarium. After a gestation period of 21-28 days, it produces at least 10-40 fry.

Girardinus metallicus

Girardinus

● **Habitat:** Cuba and Costa Rica, in small streams and ditches.
● **Length:** The male grows to 5cm (2in); the female up to 9cm (3.5in).
● **Diet:** This species eats well in captivity, taking most dry and flaked foods, live foods, algae and vegetable matter.
● **Features:** Quite a deep-bodied fish with a broad flat head and large dorsal fin. The body is typically a yellowish grey with an olive-green tinge and blue iridescence on the sides, overlaid with sickle shaped bars, those on the female being indistinct. The males are black underneath and this may extend down the front of the gonopodium.
● **Basic care and breeding:** For good breeding results maintain these fishes at a temperature of 22-25°C (72-77°F). The gestation period is about four weeks, and the female needs to be isolated in a trap or nursery tank to produce her 10-60 fry, and then replaced in the main aquarium. Although generally peaceful, these fishes eat their fry.

Heterandria formosa

Mosquito Fish; Dwarf Top-Minnow; Dwarf Livebearer

● **Habitat:** Fresh and brackish waters, North Carolina to Florida.
● **Length:** A tiny fish, the smallest livebearer, the male reaches 2cm (0.8in) and the female 3.5cm (1.4in).
● **Diet:** Despite its common name of Mosquito Fish, it eats primarily green matter.
● **Features:** The basic colour is olive-green, with a dark brown line running down each side of the body. The fins are yellowish in colour, the dorsal fin being marked with a single spot. The male has a very large gonopodium.
● **Basic care and breeding:** Keep these fishes in a species tank at a temperature of 20-24°C (68-75°F) in hard, slightly alkaline water. *Heterandria* continually produce a few fry rather than distinct broods, which allows them to bear larger fry with a better chance of survival. (This remarkable process – called superfoetation – is fully described on page 37.) Because of this 'production line' system, there is no

point in trapping the female. Ideally, use a well-planted 'species' tank for breeding and either leave the fry with the mother or remove them to another tank for greater safety when the opportunity arises.

Above: **Heterandria formosa**
A tiny livebearer best kept in a species tank. Male at bottom.

Below: **Girardinus metallicus**
The female of an iridescent species.

Heterandria bimaculata

Two-spotted Heterandria

● **Habitat:** Rivers and streams along the Atlantic coast of southern Mexico into Yucatan. Also in Guatemala, Honduras and Belize.

● **Length:** Males up to 7cm(2.75in); females up to 15cm(6in)

● **Diet:** Normal aquarium dried foods and vegetable matter.

● **Features:** The body is an attractive shade of pale rosy mauve-blue, with black edges to the scales. There are two spots: one just behind the gill cover and one on the caudal peduncle. The former is often small and may be missing in small fish.

● **Basic care and breeding:** This slim-bodied species can be very aggressive, making it unsuitable for a community tank with small fishes. Females can pose a serious threat, even to their own mates. This species is quite prolific, producing up to 100 fry at intervals of six to eight weeks. Provide a well-planted breeding tank; otherwise, the female will eat her own offspring.

Left: *A stream in eastern Mexico, a typical habitat of* Heterandria bimaculata. *This species has also been collected from the fast-flowing waters of Rio Atoyac, shown in the photograph on page 75.*

Below: **Heterandria bimaculata**
An active and aggressive species with a large mouth and appetite to match. This photograph highlights the rich coloration of both male (bottom) and females. Not suitable for a community of small fishes.

Right: **Limia melanogaster**
*In this pair, the female shows a very
prominent gravid spot. These fishes
are ideal for a community aquarium.*

Limia melanogaster

*Blue-bellied Limia; Black-bellied
Limia*

● **Habitat:** The warm, still and
rapidly flowing waters of Jamaica
and Haiti.
● **Length:** Males reach up to 4.5cm
(1.8in); females up to 6cm (2.4in).
● **Diet:** Varied aquarium foods but
with plenty of vegetable material.
● **Features:** The back is olive-
green in colour, and the large scales
over the rear part of the body are
royal blue crossed with dark bars.
The male's dorsal fin is blue-black
and the caudal fin yellow-orange
edged with black. The female has a
large blue gravid spot, which often
persists after birth.
● **Basic care and breeding:**
Ideally, keep these fishes at a
temperature of 24-26°C (75-79°F) in
a well-planted aquarium. They
produce about 20-60 quite large
young after a gestation period of
about four weeks. Fed on plenty of
live food and high-protein flakes, the
fry develop quickly into
peaceful adults that make good
community fishes.

Limia nigrofasciata

*Hump-backed Limia; Black-barred
Limia*

● **Habitat:** Slow moving or static
bodies of water in Haiti, generally
with a heavy plant growth.
● **Length:** Males up to 5cm (2in);
females up to 7cm (2.75in).
● **Diet:** Mainly vegetable matter
plus flaked food and live foods
● **Features:** The male and female
fishes are similar in colour; the
upper part of the body is olive-green
with a blue iridescence below. There

Below: **Limia nigrofasciata**
*Note the characteristic black
streaks with a hint of iridescent blue
on the flanks of this male specimen.
A prolific species in the aquarium.*

Limia vittata
Cuban Limia
● **Habitat:** Streams along the coast of Cuba, often in brackish water.
● **Length:** Males up to 6cm (2.4in); females up to 10cm (4in).
● **Diet:** A variety of aquarium foods, including vegetable and dried foods.
● **Features:** The overall coloration is olive-brown with a bluish sheen on the scales and many dark speckles and bars in a longitudinal band. The belly is a silvery pink and the fins pale yellow in colour. In the best males, and occasionally females, gold patches develop on the body. Since those that develop large patches seem short lived and sterile, it may be that these are the yellow equivalent of the melanomas in Platy/Swordtail crosses.

are black streaks on the body, and the underside is black. The hump develops in adult sexually mature males (9-12 months old); the dorsal fin also enlarges as males grow older, thus emphasizing the hump.
● **Basic care and breeding:**
Maintain the temperature at about 24-26°C (75-79°F). The males pester heavily gravid females, so the best system is to use a well-planted 60cm (24in) tank as a breeding tank for a single pair and to move the male before the female is due to give birth. Broods of 10-50 fry are born approximately every 21 to 33 days, although this is very variable. Although rather delicate at first, the fry mature fairly quickly and are able to breed at three months old.

● **Basic care and breeding:**
Cuban Limias are easy to breed and very prolific in well-planted tanks with some algal growth. They generally produce 20-60 young after a three to five week gestation period. This species prefers higher temperatures of about 25-28°C (77-82°F), and most breeders add salt to the water at the rate of 0.5-1.0gm per litre (0.5-1.0 teaspoon per gallon). The fry thrive on flaked foods and live food, taking a higher protein level than the adults.

Above: **Limia vittata**
This female shows just a trace of golden yellow markings; a bright yellow male is shown on page 59.

Phallichthys amates amates

Merry Widow
● **Habitat:** Pools and slow streams in Guatemala and Honduras south to Panama.
● **Length:** Males grow to 4cm (1.6in); females to 7cm (2.75in).
● **Diet:** All types of aquarium foods, including algae.
● **Features:** A silvery yellow fish with a black line running through the eye. An iridescence can develop which outlines the scale edges. The male may have black vertical bars and a very distinctive black edge to the dorsal fin.
● **Basic care and breeding:** This species is easy to maintain and breed. Keep it at a temperature of about 25°C (77°F) in a well-planted tank and in the company of at least a couple of its own species, although other quiet community fishes are also suitable. The 10-60 fry will need a plentiful supply of brineshrimp and then *Daphnia*. They grow slowly and are not mature until they are about six months old.

Phallichthys amates pittieri

Orange-dorsal Livebearer
● **Habitat:** Pools and slow streams in Costa Rica and Panama.
● **Length:** A little larger than the related Merry Widow, the male reaches a length of up to 5cm (2in) and the female up to 8cm (3.2in).
● **Diet:** Wide ranging dried and live foods, including algae.
● **Features:** The body is olive-green in colour fading to golden yellow on the belly. A dark line runs vertically through the eye. The male has faint vertical blue lines on the sides of the body, and a large gonopodium turned down at the tip, reaching almost to the tail.
● **Basic care and breeding:** Maintain at 20-25°G (68-77°F). After a gestation period of four to six weeks, a brood of 10-50 fry is produced. These fishes become sexually mature in six weeks.

Below:
Phallichthys amates amates
A fine pair; the male shown at top.

Above:
Phallichthys amates pittieri
A male specimen. Undemanding.

Phalloceros caudimaculatus

Caudo; One-spot Livebearer; Dusky Millions Fish
● **Habitat:** Fresh and brackish waters in Argentina, southeastern Brazil, Paraguay and Uruguay.
● **Length:** Males up to 3cm (1.2in); females up to 5cm (2in).
● **Diet:** Wide ranging; they will eat most dried and live foods.
● **Features:** A basic golden olive-green with one or more dark spots and/or markings on the body, and often a black border to the dorsal fin. Quite elongated in shape.
● **Basic care and breeding:** This fish is hardy and undemanding, although rather sensitive to water changes. It will thrive in fresh or brackish water at 20-24°C (68-75°F). After a gestation period of 21 to 28 days, approximately 20-80 young are produced. Given the opportunity, the parents will eat their young so protect them in a breeding trap or nursery tank.
● **Varieties:** *P.c.auratus* – Golden One-spot Livebearer. *P.c.reticulatus* – Spotted Livebearer. *P.c.reticulatus auratus* – Golden-spotted Livebearer. Strangely, none of these truly lives up to its name; 'caudimaculatus' means one spot on the caudal peduncle and none of them is strictly limited to one spot.

Below:
Phalloceros caudimaculatus
This is the reticulatus *variety of the species, with an abundance of black markings. Male shown at top.*

Genus POECILIA

These are generally medium-sized fishes and, as with most livebearers, the males are a little smaller than the females. The basic colour of most of the group is a green – or brown – tinged olive-yellow, the females being somewhat paler than the males. Black is a common colour in those members that were originally classified as *Mollienisia*, a colour now seen to perfection in the black forms developed from *Poecilia sphenops*. Some species have greatly enlarged dorsal fins, setting them apart from the Limias, which have more obvious humped backs and more flattened sides.

Many species come from coastal areas and so normally inhabit waters with some salt present. A number can even be kept in tropical marine tanks (as can *Gambusia affinis* if acclimatized first). They are largely herbivorous and therefore need green foods in the aquarium, although they will also take some live foods. Keep these fishes in slightly hard, alkaline water at a temperature of 25-28°C (77-82°F) with sea salt added at a rate of about 1gm per litre (1 teaspoon per gallon).

Keeping them in community tanks at lower temperatures often puts them under perpetual stress and leads to diseases; therefore it is best to keep them in a species tank, where they can be seen at their best in ideal conditions.

Poecilia formosa
Amazon Molly
● **Habitat:** Mexico and southern Texas.
● **Length:** Up to 7.5cm (3in).
● **Diet:** A wide range of vegetable-based foods, plus dried foods and a little live food.
● **Features:** Although drab in appearance, this fish is keenly kept by enthusiasts.

Above: **Poecilia formosa**
A natural all-female clone notable for its unusual breeding heritage.

● **Basic care and breeding:** It is in relation to breeding that the Amazon Molly is well known. The natural hybridization between *P.latipinna* and *P.mexicana* (or the closely related *P.sphenops*) results in an all-female population of *P.formosa*. These then reproduce gynogenetically, which means that although they mate with males of either parent species the males do not contribute towards the resulting embryo, all offspring being female clones of the mother. The eggs are simply activated by fertilization.

Poecilia latipinna
Sailfin Molly
● **Habitat:** Eastern USA in coastal and estuarine areas, often in brackish waters.
● **Length:** Males reach 10cm (4in); females 12cm (4.7in).
● **Diet:** This fish will relish green food particularly, but will take most foods willingly.
● **Features:** A fully adult male has a spectacular dorsal fin. The basic coloration is olive-yellow with bluish flecks, a mother-of-pearl sheen and coloured bands on the sides in red, blue, green and black. A very famous variety is the so-called 'Perma-black'; dappled versions are also available. The best quality fish come from the fish farms of Florida. The Black Lyretail, the Marble Sailfin and the Chocolate are all hybrid forms of *P.latipinna*.

● **Basic care and breeding:** Successful breeding calls for a large tank with a dark substrate and an abundance of plants, both rooted and floating. Small groups can be kept but males can be aggressive to each other. Maintain the temperature at about 25-28°C (77-82°F) and do not trap the adults; it is too stressful. This species is particularly sensitive to stress and chilling, which it reacts to by developing the 'shimmies', a kind of swimming on the spot.

Above: **Poecilia latipinna**
A female collected from the wild.
Many hybrids have been produced.

After a gestation period lasting about 28-35 days, up to 150 fry are produced (usually 20-80), which can normally be left with their parents if food is plentiful.

As with some other livebearers, the females produce both early developing males and late developing males. Since the latter take some time to become mature, many aquarists think that their fish have changed sex. It is these later developing males which produce the more spectacular dorsal fins.

Poecilia picta

Black-banded Poecilia
● **Habitat:** The waters of the Demerara River in British Guyana, Trinidad and Brazil.
● **Length:** Males up to 3cm (1.2in); females 4cm (1.6in).

● **Diet:** Like most of its relatives, this species will thrive on a predominantly vegetarian diet with flakes and some live food.
● **Features:** The male is basically yellowish green, dotted with large blue spots under a bronze sheen. The dorsal fin, yellow edged with blue and with a blue spot at the base, is set well back. The female is green with a mottled bronze patch in front of her dorsal fin.
● **Basic care and breeding:** This can prove a difficult fish to breed successfully; it needs salt in the water and plenty of plant cover. The gestation period is 28-31 days and the female produces only 6-15 fry per brood. It is vital to trap the female because the fry are very small and they stay close to the bottom of the tank when born.

Below: **Poecilia picta**
A male fish showing the distinctive markings in bright blue and yellow.

Poecilia reticulata

Guppy; Millions Fish

● **Habitat:** From northeastern South America (north of the Amazon) and some of the offshore islands (Leeward Islands, Barbados, Trinidad). It was named after the 19th century naturalist Robert J.L. Guppy, who settled in Trinidad. Guppies were first introduced into North America in about 1908. Like the *Gambusia* species, it has been spread around many tropical waters in an attempt to control mosquito larvae, as well as for ornamental reasons.

● **Length:** The males may grow to 3.5cm (1.4in), and the females to 6cm (2.4in).

● **Diet:** It will eat most dried foods but benefits from some green food plus live foods, such as *Daphnia* and mosquito larvae.

● **Features:** Its brilliant colours in an amazing array of varieties make the Guppy as instantly recognizable as the Goldfish. The male has a trailing tail, although there are variations even on this. The female, once a drab silver-grey, now has 'added' colour, particularly as spots on the tail.

● **Basic care and breeding:** This is a very tolerant species; it accepts a wide temperature range of 20-30°C (68-86°F) and can be acclimatized to live in seawater.

Guppies can be sexually mature at about two or three months, although six months is more usual. Six broods – each containing about 20 fry, although possibly up to 100 – may be produced from one fertilization, at intervals of about 21-28 days. (See pages 36-49 for breeding and basic genetics.)

Above: **Poecilia reticulata**
A pair collected from the waters of Rio Verde, Mexico. Male at top.

Below: **Veiltail Guppies**
These so-called 'King Cobras' are one of many aquarium-bred forms.

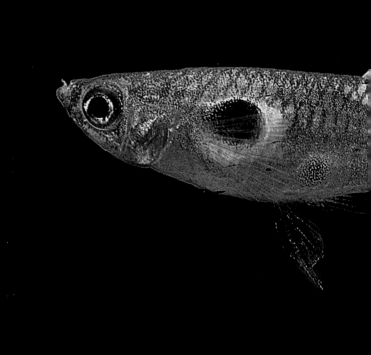

Above: **Bottom Sword Guppy**
An extension of the lower tail.

Left: **Double Sword Guppy**
Vivid yellow with a symmetrical tail.

Below: **Wild Guppy**
Wild Guppies can be as colourful as the most ornate aquarium-bred forms. Selective breeding has capitalized on this natural variation.

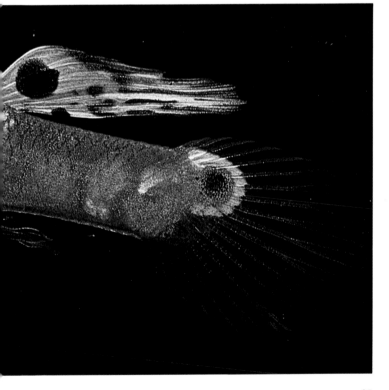

Above: **Veiltail Guppies**
Elegant males in shimmering blue.

Below: **Three-quarter Black**
A restrained but attractive form.

Below: **Spanish Skirts Guppy**
A beautiful, well-shaped tail aptly
named for the concentric stripes of
black and pink-orange it displays.

Above: **Coppertail Veiltails**
These graceful Guppies, with their

flowing tails of a subtle copper hue,
provide a stylish display in the

aquarium that never ceases to take
the eye. Guppies are justifiably

among the most popular aquarium
fishes throughout the world.

Poecilia sphenops

Short-finned Molly; Pointed Mouth Molly

● **Habitat:** Fresh and brackish waters from Venezuela to Mexico and Texas, and across to the Leeward Islands.
● **Length:** Males up to 7cm (2.75in); females 10cm (4in).
● **Diet:** Plant material is a favourite, but most dried foods are also acceptable.
● **Features:** The basic coloration is olive-green with black markings. Over the years aquarists have concentrated the black and so selected out the Yucatan Black Molly. This is not a hybrid; aquarists have simply taken advantage of individual variation. A variety called the Liberty Molly from the Yucatan peninsula is basically steel blue in colour with red fins, and the dorsal

Above: *Rio Nacome in Honduras, one of the known habitats of the widely distributed* P. sphenops.

Above: **Poecilia sphenops**
A fine pair of the natural form of this species. Male shown at top.

fin has a yellow and black crescent at the base. It is now quite uncommon, partly because it can be a pest chasing other fish.
● **Basic care and breeding:** Maintain the temperature in the region of 25-28°C (77-82°F) i.e. slightly higher than the usual community tank. These fishes also benefit from having some salt in the water (0.5-1.0gm per litre/0.5-1.0 teaspoon per gallon). Do not move pregnant females to trap them; this can cause premature birth and the death of the fry and often the mother as well. Broods contain 40-300 fry.
● **Forms and hybrids:** This species is now truly domesticated and its various forms and mutations have been well exploited, producing blacks, albinos, marbled, green, etc. Hybrids have been produced with the Sailfins *P.latipinna* and *P.velifera*; these tend to be sturdier fish than the standard *P.sphenops* and have a showy dorsal fin more like the Sailfin varieties.

Left: **Poecilia hybrid**
A black form, with P. sphenops *in its ancestry. Male at bottom.*

Poecilia velifera

Giant Sailfin Molly

● **Habitat:** Parts of Central America around Yucatan (Mexico).

● **Length:** Both sexes reach about 15cm (6in) long.

● **Diet:** Basically vegetarian, but willing to eat dried foods.

● **Features:** Similar to *P.latipinna*, although with more rays in the dorsal fin; black individuals do occur but are very rare. Males often have a spike at the end of the tail.

● **Basic care and breeding:** This species is very sensitive to water quality changes and needs a stable mature tank with salt in the water (0.5-1.0gm per litre/0.5-1.0 teaspoon per gallon). In common with *P.latipinna*, it is prone to develop the 'shimmies' when under stress. After a gestation period lasting about 28 days, 30-50 young are produced; rear in shallow water.

Poeciliopsis scarlli

Flier

● **Habitat:** The coastal freshwater canals and irrigation ditches north of the Guerrero/Michoacan State boundary in Mexico. These are mud-bottomed waters with no submerged plants but an abundance of algae.

● **Length:** Males up to 3.5cm (1.4in); females up to 4cm (1.6in).

● **Diet:** Not fully resolved. Eats algae and live foods; accepts flakes.

● **Features:** Adults of both sexes are greyish yellow with fine vertical stripes and blue eye rings. The leading ray of the dorsal fin is black. The body shape is streamlined and the set of the pectoral fins is said to make it look ready to take flight – hence its common name of 'Flier'.

● **Basic care and breeding:** This recently discovered fish, named after a British fish collector, seems

to prefer relatively low water temperatures of 22-23°C (72-73°F) and a pH value close to 7 (neutral). Small numbers of fry – four to six – are normally produced at intervals of 9-14 days. Cannibalism does not seem to be a problem in this fish.

Above: **Poecilia velifera**
Keep these Mollies in a spacious aquarium with clean mature water.

Below: **Poeciliopsis scarlli**
A relative newcomer to the hobby. The female is shown here.

Genus XIPHOPHORUS – Swordtails and Platies
These are all now members of the same genus, although originally
Xiphophorus helleri (the Swordtail) and *Platypoecilus maculatus* (the Platy)
each had its own genus. After the discovery of *Platypoecilus xiphidium* in
1932 and *P.pygmaeus* in 1943, the gap between the Swordtails and Platies
was narrowed, and the discovery of *Xiphophorus milleri* in 1960 enabled
scientists to drop the generic name *Platypoecilus* in favour of the earlier
generic name *Xiphophorus* (*Xiphos* is Greek for 'sword'), which had been
assigned to the Swordtails in 1848.

General characteristics
Since male Swordtails are aggressive to each other, keep them separately or
in groups of four or more where aggression can be spread out within the
group. Swordtails are also good jumpers, and so be sure to fit secure hoods
on their tanks. The ideal temperature is about 24°C (75°F); too high a
temperature may reduce their fertility. The gravid spot seen in many species
is less obvious in the Swordtails. They generally produce up to 150 fry per
brood, which provides an opportunity for selective breeding.

The Platy is basically vegetarian although, like most of the livebearers, it
benefits from a small amount of animal protein, such as whiteworm or a
liver-based food. The group is now considered as being split into three
complexes: Helleri, Montezumae and Maculatus.

The Helleri complex

Xiphophorus helleri
Green Swordtail
● **Habitat:** Atlantic coast of Mexico
to northern Central America.

● **Length:** Males (including sword)
up to 7.5cm (3in); females up to
11.5cm (4.5in) in overall length.
● **Diet:** Although basically
vegetarian, it will accept dried foods
readily and take some live foods.

Features: The original form – described by Heckel in 1848 – was drab green with a reddish sword. The sword is a prolongation of the lower rays of the caudal fin and is seen in the males only.

Basic care and breeding: Up to nine broods may be produced from one mating, with fry being born every four to six weeks, the average being about 29 days. Mature females usually produce 50-60 young, but up to 200 is recorded in exceptional females; younger

Above: **Xiphophorus clemenciae**
A male specimen of this relatively small but colourful Swordtail.

smaller females will produce fewer offspring. They are highly cannibalistic on fry. The best way of ensuring safety, therefore, is to maintain a pair in a well-planted tank, and when the female is due to give birth remove the male to a holding tank and put in more floating plants with the female; the fry will dash into this for cover as they are born. Alternatively, use a breeding trap. Brineshrimp and the very fine commercial dry diets are suitable to get the fry started.

In the wild, they show some seasonality in breeding, but this is not normally seen in the aquarium. Male Swordtails can be a nuisance in a community tank by pestering other fishes. Therefore, it is best to keep several in a community, when they prefer to pester each other.

Masculinization of apparent females has been seen, but cases of true sex reversal where a functional female has become a functional male seem to be more a case of legend than fact. In many cases these are late developing males, or females with inactive ovaries.

Subspecies: There are four valid subspecies: *X.helleri helleri*; *X.helleri alvarezi*; *X.h.guentheri*; *X.h.strigatus*; plus *X.clemenciae* (Yellow Swordtail), which may be a short-sworded variety of *X.helleri*.

Left: **Xiphophorus helleri**
A pair of these popular Swordtails, with the male shown at bottom.

The Montezumae complex

The species in this complex are:

X.milleri. This species from a small tributary of Lake Catemaco is an important fish in scientific terms because it 'bridges the gap' between *Xiphophorus* and *Platypoecilus*. Both sexes have a gravid spot and are similar in shape to the male Swordtail, but without the characteristic sword.

X.montezumae (Montezuma Swordtail). There are two subspecies, both from pools and slow-moving streams: *X.m.montezumae* and, with a smaller sword, *X.m.cortezi* (which is also known as *X.cortezi*).

X.pygmaeus (Pygmy Swordtail). There are two subspecies: *X.p.pygmaeus* lives along the banks of fast-flowing streams in the Rio Axtla, Mexico. It has virtually no sword. *X.p.nigrensis*, on the other hand, lives in more static waters and pools in Rio Panuco, Mexico and has quite a respectable sword.

Above: **Xiphophorus montezumae**
A pair of this amenable species, with the sworded male shown at top.

Above: **Xiphophorus cortezi**
This attractive fish is a shorter sworded subspecies of X. montezumae. *Easy to maintain.*

Right: **Xiphophorus milleri**
A female specimen of this species from eastern Mexico. The small male does not develop a sword.

Below: **Xiphophorus p.pygmaeus** *A pair of the yellow form of this subspecies – male shown at top –* *from the fast-flowing waters of Rio Axtla in Mexico. Typically, the male fish shows no sign of a sword.*

The Maculatus complex

Species in this complex are found in lowland waters on the Atlantic side of Central America. The males do not develop swords.

X. maculatus (Platy or Moon Fish). In most of the wild strains the tail has a definite moon-shaped crescent. This Platy thrives in an optimum temperature of 21-24°C (70-75°F),

Above: **Xiphophorus maculatus**
These 'Black Platies' are one of many aquarium-bred colour varieties. Male shown at left. The coloration of the wild form is dark olive above and silvery white below.

and prefers moderately hard water with a pH value of 6.8-7.4. The mean brood size is about 27, but up to 100 fry have been seen occasionally; the gestation period is usually 34 days.

X. variatus variatus (Variatus; Variatus Platy). Males grow to 5cm (2in); females to 7.5cm (3in). Optimum temperature is about 21°C (70°F). The natural form is more

Below: **Xiphophorus maculatus**
These richly coloured varieties are Red High Fin Platies, combining

intense colour with an elongated dorsal fin, particularly attractive in the male of this pair (at left).

Above: **Xiphophorus variatus**
A male of the Tuxedo Platy form.

Below: **Xiphophorus variatus**
A magnificent High Fin form.

Above: **Xiphophorus variatus**
A particularly attractive wild *specimen. Such coloration has* *been exploited in aquarium forms.*

Above: Xiphophorus couchianus
Originally from the springs around Monterrey in northeastern Mexico, their numbers in the wild have declined because of loss of habitat and interbreeding with other Xiphophorus *species. In this pair, the male is shown at bottom left.*

Above: *A typical river in Vera Cruz, eastern Mexico, the natural habitat of several* Xiphophorus *species.*

colourful than the wild Swordtail. It has been used to hybridize with the Swordtail and Platies to produce many wonderful colour varieties much in demand by fishkeepers.

X.couchianus couchianus (Monterrey Platyfish). Listed as endangered, and probably extinct in the wild. It originates from the headwaters around Monterrey, Mexico. The subspecies *X.c.gordoni* (Northern Platyfish) is also listed as endangered.

X.xiphidium (Swordtail Platy; Purple Spike-tail Platy). This species is similar in shape to *X.maculatus*. The male grows to 4cm (1.6in); the females to 5.5cm (2.2in). The basic coloration is olive-green, becoming pale underneath, and with a purple-blue iridescence. The female has a dark band along the lateral line and yellow patches above and below it at the caudal peduncle. In the male the tail is darker with a yellow crescent, and the bottom few rays extend into a spike. Both sexes have an apparent gravid spot!

The optimum temperature for keeping this species is 24-26°C (75-79°F) and they seem to do best on a high-protein diet. A well-planted tank is vital to give some protection to the 15-20 fry. These placid fishes are eminently suitable for a community tank.

Below: **Xiphophorus xiphidium**
An easy going species that will mix with community fishes. The male is much smaller than the female.

Index to fishes

Page numbers in **bold** indicate major references, including accompanying photographs. Page numbers in *italics* indicate captions to other illustrations. Less important text entries are in normal type.

115

Acknowledgements
The publishers wish to thank Dr. Peter Miller of Bristol University (for advice on modes of gestation in livebearers), Hugh Smith, SLAG London Area Group (for providing fishes for photography) and Karen Ramsay (for editorial assistance).

Picture Credits

Poecilia reticulata (Veiltail Guppy)

THE COCKIN BOOK OF STAFFORDSHIRE RECORDS

DID YOU KNOW THAT... 6

FACTS ABOUT

The Potteries,

Newcastle, Stone

A Miscellany of
NOTES, QUERIES, CLAIMS, FOLKLORE,
ODDITIES OF HUMAN LIFE
in the north west corner of Staffordshire.
Volume Six of Six. 2010.

MALTHOUSE PRESS.
GRANGE COTTAGE, MALTHOUSE LANE,
BARLASTON, STAFFORDSHIRE, ST12 9AQ

THE COCKIN BOOK OF STAFFORDSHIRE RECORDS

DID YOU KNOW THAT... 6

FACTS ABOUT

The Potteries,
Newcastle, Stone

A Miscellany of
NOTES, QUERIES, CLAIMS, FOLKLORE,
ODDITIES OF HUMAN LIFE
in the north west corner of Staffordshire.
Volume Six of Six. 2010.
Compiled by Tim Cockin.

"All knowledge is of itself of some value.
There is nothing so minute or inconsiderable,
that I would not rather know it than not."
- SAMUEL JOHNSON (1709-84)

MALTHOUSE PRESS.
GRANGE COTTAGE, MALTHOUSE LANE,
BARLASTON, STAFFORDSHIRE, ST12 9AQ

ISBN 978-0-9539018-8-3

Introduction

From time to time local historians and the general public may need to consult a book of claims, firsts, lasts etc for their area. Here is such a book. This book is one of six volumes in the series 'The Cockin Book of Staffordshire Records: Did You Know That...' covering all Staffordshire. It is part of a series with four volumes viz:- 2 (*Leek, Cheadle, Uttoxeter*), 3 (*Stafford, Cannock, Rugeley*, as yet not revised), 4 (*Lichfield, Burton, Tamworth*), and 5 (*Wolverhampton, Walsall, West Bromwich*). All are now published. In addition, there is volume 1 (*Staffordshire*), which is the general index to Staffordshire claims in the series, as well as being a Handbook to the county, and includes Calendars of events, folklore, murders, legal sessions, lists argricultural shows, connections, political representatives, sheriffs, wonders. Ancient parishes have been chosen for entry perimeters because they are static for when there were statistics. For population ratings Staffordshire had 166 ancient parishes; for dimension ratings 169; for WW1 roll of honour ratings 142.

Contents

Overview of claims

BRITISH/ UK RECORDS

Best: aqua park *S-u-T* Parks.

Convention Bureau 2006 *S-u-T* Hospitality.

baker of Hovis bread 1904 *Barlaston* Hill, George.

best hand-cycllist 2008 *Trentham* Powerlifiting.

centre-half *Sandon* Neil Franklin.

nursery *S-u-T* Horticulture.

Biggest: draw of all time to British wrestling *S-u-T* Wrestling.

ever garden festival *S-u-T* National Garden Festival.

factory shop, one of *S-u-T* Pottery Industry: Sales.

women's prison 1997 *Eccleshall* Swynnerton Royal Ordnance.

ever one-day rally of BNP supporters *Stone* Political gatherings.

flower shop *S-u-T* National Garden Festival.

sculpture display since 1951 *S-u-T* National Garden Festival.

publicly-funded NHS scheme *S-u-T* Health.

(5th) hospital 2008 *S-u-T* Health.

Bustiest: village, one of *Stone* Tittensor.

Champion: Britain in Bloom winner *Audley*.

Fire Service Cross Country championships women's team trophy 6km race winner 2008 *Newcastle* Athletics.

J12 Kayak champion 2009, J12 Canoe champion 2009, *Trentham*, Canoeing.

Junior champion 2004 *S-u-T* Pole vaulting.

No. 1 women's darts

player - Maureen Flowers *Burslem* Darts.

No. 2 female road runner 2009 *Wolstanton* Athletics.

No. 3 in U-16 list at Squash *Stone* Squash.

Young Volunteer of the Year 2007 *Trentham* Anderson, David.

Child: (2nd) diagnosed with Prader-Willi Syndrome *Stone* Stephen Shenton.

Cleanest: hospital, one of *Wolstanton*.

Deepest: colliery 1960 *S-u-T* Mining; pit 1935

S-u-T Mining.

mine by 1830s Wolstanton Apedale Colliery.

mine workings 1969-74 Trentham Mining.

Earliest: local scientific and learned societies formed, one of S-u-T Further Education.

replication of pineapples Mucklestone Lea Head Manor.

Finest: acoustics S-u-T Victoria Hall: General.

and most important (coke refinery) works c1912 Wolstanton Birchendale Colliery.

sculptor, one of S-u-T Arnold Machin.

sports meeting 1903 Stone Athletics.

Torah scroll S-u-T Judaism.

First: aerodromes, one of the Stone Meir Aerodrome.

all-electric pottery Barlaston Wedgwood Factory.

awarded a Qualification and Credit Framework (QCF) S-u-T Shopping.

bar to win the official backing of the All Party Parliamentary Save the Pub Group S-u-T Pubs.

bare foot walk Trentham Trentham Gardens; darts club S-u-T Darts.

black chairman of the Professional Footballers' Association 1988-90 S-u-T Football.

carbon positive warehouse Wolstanton Ecology.

child to die while being restrained in custody S-u-T Gareth Myatt.

circumnavigation non-stop, single-handed, with no human intervention of Britain and Ireland Wolstanton Sailing.

colliery for trainee miners S-u-T Mining.

Co-operative business college, one of Audley Schools.

disco night club, one of S-u-T Nightlife.

eco-friendly holiday complex Maer Holiday camp.

enclosure of a footpath Trentham Trentham Hall estate.

existing family-run/private narrowboat hire company Stone Canals.

football pool winner, one of S-u-T Edwin Dodd.

(4th) for the manufacture of clay pipes in C17 Newcastle Trade.

gay couple to get married, one of S-u-T Gay rights.

jet engine production site Wolstanton Engineering.

major electricity plant to be fuelled by grass Eccleshall Environment.

M.P. unable to be formally 'introduced' in the House of Commons S-u-T Dr Edward Kenealy.

men's couple Wolstanton Tennis.

Michelin Tyre factory S-u-T Tyre manufacturing.

motor hotel built in a designated green belt area S-u-T Cars.

Multiple Sclerosis Resource Centre Stone Social care.

new power station to come into operation after WW2 Stone Meaford Power Station.

new university of the C20 Keele Keele University: General.

of its kind - Normid Audley.

passenger helicopter service Trentham Sir Peter Masefield.

post-war university Keele Keele University: General.

professional company to perform permanently in-the-round in Britain S-u-T Theatre.

professional footballer to play for a foreign club Sandon Neil Franklin.

professor of Social History in a British University S-u-T Harold Perkin.

provincial town to institute communal street lightning, one of Newcastle Public services.

purpose-built occupation centre for training mentally handicapped children Wolstanton Health and well being.

purpose-built theatre in the round S-u-T Theatre.

residential adult education college Barlaston Wedgwood Memorial College.

restaurant over a motorway Keele Motorway dinning.

school for chimney sweeps Stone Schools.

(2nd) school (Stoke-on-Trent's 1st) rebuild in the Building Schools for the Future programme Stone Schools.

(2nd) shopping precinct of its kind S-u-T Shopping.

show of Buffalo Bill's last UK tour S-u-T Variety shows.

'silent peal' rung S-u-T Churches: St Mary, Bucknall.

special school to use the 'Light-Writer' Newcastle Schools.

successful production of X-ray photographs Newcastle AW Harrison.

use of Taser guns by police as handheld stun guns to break up a fight Stone Crime.

woman appointed a government whip S-u-T Harriet Slater;

geomanetic surveys carried out Swynnerton Geology.

women's amateur boxing match Wolstanton Combat sports.

Forgotten: man of music S-u-T Victoria Hall: General.

Greatest: ever private landowner to 1995 Trentham Sutherland-Leveson-Gower,

George Granville William.

freestyle swimmer S-u-T Swimming.

heiress Trentham Sutherland, Elizabeth.

Highest: ash tree Audley Natural history.

paid company chief 1979 Barlaston Wedgwood Factory.

proportion of Students and staff in residence 1986, one of Keele Keele University: General.

Largest: cable car system S-u-T National Garden Festival.

civil engineering project ever to 1777 Wolstanton Harecastle Tunnel.

Citizens Advice Bureau S-u-T Hanley.

derelict land reclamation scheme of its kind 1990 Wolstanton Business/industrial parks.

experiment of its kind in municipal history Stoke-on-Trent Civil life and Federation.

integrated green campus university Keele Keele University: General.

'police village' 1957 Eccleshall Swynnerton Royal Ordnance Factory.

(6th) collection of Charles Eamer Kempe glass Stone Church.

'stable' 1848 S-u-T Railways; brick and tile works Wolstanton.

theft from public funds brought to court after a Customs investigation - one of Stone Crime.

Union Jack flown from a public building by 1980 Newcastle Borough.

youth football tournament Keele Football.

Last: recorded cavalry charge S-u-T Trooper Harold Bradshaw.

Leading: aeronautical engineer, one of S-u-T John Lloyd.

ceramic tile manufacturer 2008 Wolstanton Pottery.

Least: affluent place *Stoke-on-Trent* Demography.

lonely area 1971-2001 *Stoke-on-Trent* Living conditions.

Longest: running record fair 2009 *S-u-T* Music and musicals.

serving poppy collectors, one of *Stone* George Murrell.

serving prisoner for a miscarriage of justice Britain's for a miscarriage of justice *S-u-T* Evans, Andrew.

serving spiritualist medium *S-u-T* Fanny Higginson.

Lowest: (15th) value postcode 2008 *S-u-T* Living conditions.

Most: advanced building of its kind *S-u-T* Buildings.

albums to reach No. 1 by a British male solo artist *Burslem* Williams, Robbie.

architecturally ambitious industrial building, one of *Burslem* Pottery.

assisted place independent school *Newcastle* Schools.

beautiful cemetery *Burslem* Cemetery; famous seet pea bloom growers *Stone* Mr and Mrs Arthur Leigh.

complete example illustrative of the whole social economy of a community which had lived and loved, worked and worshipped in the first millenium B.C. *Maer* Bronze and Iron Age.

discussed pottery designer of the C20 *Wolstanton* Clarice Cliff.

expensive single garden vendor *S-u-T* Horticulture.

famous plane - Reginald Mitchell *Audley*.

interesting mock mayoralty, historically *Newcastle* Borough.

Lord Mayors assembled together by 1929 *Stoke-on-Trent* Mayoralty.

9th, 48th, and 49th most influential gay politicians *Stoke-on-Trent* Society.

successful slalom canoe club 2008 *Stone* Canoeing.

(3rd) popular paying visitor site 1986 *S-u-T* National Garden Festival.

wanted VAT frauster, one of *S-u-T* Wooley, Ray.

Motorway: service station runner-up *Swynnerton* Motorways.

Noisiest: (10th) place *Stoke-on-Trent* Living conditions.

Oldest: bellringers 1953, one of *Wolstanton* William Fitchford.

cat living 1989 *Eccleshall* Natural history.

council houses 1976 *Wolstanton* Housing.

existing family-run/private narrowboat hire company *Stone* Canals.

family shows, one of *Betley* Community co-operation.

female organ donor by 2008 *Stone* Christine Wright.

man 2000 *S-u-T* William Lee.

parish register, one of *Betley*.

person 1999 *Newcastle* Morris, Eva.

postman 1905 *Milwich* Thomas Hough.

school of physiotherapy 1994 *Keele* Keele University: General.

(2nd) football club *S-u-T* Stoke City FC: General.

(2nd) instutution of its kind 1953 *S-u-T* Policing.

(2nd) woman 1998 *Newcastle* Morris, Eva.

stable block, one of *Whitmore* Whitmore Hall.

surviving breeders of shire horses 1921 *Stone* Joseph Harvey.

surviving fairground showman 2006 *S-u-T* Doug Camm.

surviving WW1 veteran 2000 *S-u-T* William Lee.

yew hedge, one of *Stone* Aston Hall.

Only: combined painters and plumbers association *S-u-T* Industry.

cow quads 1960 *Eccleshall* Farming.

crane tank railway engine *S-u-T* Railways.

garden created by a surgeon whilst on call for kidney transplantation *S-u-T* Horticulture.

hosting of midget car speedway league racing *S-u-T* Motor racing.

life-size cardboard cutout company *Stone* Cardboard cutout.

monkey forest *Trentham* Trentham Hall estate.

national society dealing with all aspects of solvent and volatile substance abuse *Stone* Social care.

one of few mink farmers *Madeley* Len Kelsall.

one of only two railway companies to have exclusive rights over a coalfield *S-u-T* Railways.

one of only five areas chosen for a test of a 2011 census *Stoke-on-Trent* Demography.

one of two frying pan manufacturers 1686 *Newcastle* John Holland.

soldier to win the M.M. trice in WW2 *Newcastle* Kite, Sgt Fred.

surviving C17 glass furnace *Eccleshall* Glass working.

shrine to only assasinated British Prime Minister *Sandon* Sandon Hall.

Place: with more massage parlours per head than anywhere else *Stoke-on-Trent* Society.

Politest: man *S-u-T* Rev Ian Gregory.

Purpose-built: (3rd) home for dementia suffers *Wolstanton* Health and well being.

Record: for a first cast on a new plant *S-u-T* Industry.

Richest: (6th) person 2008 *Stone* Kirsty Roper.

Safest: pit 1976 *Wolstanton* Holditch Colliery.

place for elderly people to have a thigh operation 2008 *S-u-T* Health.

Sexiest: City *Stoke-on-Trent* Society.

Sixth-Former runner-up 2004 *Stone* Louke Travlos.

Single: biggest court action against anti-social behaviour *Swynnerton* Village life.

Smallest: pub room, one of *S-u-T* Pubs.

working page boy, late 1940s *S-u-T* Ivor Jones.

Sole: surviving steam powered potters mill *S-u-T* Pottery Industry: Buildings.

Strongest: Man 1994 *Trentham* Powerlifting.

Ugliest: building *Newcastle* Built environment.

Worst: funded high schools of any unitary authority 1998 *S-u-T* Schools.

(person) of the C18 *Stone* William Augustus Cumberland, Duke of.

postal service 2007-8 *Stoke-on-Trent* Living conditions.

sports disaster to 1968 *S-u-T* Stoke City FC: Individual matches.

13th worst place to live 2007 *Stoke-on-Trent* Living conditions.

CHARACTERISTICS OF THE PARISHES

Obviously claims in themselves do not tell a proper story of the parish, but what was found by chance as information randomly accumulated (and was not searched for) unforeseen themes emerged. For instance:

Ashley: Refinement introduced.

Audley: Outstanding individual women; design sense/ collective strength of men.

Balterley: Hidden revelations.

Barlaston: Surprisingly savvy.

Betley: Kindness and charm juxta-posed rustic old lore.

Burslem: Fervour.

Chebsey: Stafford's secluded bolt-hole.

Eccleshall: Leads in rural innovation/ attracts the prestigious.

Keele: Parish of reinvention.

Madeley: Parish of piety, protest.

Maer: Geography is paramount.

Milwich: Venerable.

Mucklestone: Deceit and honesty.

Newcastle: Civility and show.

Sandon: conflict orientated (home and war fronts)/ commemoration of.

Standon: Youth verses seniority; future verses past.

Stoke-upon-Trent: A finger in a myriad of social issue pies, not least age and women.

Stone: Parish of provision and guile.

Swynnerton: Blighted by controversies.

Trentham: Pursuit in little pleasures.

Whitmore: Quietly resistant to change.

Wolstanton: Mining, methodism, families, children.

ENGLISH/ COUNTRY RECORDS

Best: England at its best, rural *Balterley* Natural history.

one of *Stoke-on-Trent* Mayoralty: Major Cecil Wedgwood.

Captain: for handicapped golf *S-u-T* Golf.

of the first ladies' darts team *Burslem* Darts.

Champion: English doubles short-mat bowls 2009 *Wolstanton* Bowls.

English Football Hall of Fame *Ashley* Football (Gordon Banks).

English singles short-mat bowls champion 2003 *Wolstanton* Bowls.

England under-15s cricket team helped to win against England under-16s by Moddershall boy *Stone* Cricket.

Ladies' FA Cup winners 1922 *S-u-T* Football.

Deepest: colliery shaft by mid 1960s *Wolstanton* Wolstanton Colliery.

Earliest: known seal of arms of a private gentleman *Swynnerton* Heraldry.

Filthiest: (5th) place *Stoke-on-Trent* Living conditions.

First: all locally-born team played in the old First Division *S-u-T* Stoke City FC: Individual matches.

coaching advertisement Stone Roads.

Danish king Swynnerton Sweyn.

house of the Passionists Stone Aston Hall.

importer of Friesian cattle from Holland Tyrley Farming.

Mother-Provincial of the English Dominican Tertiaries Stone Mother Margaret Hallahan

new museum after WW2 S-u-T Museums.

potato riddling machine Whitmore Farming.

purpose-built sixth form college S-u-T Further Education; school to get a perfect Ofsted score, one of S-u-T Schools.

sighting of a Lanthorn fly Wolstanton Natural history.

singing of the 'Contakion' Stone Performance.

transport tunnel 1777 Wolstanton Harecastle Tunnel.

WEA *S-u-T* Further Education.

Foremost: C17 theologian and Hebrew scholar *Ashley*.

Gooseberry: growers' society offering the best prizes 1905 *Stone* Gooseberries.

Greatest: Commander 1823 *Stone* John Jervis.

crowd who paid to see a league match between two provincial teams by 1950 *S-u-T* Stoke City FC: Individual matches.

Elizabethan monument of any church or cathedral, perhaps *Ashley*.

Largest: (13th) city in England and Wales 1970 *Stoke-on-Trent* Demography.

Last: wolf killed *Tyrley* Woods.

Local: authority with most derelict areas 1969 *Stoke-on-Trent* Demography.

Longest: transport tunnel 1777 *Wolstanton* Harecastle Tunnel.

serving theatre director of a provincial theatre in modern times *Wolstanton* Peter Cheeseman.

Most: boring village *Madeley* Onneley.

comfortable, convenient, substantial, tasteful village cottages *Keele* Village life.

haunted pub - one of 12 *S-u-T* Pubs.

match appearances *S-u-T* Stoke City FC: Individuals.

protracted FA Cup tie *S-u-T* Stoke City FC: Individual matches.

Oldest: industry *S-u-T* Pottery Industry: General.

player to score in the FA Cup *S-u-T* Stanley Matthews.

surviving image of Maypole dancing *Betley* Community co-operation.

Only: council of its kind

not improving adequately 2007 *Stoke-on-Trent* Civil life and Federation.

one of only two frying pan makers *Keele* Iron working.

one of only two pleasure boat firms operating on the English canal system 1948 *Stone* Canals.

weeping larch *Mucklestone* Natural history.

Record: at clay pigeon shooting *Eccleshall* Marksmanship.

Southern-most: extent of the last Ice Age *Betley*.

Swiftest: man c1825 *S-u-T* Athletics: Distance running.

Worst: place to live 2001 *Stoke-on-Trent* Living conditions.

place to place 2001 *Stoke-on-Trent* Living conditions.

EUROPEAN RECORDS

Best: Designed Newspaper 2004 *S-u-T* Newspapers.

Biggest: campus, one of *Keele* Keele University: General.

Greatest: Day out 1986 *S-u-T* National Garden Festival.

Largest: council housing estate *S-u-T* Council housing.

(and most) original skateplaza *S-u-T* Parks.

(2nd) factory of its kind *Stone* Grindley Lane works.

Champion: bantamweight champion 1921 *S-u-T* Boxing.

(unofficial) Barefoot Water Ski Championships *Trentham* Trentham Gardens.

bronze 2008 *S-u-T* Pole vaulting.

Canoe Slalom Championship women's K1 winners 2009 *Stone* Canoeing.

cross-country club championship winners 1967 *Stone* Athletics.

Footballer of the Year

1957 *S-u-T* Stanley Matthews. Grand Prix (Karate) Series champion 2000 *Stone* Martial Arts. Junior Championship 2007 200m gold medalist, 4x100m relay silver medalist *S-u-T* Athletics: Track. Junior Games 4 x 400m relay bronze medalist 1978 *Newcastle* Athletics. junior sprint hurdles champion 1993 *Eccleshall* Athletics. team weapons Junior? (Karate) champions 2009 *S-u-T* Martial Arts.

GENERAL ENTRY TOPICS

Activities: Football *Keele*: Cricket *Madeley*: Fete *Madeley*: Nudism *Eccleshall*: Holiday camp *Maer*: Nightlife *S-u-T*: Stoke City Football Club *S-u-T*: Canoeing *Stone*: Competitions Wolstanton. Archaeology: Anglo-Saxon *Barlaston*: Ice Age *Betley*: Bronze and Iron Age *Maer*: Romans *Stone*: Blore Heath Battle *Tyrley*. Arts: Singing contests *Audley*: Theatre *Burslem*: Singing *Maer*: Libraries *Newcastle*: Shows *Newcastle*: Theatre and cinema *Newcastle*: Cinemas *S-u-T*: Museums *S-u-T*: Music and musicals *S-u-T*: Public art *S-u-T*: Radio *S-u-T*: Theatre *S-u-T*: Variety shows *S-u-T*: Victoria Hall *S-u-T*: Art *Stone*: Performance *Stone*: Cinema *Wolstanton*. Buildings: *S-u-T*: Built environment *Newcastle*. Civil affairs: Borough, The *Newcastle*: Public services *Newcastle*: Civil life and Federation *Stoke-on-Trent*: Mayoralty *Stoke-on-Trent*: Freemen *Stoke-on-Trent*: Newspapers

S-u-T. Civil defence: *Standon*: Military defence *Newcastle*; *S-u-T*: *Wolstanton*. Countryside: Deer park *Eccleshall*: Environment, and built environment *Eccleshall*: (Municipal) Parks *S-u-T*; Tunstall Park *Wolstanton*: Woods *Tyrley*: Ecology *Wolstanton*. Education *Burslem*: Keele University *Keele*: Schools *Newcastle*; *Trentham*; *Stone*; *S-u-T*: Child reformatory *Standon*: Further education *S-u-T*: Keep fit classes *Stone*: Kibblestone Camp *Stone*. Farming *Eccleshall*; *Keele*; *Maer*; *Standon*; *Stone*; *Trentham*; *Tyrley*; *Whitmore*; *Wolstanton*: Horticulture *S-u-T*; *Stone*. Food and drink: *Stone*: Oatcakes *Burslem*: Gooseberries *Stone*; Joule's Brewery *Stone*: Sweets *Trentham*. Freemasonry *Newcastle*; *S-u-T*. Gardening *Sandon*; *Tyrley*; National Garden Festival *S-u-T*: Trentham Gardens *Trentham*. Headquarters Burslem Health *Burslem*; *S-u-T*: Social care *Newcastle*; *Trentham*: Maternity hospitals *S-u-T*: Health and well being *Wolstanton*. Heraldry *Swynnerton*. Housing *Burslem*; *Standon*; *Wolstanton*: Hospitality *Stoke-on-Trent*: Living conditions *Stoke-on-Trent*: Council housing *S-u-T*: Homes *Trentham*: National homes *Trentham*. Industry (other than pottery) *S-u-T*: Glass working *Eccleshall*; Swynnerton Royal Ordnance Factory *Eccleshall*: Iron working *Keele*: Trade *Newcastle*: Engineering *San-*

don: Tyre manufacturing *S-u-T*: Trades *Eccleshall*: Leather working *Stone*: Meaford Power Station *Stone*: Moddershall Valley watermills *Stone*: Quickfit and Quartz Ltd *Stone*: Brick making *Wolstanton*: Business/industrial parks *Wolstanton*: Engineering *Wolstanton*: Iron working *Wolstanton*. Law: *Audley*; *Wolstanton*: Policing *Stoke-on-Trent*: Policing *S-u-T*: Crime *Eccleshall*; *Stone*: Magistrates Court *Stone*: Manorial business *Whitmore*: Law *Wolstanton*. Mining *Audley*; *Burslem*; *Madeley*; *S-u-T*; *Trentham*; *Wolstanton*; Apedale Colliery *Wolstanton*: Birchendale Colliery *Wolstanton*; Holditch Colliery *Wolstanton*: Silverdale Colliery *Wolstanton*; Wolstanton Colliery *Wolstanton*. Natural history: *Audley*; *Balterley*; *Eccleshall*; *Madeley*; *Maer*; *Mucklestone*; *Newcastle*; *S-u-T*; *Stone*; *Wolstanton*. Nomenclature Society *Stoke-on-Trent*. People (famous) Queen Victoria *Chebsey*; Izaak Walton *Chebsey*: Stanley Matthews *S-u-T*: Josiah Wedgwood *S-u-T*: William Augustus, Duke of Cumberland *Stone*: Sir Edward Lutyens *Stone*: Sweyn Swynnerton: Sir John Soane *Tyrley*. Places: Clough Hall *Audley*: Hall o' th' Wood *Balterley*: Barlaston Hall *Barlaston*: Hulton Abbey *Burslem*: Horsley Hall *Eccleshall*: Onneley *Madeley*: Lea Head Manor *Mucklestone*: Sandon Hall *Sandon*: Fenton *S-u-T*: Hanley *S-u-T*: Longton *S-u-*

T: Stoke Town Hall *S-u-T*: Aston Hall *Stone*: Normacot *Stone*: Stone Priory *Stone*: Tittensor *Stone*: Trentham Hall *Trentham*: Trentham Hall estate *Trentham*: War memorial *Trentham*: Whitmore Hall *Whitmore*: Tunstall *Wolstanton*: Maps *Burslem*. Politics: Parish council *Eccleshall*: Councils *Stone*: Political gatherings *Stone*: Political agitation *Wolstanton*. Pottery: Pots and Potters *Burslem*: Pottery *Burslem*: Pottery Industry *S-u-T*: Wedgwood Pottery at Etruria *S-u-T*: Pottery *Wolstanton*. Pubs: *Burslem*; *Eccleshall*; *Madeley*; *Milwich*; *Newcastle*; *S-u-T*: Pubs and hotels *Wolstanton* Religion: *Newcastle*: Mormons *Burslem*: Muggletonians *Milwich*: Judaism *S-u-T*: Methodism *S-u-T*; Roman Catholicism *S-u-T*; *Wolstanton*: Non conformity, religious *Wolstanton*. Shopping and banking *Newcastle*: Shopping *S-u-T*. Societies *Audley*: Cemeteries *Burslem*: Poorest *Eccleshall*; Demography *Stoke-on-Trent*: Dialect *Stoke-on-Trent*: Gay rights *S-u-T*: Women *S-u-T*; *Stone*: Drug abuse *Stone*: Marriage *Stone*: Motherhood *Stone*: Poorest *Stone*. Transport: *Burslem*: Railways *Standon*; *S-u-T*; *Stone*; *Whitmore*: Aircraft *S-u-T*: Cars *S-u-T*: Trams and buses *S-u-T*: Waterways *S-u-T*: Aircraft *Stone*: Canals *Stone*: Meir Aerodrome *Stone*: Motorways *Swynnerton*: Motorway dinning *Keele*: Harecastle Tunnel *Wolstanton*:

Roads Wolstanton
Village life *Ashley*;
Audley; Betley; Bar-
laston; Chebsey;
Keele: Community
co-operation *Bet-*
ley; Burslem: Parish
council *Eccleshall*:
Fete *Madeley*: Con-
servation Area *Stone*:
Councils *Stone*: War
memorial *Trentham*.
WW1 *Sandon*: War me-
morial *Trentham*.

MIDLAND RECORDS
Best: laid-out and
equipped squash
court, one *Trentham*
Squash.
Biggest: suppliers of
bricks, one of *S-u-T*
Industry.
Champion: Area Mixed
Voice Choir Champi-
onship winners 1952
S-u-T Musics and
musicals.
area Coal Queen
1971 *Wolstanton* Miss
Carol Hooper.
Sports Personal-
ity 2006 *Wolstanton*
Darts.
First: Freemason Grand
Lodge *Newcastle*
Freemasonry.
Foremost: women's
swimming clubs *New-*
castle Swimming.
Largest: cinema screen
S-u-T Cinemas.
(North) industrial
wasteland 1985 *S-u-*
T National Garden
Festival.
Most: power cut capital
Stone Tittensor.
sought after town
1980 *Trentham*
Homes.
up-to-date unit in
the Central England
scheme of the Cen-
tral Electricity Board
Stone Meaford Power
Station.

NORTH
STAFFORDSHIRE
Best: distance runner
ever *Leek* (DYKT2),
Athletics.
known progressive
farmer of the younger
generation 1934, one
of *Mucklestone* Tho-
mas Bourne.
medieval church

Checkley (DYKT2)
Churches.
Cleanest: buses *S-u-T*
Trams and buses.
Deepest: pit 1869 *S-u-T*
Mining.
Earliest: blast coke-fired
furnace *Wolstanton*
Iron working.
documentation of coal
mining *Wolstanton*
Coal mining.
Fairy: godfather *Nor-*
ton-in-the-Moors
(DYKT2) Enoch
Haughton.
Field Club: their first
excursion *Biddulph*
(DYKT2).
Finest: building, one
of *S-u-T* Stoke Town
Hall.
First: amateur cinema-
tographer *Leek* Edgar
John Martin.
annual meeting of
the British Parks
Bowling Association
Norton-in-the-Moors
(DYKT2) Bowls.
bone-marrow trans-
plant patient *S-u-T*
Denise Morse.
Catholic bishop
Wolstanton Roman
Catholic.
community housing
for elderly tenants
Burslem Housing.
gathering to agitate
for trade unionism
Wolstanton Political
agitation.
known book club
Newcastle Libraries.
owner of a motor car
Newcastle Frederick
Butterworth.
pit into which a royal
descended *Trentham*
Mining.
pit to operate under-
ground conveyor belts
Norotn-in-the-Moors
(DYKT2) Mining.
Professional Golf
Championship *Wol-*
stanton Golf.
purpose-built office
block *Newcastle* Built
environment.
recorded birth of
a Jewish person
Newcastle Naomi
Francks.
space craft equip-
ment produced *S-u-T*
Industry.
Turnpike Act *Stone*

Roads.
Largest: private pho-
tographic collection
of its buildings due
for demolition *S-u-T*
Buildings.
Last: appearance of
The Beatles *Trentham*
Trentham Gardens.
bone mill, one of *Stone*
Moddershall Valley
watermills.
electric tram *S-u-T*
Trams and buses.
mineral railway
Trentham Mining.
person hung *Barlaston*
Leslie Green.
surviving independent
bus operator *Cheddle-*
ton (DYKT2) Buses.
Longest: running oper-
atic society *Burslem*
Theatre.
surviving independent
bus company *S-u-T*
Trams and buses.
Oldest: blast coke-fired
furnace *Wolstanton*
Iron working.
woman 1929 *S-u-T* Mrs
Elizabeth Legand.
Only: Communist coun-
cillor *Wolstanton* Fan-
ny Deakin.
referee of a FA Cup
Final *Burslem* Jim
Mason.
Voluntary Aided
Church of England
High School *S-u-T*
Schools.
Smallest: house *Stone*
Normacot.
Tallest:
building *S-u-T* Build-
ings.

OVERVIEW COVER-
ING THIS BOOK'S
AREA
Altitudes: The highest
point is Mow Cop,
Wolstanton, at 1,099
feet.
The lowest point is
272 feet at the Sow
and Meece conflu-
ence, Chebsey.
Churches (parish): old-
est Chebsey, 1070;
newest Balterley,
1901.
Distance to Stafford:
nearest Chebsey and
Eccleshal both 3.6m
NW; farthest Balter-
ley 19.1m NNW.
Incumbents: longest

serving James Shaw
at Milwich, 1610-
1672, 62 years.
Parish registers: earli-
est entry Betley 1538.
Latest entry Chebsey
1660.
Parish length: longest
parish entity Stone
with 7.8m; shortest
Newcastle with 1m.
Parish size: smallest
Newcastle with 554
acres; largest parish
entity Eccleshall with
21,738 acres.
Parish width: narrowest
parish entity Newcas-
tle at 1.2m; widest
parish entity S-u-T
with 8m.
Population figures
1801-1901: parish
with least Balterley
with between 237 and
253 people.
parish with most S-
u-T with between
16,414 and 140,335
people.
WW1: most killed S-
u-T with 2,377; least
killed Whitmore with
1.

VILLAINS
Allnut, Alice - Stoke's
villainess.
Barlow, Charles - Wol-
stanton's villain.
Davenport, William -
Maer's villain.
Dodsley, Rev Christo-
pher - Swynnerton's
villain.
Erdeswick, Hugh - San-
don's villain.
Florence, Henry -
Mucklestone's vil-
lain.
Green, Leslie - Barlas-
ton's villain.
Hall, John - Standon's
villain.
Higginson, Charles -
Eccleshall's villain.
Hutton, Mary Ann Tay-
lor - Eccleshall's vil-
lainess.
Jervis, James - Betley's
villain.
Knight, Kate - Meir
Hay's villainess
Stone.
Lawrence, Sarah -
Mucklestone's vil-
lainess.
Moss, Thomas - Mil-
wich's villain.

Neilson, Donald - Kidsgrove's villain Wolstanton.

Pepper, Mrs Frances M - Audley's villainess.

Punkie, Billy - Newcastle's villain.

Stafford, William - Stone's villain.

WORLD RECORDS

Best: ceramics collections *S-u-T* Pottery Industry: General.

Champion: amateur ballroom champion 1948 *S-u-T* Syd Perkins.

Championship titles by 2008, most *Wolstanton* Darts.

cycling record for over 26 miles in an hour *S-u-T* Cycling.

darts champion 1990, 1992, 1995-2002, 2004-6, 2009- *Wolstanton* Darts.

Grand Prix champion 1998-2000, 2002-03, 2005-06, 2008 *Wolstanton* Darts.

in Bloom winner *Audley*.

individual slalom kayak bronze medalist 1979, gold medalist 1981, 1983, 1985 *Stone*.

Matchplay 1995, 1997, 2000-04, 2006 *Wolstanton* Darts.

No. 19 Snooker player 2008/9 *S-u-T* Billiards.

Town Crier 1979 *Newcastle* Frank Shufflebotham.

Trial and UK Championships 2007 200m silver medalist *S-u-T* Athletics: Track.

(WWA) Heavyweight Champion 1987 *S-u-T* Wrestling.

Youth Championship 2007 100m bronze medalist *S-u-T* Athletics: Track.

Youth Triple Jump 2009 *Wolstanton* Athletics.

Eighth: wonder *Wolstanton* Harecastle Tunnel.

Finest: example of the potter's art 1789 *S-u-T* Wedgwood Pottery at Etruria.

First: female squash player to turn professional *S-u-T* Racket sports.

kidney removal day patient *Wolstanton* Helena Joines.

man to transmit a message by radio telegraphy *S-u-T* Sir Oliver Lodge.

Mormon missionary in Australia *Burslem* Barratt, William James.

Photographer *S-u-T* Thomas Wedgwood.

pottery to have an ornamental facade *S-u-T* Wedgwood Pottery at Etruria.

prove link between smoking and Rheumatoid Arthritis *Burslem* Health.

public performances *S-u-T* Victoria Hall: First performances.

radial tyre *S-u-T* Tyre manufacturing.

(rail) swing bridge *Stone* Rail.

railway canteen *Whitmore* Railways.

recipient of a unique bionic hand Stone.

portable bandstand, *Stone*, Trade.

school of Petroleum Technology, founder of *Wolstanton* John Cadman.

straight and level transport canal tunnel of more than 2600 meters *Wolstanton* Harecastle Tunnel.

to give an hypothetical structure for DNA *S-u-T* William Thomas Astbury.

to make a replica of a Gutenberg press *Stone* Alan May.

to perfect the method of multi-colour or polychrome printing *S-u-T* Pottery Industry: Processes.

to think of using light upon silver nitrate to make copies *S-u-T* Thomas Wedgwood.

Greatest: ever slalom canoeist and most decorated slalom kayaker in the history of the sport by 2008 *Stone* Canoeing.

ever slalom canoeist and most decorated slalom kayaker in the history of the sport by 2008 *Stone* Canoeing.

Wedgwood Museum *Barlaston* Wedgwood Factory.

Greenest: business parks, one of *Wolstanton* Business/ industrial parks.

Heaviest: goosberries ever grown record holders 1860-1901 *Stone* Gooseberries goosberry *Stone* Gooseberries.

Largest: all-glass heat exchanger 1960 *Stone* Quickfit and Quartz Ltd.

collection of open stock transfers *S-u-T*: Pottery Industry: Processes.

earthenware manufacturer *S-u-T* Pottery Industry: Buildings.

glass pipeline Stone Quickfit and Quartz Ltd.

manufacturers of ceramic tableware 1980, one of *Barlaston* Wedgwood Factory.

producer of coffee mugs later 1960s *Stone* Meir Aerodrome.

Last: pottery to use underglaze transfer printing from engravings *Burslem* Pottery.

surviving traditional oakcake shop *S-u-T* Shopping.

Longest: novel by an English writer to 1927 *Burslem* Arnold Bennett.

running gang show *Burslem* Theatre.

symphony ever written *S-u-T* Victoria Hall: General.

Most: agreeable member *Keele* John Sneyd.

credited trance and progressive producer-DJ, one of *S-u-T* Andy Moor.

marathons in a year by a woman. *Stone* Athletics.

modern facilities for students and a team of designers 1968 *Barlaston* Wedgwood

Factory.

prolific art dealer *Eccleshall* John Myatt.

reproduced work of art *S-u-T* Arnold Machin.

sustainable distribution centre 2009 *Wolstanton* Ecology.

Oldest: Football coach 2006 *Burslem*: Port Vale: General.

person 2000, possibly Newcastle Eva Morris

surviving football programme, one of *S-u-T* Stoke City FC: General.

(2nd) cast iron bridge ever built *Trentham* Trentham Gardens.

Prettiest: village, officially *Audley*.

Record: for drinking ale upside down *Burslem* Endurance.

for making 3,591 bowls in 72 hours *S-u-T* Pottery Industry: People.

for most clothes pegs clipped to face and neck *S-u-T* Kevin Thackwell.

for sale of a Stubbs-Wedgwood painted plaque *S-u-T* Pottery Industry: Individual Ware.

mileage bicycle endurance over 12 months *S-u-T* Cycling.

Renowned: for its Minton tiles *S-u-T* Churches: Holy Trinity.

Richest: (524th) person 2008 *Eccleshall* John Cauldwell.

Strongest: Man competitor *Wolstanton* Powerlifting.

Top: (18th) producer DJ 2009 *S-u-T* Andy Moor.

(30th) producer DJ 2005, 2006 *S-u-T* Andy Moor.

Wonders: one of *Keele* Keele University: Library holdings.

Worst: place - according to Local Government Board medical officer *Stone* Council.

Parishes of North West Staffordshire

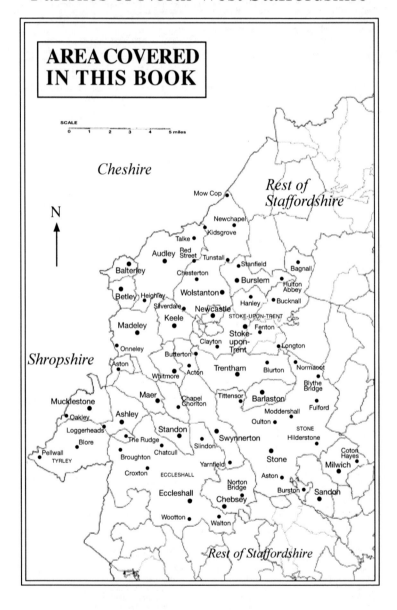

A

Acton See Swynnerton.
Almington See Tyrley.
Ashley Ashley was Staffordshire's 97th largest parish, consisting of 2821 acres; 78th closest parish to the county town, 12.2m NW; extremist length 2.4m; extremist width 2.7m. The parish's chief settlement is Ashley village in a hollow below Ashley Heath, but the most populous place is Loggerheads. Ashley is famous for the fresh air and views from Ashley Heath, which made it a popular Potteries resort in the 19th Century.

   Church *St John the Baptist* at Ashley is one of 11 such county dedications (of AP churches); 88th= oldest AP county church dating from the C14 or roughly 1350. For the founding of the church see Folklore. *'one of the most historic and lovely churches in the diocese of Lichfield'*. Ashley church (SA June 26 1948 p5 col 2). *'Perhaps the largest Elizabethan monument of any church or cathedral in England'*. That to Sir Gilbert Gerard (d1592) in Ashley church (VB p160). It is a very large alabaster 'machine' four-posted tomb (BOE p63). *Note* the Gerard arms quarter those of the family of George Washington, as they were allied by marriage (NSFCT 1924 pp94-103) (ES Feb 19 1932 p6) (STM Jan 1964 p27). *The other most interesting thing is the* Wedgwood vase made and given by Josiah Wedgwood in memory of William, 3rd Viscount Chetwynd, positioned above the arch to the chancel. Church with the 3rd most hatchments in the county Ashley with 5; there are 78 known hatchments in the county (Hatchments in Britain No. 8 p147). In the churchyard - A stone tub from the long demolished Gerrard's Bromley Hall (info Paul Everson, 2007).

   Geology The Loggerheads area is Upper Coal Measures; the N and SW areas of the parish are Bunter, part of a western outpost (TTTD p248); Ashley village, E and SE is Keuper Red Marls, surrounded by a band of Keuper Sandstones; Hookgate is Permian, reputedly highest point of the beds in Great Britain (NSFCT 1927 p171).

   Altitudes The highest point is 700 feet

on Ashley Heath. The lowest point is 370 feet by the Tern. *Highest cultivated tableland in England* is Ashley Heath, being part of England's main watershed (BPS p109), and embraces views; westwards - Berwyn Mountains, Wales; north westwards - Liverpool docks (NSFCT 1927 p171); east north eastwards - Union House, Hanley, further away, Morridge, Cloud End, and Axe Edge (BPS p112).

   Billington, Prof William *Man instrumental in founding 'the first institution in the country to provide expert medical and surgical treatment.... for the large class of patients who cannot afford high fees and yet do not wish to go into the public hospitals'*. (1876-1932). Born Sandbach, but whose father Charles had retired to White House, Ashley by 1908. William was an eminent surgeon, pioneer in bonegrafting. The hospital was St Chad's, founded 1913, later known as St Chad's Smethwick Municipal Hospital (SA Feb 13 1932 p5 col 5).

   Cradocke, John and **Alicia Lovat** *Earliest persons recorded in the parish register*. For their marriage on 20 May 1551.

   Folklore *Ashley's best, 'must be unique in ecclesiology, at least, as far as our own county is concerned'*. The building of St John's according to legend - related on a brass tablet in the nave - was achieved by a village cowman, David Kenric (*Ashley's most famous old worthy*), using plunder from the victories of Crecy and Poitiers, where he fought under the banner of the Black Prince (SA & Chron Feb 17 1955 p4 cols 4-6). The tradition is he was returning home to Flintshire in 1356 after serving in France, lost his way in Needwood Forest and emerged out of forest - then stretching across the whole of N Staffs - at Ashley and vowed to rebuild the church herein thanksgiving for his safe delivery. Another story tells he was an Ashley native and, before leaving home for a war, stuck a spear into the soil where the church now lies and solemnly vowed that should God restore him to his friends after the war he would build a church on the spot.

   Football *'Safe as the Banks of Eng-*

land', 2nd best goalkeeper of the C20, an inaugural inductee in the English Football Hall of Fame (2002). Gordon Banks, born near Rotherlam 1937. When he was with Stoke City 1967-72, he lived at Ashley Heath. He won 73 England caps, 1963-72; received an honorary doctorate from Keele University 2006. A poll by the International Federation of Football History & Statistics elected him as the second best goalkeeper of the C20 after Lev Yashin. A statue of him erected in his honour at Britannia Stadium, Stoke, had been moved to Madeley High School by 2009, by then Banks was living at Madeley (Wikipedia 2010) (ES Feb 6 2010 p27p) (info John Griffiths).

Lawrence *2nd earliest parish register entry in Staffordshire of a black person,* 'an African by nationality, a Christian by profession' servant of Lord Gerard of Willoughbridge was buried (1)6th April 1668; it has been claimed the black-shrouded figure at the foot of the Sir Gilbert Gerard tomb in the church represents him, but the most likely explanation is that the object is an unpainted 'cadaver' or corpse in its winding-sheet; his marriage is said to be recorded in Eccleshall PR and some of his descendants still (1917) live in The Potteries (NSFCT 1917 p139) (STM Jan 1964 p27) (VB p161). The earliest is at Wolverhampton.

Lightfoot, Dr John *England's foremost C17 theologian and Hebrew scholar, 'the most famous Rector of Ashley'.* Rector of Ashley, 1629-75. Died 1675; the 2nd claim was made by local historian, D Goronwy Harnaman in Six Towns Magazine Jan 1964 pp26-27 (Burrow's Reference Map of Stoke-on-Trent 2nd ed 1970 p7).

Place-name Ashley first appears in Domesday Book, 1086, and means 'the leah growing with ash-trees' (PNSZ p92).

Poorest There was an agreement for maintenance of Ashley poor in Audley workhouse 1773; later there was an Ashley parish workhouse, which Thomas Kinnersley had a hand in erecting; a special meeting of the vestry met June 1 1838 to discuss its dispersal (D44/A/PO/33) (D44/A/PV/1). After 1836 Ashley poor, unable to support themselves, went to Market Drayton Union workhouse in Shropshire Street; it was enlarged in 1839. A new workhouse was built c1851 on Little Drayton Common, SW of Market Drayton. It became Quarry House, and is now demolished.

Population Ashley was: 82nd most-populated Staffordshire parish in 1801 with 605 people; 83rd in 1811 with 616; 83rd in 1821 with 729; 78th in 1831 with 825; 79th in 1841 with 853; 79th in 1851 with 896; 82nd in 1861 with 870; 79th in 1871 with 903; 83rd in 1881 with 806; 82nd in 1891 with 797; 87th in 1901 with 725. Ashley could be ranked 80th= worst-affected Staffordshire parish for loss of men in WW1, with 14 lives taken.

Quote *Choicest.* Weston E Vernon-Yonge in his quirky Bye-paths of Staffordshire, 1911, writes 'The more pastoral bits about Ashley proper contrast well with the woods and park of Willoughbridge, and the more bold and bracing tableland of Ashley Heath.'

Village life *'one of the prettiest of North Staffordshire villages'.* Ashley in the opinion of 'Wayfarer' the columnist for 'Random Notes' in The Staffordshire Advertiser (SA May 10 1947 p5), *'one of the beauty spots of England'.* Ashley, in the opinion of an Ashley Parish Councillor at a council meeting on April 23 1955, worried that the village was being 'flooded' with caravan dwellers from the Potteries (SA & Chron April 28 1955 p8 col 6-7). *One of the first places in Staffordshire to have an automatic telephone exchange.* Ashley in or by 1930, along with Hollington (Checkley), with Sandon next, and Seighford, Bradley, Hamstall Ridware, and Dapple Heath (Admaston) earmarked for the service in the future (SA Sept 27 1930 p9 cols 3-4).

Willoughbridge *'exceedingly rare' book.'* Samuel Gilbert's 'Fors Sanitatis; or, The Healing Spring at Willowbridge, Staffordshire' 1678, according to Rupert

James I stayed at Gerard's Bromley Hall (Eccleshall) for two days in 1617. There is a tradition he bathed in Willoughbridge spring for his rheumatism. Lady Gerard built a bath house (below) and lodgings for the sick in her attempt to create a large fashionable spa resort.

Simms in his Bibliotheca Staffordiensis (1894).

Aston See Mucklestone.

Aston-by-Stone See Stone.

Audley Audley was Staffordshire's 21st largest parish, consisting of 8727 acres; 49th= farthest parish away from the county town, 16.6m NW; extremist length 5.6m, making it 22nd= longest parish in the county; extremist width 5.3m, making it 23rd= widest parish in the county. The parish's chief settlement is the old mining village of Audley. The parish is famous for its views over the Cheshire plain, the great old county family of Audley, its higgledy-piggledy former mining communities.

Abnett, Alice *Person with Audley's earliest-surviving will.* It is dated Oct 22 1524.

Altitudes The highest point is 728 feet near Ashenough Farm. The lowest point is 295 feet on Cheshire border at Domvilles Wood, and also at Foxley Drumble.

Audley, Henry de *Audley's most famous old worthy.* (c1175-1246). He was the most illustrious of the great Audley family, lords of Audley. By the 1220s "Henry had become by inheritance, gift, marriage and purchase one of the most important men in North Staffordshire" and Henry III often trusted him with governorship of strongholds on the Welsh marches. He founded Hulton Abbey, near Burslem (1223), built Heighley Castle (1226), and created Heighley Park (1222) in the Silverdale area, which was stocked with 12 hinds given by the King. In 1237 he twice met Prince Llewellyn of Wales to treat for peace. He was sheriff of Staffordshire 1227-29, 1229~32.

Audley, Sir James de *Most famous member of the Audley family, founder of the Order of the Garter.* KG. (c1322-1369). Son of James de Audley of Stretton (Salop), hero of Poitiers (1356), who led the Black Prince's forces (Wikipedia, 2006). *Most erroneously identified Staffordshire luminary.* He was long mistaken for Staffordshire's James de Audley (1312/3-1386), 2nd Lord Audley until GF Beltz, Lancaster Herald, in 'Memorials of the Order of the Garter' (1841) made the correct identification.

Audley, Katherine *The anchorite.* (b1272). Daughter and coheiress of John Giffard - Baron of Brimsfield - by Matilda de Clifford, widow of William Longespee III, Earl of Salisbury. She married Nicholas de Audley (1258-99), lord of

Audley 1282-99. In widowhood she reputedly wandered with her maid, Mabel, to a town 'where the bells should ring untouched by man' following her stolen mare's hoof-marks. At such a place - Ledbury, Heres (there perhaps by 1312) - she stayed; described as 'recluse of Ledbury' 1323; Wordsworth writes of her in a sonnet (SHC 1906 p264. 1917-8 p7) (HAOE pp74-5).

Burrows, Mary Jane *'Princess Tiny, the renowned lady midget'* according to show advertisements. (1869-1917). Dwarf born in Halmerend who joined Wall's (or Well's) Ghost Show at Tunstall in c1896, and became something of a celebrity. She was only 42 inches high and 48 lb in weight. She was known in the Halmerend district as 'Little Polly' and in the Potteries as 'Dot,'. Died 1917 (Weekly Sentinel. March 3 1918) (AHJ 1998 p90).

CHURCHES St James the Great at Audley is the only such county dedication (for AP churches); 37th= oldest county church dating from 1170. *'one of the most interesting in Staffordshire, both from an architectural and historical point of view'.* Audley church (SA June 1 1946 p5 col 4). *Staffordshire's earliest brass (with figure in Military Costume) and one of the last uses of Norman-French on a memorial inscription.* The brass of Sir Thomas de Audley (d1385) in the south floor of the chancel. Apparently, the brass, at one time or another, had been thrown out of the church, and after several years lying in the Vicarage stable, it was rescued badly damaged. It has been subsequently restored as far as possible at the expense of the North Staffs Field Club (Audley PR) (STM Feb 1964 p35il) (Catalogue of Rubbings of Brasses and Incised Slabs. Muriel Clayton. 1968). *Note* the little metal plaque in memorandum of Queen Victoria's death - a flag - no longer existing - was hoisted up halfmast on the tower. *In the churchyard* note the grave of the daughters of John and Mary Taylor:

Sir Thomas de Audley - Staffordshire's earliest brass.

'...Ann died 16 Oct 1770 aged 13 years.
Hannah died 28 Oct 1770 aged 7 years.

Hannah in her ilnes said, Frett not dear parents for Nancy and me for if I die we two pretty little angels shall bee.' (info Ian Bailey).

St John at Alsagers Bank was built in 1875 and entirely rebuilt in 1911. *In the churchyard* are memorials to victims of the 1st and 2nd Minnie Pit disasters 1915 and 1918.

Clough Hall *'Paradise of the Potteries'*. What Clough Hall grounds was known as in the later C19; here was Staffordshire's Great Exhibition, staged in 1899 (ES Your Week July 29 2006 p9. April 25 2009 p23).

Downing, Paul and **Charles Powys** *Audley's villains*. Poachers. They shot dead William Cooper, the son of one of the gamekeepers of Sir TFF Boughey, Bt, aged 23, in the doorway or threshold of the house called The Hays, near Minnie Pit, in Aug 1844. Downing, a miner aged about 20, and his cousin Charles Powys were convicted on the evidence of the prints on their boots ; that they matched those found in mud leading up to the house. Added to this Downing had just completed a two month prison sentence for poaching on the evidence of the deceased's father. Despite the fact that the two maintained their innocence they were convicted of murder and hung in early 1845.

Emberton, Joseph *'one of Britain's most significant architects during the inter-war period'* (University of Brighton, Faculty of Arts website 2010). Born at Shraley House, Audley parish. Attended Orme Boys' School in Newcastle; apprentice to local architects, Chapman and Snape. Whilst working in the early modernist style he designed the British Empire Exhibition at Wembley (1924-25), the Royal Corinthian Yacht Club, Burnham-on-Crouch (1931), Blackpool Pleasure Beach (1935-39), and Simpson's department store, Piccadilly (1936) (ES May 29 2010 p29) (DNB).

Fenton, William de *Audley's longest serving vicar*. He served for 48 years, 1258-1306.

Folklore *Audley's best*. There is a local tradition Red Street, partly in Wolstanton ancient parish, is named 'red' after a battle here in ancient times (The Times Nov 22 1967). Also a white rabbit ghost crossing the avenue leading to Clough Hall was said by the late C19 to predict a death in the family of the one seeing it (NSFCT 1900 p144).

Garrett, Agneta *Earliest recorded person in the parish register*. For her baptism on Nov 7 1538.

Geology Talke is entirely Middle

Coal Measures; Audley is Keuper Red Marls and Sandstones band (by Cheshire border), Bunter band (Knowl Bank-Mosshouse), Upper Coal Measures band (Heighley-Dunkirk), Middle Coal Measures band (Scot Hay-Bignall Hill).

Griffiths, Keith *Talke's villain*. In 2003, aged 24, of Crystal Street, Cobridge, admitted murdering his grandfather Harold Bunn, aged 59, at his bungalow in sheltered housing complex at Hollinwood Close, Talke, on Dec 30 2003 (BBC news Sept 30 2004).

Law *Fancy that!* Emma Knight, widow, of Audley, sued Thomas Brassington, greengrocer, Fletcher Street, for 14s. 9d. damages sustained by his dog tearing her dress on Aug 18 1896. But the defendant's wife appeared at the County Court in Newcastle before Hon Judge Jordan and raised the objection that the dog was hers, and that the licence was in her name. Judge Jordan said: "That doesn't matter; when your husband married you he married your dogs as well." (Laughter). The dog was declared of a good character, and his Honour said that the state of the law compelled him to nonsuit her. As Mrs Brassington had paid 6s. into court the Judge suggested that this should be allowed as compensation to the plaintiff, who lost her husband in the Diglake colliery disaster. After some hesitation and some ironical observations Mrs Brassington agreed to forgo the return of the 6s (SA Nov 7 1896 p7 col 3).

Lewis, Rev JLD *Youngest vicar in England*. Vicar of Audley 1935-71 (Weekly Sentinel March 2 1979) (A p91).

Mitchell, Reginald J *Designer of Britain's most famous plane*. (1895-1937). He designed The Spitfire aircraft in the 1930s. Born Butt Lane; awarded CBE 1931; in 1951 a plaque was unveiled on his birthplace by Air Marshall R.I.I. Atherley, one-time holder of the world air speed record (SLM Nov 2005 p13) (TB March 16 2006 p24). *Royal Aeronautical Society Silver Medalist 1927*. Reginald Mitchell (TB March 16 2006 p24p). *Spitfire's maiden flight*. March 5 1936 (TB

Reginald Mitchell - Designer of Britain's most famous plane.

March 16 2006 p24). *World's oldest surviving Spitfire* is Spitfire K9942, built at
Eastleigh, Hants, in 1939. It went to RAF
Museum, Cosford, Salop, in Nov 2002
(TB Dec 12 2002 p25). *First Reginald
Mitchell Memorial Lecture* was The Ad-
vent of The Aircraft Gas Turbine by Air
Commodore F Whittle CBE, held in Oct
1946 at Victoria Hall, Hanley (ES Aug
26 2006 p5p). The *only-Potteries-born
lecturer* was Dr Arnold Green, ceramic
scientist, 1957 (ES March 27 2010 p25);
the *first female lecturer* was Mrs Margaret
Rule with Excavation and the Raising of
the Tudor Warship Mary Rose, 1983; the
lectures are run by Stoke-on-Trent Association of Engineers. For *Stoke-on-Trent's
other great aircraft designer* see John
'Jimmy' Lloyd, under Stoke-upon-Trent.
  Mining *North Staffordshire's worst-ever
mining disaster.* 155 men at the Minnie
Pit, Halmer End, mid Jan 1918; the last
body was not recovered until Aug 19
1919 (IANS p36) (LMV pp29-33) (ES
April 14 2006 p41). *Staffordshire's only
recipient of the Albert Medal for bravery.*
Perhaps William Dodd, Diglake Colliery
under-manager, for his part in the rescue
at the colliery 1895 (SVB p34). *'One of
the UK's biggest memorials'.* The Apedale
Memorial Pit Wheel in Apedale Country
Park, unveiled in 2004 (BBC news Sept
24 2004).
  Natural history *Highest ash tree in the
country.* Claimed by Richard Parrott of
The Talke Ash, which fell in c1683; it
could be seen from Delamere Forest and
most of the hills in Cheshire (SHC 1944
p62). *Very rare plant.* Common Navel
Wort (Cotyledon Umbilicus) found growing in rocks under Heighley Castle Bank
(SHOS vol 1 part i p102). *Strange but true!*
In an issue of the Staffordshire Advertiser
of the first two weeks of Feb 1796 it was
recorded 'A robin's nest with six eggs
was last week found near Audley, in this
county' (SA March 31 1888 p5 col 5). At
Wood Lane was grown a turnip in 1921
with six smaller turnips at its roots (SA
Oct 29 1921 p4p). *Audley Tandridge* had
a 2-year old filly belonging to T Wannop,
which won 1st prize in the Open Class for
Brood Mares and Shire Horse Society's
Silver Medal at the West Staffordshire
Shire Horse Society Show, 1918 (SA Sept
28 1918 p6p).
  Pepper, Mrs Frances M *Audley's villainess.* In 1936 when aged 46, of Church
Street, Wood Lane, she ill-treated and
bruised her three year old daughter,

Frances, born with a split lip and cleft pal-
ate. The NSPCC prosecuted Pepper and
Frances was taken into care (SA Feb 29
1936 p4 col 6).
  Place names Audley first appears in
Domesday Book, 1086, and means 'the
leah of Aldgyp'; Aldgyp is an Anglo-Saxon feminine name (PNSZ p95). *Unique
derivation for a surname.* Eardley will be
from Eardley in this parish (PDS).
  Poole, George William *Audley's hero.*
(1893-1955). Of Wesley Street, Wood
Lane, Bignall End, 2nd Lieut (Acting
Capt) South Staffs Regt, awarded M.C.
in King's Birthday Honours List 3 June
1919. After WWI he was a manager at
the Minnie Pit, and died in Anglesey (EL-
SONSS p62p).
  Poorest Audley workhouse, Alsager
Road, which succeeded an earlier workhouse, was built 1733. It started receiving inmates from May 1734. It was held
by the Trustee of the Audley Grammar
School until 1900, and became known as
Workhouse Farm (A pp43-46). After 1838
Audley poor, unable to support themselves, went to Newcastle Union workhouse on the south side of Keele Road,
Thistleberry.
  Population Audley was 28th= most-
populated Staffordshire parish in 1801
with 2,246 people; 25th in 1811 with
2,618; 25th in 1821 with 2,940; 25th in
1831 with 3,617; 23rd in 1841 with 4,474;
20th in 1851 with 5,180; 20th in 1861
with 6,494; 20th in 1871 with 8,955; 21st
in 1881 with 11,505; 21st in 1891 with
12,936; 21st in 1901 with 13,918. Audley
could be ranked 19th most-affected Staffordshire parish for loss of men in WW1,
with 219 lives lost.
  Quote *Choicest.* The Audley branch of
the Staffordshire Federation of Women's
Institutes in The Staffordshire Village
Book, 1988, said of their area 'Situated on
a southern spur of the Pennine Chain, the
village (Alsagers Bank) enjoys a view un-
rivalled for miles. To the west the fertile
plains of Cheshire, bisected by the M6.'
  Registers *Staffordshire's richest parish
register for uncommon Christian names.*
Audley (for instance Walburgis, Mirable,
Griffin, Kattorn, Euphemia, Audelia etc)
(Audley PR).
  Singing contests *Welsh National Ei-
steddfod winners 1933.* Talke o' th' Hill
Male Voice Choir, their winning (at
Wrexham) resulted in a change of rules to
ban English choirs from competing (ES
Your Week March 3 2007 p9). *Channel*

4's 'Operatunity' joint winner 2003. Denise Leigh (nee Moss) (b1972), native of Audley, blind opera singer (ES May 11 2004 p21pc).

Denise Leigh with her joint-winner, Jane Gilchrist, in the T.V. contest Operatunity 2003, on the sleeve of their album.

Schools *Staffordshire's longest school strike ever (probably)*. Audley School Strike which was a strike against reorganisation of schooling in Audley district lasting eight months 1938-9. It involved the transfer of senior children in Bignall End from Ravens Lane school (later Ravens Lane Primary) to Halmerend school (later Sir Thomas Boughey High School) and infants from Halmerend school to Alsagers Bank, Wood Lane, or Audley schools. On Aug 22 1938 there was a protest procession by parents from Bignall End through Audley, Ryehills and Miles Green to Halmerend, where a meeting was held with Col Rt Hon Josiah Wedgwood as principal speaker. Many parents were at length prosecuted by Staffs County Council (SA Aug 27 1938) (The Staffordshire Weekly Sentinel Aug 27 1938 p4. Sept 3 1938 p11p of Mr Bowers, with whom is Mr 'J' Riley Chairman of the Parents' Committee addressing parents & scholars) (Hooligans and Rebels. Stephen Hum-

phries). One of the first Co-operative business colleges in the UK. Sir Thomas Boughey High School, Halmerend (ES Nov 4 2009 p12).

Mr Bowers, headmaster of the Ravens Lane junior school (formerly a senior school) taking names of senior scholars, who presented themselves but were refused admission during the Audley School Strike - perhaps Staffordshire's longest school strike ever.

In late 2003, the Co-operative Group, the UK's largest co-

operative business, agreed to sponsor a number of secondary schools. Thomas Boughey School was one of the original seven schools - in the Group's six regions of England, together with an additional school in London - sponsored by the Co-operative in summer 2004 (Co-operative websites, 2009).

Societies *First meeting of the Audley Rifle Volunteers*. Took place on Dec 23 1859 at the National Schoolroom, Audley (SA Jan 14 1860 p5 col 4). *Last procession of the Audley Court of the Ancient Order of Foresters*. 1928 (NSFCT 1984 p20) (AHJ 1996 pp58-78).

Sport *First Audley Races*. Were held at Kent Hills on Friday before Aug 19 1854. The handicap hurdle race was won by Mr Ginders's horse. The Match Race was won by Mr Colclough's horse. The third stake was won by Mr William Goodall's horse (SA Aug 19 1854. SA Aug 20 1954 p2 col 3). *Record for playing competitive cricket*. 55 years in league matches by Aaron Lockett of Bignall End 1906-61 (ES Your Week Aug 5 2006 p9. May 2 2009 p23). *Represented England at cricket*. John Thomas Ikin (1918-81), born Bignall End, played for Staffs CC, and England 1946-55.

Normid *'the first of its kind in the country'*. A hypermarket, warehouses and services all under one roof built by The North Midland Co-operative Society Ltd (Normid), opened just off Jamage Road, Talke, in Spring 1975 (ES Oct 14 1975).

Village life *'Officially the prettiest village in the world'*. Audley for winning so many Best Kept Village competitions (ES Feb 2 2000 p15). *World in Bloom winner 1999, 2001, 2002, runner-up 2000. Britain in Bloom (National Urban Area) 1st Best Kept Village 1998, 2000; 2nd Best Kept Village 1999, 2001, 2002; 3rd Best Kept Village 1997. Britain in Bloom (Regional Urban Area) winner 1998, 1999, 2000, (Regional Gold Medal) holder 2002. Britain in Bloom Subaru Trophy for Exceptional Community Achievement 1997*. Audley; their 2001 World in Bloom (or called that year 'International in Bloom Challenge') win was the first time a contestant had won twice in the competition's history (ES Oct 1 1998 p1pc. Sept 28 2001 p9pc) (Audley Village Network website, 2009). *Staffordshire Best Kept Village Newcastle District (Large Village) winner 1999, 2004, (soul) winner in 2005: County winner (Small Village) 1999, 2002, Newcastle District (Small Village) winner in 1999,*

2001, 2002. Scot Hay: *Newcastle District (Large Village) winner 2002, 2003.* Wood Lane. *Potteries Community Pub 2000 and 2002.* Blue Bell Inn, Hardingswood, claiming the Potteries Pub Preservation Group's Titanic (Brewery) Trophy. *Longest unmade road in Staffordshire.* Perhaps The Drive, running from Alsagers Bank through Apedale to Chesterton; it led to Apedale Hall (AOPP pl 32).

B

Balterley Balterley was Staffordshire's 133rd largest parish (actually a township of Barthomley in Cheshire), consisting of 1,235 acres; 31st= farthest parish away from the county town, 19.1m NNW; extremist length 1.5m, making it 22nd= shortest parish in Staffordshire; extremist width 2m. The township's chief settlement is the rural scattered hamlet of Balterley. Balterley is famous for the superb C16 timber-framed house Hall o' th' Wood.
  Altitudes The highest point is 377 feet above Dean Brook. The lowest point is 197 feet on Cheshire border N of Betley Common.
  Church *All Saints* is one of 19 such county dedications (of AP churches); 4th last AP county church built dating from 1901 (if Balterley is accepted as an original parish!). *Only place of worship in Staffordshire in the Province of York.* Balterley chapel. *Only church vestry left unconsecrated in Staffordshire.* Balterley chapel, so the rector could smoke his pipe there (info Beryl Fox).
  Folklore *Balterley's best.* There is little, of course, owing to the small size of the township, except Doddlespool Hall, 1m SW of Balterley, built 1605, with additions made in blue and red brick in c1700, known locally as Toad's-pool Hall (BART p203).
  Geology Balterley township is Keuper Red Marls (W), Bunter (E). Barthomley township (entirely in Cheshire) is Keuper Red Marls.
  Hall o' th' Wood *'One of the most delightful black and white houses in the county'.* This rambling black and white timber-framed C16 hall lies half a mile east of Balterley. It was built by George Wood, a judge of Chester, in 1557 (BOE p65).
  Holland, Samuel *'the Miracle Mite'.* Born 1981. Of Mill Dale Farm, Deans Lane, who survived to celebrate a healthy first birthday weighing 18 lbs, despite being born 10 weeks premature, weighing only 4 lbs and with lungs not fully developed. He had an emergency baptism and 'died' for an astonishing 20 minutes, stunning medical experts he revived to spend five and half months in an incubator. In his first weeks he stopped breathing sometimes as often as twice a night (ES Nov 1 1982 p1p).
  Kelsall, William *Balterley's most famous old worthy.* (fl 1703). Of Hall o' th' Wood, Balterley. He produced a 700-page manuscript, dated 25th March 1703, on the kinship of people of Balterley and Audley, based entirely on the parish registers.
  Natural history *First nature reserve managed by Staffordshire Wildlife Trust.* Black Firs and Cranberry Bog, from Oct 10 1968. The Trust was then the Staffordshire Sites Committee (of the West Midlands Nature Conservation Trust). The first site they owned was Loynton Moss, Norbury, 1970 (Staffs Wildlife. No. 76 May 1999 p15). *Perhaps earliest date for cereal cultivation in the British Isles.* Cultivated cereal pollen of possibly c6000 to 5500 BC found in Black Firs relic basin mire (WSS p104). *'a walk with splendid views and shows rural England at its best'.* A figure of eight-shaped walk starting and ending at Barthomley contributed

Hall o' th'
Wood C16
mansion.

to The Sentinel in 2006 by Peter Matthews of the Staffordshire Area Ramblers' Association. It passes through Mill Dale, by Waggon and Horses Inn, Hall o' th' Wood, and Dean Brook (ES Your Week July 8 2006 p4. Aug 5 2006 p4).

Place name First appearance of the name 1004, and means 'Baldpryp's leah', but this Anglo-Saxon female name is otherwise unrecorded (PNSZ p100).

Poorest Since Balterley was a township of Barthomley parish, it used its workhouse. It existed in an unknown location by 1767 (Barthomley: The Story of an estate village. Robert Speake. 1995. pp228-9). After 1838 all Barthomley poor, unable to support themselves, went to Newcastle Union workhouse on the south side of Keele Road, Thistleberry.

Population Balterley could be said to be 130th most-populated Staffordshire parish entity in 1801 with 237 people; 131st in 1811 with 249; 133rd in 1821 with 242; 125th in 1831 with 305; 126th in 1841 with 316; 129th in 1851 with 299; 131st in 1861 with 281; 129th in 1871 with 273; 131th in 1881 with 253; 128th in 1891 with 273; 129th in 1901 with 253. Balterley could be ranked 110th= most-affected Staffordshire parish for loss of men in WW1, with six lives lost.

Quote *Choicest*. The historian of Barthomley, Rev Edward Hinchliffe, in his Barthomley: In Letters from a former Rector to his eldest son, 1856, writes 'Here is neither church, nor chapel, nor school.'

Tatham, Capt Basil Owen *Balterley's WW1 hero*. Son of Arthur Thomas Tatham of Doddlespool Hall, a director of Eley's Stafford Brewery Ltd. 3rd Battalion East Yorkshire Regt; killed in action during the second battle of Ypres, April 22 1915; awarded British War, Victory Medals and the 1915 Star Medal; he is commemorated on the Menim Gate, Ypres (Lest We Forget. Philip M Coops. 2003).

Barlaston Barlaston was Staffordshire's 114th largest parish, consisting of 2,184 acres; 58th closest parish to the county town, 9.5m N; extremist length 2.2m; extremist width 3.2m. The parish's chief settlement is Barlaston, a large residentially-desirable village on the edge of the Potteries. It is famous for The Wedgwood Factory.

Adams, Benjamin *Barlaston's longest serving vicar*. He held the cure by 1783 to 1834, serving at least 51 years. For most of this period he lived at Newcastle, com-

ing over to Barlaston every Sunday. During his last years he lived in an old house behind the Plume of Feathers Inn. Died 1834 (BAH p26).

Altitudes The highest point is Hartwell Hills at 738 ft. The lowest point is 295 feet by the Trent.

Anglo-Saxon *Last identified pagan burial in Mercia*. A rock-cut grave of an Anglian warrior of the C7 near Upper House, on ground above the village green, according Dr Philip Morgan's lecture 'Boundaries and their historical significance etc'. It was discovered in 1850, and the finds went to the British Museum (Border History Exploration Day report 2007 p7).

Barlaston Hall *One of the best examples of country villas pioneered by architect Sir Robert Taylor (1714-1788)*. Barlaston Hall, built 1756-8 (StE). *Rare phenomenon in England for a Palladian house*. The no gates, wall, or fence, and simply a stretch of lawn running back from the road for Barlaston Hall; on the E coast of America this landscaping is common (OVH pp64-65).

Church *St John the Baptist* (the redundant church by Barlaston Hall) is one of 11 such county dedications (of AP churches); 60th oldest AP county church dating from 1225. *In the churchyard* is the earliest appearance of 'The Potteries' on a gravestone 1794, on that of Jonathan Shelley, Barlaston churchyard (PNSZ p444). Also the grave of John Blunt, Prof. of Divinity at Cambridge, rebuilder of the church 1880s (SDOPP p64). Because of mining subsidence this church is now redundant, and the most interesting memorials in the new church in Station Road are to recent Wedgwood family members, including Camilla Hildegarde Wedgwood, anthropologist, daughter of 1st Lord Wedgwood d1955, and Adrian Charles Hamilton, son of Sir John Wedgwood drowned at sea in a storm off Sydney Harbour, Australia 1974 aged 26.

Davies, Howard *Olympic hockey player 1956, 1960, 1964 (Capt)*. Born 1933. Residing by The Green, Barlaston, in 2000s. In all, he gained 81 international caps, 41 playing for Britain and 40 with England. A fine all-round sportsman, he played cricket for Longton and Staffordshire in the 1950s (ES May 29 2010 p36p).

Dix, Henry *Head of the first year list at Saltley College 1888*. Youngest son of Thomas Dix, coachman to Mrs Brownfield of Hartwell Hall, was said to stand at the head of the first year list at Saltley College (St Peter's College?, Saltley, Birmingham, founded 1852), having gained a first class in scripture and several prizes (SA March 10 1888 p7 col 4).

Broughton-Adderley, Peter *He had the first portrait photograph relevant to a news story to appear in the Staffordshire Advertiser.* Born 1891. Of Barlaston Hall; in the edition of 5 October 1912 p10 to accompany a story about of his coming-of-age festival on Sept 30 1912.

Dickson, Ruth *First mayor of the present enlarged borough of Stafford.* Of Barlaston, in 1974 (ES Your Week May 20 2006 p11).

Folklore *Barlaston's best.* According to legend Madam's Bridge, a C17 brick bridge over the Trent below Tittensor, upstream from the present road bridge, was destroyed by a maiden, Miss Ann Aston of Parkfields, Barlaston, on Nov 15 1834 at night because she disapproved of two young ladies who were paying attentions to her bachelor brother and used the bridge to come to see him (NSFCT 1940 p34) (STM May 1964 p33).

The tale of Madam's Bridge.

Geology The centre of the parish is Upper Coal Measures; E and W extremities are Bunter.

Barlaston's villain - Leslie Green.

Green, Leslie *Barlaston's villain, last North Staffordshire person hung.* Chauffeur and handyman who murdered his employer's wife, Maud Alice Wilshaw at Estroil, Station Rd, on July 16 1952, in an attempt to steal £3,500 worth of jewellery; he was hung at Winson Green Prison, Birmingham, on Dec 23 1952 (ES Your Week Sept 2 2006 p9).

Griffiths, Philip H *Stock Exchange Challenge Cup winner 1951, Wimbledon Challenge Cup winner 1957, 2nd 1955.* Of Park Drive, Barlaston. Born Handsworth 1892. He represented Britain in marksmanship in the Olympics 1924, and at the Empire Games 1929, 1946; awarded DSM for service in East Africa in WW1, being one of a small party which rooted out the German cruiser 'Konigsberg' up Rufiji River 1915. When on tour with George VI in 1927 he was invited to compete in an Army Championship; thereafter he believed he was the only sailor to win an Army Championship. When asked by Staffordshire Advertiser how he got his practice in he answered laconically 'I never practice between competitions" Employed at Swynnerton Royal Ordnance Factory from 1955 (SA & Chron Feb 14 1957 pp1p,6 col 3).

Hand, Katherine *Barlaston's kindest.* (1672-1756). She has an unusual long eulogy in the parish register, which says she was a virtuous, benevolent farmer's daughter and shoemaker. She was the sister-in-law of James Stevenson with whom she resided at The Waste, and was commonly known as the Poetess.

Hargreaves, John *Most gossipy incumbent parish register entry-keeper in Staffordshire.* His explanatory footnotes, 1722-59, about person's characters are quite revealing; for instance 'Jonathan Shelley, of B. Victualer, aged 44; accidentally killed by the fall of a tree' Feb 11 1738.

Hill, George *Baked the best Hovis bread in the country 1904.* Born 1873. Barlaston village baker (originally of Lichfield?), who won a diploma in 1904 for making the best type Hovis in the country, scoring 96 points out of the possible 100 (SA July 9 1949 p7 col 3).

Lowe, Billy *Barlaston's hero.* He lost an arm and an eye in WW1, and had the honour of unveiling the war memorial on the village green, 1926. He lived in a cottage (since demolished) which adjoined the Duke of York Inn, Longton Road (info Ernest Hawkins) (Yesterday's Country Village. Henry Buckton. 2005 p179).

Morgan, Miss Susanna *Pioneer of savings banks.* Died 1856. Of Parkfields Cottage, Parkfields, by 1834. Formerly of Clifton, Bristol, in which city she helped found a savings bank. On her removal to Staffordshire she was mainly instrumental in founding a savings bank in Stone; perhaps, the Pirehill and Meaford Savings

Bank, 1818. She had taken an interest in savings banks 'when very few were established, and their advantages but little known, believing if the working-classes could be induced to commerce the work of saving' their lives would be enhanced (SA Feb 2 1856 p4 col 5) (White's Directory 1834, 1851).

Place-name Barlaston first appears in Domesday Book, 1086, and means 'Beornwulf's tun' (PNSZ p101).

Poorest There is no evidence for a Barlaston workhouse. After 1838 Barlaston poor, unable to support themselves, went to Stone Union workhouse.

Population Barlaston was 117th most populated Staffordshire parish in 1801 with 349 people; 116th in 1811 with 396; 109th in 1821 with 462; 106th in 1831 with 514; 99th in 1841 with 591; 97th in 1851 with 617; 95th in 1861 with 637; 91st in 1871 with 733; 81st in 1881 with 821; 85th in 1891 with 782; 84th in 1901 with 744. Barlaston could be ranked 67th worst affected Staffordshire parish for loss of men in WW1 with 24 lives lost.

Pugilism *Fancy that!* A man lost his life in a pugilist combat at Barlaston. The 'battle' took place between labouring men John Slaney and Richard Harvey in a field in the parish on Nov 2 1841. In the 43rd round Slaney was carried off in a state of 'insensibility' to the Sutherland Arms Inn at Tittensor (suggesting the site was near the Trent). There he languished until he died two days later. An inquest returned a verdict of manslaughter against Harvey, but he had absconded (SA Nov 13 1841 p4 col 3).

Quote *Choicest.* Charles Masefield (d1917) in his Staffordshire (Little Guide series), 1910, wrote 'Barlaston is a pleasant village which is fortunate enough to have retained, in spite of Inclosure Acts, its village green.' (Incidentally, his cousin John Masefield OM (1878-1967), Poet Laureate, is said to have stayed with the Warners at The Mount in Barlaston).

Village life *'one of the gems of rural England'.* Stated of Barlaston at a licensing session at Stone in 1939 by Mr F Livingston Dickson on behalf of 192 residents of Barlaston against the proposal for Sunday opening of The Duke of York Inn, as it would encourage day trippers (SA March 4 1939 p4 col 4). *'one of the prettiest (country lanes) to be found in Staffordshire'* 1948. The mile-long lane from Barlaston to Hartwell (SLM April 1948 p90). *One of 50 villages in England and Wales chosen to test for poliomyelitis 1952.* Barlaston, chosen by Staffordshire Health Dept in conjunction with the director of the Virus Reference Laboratory, on behalf of the Medical Research Council, to determine the distribution of the virus during epidemic and non-epidemic periods. Barlaston was selected in the 'positive' category, in view of the cases of poliomyelitis that had occurred there. 50 towns were also chosen (SA Dec 19 1952 p4 cols 2-3). *Staffordshire Best Kept Village County winner (Large Village category) 1979, 1980, 1984, finalist 1956, 2nd= 1985.* Barlaston; the certificates used to be displayed in the village library.

Wardle, James *The 'celebrated pedestrian'.* James Wardle of Barlaston, according to The Staffordshire Advertiser. He took on fellow 'celebrated pedestrian' Arthur Akers of Birmingham at Endon on April 2 1855 and lost. In his running style Wardle resembled the celebrated Sheppard of Birmingham. The locals in the Leek area supported Wardle 'for, on stripping, he was the theme of admiration' (SA April 7 1855 p4 col 6).

Webb, Agnete *Earliest person recorded in the parish register.* For her baptism on Nov 10 1573; she was the daughter of Robert and Ellen Webb.

Wedgwood Factory *First all-electric pottery in the country.* Wedgwood Factory, 1938 (Staffordshire County Handbook c1958 p135). *Largest pottery export order ever placed with one firm.* Order made to the firm in 1950 by the Roman Catholic Archbishop of Boston, U.S.A. Most Rev Richard J Cushing, for 250,000 10-inch decorated service plates in the celebrated ivory Queensware (with views of Rome by Giovanni Battista Piranesi, contemporary of Josiah I Wedgwood), to commemorate Holy year and raise funds for physically and mentally handicapped poor children (SA Nov 11 1950 p8 col 8). *First reigning British monarch to participate in a pottery process.* Elizabeth II when she tried her hand at turning a dish at the Factory on a visit in 1955 (ES Nov 21 2009 p25). *Wedgwood group's trading highest profit since firm's foundation to 1961.* £444,293 annual sales in 1961, since 1758 (SA & Chron March 15 1961 p1). *'one of the most modern facilities in the world for students and a team of designers'.* The design centre at Wedgwood, built 1968 (Staffs Illustrated April 1969. Staffs Scene). *Britain's highest paid* *company chief 1979.* Believed to be Sir Arthur Bryan, chairman of Wedgwood, on £64,000. For the following year (1980), he faced a pay cut after Wedgwood's profits fell from £1.68 million to £500,000 (E&S Aug 22 2009 p8). *'one of the world's largest manufacturers of ceramic tableware' 1980.* Wedgwood, with exports to more than 60 countries (SN July 25 1980 p55). *The greatest Wedgwood Museum in the World'.* Work began in 2006 at the Wedgwood Factory on what was thought to become the greatest Wedgwood Museum in the world, creating a home for a number of collections (SLM June 2006 p43). *Queen's Award for Industry 1966, 1971, 1976, 1980.* Wedgwood (SN May 14 1976, Business Newsletter p2. July 25 1980 p55). *Art Fund Prize winner 2009.* Wedgwood Museum. Worth £100,000, it is Britain's biggest arts prize (ES June 19 2009 p1).

Wedgwood Memorial College *Country's first residential adult education college.* Wedgwood Memorial College, Station Road, named in memory of the late Lord Wedgwood, due to open in early 1947 with accommodation for 28 full time students (SA Dec 7 1946 p5 col 7). *Longest continuous series of lectures in Staffordshire.* 24 hour-talkathon on Staffordshire history organised by the Staffordshire Guild of Historians at the Wedgwood Memorial College, in aid of saving the Sutherland Collection of papers for the county, 5-6 Sept 2005. *National homes of Esperanto Association of Britain (Esperanto-Asocio de Britio, 1904).* Esperanto House, an annex at the Wedgwood Memorial College, Station Rd, 2002-, in 2006. *Crufts Samoyed open bitch class winner 1955.* 'Pat', Champion Snowland Dorva, owned by Mr William E Lloyd of The Limes, Station Road, Barlaston. In addition, the dog also won a special prize for the best bitch. It was her 8th championship win and only two other bitches had won more championship certificates since the breed was introduced into this country in 1895. Mr Lloyd was the first warden of the Wedgwood Memorial College at its new present site in Station Road (info Ernest Hawkins) (SA & Chron Feb 17 1955 p1p).

Beech See Stone.

Betley Betley was Staffordshire's 131st largest parish, consisting of 1,463 acres; 42nd= farthest parish away from the county town, 17.7m NNW; extremist length 1.6m, making it 26th= shortest par-

ish in the county; extremist width 1.8m. The chief settlement is Betley, a pretty residentally-desirable linear village. Betley is famous for The Betley Window, a C16/C17 stained glass famous for showing early morris dancers. *One of the oldest parish registers in the country.* Betley's dates from 1537 (NSFCT 1917 p141).

Altitudes Highest point 492 feet on the E boundary at Sargents Wood. The lowest point is Betley Mere at 181 feet.

Church *St Margaret* is one of 4 such county dedications (of AP churches); 50th= last AP county church built dating from 1490. *Very first church restored by Sir Gilbert Scott.* Perhaps St Margaret's, restored 1842 (NSFCT 1917 p141). *Most curious memorial.* The east window is to the memory of Thomas William who was hit on the head and killed by a cricket ball on playing fields of Eton College 1902. *In the churchyard* the grave of Mary Malpas with an unusual accusation in the inscription:

THIS STONE
is erected by Subscription
To the Memory of
MARY MALPAS
the beloved Daughter of
JOHN & ANNE MALPAS
who at the early age of 15 Years
& 10 Months
was on the night of June 20th 1835,
most basely and cruelly murdered
in CHAPEL FIELD HUNSTERSTON.
by *THOMAS BAGGULEY.*
An elderly Married MAN
He escaped the punishment of
the law by adding his own
Death to that of his
INNOCENT VICTIM
Lone was the place and dark the midnight hour
Which gave sweet MARY to the Ruffians power
Stediest in faith and strong in virtue might
She fell a Martyr on that awfull Night
Now safe from sin and harm She rests secure
Among the blessed who in heart are pure.

For the renowned Staffordshire Art Thomas Peploe Wood (1817-45) to make a sketch of the grave shows the amount of publicity the case received. Today, some are trying to prove Bagguley's innocence (SP-t illus 2009) (info Mavis Smith).

Community co-operation *Oldest surviving image in England of Maypole dancing.* May be that on the C16 Betley Window, a famous stained glass window portraying 11 dancers of the C16 or C17 period long housed at Betley Old Hall and then at Betley Hall; the dancers themselves are believed to be those from the Betley Morris Dance (SCSF p17). *'one of the oldest (friendly societies) in the coun-*

The famous Betley window.

ty'. Betley Friend Society, which celebrated its anniversary on Whit Tuesday 1856 with a procession to the parish church (SA May 17 1856 p5 col 2). *'One of the country's oldest family shows'*. The Betley Show, held on the first Saturday in August since 1856 (ES Aug 4 2008 p2).

Eggerton, Randall *Person with the earliest-surviving will*. Of Wrinehill. Dated July 5 1518.

Folklore *Betley's best*. There is a rhyme that implies the natural ruggedness of the road passing through Betley is, if not created by God, then made by the devil.

Aidley, Madeley, Keele and 'Castle,
Huxon, Muxon, Woore and Asson
Rainscliffe rugged and Wrinehill's rough.
But Betley's the place where the devil came through.

(NSFCT 1886 p59) (M p29) (NSSG p7) (SCSF p166) (SJC pp2,3) (FOS p34).

Geology Betley village, S and E is Bunter; Betley Common is Keuper Red Marls.

Holdsworth, Lance Corp Frederick William *Betley's WW1 hero*. (1883-1918). School teacher, and church organist of White Cottage, Betley. Enlisted in the 11th Battalion Cheshire Regt 1915. Killed in action on April 20 1918 shortly after returning to the Front. Awarded the British War and the Victory Medals. There is also Pte George Bailey (d1918), also so awarded. He was born at Betley, son of a colliery banksman, but his family moved to Oldham, Lancs, when he was a child (Lest We Forget. Philip M Coops. 2003).

Ice Age *Southern most extent of the last Ice Age* reached Betley parish (BVC p12).

Jervis, James *Betley's villain*. A pointsman at Betley Road Station signal box, who when aged 34 on Dec 1 1888 killed, in an unaccountable frenzied attack, his wife, Sarah Ann aged 36, and two of his eight children, Harry aged four and Mabel aged 14 months, at his cottage. Having had a mind to take the lives of all his family Jervis died of wounds to the throat he had inflicted upon himself in the attack (DMF pp19-32).

Mills *Earliest recorded fulling mill in Staffordshire*. Betley, in the 1270s (HOS p42).

Old Wood *Property Robbie Williams bought for his mum as a thank-you*

present. The famous pop star of Burslem (see) bought this house beside Betley Hall lake in April 1999 for £975,000 as a thank-you present to his mother, Jan. The Williams' sold the property in Nov 2001 for £1.25 million. Coincidentally, the new owners were called Williams (ES Aug 31 2000 p13p. Nov 30 2001 p15).

Place name Betley first appears in Domesday Book, 1086, and means 'Betta leah'; Betta may not be a personal name (PNSZ p117). *Unique in England*. Are the names Betley, and Hand and Trumpet Inn, on The Main Road, Wrinehill (ES May 26 2000 p75).

Poorest Betley overseers' accounts for 1748 state 'For removing the poor from Betley to Audley poorhouse 12-0'; there are references to the poorhouse (at Betley?) 1767. In 1774 approval was given and progress made in building of two houses (for the poor) at Betley Common (BVC pp127-9). After 1838 Betley poor, unable to support themselves, went to Newcastle Union workhouse on the south side of Keele Road, Thistleberry.

Population Betley was 78th most-populated Staffordshire parish in in 1801 with 670 people; 74th in 1811 with 761; 69th in 1821 with 932; 75th in 1831 with 870; 77th in 1841 with 884; 80th in 1851 with 882; 83rd= in 1861 with 850; 83rd in 1871 with 826; 80th in 1881 with 821; 81st in 1891 with 827; 80th in 1901 with 837. Betley could be ranked 120th= worst affected Staffordshire parish for loss of men in WW1, with four lives lost.

Quote *Choicest*. Celia Fiennes in her Diary, 1698, wrote 'this town is halfe in Staffordshire and halfe in Cheshire one side of the streete in the one and the other in the latter, so that they often jest on it in travelling one wheele goes in Staffordshire the other wheele in Cheshire:'

Celia Fiennes passes through Betley, 1698.

Tollet, Elizabeth *'The new Newtonian woman'*. (1694-1754). Poet, and an acquaintance of Sir Issac Newton, she is remarkable for her interest in scientific investigation and natural philosophy; brought up in London, the eldest of three surviving children. From 1702-14 her father, George (d1719), served as Extra Commissioner of the Navy, and the family resided in the Tower of London; later she moved to her father's country seat Betley Hall, later returning to seats in the south of England. In 'The Microcosm' (1727 or later) she reveals her familiarity with the natural philosopher Robert Hooke's magnificent illustrations of the insects and plants he examined through a microscope. And in an elegy to Newton (1727) she summaries his experiment showing how light is refracted into coloured rays as it passes through a prism (History Today April 2009 pp52-58 ils) (quote from Mavis Smith, author of 'Ellen Tollet of Betley Hall: Journals and Letters from 1835. Mavis E Smith. 2008).

Tollet, George *Betley's most famous old worthy, Pepys said of him "a worthy gentleman, my friend Mr Tolot."* Civil servant. Secretary to the Commission in Public Accounts, 1691; Comptroller-General and Accomptant General for Ireland, 1691; Secretary to the Excise Commissioners, 1700; Extra Commissioner in the Navy Office, 1701/2. He lived near Samuel Pepys in York Buildings off The Strand, London, and was one of Pepys' pall bearers at his funeral: Pepys described him in his diary. He bought Betley Hall, later known as Old Hall Farm in 1718, and died about this time. His grandson, George of Betley (d1779) was the local antiquarian and bibliophile.

Tollet, Georgina *She proof read Darwin's 'On the Origins of Species by Natural Selection'.* (1808-72). Of Betley Hall, sister of George, for Charles Darwin, prior to its publication in 1859, by then she was residing at 14 Queen Anne Street, London; she had had an arm amputated in 1826 due to an abscess (Ellen Tollet of Betley Hall etc. Mavis E Smith. 2008 p219).

Turner, Sapper Cyril *Betley's WW2 hero.* (1919-1941). Of Common Lane, Betley. He saw action in Cyprus, before going to North Africa; missing in action during the Desert campaign; commemorated at the Alamein Memorial, Egypt; awarded the 1939-45 Star, the Africa Star and the 1939-45 War Medal (Lest We Forget. Philip M Coops. 2003).

Village life *Prettiest village in Stafford-*

shire. Betley, according to Edward John Littleton (1791-1863) of Hatherton Hall, MP for Staffordshire 1812-37 (SA Nov 24 1934 p10 col 4). *Only village in Staffordshire to have a boulevard.* Perhaps Betley (NSFCT 1886 p57). *Fancy that!* The county boundary ran through The Crown Inn, Den Lane, Wrinehill, until 1965. The bar lay in Staffordshire, whilst the smoke room lay in Cheshire. When time was called at 10.30pm in the bar to comply with Staffordshire licensing laws drinkers could decamp to the smoke room to continue drinking by Cheshire licensing laws until 11pm (info John Griffiths). *Good Pub Guide 2008's Best Staffordshire pub for food.* The Hand & Trumpet Inn, Wrinehill, winning their Staffordshire County Dining Pub of the Year award (ES Oct 16 2007 p7pc). *National home of the Cottage Garden Society,* founded 1982, Brandon, Main Road, Betley, in 2008.

Walwyn, Elizabeth *Earliest recorded person in the parish register.* Baptised Nov 24 1538. Daughter of Richard Walwyn.

Wicksted, Charles (formerly Tollet). *'second to none in all fox-hunting knowledge'.* (1796-1870). Son of George Tollet (d1855) of Betley Hall. He rode with the Tarporley Hunt from 1817. His poems on hunting still survive (The Green Collars: Tarporley Hunt Club and Cheshire Hunting History. Fergusson Gordon. 1993. pp458,459) (Ellen Tollet of Betley Hall, etc p10).

Blackbrook See Maer.
Blore See Tyrley.
Blurton See Trentham.
Blythe Bridge See Stone.
Broughton See Eccleshall.
Bucknall See Stoke-upon-Trent.
Burslem Burslem was Staffordshire's 86th largest parish, consisting of 3,122 acres; 60th= farthest parish away from the county town, 15.5m N; extremist length 2.2m; extremist width 4.2m. The parish's chief settlement is Burslem, the mother town of the Potteries. Burslem was famous for pottery making and its native Arnold Bennett, the novelist.

Altitudes Highest point is 787 feet to E of Woodhead. The lowest point is 400 feet by Fowlea Brook on the SW boundary.

Barratt, William James *First Mormon missionary in Australia.* (1823-89). Born Burslem. He converted to Mormonism possibly in 1839 when Latter Day Saint missionaries first preached in the town. Barratt's parents had already decided to emigrate there. Barratt arrived in Adelaide in Nov 1840, finding employment as a shepherd's cook in Mount Barker. He tried preaching, and was successful in baptising a few people, but quickly became discouraged at the moral tone of the settlers. Shortly, after 1842 he lost interest in Mormonism and became involved in the Congregational church in Encounter Bay; the leadership of the movement then passed to others. Barratt became a prominent landowner in the Bald Hills and Inman Vallery areas of South Australia (info Katherine Cartwright, 2009) (Wikipedia, from various sources including BYU Studies, vol 28, no. 3 (June 2007) pp53-66).

Baskeyfield, Lance-sergeant John (Jack) Daniel *Burslem's hero.* VC, born on Nov 18 1922 in Burslem. Of Carson Road, Stanfield. Butcher, later serving in the Staffordshire Regiment and was posthumously awarded the V.C. for heroically manning an anti-tank gun at Oosterbeck in the battle of Arnhem in WW2 on Sept 20 1944. In spring 1969 a film entitled 'Baskeyfield V.C.' was shown at the Manchester Film Theatre. On Sept 20 1969 a plaque to his memory was unveiled in the Market Square Gardens, Burslem. In 1996 a bronze statue of Baskeyfield was unveiled at Festival Heights.

Bennett, Arnold *Greatest West Midlands writer, Burslem's most famous old worthy, Novelist of The Potteries.* (1867-1931). Born Burslem, as polled in

Arnold Bennett - The West Midlands' greatest writer.

a competition for the first Regional Wall of Fame in Birmingham's City Plaza (ES March 27 2006 p12). *His first published article* was in the Sentinel 1887 (ES Your Week July 29 2006 p9). *Longest novel by an English writer to 1927.* Old Wives Tale (1908); in 1927 it was surpassed in length by Francis Brett Young's 'Love is not Enough' (Francs Brett Young: A Bi-

ography. JB Young. 1962 p150). *His only film script which reached the screen.* The silent 'Piccadilly', 1929 (ES Your Week June 3 2006 p11). First annual dinner of the Arnold Bennett Society was in 1956 (ES Your Week March 25 2006 p8). *First Arnold Bennett Memorial Lecture.* 1990, given by John Wain (d1994), poet and novelist of Newcastle under Lyme, whose final work was '(Dr) Johnson is Leaving', the preface of which he completed just days before he died (ES Dec 7 1994) .

Bennett, Sarah *Perhaps first woman to stand for an elected council in the Potteries.* She stood at the Burslem Borough council elections in November 1907 (POTP p32).

Bennions, George Herman 'Ben' *'one of the leading Battle of Britain Spitfire pilots', one of the first pilots to have plastic surgery by the pioneer of plastic surgery Sir Archibald McIndoe.* (1913-2004). Born Burslem. RAF Squadron Leader. On Oct 1 1940, the day he was awarded the Distinguished Flying Cross he was severely burnt by an enemy shell exploding in his cockpit. At Queen Victoria Hospital, East Grinstead, he received the pioneering plastic surgery (Wikipedia 2008).

Bowling *Record score for a single game of ten pin bowling.* 300 by Albert Kirkham, 34, of Burslem, on Dec 5 1965 (GBR 1970 p241. 1981 p248).

Cemeteries *'one of the most beautiful in the country'.* A journal on Burslem Cemetery. It opened 1879, on about 28 acres on the east side of Sneyd Hill Park (ES Sept 15 2008 p14).

CHURCHES St John the Baptist is one of 11 such county dedications (of AP churches); 49th last AP county church built dating from 1536. *A notable thing* are two pieces of pottery taken out of tomb of Enoch Wood, both modelled by Enoch Wood: i) The Representation of Rubens's 'The Descent from the Cross' 1772, ii) Figure of Our Saviour. *In the churchyard* are the graves of Elizabeth de Aldithley (d1400), wife of the 5th Lord Audley, originally at Hulton Abbey, and Molly Leigh d1748, aligned North-South because she was a reputed witch.

Holy Trinity Nile Street. Built in 1852; the last service was in 1956. It was demolished in 1959.

Holy Trinity *'architecturally one of the nicest churches in the Potteries' 1959*, according to Rural Dean of Stoke, Preb Jesse Howse. The congregation was transferred to St Werburgh's, Hamil Road, which was reconsecrated as the church of the Holy Trinity, Sneyd, in 1958 (VCH vol 8 p124).

St Paul at Dale Hall, was built in 1831, demolished 1974. *'an outsize hot dog stall'* is how historian Bill Morland described the new St Paul's (TWWW Nov 1 2008 p16).

Clowes, William *'The Evangelist of the Fields'.* (1780-1851). Born Ball Bank, Burslem, has been described as 'one of the most successful evangelists in religious history' (KES p52). His followers, with those of Hugh Bourne, began the Primitive Methodist movement in 1811.

Community co-operation *First prize at the Crystal Palace Competition 1884.* Burslem Tonic Sol-fa Choir, winning £20 (SA review of the year 1884). *Oldest surviving Freemason lodge in Staffordshire 1917.* St Martin's Lodge, Burslem, No. 98, founded by at least 1817; the only other oldest lodge by 1917 was Noah's Ark, Tipton (SA Dec 29 1917 p7 col 7). *First meeting of the Burslem Rifle Volunteers* took place on Nov 11 1859 (SA Jan 14 1860 p5 col 4). *5th oldest St John Ambulance Brigade division in the British Commonwealth 1954.* Burslem Division; it grew out of the first public first-aid classes held in the Potteries in the Victorian era (SA March 12 1954 p4 col 5).

Cycling *National cycling endurance record holders.* Thomas Francis Finney (1947-2008), of Murhall Street, Burslem, with a team, who achieved 1,441 miles in 24 hours in 1980. The record still stood in 2008 (ES Aug 13 2008 p11).

Darts *Captain of the first England ladies' darts team 1977, Swedish Open ladies champion 1978, 1979, 1980, 1981, Denmark Open ladies champion 1980, 1981, 1982, 1983, World Cup Ladies pairs champion (with Audrey Derham) 1983, Pacific (Aus) Masters ladies winner 1986.* Maureen Flowers, grew up at the Foaming Quart Inn, Burslem; UK's number one as soon as women's rankings were announced; after retirement from darts in 1988 she went on to run the Crafty Cockney Inn, Smallthorne, with her then partner, darts legend Eric Bristow. She has been landlady at the Sneyd Arms Hotel, Tunstall, from 1991; entered U.S. Darts Hall of Fame, Martinsburg, West Virginia, 1996 (The North Staffordshire Magazine. Feb 2008. p120).

Dawson, Scott *Brain of Britain runner-up 2007* when he was aged 29, of Dartmouth Street, Burslem. This is a BBC Radio 4 general knowledge quiz (ES Jan 7 2008 p12pc).

Education *First school to offer midday meals for children during the pottery strike in the 1890s* was Hill Top Boys' Board School (POTP p24).

Endurance *World record for drinking ale upside down.* Richard Stanley (b1945), who drank a record 2 pints of ale in 22 seconds upside down at Barons Disco in Market Place (Co-op Travel agency in 2007) where he was a doorman in 1974 (Book of Alternative Records) (ES Sept 5 1974. Your Week July 7 2007 p9p).

Fellows, Roy *Man who drove back to Burslem from Singapore 1958.* Of Burslem, in an American army jeep (Four Wheels and Frontiers. Roy Fellows. 2008).

Finney, Samuel *First Labour Party candidate in the Potteries.* Miner and trade union official, returned for Burslem 1918 (HOS 1998 p84).

Fishing GF Butter and F Hall, anglers of Burslem, achieved a unique feat in the season leading up to spring 1904 when they caught a quarter of a ton of pike in 12 days, totalling a weight of 566 lb, in the presence of an appointed referee (SA March 19 1904 p5 col 5).

Folklore *Burslem's best.* The story of the witch, 'Molly' Margaret Leigh (1723-48), whose chest tomb in St John's churchyard, lies on a N-S axis. According to tradition she had a smallholding at Jackfields, east of Burslem; sold milk and butter; was ridiculed for being very ugly and consequently never attended church; was an outcast. After being buried on April 1

St John's churchyard. Molly Leigh's chest tomb is to the right by the church.

her ghost appeared in the churchyard and at her cottage where it was found knitting by the fire mumbling to itself
'Weight and measure sold I never,
Milk and water sold I ever.'
To lay the ghost, Burslem vicar, Rev Thomas Spencer, embarked on an elaborate exorcism service involving her re-inter-

ment and a caged blackbird placed in her coffin. Ever since, Burslem children have challenged each other to chant a jingle whilst walking round her tomb

'Molly Leigh, follow me
Molly Leigh, follow me'

(MMM p71) (TFTP pp14-18 il). In recent years the story has been totally revised by historian, Andrew Dobraszczyc, who shows through documentary evidence her reputation was deliberately tarnished by her stepfather in order to reverse her will and prevent her estate being bequeathed to the poor in Burslem.

Fradley, Sarah *She had one of Stafford-shire's last wills proved in the bishop's consistory court*. Of Burslem. Her will, and three others at Leek and Longton, was proved on Jan 9 1858. Wills on and from Jan 12 1858 were proved in a civil District Probate Registry.

Gambling *Biggest football pools win by 1986*. One of £937,807 for a 36p stake on Littlewoods Pools won by Dennis Turner of Burslem on April 13 1985 (GBR 1986 p258).

Geology Burslem town and W is Upper Coal Measures containing Etruria Marl and purple-coloured sandstones: the east side of the parish is Middle Coal Measures; the east tip is Millstone Grit.

Hales, Harold Keates *Model for Arnold Bennett's 'The Card', first to drive in a motor car non-stop between London and Edinburgh.* (1868-1942). Motor agent, early aeroplane owner, shipowner, politician. Moved to Burslem in childhood. He claimed himself he was the original of Bennett's 'The Card', and asked for royalties; Bennett replied that Hales should pay him for the free publicity he had enjoyed (POTP pp109-110). He possibly achieved the motoring feat with JW Stocks, a well-known motorist, from Friday 4.17pm on Feb 26 to 5pm on Saturday Feb 27 1904, covering just over 402 miles (SA March 5 1904 p7 col 7).

Headquarters *National home of the Federation of Worker Writers & Community Publishers (FWWCP, 1976)*. Burslem School of Art, Queen Street, Burslem, in 2008.

Health *First in world to prove link between smoking and Rheumatoid Arthritis*. Doctors at Haywood Hospital, Stanfield, noting smokers who develop RA develop it much more seriously than non-smokers (Sentinel Sunday Nov 19 2006 pp1,4).

Heath, Noah *Burslem's poet*. Of Sneyd Green. His 'Miscellaneous Poems' vol 1

1823 and vol 2 1829 were declared by Rupert Simms in his Bibliotheca Staffordiensis (1894) as very rare (BS p219).

Housing *Smallest occupied dwellings in the Potteries*. Some 19th Century cottages in Sneyd Street, demolished 1956 (TWWW in the 1950s p74p). *First Burslem brick house built*. Brick House St John's Square, early C17 (VCH vol 8 p117). *Potteries' oldest terraces*. One-storey brick cottages between Orme and Reid Streets, south side of Newcastle Street, Middleport. Existing by 1777, they were not built for canal navvies, as legend has it. In the 1880s they were converted into the present shops (info Andrew Dobraszczyc, 2009). *First North Staffordshire community housing for elderly tenants*. Barratt Gardens, Leek Road, Milton 1955, named after Burslem philanthropist William George Barratt (d1962) who had them built (ES Your Week March 25 2006 p11).

Hughes, Fred *Made the longest continuous talk in Staffordshire*. Born c1938. Of High Lane, Burslem. Former policeman; journalist, local historian, and author of *'the first book to be dedicated solely to the history of Burslem'* - 'Mother Town' (2000). He spoke for 12 hours on Burslem history at the Ceramic shop in Burslem on Whitsun weekend May 2006, raising £170 for charity (ES Oct 13 2000 p12p. May 30 2006 p15).

Hulme, Thomas *Last Chief Bailiff and first Mayor of Burslem*. (1808-84). Draper. He served as Chief Bailiff to 1878, when Burslem was incorporated as a borough.

Hulton Abbey *Poorest of the three Staffordshire Cistercian houses*. Hulton Abbey (VCH vol 3 pp235-237). *First skeletal remains of a Medieval executed person identified*. Sir Hugh Despenser the Younger, gay lover of Edward II, executed as a traitor in 1326. The remains were uncovered from a burial site at Hulton Abbey in the 1970s. They were pronounced to be probably his in 2008 after accumulative evidence: the manner of execution, carbon-dating of the bones, the fact that Hulton forms part of the estate of Sir Hugh's brother-in-law, Hugh Audley, and that only Sir Hugh's head, a thigh bone and a few vertebrae were returned to his wife (and these are the bones missing from the Hulton skeleton) (Daily Telegraph Feb 18 2008 p3).

Jones, Rev Christine *First Methodist minister to give birth* when she gave birth in July 1981; of Abbey Hulton (ES Your

Week July 8 2006 p11).

Maps *First map of Burslem* was one which tried to show how Burslem looked c1700. It was commissioned by Enoch Wood (d1840), pottery manufacturer, and made by a surveyor called McPhail, 1816. Various copies of it have been passed off as predating this map (Andrew Dobraszczyc, 2008).

Mason, Jim *Only North Staffordshirian to referee a FA Cup Final*. Of Burslem, at Crystal Palace, 1909 (ES Your Week Jan 20 2007 p9).

Mining *'a Million to One Chance' mining fatality*. When one of the picks on the jib of a coal-cutter caught the end of a metal crossbar supporting the roof at West Cockshead Seam of No. 4 Pit at Sneyd Colliery on Aug 9 1937. The bar was displaced and swung round and hit William Embury, a 31-year old coal cutter's assistant of Mill Hayes Road, Burslem, on the head. He later died of a fractured skull (SA Sept 25 1937 p11 col 5). *First pit to stage an underground open day for miners' families*. Sneyd Colliery at Sneyd Green, 1950 (ES Your Week July 1 2006 p11).

Mormons *Staffordshire's first branch of Mormons*. Burslem branch, set up 1839; the driving force behind it came from local potter, Alfred Corden, who converted to the movement at the Manchester branch. He was the first president of the Staffordshire Conference of Mormons (the Conference dissolved in 1869) (info Catherine Cartwright. Jack Leighton Seminar, Keele University. 2009).

Oatcakes *Burslem's first oatcake shop* was a small cottage on the west side of St

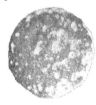

The North Staffordshire oatcake is at least 9 inches in diameter, crepe-like, and almost entirely unknown outside this district. It has been called a 'Tunstall tortilla,' 'a Potteries poppadom', a 'clay suzette' and an 'oat flannel'. Its origins are said to lie in Colonial India. Staffordshire soldiers who served there had the local flat-bread, and tried to duplicate on their return. The main ingredients are oatmeal and wholewheat, then cooked on a well-greased griddle, orginally placed on a bakestone. The Hole in the Wall Oatcake Shop in Hanley claims North Staffordshire oakcakes are *Britain's longest surviving food industry proper*.

John's Square in the earlier C19. A picture of it appears in the Warrillow Collection in Keele University. In 1884 it was replaced with the present shop, which in 2009 was occupied by the ladies clothes outlet 'What Women Want' (Burslem: Georgian Pottery Town. Andrew Dobraszczyc. 2009). See also Trentham (Sweets).

Oclott, Thomas and **Alice Wattson** *Earliest people recorded in the parish register*. For their marriage on Dec 16 1578.

Oliver, Dr Thomas Milward *Burslem's villain*. (1769/70-97). He shot dead John Wood at his house on Jan 27 1797 in reprisal for Wood's attempt to terminate the relationship between Oliver and Wood's daughter, Maria. Oliver had come to Burslem in c1792 to be partner to Dr Hickman and after being prevented from seeing Maria had gone to her house intending to commit suicide with a gun but instead shot Wood. Oliver was hung on Aug 28 1797.

The shooting of John Wood by Dr Thomas Milward Oliver of Burslem.

Place-name Burslem first appears in Domesday Book, 1086, and means 'estate in the district called Lyme belonging to a fort-guardian' or 'estate in the district called Lyme belonging to Burgweard' (PNSZ p163). *First record of Burslem as a surname*. Thomas Burslem in 1416; the first in Burslem itself was John Burslem, a foreman of the local court, temp Elizabeth I (ES Aug 18 2008 p14).

Poorest There was a workhouse at Burslem by 1741, with a capacity of 60 in 1775. A new workhouse was built at Greenhead in 1780. It was enlarged in 1835 to hold up to 300 inmates. It was later a barracks, and a pottery until demolished in 1958 (VCH vol 8 pp129-30) (WITP p11 fig 8). From 1838 Burslem entered Wolstanton Poor Law Union at Chell.

Population Burlsem was 6th in 1801 with 6,578 people; 5th in 1811 with 8,625;

7th in 1821 with 10,176; 8th in 1831 with 12,714; 9th in 1841 with 16,091; 9th in 1851 with 19,725; 9th in 1861 with 22,327; 9th in 1871 with 27,108; 11th in 1881 with 28,249; 11th in 1891 with 32,767; 9th in 1901 with 40,234.

PORT VALE FOOTBALL CLUB

The badge of Port Vale Football Club.

General. *First HQ of Longport Football Club.* Port Vale House, Scott Lidgett Road, Longport, in 1876. *Man who scored a hat-trick in a Staffordshire Cup-tie.* Billy Beats born Wolstanton (1871-1939), against Wolves, when playing for Port Vale, who he joined in 1891 (TB Oct 18 2007 p31). *Last surviving player of Vale's first recognised team.* Tom Hodgkinson (1861/62-1945); he played at Longport in the 1870s (ES March 14 2009 p25). *First player in two teams at the same time in a National football fixture.* Jimmy Oakes who played for Vale and Charlton Athletic in April 1933; the first meeting between the clubs was abandoned. When the match was played again Oakes had been transferred to Charlton (ES Your Week April 22 2006 p11). *Former player who died in the Munich air crash 1958.* Harold 'Donny' Davies, born Pendleton, Salford 1892, played for Vale in the 1914/15 season; sports reporter for the Manchester Guardian on the flight with Manchester United when their plane crashed in the snow at the stopover at Munich going to play Red Star Belgrade (ES Feb 5 2009 p35p). *Player who became a Methodist minister* was Norman Hallam, who gave up football in the late 1940s (ES April 11 2009 p27). *First champions of the Football League new Fourth Division.* Port Vale, 1958, comprising the lower ranking clubs from the old Third Divisions North and South (ES Sept 27 2008 p27). *Giant Killers' Cup holders 1962.* Port Vale; this was a short-lived trophy, awarded for their FA Cup exploits (ES Oct 10 2009 p25). *Greatest number of appearances in Association Football for Ireland by 1969.* 56 by Billy Bingham (a player for Sutherland, Luton, Everton, and Port Vale) (GBR 1969 p311). *UK's first children's centre built in a football stadium.* A one stop shop for children in partnership with Stoke CC due to

open at Port Vale from in March 2008. It will form part of the Lorne Street Stand (ES Sept 22 2007 p15). *Only Port Vale player to appear in an England team.* Ray King, goalkeeper, who played for England B against Switzerland at Basle in 1954 (ES Your Week. June 30 2007 p9). *World's oldest football coach 2006.* Ivor Powell (c1917-2010), when aged 90; he had managed the club for six months in 1951 (GBR) (ES May 27 2010 p12).

Ivor Powell aged 90.

Club Records *Record transfer deal* was when Vale signed two Liverpool players, Stan Polk and Mick Hulligan for £10,000, 1948 (ES Your Week July 29 2006 p9). *Record crowd* was when 6,000 filled the stands at Vale Park in Feb 1954 for the cup-tie against Blackpool, because tickets were on sale at the turnstiles (ES Oct 11 2008 p27). *Port Vale's official ground record* is 49,768 spectators on Feb 20 1960 when Aston Villa won 2-1 at Vale Park in the 5th round of the FA cup (ES Sept 26 2009 p25). *Worst match* was perhaps when Vale lost 7-1 at home to Nottingham Forest Feb 2 1957 (ES Your Week Aug 26 2006 p7). *'Club's greatest servant'.* Roy Sproson who made 837 appearances over 30 years and managed the club 1974-77, according to Michael Baggaley in The Sentinel May 27 2010 p46). *Longest-serving manager in C20* was John Rudge, born Wolverhampton, who served 1980-99 (BBC internet site: Stoke & Staffordshire).

Pots and Potters *Largest piece of porcelain ever made 11-foot.* Earth Vase produced by William Brownfield & Son, Cobridge, exhibited in Paris, 1889 (ES Your Week April 8 2006 p11). *Most famous piece of pottery made by the Hill Pottery.* Copy of the Vase of Lecythus discovered by his Royal Highness, the count of Syracuse (SHST pp657il,658,659). (OTP pp92-93). *Inventor of a cup and bowl making machine, and pottery drying appliances.* Thomas Willett, born Burslem 1847, founder of the firm of Messrs Thomas Willett and Co in Liverpool Road, Burslem, retired in 1917, and was still living in 1938 (SA March 19 1938 p4 col 6). *First Florian ware* was developed by William Moorcroft (d1945), a Burslem potter (POTP p158). *Best-known work of Clarice Cliff (1899-1972)* was for the Newport Pottery. *Only person Jacob Epstein, a sculptor, allowed to copy his work for the pottery industry.* Jessie Van Hallen of George Wade & Sons of Burslem (ES Your Week Aug 5 2006 p9).

Pottery *Greatest pottery centre in Staffordshire.* Burslem, according to Dr Plot (NHS p422). *'Mother of the Potteries'* *'The Mother of the Potteries'.* Reference to Burslem, being the oldest of the pottery towns, the expression was occurring by 1884 (SA June 21 1884. June 23 p12 col 5) (KES p50). *Burslem's oldest potteries.* Knowle Works, west end of Hamil Road, can be traced back to 1651 (VCH vol 8 p132); Overhouse Manufactory Wedgwood Street, in existence by c1700; Brickhouse Works, on the site of the Wedgwood Memorial Institute (VCH vol 8 p117) (NSSG p6). *First works bell in the Potteries.* At Brickhouse Works. *Architecturally one of the most ambitious industrial buildings anywhere in the country.* Royal Pottery, Westport Road. *"the wonder of the Pottery Industry"* Moorcroft Factory, Sandbach Road, Cobridge, when built 1913, for its innovative modern layout - the single storey, skylights but no windows, use of steel girders (Andrew Dobraszczyc on a social history walk, May 2007). *'the 'Model Pottery' of Staffordshire'.* Middleport Pottery, Port Street, Middleport, built for Burgess & Leigh pottery company in 1888-9. 'A Graphic Description of the Potteries' (1893) described the building thus 'What may be styled the 'Model Pottery' of Staffordshire...' (info Andrew Dobraszczyc, 2009). *Last pottery in the world to use underglaze transfer printing from engravings.* Burgess, Dorling & Leigh Pottery, Middleport, as claimed by Michael Aspel on BBC's Antiques Roadshow Sept 2007, after Wedgwoods ceased the process earlier in 2007 (info William Dorling, and Ian Dale of Wedgwood).

Pubs *Burslem's oldest house* is probably the Red Lion Inn (VCH vol 8 p110). *Burslem's oldest inn* is reputedly Mitre Inn, Pitt Street, in existence as an inn by the C16 (ES Oct 16 1995 p8). *Burslem's most important inn c1770-1830.* The Legs of Man Inn, north side of Market Place. Also the town's first coaching inn, shutting down in the 1840s (Burslem: Georgian Pottery Town. Andrew Do-

braszczyc. 2009). *'The Savoy of the Midlands'.* Reference to The Leopard Inn, Market Place, Burslem, which became Burslem's principal inn from c1830 (BBC Stoke & Staffordshire website, June 2007). *Burslem's most haunted place 2009.* The Leopard Inn, after ghost hunters found an angry, aggressive spirit there; one ghost hunter was possessed by a growling man. The incident was caught on film and the footage shows the ghost hunter's face becoming distort as the spirit inhabited his body (ES Feb 7 2009 p6). *Potteries Community Pub 2004 and 2005.* Bulls Head Inn, Burslem, claiming the Potteries Pub Preservation Group's Titanic (Brewery) Trophy.

Quote *Choicest.* Arnold Bennett wrote in his most acclaimed novel, The Old Wives' Tale., 1908, 'Bursley (Burslem) has the honours of antiquity in the Five Towns. No industrial development can ever rob it of its superiority in age, which makes its absolutely sure in its conceit..'

Riley (perhaps Kilkenny), Vincent *Potteries' greatest drunk.* He made hundreds of court appearances, nearly all for drunkenness. In 1937, when of no fixed abode, he was charged and convicted - for the 155th time by Hanley magistrates - with being drunk and incapable on his way to London

Vincent Riley in his later years.

to see the Coronation, having been only discharged from prison a few weeks earlier. He was fined 40s with an alternative of one month's imprisonment. He died in 1951 perhaps overcome by fumes while spending a night in Sneyd Brick Works, Nile Street, Burslem, with a record of more than 300 convictions for drunkenness. In good weather the police would bed him down for the night, inebriated, in a Hanley graveyard, so that he'd have an awful shock when he awoke among gravestones (SA May 8 1937 p5 col 1) (TWWW in the 1950s p8p) (Vincent Riley, The Life of a Meth-Elated Spirit. Fred Glen) (ES Feb 10 2001 p18p. Nov 23 2002 p23p. Your Week Sept 25 2004 p10p).

Slater, Harriet *First woman appointed a party whip in the House of Commons.* MP for Stoke North (ES Your Week Aug 5 2006 p9).

Swimming *Northern Counties Championship Polo winners 1946.* Burslem Swimming Club (ES Your Week March 17 2007 p9).

Theatre *Longest running North Staffordshire operatic society.* The North Staffordshire Operatic Society, founded 1892, whose first productions were at Queen's Theatre; Stoke-on-Trent Amateur Operatic Society was founded in 1896 (ES April 6 2006 p11). *World's longest-running gang show.* The Potteries scouts production of Screamline, from 1934 to present; staged at Burslem (Queen's Hall) 1934-1950s, 1964-, Hanley 1950s-64. Girls first joined the cast in 1980s (ES Your Week Oct 28 2006 p5p). *Royal Doulton Choir's smallest audience for a performance.* One, Princess Elizabeth (later Elizabeth II), who listened to a recital alone, when visiting the Potteries 1949 (ES Your Week Feb 24 2007 p5).

Transport *First sod cut of the Trent and Mersey Canal.* Occurred at Brownhills by Josiah Wedgwood I, July 26 1766 (NSFCT 1938 p60). *First horse-drawn trams in the Potteries* was introduced by George Francis Train between Hanley and Burslem in 1862 (ES Your Week April 22 2006 p11). *First garage in the Potteries* was reputedly, that built by HK Hales of Burslem in late C19 (POTP p109). *The warship named after Burslem* was the H.M.S. Burslem, launched 1918 (SA Sept 21 1918 p7 col 6).

Unwyn, George *Burslem person with the earliest-surviving will.* It is dated April 26 1537.

Walker, Roger *First Staffordshire man to be elected chairman of the British Legal Association.* (1932-99). Solicitor with Abberley and Walker, Burslem (ES Your Week Oct 28 2006 p9p).

Ward, John *Burslem solicitor who had an ancient fish fossil named after him.* (1781-1870). Born Leics. Author History of the Borough of Stoke-upon-trent etc 1844, and fossil hunter, having the Acanthodes Wardi named after him (ES Your Week Jan 20 2007 p9).

Whieldon, Edward *Burslem's longest-serving vicar.* He served for 39 years, 1811-50.

Williams, Robbie *20th greatest sexiest celebrity of all time* (Channel 4 TV Feb 24 2007), *world's sexiest man.* Of Stanfield, pop musician, 1999 and 2000; by 2002 he had more BRIT (British Record Industry Trust) awards than any other

artist or act (info Hanley Library) (The Encyclopaedia of Popular Music. Colin Larkin. 1998) (ES May 31 2000 p4p) (GBR 2002 p36). He had the *best UK Solo Album Chart Show* with five successive Number Ones on the UK album chart. The albums released between Sept 1997 - Nov 2002 are: Life Through A Lens 1997; I've Been Expecting You 1998; Sing When You're Winning 2000; Swing When You're Winning 2001; Escapology 2002. One of his songs is called 'Burslem Normals'. From 1 Jan 2000 - 31 Dec 2003 he sold 5,608,000 albums in the UK - more than any other UK album act. He has also won a record 14 BRIT awards (GBR 2005 p193). He had the *most albums to reach No. 1 in the UK by a British male solo artist* when his album 'Rudebox' topped the UK charts on Nov 4 2006, giving him his 8th No. 1 as a solo artist - equalling a record set in 1983 by David Bowie (GBR 2008 p179).

Robbie Williams - Staffordshire's greatest pop star.

Wood, Enoch *'Father of the Potteries,' 'Father of 'The Mother of the Potteries''.* (1759-1840). Pottery manufacturer of Burslem. The first claim was made by Frank Falkner in his 'The Wood Family of Burslem' (1912) p6 by reason of his sterling character, his sincere lover for local lore, and his long life devoted to the Art of Potting. The second claim was made by historian Andrew Dobraszczyc at a lecture in 2008, considering Wood was the first promoter of Burslem as the oldest, or Mother, town of the Potteries, in its C19 rivalry with Hanley, for which cause Wood collected a great deal of historical material.

Wood, Levison *Burslem's bravest.* When aged 50, of Prospect Street, Burslem, he saved a blind man from drowning in the canal at Middleport. Albert Llewellyn, 37, employed at the workshops for the blind at Shelton, left his Burslem lodging house to visit friends at Middleport on Dec 30 1928, lost his way and walked into the canal. Mr Wood, a rheumatism sufferer, at the Bridge Inn, nearby, came to his assistance (Staffordshire Weekly Sentinel Jan 5 1929 p10p).

Burston See Stone.

Butterton See Trentham.

C-D

Chapel Chorlton See Eccleshall.
Chatcull See Eccleshall.
Chebsey Chebsey was Staffordshire's 63rd largest parish, consisting of 4,172 acres; 16th= closest parish to the county town, 3.6m NW; extremist length 2.9m; extremist width 3m. The parish's chief settlement is Chebsey, a small rural village, but the population centre is Norton Bridge by the North West railway line. The parish is famous for Izaak Walton's Cottage.
  Altitudes Highest point in the parish is 400 feet at Rodgeley Lodge and the lowest point is 272 feet at the Sow and Meece confluence.
  Bennett, Mrs Elizabeth *Oldest resident of Chebsey 1929.* She died aged 96 in Jan 1929. She was born at Wootton, Eccleshall, and lived for many years with her brother, Ben Milner, at Scamnells (Staffordshire Weekly Sentinel. Jan 26 1929 p4p).
  Boyd, Mrs *Chebsey's kindest.* Of Hilcot. She was the last surviving member of the Ripley family, and gave £1,000 towards restoration of the church, and gave £20 to the Soldiers and Sailors Families Association Funds (Eccleshall Division) in 1900; and placed in the church a stain glass window in memory of her sister Miss Ripley (SA July 7 1900 p4 col 7. Aug 10 1901 p5 col 1).
  Church *All Saints* is one of 19 such county dedications (of AP churches); 3rd oldest county church dating from 1070. *Parish registers* were stolen when the thieves broke into the church in 1958 and stole some silver plate (SN Jan 17 1959 p14). *In the churchyard* note the Anglo-Saxon cross, an undecorated fat round shaft turning square and then decorated, mainly with (decayed) interlace (BOE p99). There are similar ones at Leek and Clewlow (NSFCT 1908 p170). (NHS p432) (CHMS p24) (STM Jan 1965 p41p).
  Farming *One of Staffordshire's few new farms built since WW2 - Staffs CC smallholdings excepted.* Whitehouse Farm, Cold Norton, of 190 acres, built by Mr T

Ball in c1956, a dairy farm (SA & Chron March 15 1956 p8ps).
  Folklore *Chebsey's best.* The Quaker burial ground at Shallowford (SJ 872292) (the last burial was in 1859) is said to be haunted by the ghosts of those buried; one sighting was made by a couple in 1969, and there has been at least one further sighting (ROT p30) (SN April 15 1994 p5) (further info from Bruce Braithwaite). In addition, in the early C19 a skeleton was found in a field at Shallowford at a depth of four feet; it was thought to have been that of someone murdered (Broughton's Scrapbook p171; article is dated Sept 22 1814).
  Garnett, Rev Richard *'one of the most eminent of British philologists', almost presented the first introduction of German philological research to the English public (1835-36), 'I do not know any man who has read so much which you would not expect him to have read'.* (1789-1850). Born Otley, Yorks, vicar of Chebsey 1836-38, later Assistant Keeper of Printed Books at the British Museum. His articles on German philological research appeared in the Quarterly Review (DNB). The second quote on him is from Southey (SA Dec 31 1949 p6 col 6).
  Geology The whole parish is Keuper Red Marls, with the Dolerite Butterton dyke running through the centre from N-S.
  Johnson, Joane *Earliest person recorded in the parish register.* For her baptism on April 8 1660. She was the daughter of Richard and Joyce Johnson. This is the Bishop's transcript register; earlier registers must be lost.
  Morton, Thomas de *First-known vicar* of Chebsey, in 1321.
  Mould, David *Chebsey's saddest.* When aged 23, a mechanic of Fancy Walk, Stafford, former Seimens employee, who called with an 'unsound mind' at the house of his sweetheart, Sarah Ann Latham of Chebsey, on April 25 1910 with a revolver. He hoped to take her away to take her life and commit suicide, after her parents disapproved of their proposed marriage.

He threatened Sarah with the gun in the presence of her mother, made off, took a mixture of carbolic acid and spirits, threw himself off a bridge into the Sow, was rescued by a youth, but subsequently died of poisoning in Stone Workhouse (SA April 30 1910 p5 cols 3-4).

Nelson, Sir George *'one of the greatest industrial leaders of the present time' 1960.* (1887-1962). Baronet. Of Hilcot Hall by 1960, Chairman of English Electric Co Ltd, Stafford; past President of the Institution of Electrical Engineers; past President of the Institution of Mechanical Engineers; and elected President of the Locomotive and Allied Manufacturers Association. Freeman of Stafford 1956; Prime Warden of the Goldsmiths Company 1960 (SA & Chron Jan 7 1960 p6p. July 19 1962 pp1p,9).

Panting, Laurence *Chebsey's longest-serving vicar.* He served for 52 years, 1838-90.

Place-name Chebsey first appears in Domesday Book, 1086, and means 'Cebbi's island or raised dry area' (PNSZ p186).

Poorest There is no evidence for a Chebsey workhouse.

Population Chebsey was 103rd= most populated Staffordshire parish in 1801 with 441 people; 113rd in 1811 with 406; 117th in 1821 with 421; 120th in 1831 with 414; 110th in 1841 with 442; 113th in 1851 with 466; 106th in 1861 with 514; 107th in 1871 with 487; 105th in 1881 with 503; 100th in 1891 with 536; 96th in 1901 with 566. Chebsey could be ranked 94th= worst affected Staffordshire parish for loss of men in WW1, with 10 lives taken.

Quote *Choicest.* Horne & Bennion's 'Advertiser' Almanack 1895, Stone & Eccleshall edition, tells 'Chebsey is an ancient village situate in the narrow valley near the confluence of the Eccleshall brook with the river Sow...'

Shaw, William *Chebsey person with the earliest-surviving will.* It is dated Oct 7 1534/3.

Tinsley, Capt WH *Chebsey's hero.* Son of Thomas Tinsley of Chebsey. After serving in Northern France in WW1 he returned to work for the North Staffs Railway. In c1925 he was British Pro-Consul at St Malo, and representative of the LMS Railway for the West of France and Spain, and by whose efforts the commercial relations with Britain and France were greatly developed. In 1935 the French Government awarded him the Chevalier due Merite Agricole (SA April 20 1935 p6p).

Victoria, Queen *First memorial to her discussed in Staffordshire.* Was an organ for the church at Chebsey, as unanimously agreed at a meeting on Jan 21 1901, as reported in The Staffordshire Advertiser Feb 23 1901 p7 col 5.

Village life *One of Staffordshire's prettiest villages* is Chebsey, according to Staffordshire County Handbook c1958 p92. *'a rather sleepy village. At times it is almost dead.'* Gladys May Davies, village postmistress and Chebsey resident since 1911, when asked her opinion about the village in 1950 for The Stafford Advertiser feature 'My village as I see it' (SA Feb 4 1950 p7). *Village forbidden from having a public house.* Chebsey, as somewhere in the ancient Deeds there is a clause forbidding the promotion of a public house (SA & Chron Aug 31 1961 p8 col 1).

WALTON, IZAAK *Chebsey's most famous old worthy, 'one of the the greatest citizens we (Stafford) has ever produced'.* (1593-1683), mercer, author, steward, helped secret royal jewels out of the country to Charles II during the Commonwealth. In c1654 he bought Halfhead Farm at Shallowford in Chebsey parish. The second quote is by Philip Thomas Dale (1876-1953), trustee of the Izaak Walton Trust, of Stafford, when he unveiled in Sept 1953 a plaque to mark the birthplace of Izaak Walton at 62 Eastgate Street, St Chad's (parish), Stafford (SA Nov 6 1953 p1 cols 3-4). *First open contest of Izaak Walton Angling Association* was held at

Izaak Walton (above). Title page of his 'The Compleat Angler'.

the canal at Radford, near Stafford on Oct 12 1901. There were 79 competitors. The HQ of the association was at the Dolphin Hotel (SA Oct 19 1901 p4 col 6). **The Compleat Angler** *3rd most reprinted book in the English language*. Walton's fishing manuel first published in 1653 (BBC Midlands Today. July 31 2009). *The man who put Walton's 'The Compleat Angler' into verse* was Paul Brett in 2009

(BBC Midlands Today. July 31 2009).
Chell See Chell.
Chesterton See Wolstanton.
Clayton See Stoke-upon-Trent.
Clayton Griffith See Trentham.
Cobridge See Burslem.
Cold Norton See Chebsey.
Cotes Heath See Eccleshall.
Croxton See Eccleshall.
Darlaston See Stone.

E-J

Eccleshall Eccleshall was Staffordshire's 3rd largest parish, consisting of 21,738 acres; 16th= closest parish to the county town, 3.6m NW; extremist length 6.5m, making it 13th= longest parish in the county; extremist width 7.7m, making it 4th widest parish in Staffordshire. The parish's chief settlement is Eccleshall, a

A few Staffordshire villages now have pictorial signs like this, common in East Anglia. Barlaston has one too.

small, very pretty market town, in a shallow curve of gently rising ground south of the river Sow. The parish is famous for being the principal diocesan estate outside Lichfield and having a bishop's seat, Eccleshall Castle.

Allen, Annie E *Eccleshall's heroine, one of the few women commemorated on a Staffordshire WW1 war memorial*. VAD, on the one in Eccleshall churchyard. Born Walsall c1872, second daughter of Rev William Allen, vicar of Eccleshall from 1882 to his death in 1913, prebendary of Lichfield (Sandiacre) from 1880. At a parochial tea party he is reputed to have said "Now, the next item will be sung by Miss Gosse, 'O put me in My Little Bed' accompanied by the curate" to which everyone laughed, but the vicar was horrified (Victorian Eccleshall. David Vincent. 1982. p151). He appears to have founded St Chad's, Slindon, earning the nickname 'Begging Billy', presumably for his soliciting for funds.

Altitudes Eccleshall parish's highest point is 668 feet at Broughton Birches, Broughton. The lowest point is 264 feet by the Sow north of Waltonbank, Walton.
Athletics *London-Brighton Road Race 7th place 1978*. George Kay of Eccleshall, at the remarkable age of 42, in 5 hours 45 minutes 53 seconds; member of Stafford AC (SN Oct 2 2008 p73). *First ever North Staffordshire Road Runners Eccleshall 15 mile race*. Saturday Sept 13 1980. Martin Bishop of Staffordshire Moorlands AC won the men's race; Brenda Cook of Stafford AC won the ladies race (SN Sept 19 1980 p57ps). *European junior sprint hurdles champion 1993, British Women's Hurdle Championship silver medalist 1993*. Keri Maddox of Eccleshall, member of Cannock and Stafford AC, failing to win gold by two hundredths of a second (SN June 15 2009 p58pc).
Broughton Hall *'the most spectacular piece of black and white in the county'*. Nikolaus Pevsner's description of the house (BOE p81). *First flower crowning of the Blessed Virgin Mary statue on first Sunday in May at Broughton Hall*. This traditional Catholic custom first took place in the hall gardens in May 1953 when occupied as the Mother House of the Franciscan Missionaries of St Joseph. The statue of Our Lady of Walsingham was carried by cadets of Pell Well Hall College, near Market Drayton, and crowned by Anne Wilson of Ashley (SLM June 1953 p25).
Carter family *Eccleshall's saddest*. On Jan 17 1935 Edward C Carter, 17 year old son of Mr WE Carter of Eccleshall Castle, was accidentally shot dead by his little

sister Daphne with his double barrel 4.10 gun, left in his bedroom. WWM Morgan, Stafford District Coroner, said the case was 'the very saddest case I have ever had to deal with' (SA Jan 19 1935 p7 col 5).

Cauldwell, John *Richest person in the West Midlands 2006, 524th richest person in the world 2008, 245th richest person in the world 2009, 35th= richest person in Britain 2010.* Mobile phone entrepreneur, formerly with headquarters in the Potteries. Of Broughton Hall; his value in 2008 was £1.7 billion; in 2009 £1.2 billion; in 2010 £1.4 billion (UAd April 26 2006 p5) (ES March 13 2009 p6) (Sunday Times Rich List 2010).

CHURCHES Holy Trinity is one of 4 such county dedications (of AP churches); 41st= oldest county church dating from 1190. 'one of the most perfect C13 churches in Staffordshire', in what Pevsner thought according to Pevsner in his The Buildings of England series, 1974. *Most interesting thing.* A bishop's throne (STM June 1965 p40p), rare for a parish church, and probably exists because Eccleshall was an estate held by the bishops of Lichfield from the C7 and their formerly residing at Eccleshall. *2nd place with most Bishops of Lichfield buried.* Eccleshall church with six, the first being Lichfield Cathedral. At Eccleshall there is a table tomb which once bore an incised effigy of the bishop in his vestments to Richard Sampson, bishop 1543-54; Thomas Bentham, bishop 1559-79, in the chancel; William Overton bishop 1580-1609, a table-tomb with an effigy, and, in recesses above, kneeling figures of the bishop's two wives; Robert Wright, bishop 1632-43; James Bowstead, bishop 1839-43, tomb with an effigy, a sixth bishop may be represented by the battered figure brought in from the churchyard John Lonsdale, bishop of Lichfield 1843-67 (GNHS pp117,118) (JME part i p12) (VCH vol 3 pp44-46) (LGS pp129-130). *The churchyard* was Lichfield Diocese Best Kept Churchyard winner 1998.

St Chad at Slindon, was built 1894 and described by Henry Thorold as 'A little church of rare beauty' (SGS p148).

St Paul at Croxton, built 1853-4. *In the churchyard* the grave of Able Seaman Thomas Oldbury who served on HMS Bellrophon when Napolean surrendered to the British on July 1 1815 and was taken to St Helena (BOV p18).

St Peter at Broughton, built in 1634, and with the C17 high box pews still in place.

In the churchyard there a number of interesting epitaphs on grave: Mrs Elizabeth Broughton (d c1649), which desires all persons to 'forbeare to stir her bones', and similarly Thomas Nevill (d1749) of Wetwood, gent, 'I desire all persons to forbear removing my body' (BOV p2).

Crime *Staffordshire's last highway robbery.* Perhaps that at Slindon at 10pm on June 27 1837 when Charles Fearns was attacked and robbed by three men, thought to be navvies, on his way home from the White Lion Inn, Eccleshall. They stole £2 16s, beat him in a most unmerciful manner, and threw him into a pond of water, where they left him (SA July 1 1837. July 3 1937 p6 col 8). However, there are a number of later cases (SA March 14 1840 p2 col 3. Oct 24 1840 p3 col 4).

Deer park *Largest in Staffordshire.* Blore Park at 1500 acres (info David Jacques, 2006).

Egerton, Rev William Henry *Oldest Fellow of the Geological Society 1910.* (1811-1910). Prebendary of Eccleshall from 1896 (SA March 19 1910 p4 col 4).

Environment, and built environment *Britain's first major electricity plant to be fuelled by grass* was to be built at Eccleshall (BBC Midlands Today May 30 2005). *An original Staffordshire Conservation Area.* Eccleshall in 1969, one of the first four areas to come before the Subcommittee (of the Town and Country Planning Committee). In total 51 Staffordshire Areas were created under the Civic Amenities Act 1967. The Act enabled planning authorities to provide for the protection of whole Areas of towns and villages if they were of a special architectural or historic interest (BOb Aug 7 1969 p1) (TH Aug 8 1969 p1 cols 6-9).

Farming *Staffordshire's 1st enclosure by Private Act of land not including some open field arable.* Gratwood Heath; 1,000 acres awarded by an Act of 1719 (A Domesday of English enclosure acts and awards. WE Tate. 1978). *Only cow quads in the country 1960.* Possibly Friesian quads achieved by artificial insemination belonging to Roland Shelley of Wetwood Farm, born Feb 10 1960; they appeared at the Staffordshire County Show 1960 (SA & Chron June 2 1960 p5p). *The first Eccleshall Flower Show.* The first annual exhibition of the Eccleshall and District Horticultural Show took place in 1890 (SA Aug 8 1896 p2 col 6). *First Farmers' Market in Eccleshall* was on April 23 2006 (The Stone & Eccleshall Gazette.

May 2006 p37).

Folklore Some of the 20 former townships have their best stories. *Broughton's best.* There is a tradition in the Civil War the young heir to Broughton Hall leaned out of the Long Gallery window to shout at some marauding parliamentarians 'I am for the King.' They shot him dead and his blood, long stained the Long Gallery floor. His ghost is called 'Redstockings,' after the red socks worn by it. Blood-stained floor boards were replaced during the reconstructions of the hall in 1926. The story may be a Victorian invention to explain sightings of the ghost of a boy in blood-stained stockings. *Charnes' best.* Charnes Hall is reputedly haunted by the wife of a member of the Yonge family, who is said to have lived in the later C17, and who, when young, was thought to have died after an illness. Shortly after the funeral her grave in Chapel Wood, opposite the hall entrance, was robbed and a ring taken from her finger. She had in fact been buried alive and was revived when her finger was cut off. After death in old age she returned as a ghost to look for the ring. The rustling and sight of her silk shroud in the hall and grounds is why the ghost is called 'Silkie.' Rev WE Vernon Yonge was told that the thief was the family coachman. *Croxton's best.* In Offley Hay there is a sycamore tree which is said to have grown from the stake that was driven through the body of a giant in an attempt to keep him down (FOS p42) (MR p250). *Eccleshall town's best.* Eccleshall Castle grounds are said to be haunted by the ghosts of a grey lady, a white lady, a spectral cavalier and a black dog. *Great Sugnall's best.* Local tradition asserts Holy Well, a well surrounded by stonework surmounted by a cross in woods between Cop Mere and Sugnall was blessed by one of the Popes (NSFCT 1884 p32. 1910 p198) (NSSG

Parliamentarian marauders fire on the young squire of Broughton Hall.

p18). *Horsley's best.* A former stile called Jacob's Ladder at NE corner of Cop Mere is where a gamekeeper is supposed to have hung himself from; his ghost is said to haunt the spot. *Most haunted village in Staffordshire.* Perhaps the Broughton-Charnes area, with nearly every corner of the neighbourhood reputedly having supernatural associations, according to local ghost-collector Mrs Mary Palmer of Fairoak in 1949. As well as Broughton and Charnes Halls being haunted, there is the 'Dark Lane' with its phantom horse-drawn coach, perhaps the same as a spectral coach, which is supposed to be a warning of impending family disaster at Charnes (SA July 14 1949 p7).

Rev Kenneth Hunt. The Blue Plaque commemorates his family home 1898-1920s at St Mark's Vicarage, Chapel Ash, Wolverhampton. He played for 'Eccleshall Comrades' after his father, Rev Robert George Hunt, retired to Eccleshall Vicarage, where he was living by 1922.

Football *Eccleshall Comrades player in FA Cup final 1908.* Rev Kenneth Hunt (1884-1949), an amateur footballer, who also played for Stafford Rangers as well as for Wolverhampton Wanderers when they won the FA Cup in 1908; England International 1907-20 (TB Aug 23 2007 p16p). *Played football for England.* George Luxton Jeffery (d c1937) of The Mount, Eccleshall, and formerly of The Royal Pavilion Hotel, Folkestone, for many years a member of the London Stock Exchange, who played football for England, Cambridge University, and Blackheath (SA Feb 5 1938 p6 col 4).

Geology The townships of Aspley, Charnes, Chatcull, Coldmeece, Eccleshall, Gerard's Bromley, Pershall, Podmore, Little Sugnall, Slindon, Three Farms, Walton, Wootton are entirely Keuper Red Marls; Broughton township is Keuper Sandstones (most, with an E-W central intrusion of Keuper Red Marls), Bunter (S fringe); Chapel Chorlton is Keuper Red Marls (W, surrounded by a band of Keuper Sandstones on which lies Chapel Chorlton village), Bunter (Meece valley); The Chapel Chorlton detached area is entirely Upper Coal Measures; Cotes township is Bunter (most and N),

Keuper Sandstones (Cotes Heath chapel), Keuper Red Marls (S fringe); Croxton township is Permian (S), Bunter (most with N-S intrusions of Keuper Sandstones in the E), Keuper Red Marls (extreme E); Great Sugnall is Bunter (W), Keuper Red Marls (E); Hill Chorlton is Bunter (N and most), Keuper Sandstones (SW corner); Horsley is Keuper Red Marls (most and E), Bunter (Lea Knowl), Keuper Sandstones (Offley Hay); Millmeece is Bunter (N), Keuper (S).

Gerrard, Sir Gilbert *46th Master of the Rolls, Eccleshall's most famous old worthy.* Serving as Master of the Rolls 1581-1593/4. He bought Bromley in Eccleshall from his kinsman, Sir Thomas Gerard of Etwall, Derbyshire, and built Gerards Bromley Hall which Dr Robert Plot in his 'Natural History of Staffordshire' (1686) described as "the most magnificent structure of all this county." It was built in c1575 or after his appointment as Master of the Rolls in 1581, in expectation of entertaining Elizabeth I. The hall was demolished in c1750, though some fabulous plaster work depicting a hunting scene survives in a barn.

Glass working *Only surviving C17 glass furnace in the UK and best preserved in Europe.* The one in Bishop's Wood, Fairoak, at SJ 759313 or 759312.

Higginson, Charles *Eccleshall's villain.* He murdered his five-year old son on April 2 1843 in the Moss Lane area. By its own admission this was one of the most cold-blooded and heartless murders ever reported by the Staffordshire Advertiser (SA May 13 1843) (BPS p89).

Horsley Hall *Fancy that!* Eric Wildman, cane manufacturer and president of the National Society for the Retention of Corporal Punishment in School, was seized and beaten with one of his own canes in front of the national press by pupils of Horsley Hall School on Nov 24 1948. He left prematurely in the protection of a journalist's car, in disgust cursing his naivety to accept an invitation to the school, not expecting the reception he got, and threatening to take legal action for assault. This was the co-educational senior section (ages 12-16) of a fee-paying progressive educational institution run on the lines of 'self-expression' for upper middle class children, under the principal, Robert Copping, aged 28; it opened c1945 (SA Nov 27 1948 p5 cols 2-3).

Hutton, Mary Ann Taylor *Eccleshall's* *villainess.* She was a young woman of Burslem, 'a gross impostor and vagrant' found on the High Street on May 22 1863 claiming to passers-by "I'll destroy myself", and on being asked what had she done, replying "Oh, dear, I wish I had never done it." - but would not state what she had done. Taken to the police station and locked up, the next morning she appeared very ill, and pretended to a surgeon she had been duped into taking arsenic for her health at Shifnal. This led to her being given a great deal of attention and cures. The following Monday - having made a 'dying declaration' and drawn on the resources of the locality - she was exposed by a letter from Burslem police which said she had recently been released from Stafford Prison, and was of a very bad and wicked character, having formerly accused men of raping her and of murdering another in the Stone area. She was sentenced to three months prison under the Vagrant Act to Stafford gaol, her fourth spell there (SA May 30 1863 p5 col 4).

Kent, Jeff *A Great Mind of the 21st Century.* Mystic and writer of Cotes Heath, lecturer at Stoke-on-Trent College, who occurs in the American Biographical Institute's 'Great Minds of the 21st Century' 2006; he is one of only 1000 biographical entries listed (SN Aug 31 2006 p10pc).

Lonsdale, Bishop *Last bishop to live at Eccleshall Castle.* He was in residence by at least 1851, and died in its parlour in Oct 1867. Full of harmonious contradictions he was renowned for being quite unlike anybody else. He hated any kind of grandeur or flunkyism, and delighted in shocking people by disregarding conventions of all kinds. He once went to Eccleshall on the railway with his scanty wardrobe done up in a blue pocket-handkerchief. Arriving at Norton Bridge station his blue-liveried footman had the indignity of having to help his master from the third-class carriage with the offending handkerchief to the Episcopal carriage (SA Aug 1 1936 p5 col 2).

Lowe, Mrs Susan Anne *First Welsh woman to qualify with the highest surgical degrees.* (1868-1959). Of Sugnall Hall. Born Barmouth; lived Wincote with her husband 1896-98, thereafter at Sugnall (SA & Chron Oct 15 1959 p1 cols 6-7).

Macham, Miss Marjorie *2nd ever Deputy Miss Staffordshire.* She was so crowned in 1947, when she reigned as Miss Eccleshall (Stafford Pageant: The Exciting Innovative Years 1901-1952. Gordon Henry Loach. 2007).

Marksmanship *English record at clay pigeon shooting*. Duncan Lawton, aged 21, of Croxton, with a maximum 100 marks using a Remington automatic shotgun, breaking the previous record of 99 held by a Gloucester marksman Brian Wells. By 1980 Lawton had represented England and Staffordshire at clay pigeon shooting (SN June 27 1980 p64).

Moore, Henry *Eccleshall's longest-serving vicar*. He served for only 34 years, 1822-1856.

Myatt, John *'one of the greatest art forgers ever', 'the most prolific art dealer in the world'*. Born 1945. Of Sugnall, art forger, who with John Drewe sold many forged paintings as the work of great artists 1984-95, and he was imprisoned for forgery c1999. The second claim was made by Scotland Yard (The Times magazine Jan 22 2005 pp45-7pc) (Stone Post Nov 30 2006 p12). Myatt's activities have been called the *'biggest art con of the C20'* (BBC 1 Midlands Today Oct 25 2007).

John Myatt - World's most prolific art dealer.

Natural history *Rare species of dwarf elder*. Danewort, Dane's bane, Dane's blood, or Sambucus Ebulus is only found in the county at Wootton and at Tutbury Castle (NSFCT 1885 pp69-70). *Fancy that!* Eccleshall Cricket Club were able to play on iced-over Copmere on Jan 23 1850 (SA Jan 26 1850. Feb 4 1850 p6 col 4). *Oldest cat living in Britain 1989* was believed to be a female black moggy 'Kitty' owned by George Johnston of Croxton, who celebrated her 31st birthday in 1988 (GBR 1989 p30. 1998 p242).

Nudism *Staffordshire's earliest documentary-evidence of alleged mass nudism*. In Aug 1937 the Chief Supt of Newcastle Division of Staffs Police wrote to Newcastle RDC passing on local complaints of nudism practised among campers at the holiday camp by The Cock Inn, Stableford (SA Aug 21 1937 p10).

Parish council *One of Staffordshire's first 'Quality' parish councils*. Eccleshall Parish Council as awarded by Staffordshire's County Accreditation Panel. The scheme was launched in March 2003; there are two other Staffordshire parish councils awarded this Status, as well as one town council; there are only a hundred other councils with Quality Status in the country (info Mary Booth).

Parris, John Barrister *Textbook of the year award winner 1973*. Of Eccleshall. He won this with his 'Commercial Law Made Simple' (SN Nov 13 2003 p8).

Place-names Eccleshall first appears possibly in 1002-4, certainly in Domesday Book, 1086, and means something like 'sheltered place of a body of Christians, a church' (PNSZ p243). *Unique derivations for surnames*. Podmore (chiefly a Shropshire surname) will be from Podmore in this parish, and Meece will be from the Meece which runs through this parish (PDS).

Poorest The old Eccleshall parish workhouse was dilapidated in 1810. Shortly afterwards it was rebuilt at Goal Butts in the town; later becoming Eagle House (VE p92). After Aug 1839 Eccleshall poor, unable to support themselves, went to Stone Union workhouse in Stone. Whilst the poor of out-township Chorlton went to Newcastle Union workhouse. In 1888 ratepayers met to consider breaking away from Stone Poor Law Union, and forming a separate union for Eccleshall, containing parishes like Chebsey and Standon, but it never got considered by the boundary committee (SA Jan 21 1888 p5 col 3. Jan 28 1888 p4 col 7). *Sixteen of Eccleshall town's poorest* householders could expect annual pasturing for a cow each as bequeathed by Sir John Pershall 1611-2 (RCACEW). *Strange but true!* Of Stoke-upon-Trent parish. In 1813 William Allington of Stoke-upon-Trent went to Eccleshall poorhouse with the intention of falling in love and marrying a pauper by the name of Cotton, but when he got there he had amorous desires for one Sarah Rose who he married instead after a 'short but sweet' courtship (SA April 26 1913 p5 col 2).

Population Eccleshall was 19th most populated Staffordshire parish in 1801 with 3,734 people; 20th in 1811 with 3,801; 20th in 1821 with 4,227; 21st in 1831 with 4,471; 21st in 1841 with 4,730; 22nd in 1851 with 4,696; 22nd in 1861 with 4,882; 26th in 1871 with 4,827; 33rd in 1881 with 4,455; 34th in 1891 with 4,251; 36th in 1901 with 4,186. Eccleshall could be ranked 32nd= worst affected Staffordshire parish for loss of men and women in WW1, with 68 lives lost.

Pubs *One of the AA's 1001 Great Family Pubs*. The George Inn, Eccleshall, a C16 former coaching inn (book of the above title, 2005).

Quotes *Choicest*. Bruce Braithwaite in Ripples of Time, 1987, wrote 'One mile beyond Pershall the river (Sow) reaches its first town, and what an historicial town it is.' *'God's own country'* is said to have been a reference to the upper Sow valley as a choice area to live by local outsiders before the mid C20, though it is now obsolete (info Mrs L Cockin).

Sampson, Bishop Richard *First bishop of Lichfield to live mainly at Eccleshall Castle*. Possibly; he served as bishop 1543-54 (ECC pp36-37).

Sport See Athletics, Football, Marksmanship.

Swynnerton Royal Ordnance Factory *'Swynnerton Roses'*. Local name for its female munition workers in and after WW2 (ES Oct 10 2009 p27). *Railway station for 8,000 passengers a day, but was never on a timetable*. Cold Meece, which opened August 1941 to carry workers to and from ROF. At peak production at the factory in WW2 about 8,000 used the station, which was kept secret for national security reasons. In all, somewhere in the region of 13,000,000 had used it by the time the last train stopped on June 27 1958 (SA & Chron June 26 1958 p6 cols 7-9). *Country's largest 'police village' 1957*. No. 4 District Police Training Centre at Mill Meece (formerly part of ROF) founded 1948, the largest of eight in the country. The 'village' for 300-400 people, had its own facilities such as courtroom, cinema, pub, hospital, etc, with a constant turnover in residents. The 13,000th recruit 'passed out' in June 1960 (SA & Chron Jan 17 1957 p9. June 30 1960 p7). *1st North Staffordshire Drama Association Festival* was staged at Nelson Hall, the County Training College (formerly part of ROF), in March 1954, at which 12 amateur dramatic groups competed: Basford St Marks and the North Staffordshire University College (Keele University) were selected to go forward to the divisional finals (SA March

19 1954 p4). This event later moved to the Mitchell Memorial Theatre, Hanley. *First baby born to Vietnamese refugees at Nelson Hall*. A baby called Nelson to Tran Thi Xuan Hoang and Huynh Chi Dung who met and lived at Nelson Hall, Cotes Heath, 1982 (SN Nov 15 2007 p6). *Biggest women's prison in Britain 1997*. Drake Hall (formerly part of ROF) (ES Nov 7 1997 p2).

Tildesley, Harry *Eccleshall's bravest*. Of 70 High Street, Eccleshall, polio sufferer and author. His first book 'Polio and I' was based on on his personal endeavours to combat his crippling affliction through the medium of invigorating outdoor life, as an aid to fellow sufferers. His second book 'Gear Bottom Stew', still being written in 1961, was on a similar theme, depicting his travels in Cornwall (SA & Chron Feb 23 1961 p8 col 2).

Trades *4th silencing of Big Ben for repairs* was undertaken by Total Access UK of Eccleshall in 2007; other silencing for repairs have been in 1934, 1956 and 1990 (SN Aug 16 2007 p3pc). *Pharmacy of the Year 2008*. Eccleshall Pharmacy Ltd 11 High Street, Eccleshall, awarded by pharmaceutical company Numark (The Stone & Eccleshall Gazette. Nov 2008 p25). *National home* of the Basketmakers Association (1975) in 2002 was Highlanes Farm, Brockton; of the Clarice Cliff Collectors Club (1982), and of the Keith Murray Collectors Club, was Eccleshall, in 2008.

Walton, Cisselye *Eccleshall's earliest person recorded in the parish register*. For her baptism on Dec 6 1573.

Wright, David *A statue of him should occupy the 4th plinth in Trafalar Square*, according to Tom Utley, columnist in the Daily Mail Sept 5 2008 p14. After he was so impressed by a letter of Mr Wright of Eccleshall to The Times Sept 3 2008 on the subject of whether the National Gallery of Scotland should buy Titian paintings, he recommended in jest a statute of Wright be made and placed on the vacant plinth in Trafalar Square.

Etruria See Stoke-upon-Trent.
Fenton See Stoke-upon-Trent.
Fulford See Stone.
Garshall Green See Milwich.
Gerrard's Bromley See Eccleshall.
Halmer End See Audley.
Hanford See Trentham.
Hanley See Stoke-upon-Trent.
Hilderstone See Stone.

K-L

Keele Keele was Staffordshire's 103rd largest parish, consisting of 2,613 acres; 76th farthest parish away from the county town, 14.1m NNW; extremist length 2.4m; extremist width 2.2m. The parish's chief settlement is Keele, a Victorian village, but now surpassed by the neighbouring university campus. The parish is famous for Keele University.

Altitudes The highest point is Bank Top Farm at 705 feet. The lowest point is 443 feet in Spring Pool Wood.

Church *St John the Baptist* is one of 11 such county dedications (of AP churches); 11th last AP county church built dating from 1868-70. *One of only two Royal Arms of William & Mary in Staffordshire* is in the church at Keele; the other is at Brewood (Church Guide. Christopher Harrison. 1988. p4). *Note* the chest tomb to William Sneyd (d1613) with effigies of Sir William and his wife Clare, daughter of Sir Anthony Colclough knt. The tomb chest was made up with panels discovered beneath the floor together with the effigies during the rebuilding of the church in 1790, thus the figures are much mutilated (LGS p155) (SLM winter 1955 pp19,20p) (JME part iii pp13-14) (CHMS p36). *First church to have Hollins' Minton tiles* was probably Keele, in the chancel and altar platform. Colin Minton Campbell (d1885) and Michael Daintry Hollins (d1898) having dissolved their partnership in 1868, Campbell took the china works and Hollins the tile works, with production at a new factory at Cliff Vale (Andrew Dobraszczyc, 2008). Six bells were restored 1956 dedicated by Rev T.H. Brookes; bell number five was adopted by the undergraduates of University College Keele. *In the churchyard* there is a grave on the south side of the church to William Pepper, deported for sheep stealing. Apparently Pepper Street is named after him (SLM Winter 1955 p18). The inscription reads:-

'In memory of Faithful
Pepper who died April the 21st
180 Aged 81 years
Befool'd by sin from childhood to three
score
The yoke of Satan willingly he bore
He boldly brav'd the terrors of the Lord

Dispis'd his threatenings and defied his
sword
But Heaven with pity his delusion saw
Awak'd whim with the thunders of the Law
Shame and remorse now stung his alter'd
mind
He felt his wretchedness and long'd to find
A shelter from the impending wrath of God
He sought and found it in his saviours
blood
Holy and happy were his following years
Till Death remov'd him from the vale of
tears.'
'Ann Pepper his wife who died
Nov the 30th 1790 Aged 67 years.'

Farming *'Keele Paxton', 'Keele Patchwork'* were stallions of the stud of G Holland of Top Farm, Keele, used c1901 to impregnate local mares (SA April 27 1901 p8).

Folklore *Keele's best.* The M6 Keele service station is reputed to be haunted by a Puritan-looking gentleman who frequents the toilets. He was seen by Geoffrey White in Jan 1974 and the same ghost was seen by him at his home in Colchester; his home facing the Siege House (one of the last strongholds of supporters of Charles I) (EGH pp148-149).

Football *Largest youth football tournament in Britain.* The Wedgwood Keele Classic, in its 15th year in 1994, when it was held at Keele University, attracting 150 teams from 10 different countries (ES Aug 5 1994).

Geology Keele village, centre and south of the parish is Upper Coal Measures; Silverdale (W) and the north of the parish is Middle Coal Measures.

Iron working *'one of only two frying-pan makers in England'.* Keele, by later C17 (HOS 1998 p97).

Hollywood Music Festival *'Staffordshire's Woodstock', Grateful Dead's first appearance outside USA.* Hollywood Music Festival was held over Whitsun Bank Holiday weekend 1970, at Lower Farm, Finney Green. The first claim is by Garry Marsh, a pop music historian from Wolstanton, who attended the Festival. Here John Peel first saw and later promoted the group, Mungo Jerry, who launched here their hit 'In The Summertime', which reached No. 1 in the Charts (Borough Focus: Newcastle Borough's independent magazine. March 2006) (ES June 13 2009 p26p).

KEELE UNIVERSITY Activities *Staffordshire history's premier lecture.* The Earl Lecture, occurring biennially at Keele University. Founded by Jack Leighton, a local tax inspector, in memory of his wife (Earl being her maiden name). The first lecture was on the Sneyd family of Keele c1530-1949 by JW Blake MA FR Hist, Prof of History in the Sir Walter Moberley Hall, University College of North Staffordshire on Dec 1 1961. Subsequent speakers have included Rodney Hilton, Margaret Spufford, David Hey, Joan Thirsk, and Chris Dyer. *One of the 1st centres for the Open University summer school scheme.* Keele, the first courses started in summer 1971 (Staffs Illustrated. March 1970. Staffs Scene). *2nd performance ever of Handel's opera Berenice.* By Keele University's Music Dept to celebrate European Music Year 1985, on 26, 27, 28 April at Walter Moberley Hall. It was first and last performed in 1737 - and was the only one of Handel's 39 operas not staged in the 20th Century (STODAY April/ May 1985 p12). **General** *Oldest school of physiotherapy in Britain 1994.* The Oswestry and North Shropshire School of Physiotherapy founded by Dame Agnes Hunt in 1909. In Sept 1994 it relocated from The Robert Jones and Agnes Hunt Orthopaedic Hospital, Oswestry, to Keele University (ES Aug 31 1994). *'First new UK university of the twentieth century', 'first of Britain's post-war universities', one of the biggest campus' in Europe, with one of the highest proportions of students and staff in residence in Britain with some 85% in 1986* (Staffordshire: Shire County Guide. Peter Heaton. 1986) (Staffordshire County Guide 2006/7 pp62-63). *UK's largest integrated green campus university.* Covers Keele Hall grounds (ES Oct 27 1999 p18). *'one of the few places in the British Isles I haven't yet insulted'.* Keele University, according to then Tory M.P. and Shadow Higher Education Minister, renowned for his gaffes, Boris Johnson, in June 2007 (ES June 9 2007 p12). **Library holdings** *'One of the wonders of the world, not to say the monstrosities of the world'* is how an article by Sam Johnson in Staffordshire Studies xii (2000) pp109-119 was entitled. This is the Sarolea Collection which forms the basis of

the University Library. It was acquired by Stanley Stewart (d1995), librarian, himself *one of the first staff appointments of the university*; it was during his tenure (1949-81) the book stock went from nothing to around half a million volumes. In 1954 he purchased some 120,000 of 200,000 items of the vast library of Prof Charles Sarolea (1870-1953), Prof of French at University of Edinburgh, Belgium Consul in Edinburgh 1908-53, intellectual, charismatic and bibliomaniac at his home, 21-22 Royal Terrace, Edinburgh. Sarolea proclaimed his library 'the largest private library in the British Empire'. The cost was £1,348, and the books were housed in Madeley brick works until long after the library was built, 1960-1. Today 60,000 items survive as the founding stock; the term 'Collection' is a misnomer as the books do not exist separately from the main body of the library. Sarolea books can be identified by his signature on the title pages, or by his bookplate on the inside cover, or traced through their accession mark (ES Nov 22 1995 photo). *Some first edition proof sheets of Dr Johnson's Dictionary (1755)* are held in the University library (NSFCT 1927 p164) (HOK pp125,130). *First dissertations for M.A. in Local History.* 'Privilege, Property and Prosecution in Staffordshire: A Study of the County's Associations for the Prosecutions of Felons 1700-1850.' JC Sutton. 1993. "The Nailmaking Industry in Audley in the Later Charcoal Period circa 1550 to 1750. L Williams. 1993. 'North Staffordshire Professional Photographers 1850-1940.' GA Jones. 1993: *Certificate in Local History* 'Repeal of the Corn Laws in Staffordshire 1838-50.' Beryl Daniels. 1971. *Oldest publication in the Special Collections Library.* This local history library within the main library has some 600 works published before 1700, but the oldest Staffordshire book is Plot's 'Natural History of Staffordshire' (1686). **Staff** *First principal of the University.* Alexander D Lindsay (1879-1952); many of his academic ideas for the university were unique. *'The radio professor'.* The name students gave to Professor Alan Gemmell, head of the Biology department 1950-76, a radio programme panellist, appearing on the 1000th edition of Gardeners' Question Time, 1972 (ES Your Week July 8 2006 p11. Feb 17 2007 p9). It was he who said in 1970 it was the first time he could distinguish between male and female students (such was the similarity between the young of either sex in dress and hairstyles at the time), when students protested in the nude for more rights (ES April 12 2008 p30p).

First recipient of a PhD awarded by Keele University, 'among the first scholars in Britain to exploit the possibilities of computers,' 'among the first researchers to work with automatic speech recognition by computers'. Prof William 'Bill' Ainsworth (1939-2002), born Stoke-on-Trent, speech recognition researcher whose work led to the cochlear implant. His PhD (on neural networks - at that time a novel field) was awarded in 1963 just after University College of North Staffordshire had become University of Keele. The computer in question, was the PDP-8, the first general-purpose laboratory computer, which Ainsworth began work with in 1967. In 1998 he was awarded the Rayleigh Gold Medal by the Institute of Acoustics (The Daily Telegraph May 10 2002 p29p). *First Russian 'poet in residence' at a British university.* Dr Olga Sedakova, aged 44 when appointed at the university in 1994. Former lecturer at Moscow University, she was invited to Keele by Dr Valentina Polukhina, Reader in Russian Studies at the Department of Modern Languages (ES Feb 19 1994 photo).

Students *First cohort in 1949* numbered 148, and Bill Lighten was one of the first students. First multi-denominational chapel in the country Keele University chapel; opened 1965. *Staffordshire's worst paid job* is the VIP Student Ambassador, which pays 1 pence per annum; Spike Milligan was sacked from the post in 1982 for failing to write for the rag magazine (BBC internet site: Stoke & Staffordshire). *University Challenge winners 1968.* Keele in the 5th series of what has been daubed as TV's toughest general knowledge quiz show, defeating Jesus College, Cambridge. The contestants were Paul Brownsey, Pamela

KEELE UNIVERSITY

Keele University contestants on University Challenge in 1968.

Maddison, Aubrey Lawrence (later BBC Radio's Brain of Britain), and Andrew MacMullen (ES Aug 2 2008 p25p). *First person born on the campus to graduate from Keele.* Frances Anne Moseley. In 1975 she gained a Class Two Division One B.A. degree in English and Psychology; her father was a lecturer in geology, then (1975) at Birmingham University (ES July 2 1975).

Motorway dining *First UK restaurant over a motorway.* Keele services, M6 (ES Sept 18 1962) (Weekly Sentinel Aug 2 1963).

Keele Services shortly after its opening in 1962.

Place name Keele first appears in 1156, and means 'cow's hill' or possibly 'keel (ridge) hill' (PNSZ p338).

Poorest There was a Keele workhouse from 1737 (Keele Parish Book 1693-1770). After 1838 Keele poor, unable to support themselves, went to Newcastle Union workhouse on the south side of Keele Road, Thistleberry.

Population Keele was 61st most populated Staffordshire parish in 1801 with 904 people; 62nd in 1811 with 944; 65th in 1821 with 1,061; 65th in 1831 with 1,130; 65th in 1841 with 1,194; 65th in 1851 with 1,232; 72nd in 1861 with 1,062; 74th in 1871 with 1,052; 76th in 1881 with 1,048; 74th in 1891 with 1,090; 74th in 1901 with 1,080. Keele could be ranked 90th= worst affected Staffordshire parish for loss of men in WW1, with 11 lives lost.

Quote *Choicest.* The university is based round Keele Hall, the seat since the late C16 of the old staffordshire family of Sneyd. In a letter to HW Vincent dated 9 May 1862 Ralph Sneyd wrote about the grounds being open to the public 'I am in such beauty that I am drawn like a double tooth. My beauty indeed entails some inconvenience, for people flock from all quarters to see the red Rhododendrons which are a perfect conflagration (I really never saw a more splendid sight) and I am headed by beards and crinolines on every gravel walk.'

Smith, John *Earliest person recorded in the parish register.* For his baptism on May 1 1540. He was the son of John Smith.

Sneyd, John *Most agreeable member of the world,* according to society beauty Lady Wilmot Horton of Catton, Derbys, without hesitation when asked by Mrs Charles Bagot who she would prefer to call back to this world as the most agreeable member of it she had known in her life (Links with the Past. Mrs Charles Bagot. 1901. p131).

Sneyd, Rev John *The Anti-Jacobin.* Son of Ralph Sneyd (d1793). Founder of The Anti-Jacobin (or Weekly Examiner) Newspaper (later The Anti-Jacobin Review) 1797-8. Rector of Elford. High Tory, friend of Canning.

Sneyd, Georgina Mary Sophia Sneyd *George III sponsored her* (SLM Winter 1955 p19).

Sneyd, Charlotte *The artist.* (1800-82). Daughter of Lt Col Walter Sneyd and Louisa, eldest daughter of 1st Lord Bagot. She was named after the Queen, who was her godmother. In c1830 she, her mother, and two unmarried sisters moved to Cheverells, near Markyate, Herts (CL April 17 1997 pp50-53 ils).

Sneyd, Ralph *The Royalist.* (c1612-1649~50). MP for Stafford 1640, 1640-3. He took the Protestation 1641, but joined the King at Oxford; taken prisoner at Stafford in 1643. He was a colonel in the Royal army, raised a troop of horse and commanded Royalist troops in Staffordshire, attempting to relieve Rushall Hall in May 1644. In 1645 he was taken prisoner. He rose in arms again in the second rebellion and was slain in the Isle of Man (SHC 1922 pp61-2).

Sneyd, Ralph *He landscaped the park.* (1723-93). Father of Col Walter Sneyd.

Sneyd, Ralph *He built the present Keele Hall.* (1793-1870). Son of Col Walter Sneyd (d1829). The hall was built 1855-60 to designs by Anthony Salvin.

Sneyd, Col Ralph *Arrested Mata Hari, sold Keele Hall to University College of North Staffordshire.* (1863-1949). Son of Rev Walter Sneyd (1809-88), son of Col Walter (d1829). He arrested the notorious spy when DAPM in Paris in WW1.

Sneyd, Lt Col Walter *'not known to have spoken in the House', improved old Keele Hall.* (1852-1829). Succeeded to Keele estate in 1793. Commanded the Staffs Militia who served as George III's personal bodyguard. The claim is made in RG Thorne's 'The House of Commons 1790-1820.' 1896 vol 5. p457.

Sneyd, Sir William *Keele's most famous old worthy.* He was the Sneyd of Bradwell Hall who bought Keele. Recorder of Chester 1518/9-37/8; mayor of Chester 1543, 1566; sheriff of Staffordshire 1549-50, 1558-9; J.P. in the reigns from Edward VI to Elizabeth I; purchased Keele from the Crown 1544/45; engaged in the Scottish Wars, being at the battle of Pinkey, 1547. He died 1571 and was buried in Wolstanton parish church, under an elaborate canopied table-tomb, with effigies; figures of his fifteen children adorn the sides of the tomb.

Village life *'...no village in England where the cottages are more comfortable, more convenient, more substantial or in better taste..' 1856.* Keele village according to W Rothwell in his article 'Farming in Staffordshire' in Agricultural Gazette Nov 24 1856 p779. Rothwell was a land agent by profession and had published a detailed account of Lancashire farming (1850) (HOK p104). *Staffordshire Best Kept Village Newcastle District (Small Village) winner 1996, 1997, 2000, 2003.* Keele village.

Kibblestone See Stone.

Knutton See Wolstanton.

Longton See Stoke-upon-Trent.

M

Madeley Madeley was Staffordshire's 43rd largest parish, consisting of 5,864 acres; 82nd farthest parish away from the county town, 13.4m NW; extremist length 4.6m; extremist width 2.9m. The parish's chief settlement is Madeley and its satellite villages of Little and Middle Madeley, now all continuous through residential growth; the only one that isn't is Madeley Heath. The parish is famous for being the seat of the old county family of Offley, the village millpool, black and white timber framed buildings, mining, the railway and the teacher training college.

Altitudes The highest point is 620 feet on the south boundary below Camp Hill. The lowest point is 246 feet by Checkley Brook north of Wrinehill Mill.

Barnish, David *Fancy that!* On May 29 2008 David, aged 47, and his family of Hillwood Drive, Madeley, claimed £750 compensation for a £4,000 holiday to the Grecotel Park Royal, Kos, Greece, from their operator, Thomson Holidays, because they had failed to state that entertainment and activities were offered only in German, and the hotel was full of Germans (ES May 30 2008 p1pc) (Daily Telegraph May 31 2008 p1).

Church *All Saints* is one of 19 such county dedications (of AP churches); 23rd= oldest county church dating from the C12 or roughly 1150. *In the churchyard* the grave of Joseph Elkington (d1806), land drainer (see below).

Cricket *Staffordshire's longest six!* Probably that hit by Dennis Downend of Bar Hill Farm for Onneley Cricket Club in the early 1960s. The Club's ground then lay by the Wheatsheaf Inn and Downend's six reached the nearby Woore-Madeley road where it smashed through an upper window of a passing Crossville doubledecker bus. There lodged, it reached Newcastle-under-Lyme, the bus's destination. The Club has since amalgamated with Maer (info John Griffiths). *First club from outside the Premier Division to win the Hanley Economic Talbot Cup.* Leycett in 1990 (ES Sept 15 200? p42). See also John 'Jack' Iddon.

Deer park *Smallest and shortest-lived of the Earls of Stafford's deer parks at Madeley.* Netherset Hay Park which was about 430 acres.

Elkington, Joseph

Joseph Elkington's memorial in Stretton-on-Dunsmore churchyard, Warws.

George III paid him £1,000 for his drainage secrets. (1738-1806). Farmer of Madeley, who was such a pioneer in land drainage the House of Commons voted an inducement of £1,000 to discover his mode of drainage. Subsequently, Elkington, went about the country putting his methods to the test, and an official report published in 1797, with a 3rd and last edition appearing in 1808. He has a monument celebrating his achievements in Stretton-on-Dunsmore churchyard, Warws. His grandsons were inventors of a process of electro-plating and were the founders of a well-known firm of Birmingham silversmiths (SA Aug 15 1936 p10 col 7).

Fete *'the Greatest Fete in the District'.* Madeley Fete, as stated in an advertisement for it in 1893, beginning 'The Madeley Fete has been widely acknowledged for years as the Greatest Fete in the District'. In 1893 it was held over two days on Whit

Monday and Tuesday in the Park at Madeley Manor (SA May 20 1893 p1 col 2).

Folklore *Madeley's best.* Madeley Old Hall is a timber-framed black and white house on the Woore-Newcastle road in the village. According to tradition Queen Margaret of Anjou stayed here on her way to

Gawping at Madeley Old Hall in the 16th Century.

Eccleshall after the battle of Blore Heath (1459) in the Wars of the Roses. According to further tradition in consequence of this passers-by started to stare at the house in awe. By the middle of the C17 the owner was got so fed up he had a curious mocking inscription carved into the wood at the front of the house:

16 Wallk k nave what look est at 47. ISB

Or is this inscription to fool local parliamentarians into thinking the owners were loyal while in reality they were royalist? Or simply a reflection of the pride of the new owner?

Geology Madeley township is Upper Coal Measure (Finney Green and NE), Middle Coal Measures (Madeley Old Manor-Great Madeley-Little Madeley, and all E), Bunter (Wrinehill Hall and W); Onneley township is entirely Bunter.

Greville, James *Madeley's longest serving vicar.* He served for 35 years, c1782-c1817.

Iddon, John alias 'Jack' *England cricketer killed in a car crash in the parish.* Born Lancs 1902. English cricketer who played in five Tests in 1935. He was a right-handed middle-order batsman who hit the ball hard and a slow left-arm bowler who achieved a lot of turn on wearing pitches. He was integral to the successful of Lancashire teams 1926-39. On April 17 1946 he was working as a technical representative for a company making linings in Manchester, and he was on his way home from a business meeting at Rolls-Royce in Crewe when he was killed in a road accident at Madeley Heath (ES Your Week

Dec 23 2006 p9) (Wikipedia, 2009).

Kelsall, Len *One of only 10 mink farmers left in UK 1998.* Mink farmer at Kelbain Fur Farm, Onneley, by 1998; in the mink fur farming business since the late 1960s. Demonstrations against his fur farm by animal rights activists in 1998 included a break in at Onneley and the release of 2,000 mink, as well as a naked protest outside his home in Hempstalls Lane, Newcastle-under-Lyme. In 2003, he and the 10 other mink farmers in the UK, were forced to quit under the Fur Farming (Prohibition) Bill (2002) (ES March 23 1998. April 18 2001 p9p).

Kilmister, Ian Fraser *Alias 'Lemmy', 'bedded' in excess of 2,000 women.* Bass guitarist with Hawkwind (1970-75), and Motorhead (1975-). 'His appearance, facial moles, mutton chops, and gravelly voice have made him an instantly recognisable cult figure'. Born in Stoke-on-Trent, 1945. After his parents separated, he, his mother and grandmother moved to Newcastle-under-Lyme, then to Madeley, where he lived until the age of 10. In c1955 his family moved to Benllech, Anglesey. In the Channel 4 documentary called 'Motorhead: Live Fast, Die Old' broadcast on Aug 22 2005, it was claimed Lemmy had 'bedded' in excess of 2,000 women. Maxim magazine has him at No. 8 on its top ten 'Living Sex Legends' list, as they claim he has slept with around 1,200 women (Wikipedia, 2009).

Mining *Pevsner's most acclaimed Staffordshire building of the 1930s.* Madeley Colliery pithead baths, 1935, by WA Woodland; demolished by 1974 (BOE pp43,200).

Moreton, Rev William *Staffordshire's worst clergyman ever.* (1759-1834). Born Madeley; curate of Willenhall 1789-95, vicar 1795-. He would deliver his sermons inebriated and then go off to cock fights; alias 'Old Mowton'; he was even fined for sporting 1791; declared bankrupt 1812.

Natural history *Rare bird.* Coccothraustes or Gross-beak bird had been found and killed at about Madeley Old Manor and had been preserved in the collection of Madam Offley (NHS p230).

Offley, Sir Thomas *295th Lord Mayor of London, Madeley's most famous old worthy.* (?1505-1582/3). He served in 1556-7; Native of Stafford. He bought the manor of Madeley in 1547; during his tenure as London mayor he introduced bellmen to alert Londoners in time of fire or theft; renowned for his frugality as stated in the verse "Offley three dishes had of daily roast/ An egg, an apple, and (the third) a toast." Yet he was charitable and Fuller called him the Zaccheus of London.

Onneley *'most boring village in England'.* Onneley in 1996 after a new road sign for Onneley was erected on the A525 prankster put up an addition handwritten notice underneath declaring

'BEWARE! YOUR ARE NOW ENTERING THE MOST BORING VILLAGE IN ENGLAND'.

Mark Bittner, landlord of The Wheatsheaf Inn said "The village shop closed down several years ago and our most colourful claim to fame - a local nudist club - packed up too' (ES May 1 1996. May 10 1996. Aug 4 1998 p9).

Place-name Madeley first appears in 975, and means 'Mad(d)a's leah or clearing' (PNSZ p380).

Poorest Madeley, having used Audley workhouse (A pp43-6), set up its own in 1832 in the Holborn premises of J Cunliffe Offley. Madeley vestry committee book 1831-54 has the rules, orders and regulations, including the Bill of Fare intended for inmates (D3412/4/4). After 1838 Madeley poor, unable to support themselves, went to Newcastle Union workhouse on the south side of Keele Road, Thistleberry.

Population Madeley was 58th most populated Staffordshire parish in 1801 with 945 people; 60th in 1811 with 1,018; 60th in 1821 with 1,166; 63rd in 1831 with 1,190; 58th in 1841 with 1,492; 52nd in 1851 with 1,655; 54th in 1861 with 1,940; 46th in 1871 with 2,387; 50th in 1881 with 2,457; 41st in 1891 with 2,904; 43rd in 1901 with 2,909. Madeley could be ranked 49th= worst affected Staffordshire parish for loss of men in WW1, with 44 lives lost.

Pubs *One of the AA's 1001 Great Family Pubs.* The Wheatsheaf Inn, Barhill Rd, near Onneley, gets a high rating for its accommodation (book of the above title, 2005).

Quote *Choicest.* J Kennedy in his 'Madeley: A History of a Staffordshire Parish, 1970, p81, writes "As for Madeley village, it continued to grow and to change. The new buildings of the College of Education, begun in 1961, were sited on the lower slopes of the former Regency manor parkland. A new secondary school had been built a little earlier and a new shopping precinct was to follow. It was part of Madeley's past that it had never been a 'closed' village for long periods, but had changed with the times: the 1960's were witnessing a new phase of this process".

Riley, George *Council for the Protection of Rural England Merit Award holder.* (b1917/18). Awarded 1990, for producing guide books to 32 walks; his first book was 'Five Walks Around Madeley' published by Newcastle MB, 1984.

Snape, Ellen *Earliest person recorded in the parish register.* Wife of John Snape, husbandman, for her burial on May 3 1567.

Maer Maer was Staffordshire's 99th largest parish, consisting of 2,750 acres; 70th= closest parish to the county town, 11.5m NW; extremist length 3.4m; extremist width 3m. The parish's chief settlement Maer, a tiny pretty rustic village; Blackbrook, aligned along the Nantwich road, has been more the commercial centre. The parish is famous for Maer Hall, Pool and associations with Charles Darwin.

Altitudes The highest point Camp Hill at 709 feet. the lowest point is 370 feet by the Tern at Willoughbridge.

Bronze and Iron Age *'the most complete example illustrative of the whole social economy of a community which had lived and loved, worked and worshipped in the first millennium B.C.' in Britain.* The Bronze Age or early Iron Age settlement covering nine acres of the parish, including Camp, Red, War, Berry and Byrth Hills, with remnants of their husbandry (a feature unique to Maer), copper and iron foundries, military enclosures (fort on Bryth Hill) with its associated parliament house and temple (SA & Chron Feb 21 1957 p6).

Church *St Peter* is one of 15 such county dedications (of AP churches); 54th oldest AP county church dating from 1210.

Clive, Miss Dorothy *Maer's heroine.* Daughter of Col and Mrs Harry Clive, an experienced pilot, whose aeroplane crashed landed at Stoke-on-Trent municipal aerodrome at Meir in a severe snow storm on Dec 15 1935. Deciding it was impossible to make a safe landing, she tried to rise again and keep above the storm, but the plane struck a high tree about 200 yards from the aerodrome boundary. Miss Clive was thrown from the cockpit, but despite the fact that she was suffering from cuts on the head, her first thoughts were for her passenger, Roger David Clive, her 21-year old cousin, pinned underneath the wreckage, he subsequently died in Longton Cottage Hospital. The inquest exonerated Miss Clive from any blame (SA Dec 21 1935 p7ps. Dec 28 1935 p9 col 6).

Clive, Col Harry *First Territorial officer to take command of the 137th Staffordshire Infantry Brigade.* Of Willoughbridge, between 1927-31; he is the 2nd son of Col RC Clive (SA Aug 11 1934 p9p).

Charles Darwin. Cutting from an unidentified newspaper, showing The Famous Merry Tree, near Maer Hills.

Darwin, Charles (1809-82) and **Emma Wedgwood** (1808-96). *Maer's most famous old worthies, he developed 'Ye Maer Hypothesis'.* According to the parish register the natural historian married his cousin at Maer church on January 29 1839. She was the youngest daughter of Josiah Wedgwood II of Maer Hall. Darwin frequently visited his cousins and uncle at Maer for social reasons. In the mid 1820s, 1836-42, he took a close interest in Maer's flora, fauna, and geology. He developed this hypothesis there after 1842. It was the influence of earthworms on the generation of soils. At the suggestion of his uncle, Josiah Wedgwood II, Darwin investigated a peaty meadow at SJ 780384 by William Dabb's cottage and croft where debris scattered on the surface to counteract poor drainage 80 years earlier had become buried 12-14 inches deep due to the action of earthworms (Staffordshire Encyclopaedia).

Davenport, William *Maer's villain.* (1805-69). Pottery manufacturer of Maer Hall, who put Charles 'When I was a Child' Shaw's family in the workhouse (see Wolstanton under poorest).

Farming *Windsor Royal Show 1st prize 1939.* For a shorthorn bull called Maerfield Sultan, belonging to Miss Harrison of Maer Hall; the bull winning a prize at the Show (SA Sept 16 1939 p5p). *Staffordshire Agricultural Society Best Farmed Farm 1950* was Bates Farm, Maer, occupied by Mr JH Cooke, belonging to the Maer Hall estate (SCP Sept 1950 pp26-

27ps). *Staffordshire's small-bore shooting range* opened at Baldwin's Gate on land provided by Miss Harrison of Maer Hall, Aug 31 1951 (SA Sept 7 1951 p1p).

Folklore *Maer's best.* Various battles are said to have taken place at or near Maer in the Anglo-Saxon period. Penda, king of Mercia, reputedly killed Oswald, king of Northumbria, in one in 635 (ES Sept 1936 p4). In a battle in 642 Penda slew Maser or Maserfield at Maerfield (GNHS p74) near Maer. King's Bank in the Maer Hills is the tradition resting place of Oswy, Christian king of Northumbria, slain in a battle in 642 (STM June 1967 p27p).

Geology Maer Hills is Bunter; Maer village is Keuper Sandstones; Maerway Lane-Sidway is Upper Coal Measures; Minnbank is Bunter; Western Meres is Keuper Red Marls.

Goodwin, Raphe *Earliest person recorded in the parish register.* For his baptism on Jan 23 1558.

Holiday camp *Britain's first eco-friendly holiday complex.* Evolution Leisure Village on Maer Hills above Blackbrook, as proposed by Claymoss Properties in 2006 (ES Sept 8 2006 pp1-2map).

Natural history *Last remnant of an Ice Age lake covering the whole Maer valley.* Maer Pool (TTTD p241). *Rare plants.* Hybrids of bilberries as studied by Charles Darwin 1836-42; rhododendrons at Dorothy Clive Garden, Willoughbridge (NSFCT 1983 p33). *'The famous merry tree, near Maer Hills'.* A tree by Maer Pool noted for it blossom (photo & quote from unknown local newspaper of about April 17 1926).

Place-name Maer first appears in Domesday Book, 1086, and means 'lake, mere' (PNSZ p380).

Poorest There is no evidence for a Maer parish workhouse. After 1838 Maer poor, unable to support themselves, went to Newcastle Union workhouse on the south side of Keele Road, Thistleberry.

Population Maer was 113th most populated Staffordshire parish in 1801 with 382 people; 108th in 1811 with 454; 112th in 1821 with 451; 107th in 1831 with 505; 103rd in 1841 with 559; 108th in 1851 with 515; 108th in 1861 with 473; 118th in 1871 with 387; 115th in 1881 with 393; 114th in 1891 with 389; 108th= in 1901 with 436. Maer could be ranked 85th= worst affected Staffordshire parish for loss of men in WW1, with 12 lives lost.

Quote *Choicest.* Michael Raven in his Staffordshire and the Black Country

(1988) writes 'Between Stableford and Blackbrook the A51 passes through a beautiful valley of curving wooded hills. These are the Maer Hills.'

Singing *Staffordshire Musical Festival (Adult Section) winners 1923.* Maer Choir with three 1st prizes and one 2nd prize. The event, organised by the Staffordshire County Musical Association, was held on March 23-24 1923 at The Corporation Street Schools, Stafford. It appears to have been superseded by the Staffordshire Schools Music Festival from 1924, and to have developed out of the county musical competitions, begun by Haughton Musical Association as the Haughton and District Musical Society Competitions in 1913, largely through the efforts of Miss BE Royds of Haughton with the object of fostering the study of choral singing by village choirs. The festival was revived by the Staffordshire Federation of Women's Institutes in 1922 when Maer Choir won the part-song for female voices and the female voices contests (SA May 23 1914 p5 col 6. April 15 1922 p11p. March 31 1923 p4ps).

Wilson, Richard *3rd oldest Staffordshire man ever.* Of Maer, who lived to the age of 138 (Maer PR 1639; but the clerk evidently had his doubts as he entered in brackets (ut ipse dixit) (so he said himself)) (MJW p15).

Village life *Staffordshire Best Kept Village County winner (Small Village category) 1961, 1990, Newcastle District (Small Village) winner in 1990, 1993.* Maer village.

Meaford See Stone.

Meir Heath See Stone.

Meir Park See Stone.

Milwich Milwich was Staffordshire's 87th largest parish, consisting of 3,042 acres; 30th closest parish to the county town, 5.6m NNE; extremist length 2.6m; extremist width 2.7m. The parish's chief settlement is Milwich; there is none bigger and more compact than this small village; Garshall Green with Wheatlow Brooks is a very fragmented settlement in the north of the parish. Milwich is famous for the church bell.

Aler, John *Milwich's person with the earliest-surviving will.* It is dated July 18 1524.

Altitudes The highest point is 672 feet at Highpark. The lowest point is 361 feet by Wall Brook below Coton Hill Farm.

Church *All Saints* is one of 19 such county dedications (of AP churches); 50th= last

AP county church built dating from 1490. *Staffordshire's oldest church bell, and certainly the earliest dated.* No. 3 bell at Milwich's, dated 1409 (LGS p188) (SA Dec 28 1951 p3p of church. July 17 1953 p4 col 4). But it could be superseded by the mid C13 or earlier bells at St Chad's, Lichfield, and Farewell, only they are neither dated, nor named, accordingly this would make the Milwich bell the 3rd oldest in the county.

A model carved from the axle of the 1409 Milwich church bell

Clewlow, George *Milwich's saddest.* He was landlord of the Green Man Inn, Milwich, prior to WW1, and subject to deep fits of depression. In one such fit he popped across the road to the wheelwrights, borrowed his pliers, and pulled out all his own teeth. This may have cheered him up a bit, but the depression returned and, with no more teeth to extract, he tried to drown his wife in the water tank (notice in the Green Man, taken from *Timpson's English Country Inns*).

Davall, Miss Nellie *First Milwich person to broadcast.* Of Milwich. She may have this claim to fame, as she described modern dairying on air during Uttoxeter's first radio broadcast from the Market Room, at the White Hart Hotel, Feb 10 1938 (SA Feb 19 1938 p11 col 5).

Folklore *Milwich's best.* According to local legend some parliamentarian stragglers returning to Derby after losing the battle of Hopton Heath in March 1643 broke into Milwich church and attempted to loot the church plate. The churchwardens, however, put up a spirited defence putting soldiers to flight. The only casualty in the 'Battle of Milwich' was a dented chalice which was buried until after the Restoration (BFS p18). The story is doubted by some in the village (local info).

Garle, William *Rare example of early ecumenism.* Churchwarden of All Saints, c1900, who was also steward of the Wesleyan Methodist circuit (notice in the Green Man Inn, taken from *Timpson's English Country Inns*).

Geology All the parish is Keuper Red Marls.

Greaves, Dorothy *Earliest person recorded in the parish register.* For his baptism on May 15 1573.

Hough, Thomas *'The oldest British postman' 1905.* (1820-1908). Born Hilderstone. Blacksmith and postmaster at Milwich 1844-1901 and 1860-1902, respectively; although he must have still been delivering post in 1905. He lived at The Forge, a few doors away from The Green Man Inn in the heart of the village (The Stone Weekly News March 17 1905 p 5 col 1) (info Randle Knight).

Hulme, Miss Nancy Violet *'Dairy Maid of Stafford' 1959.* Of Coton Mill Farm, Coton, Milwich; she married James William Gregson at Gayton in 1960 (SA & Chron Jan 28 1960 p1).

Martin, Edgar Shemilt *Milwich's hero.* Son of Mr & Mrs Martin of Whitelow Brooks, Milwich. He was awarded the Military Medal, and was the first Milwich man to obtain this distinction (SA May 25 1918 p7 col 7).

Moss, Thomas *Milwich's villain.* Of Cheadle. While serving as a soldier in Germany, he encouraged friends to spread rumours of his death to his wife, Mary. Then on his returned in 1763 he entered into an 'agreement' with John Keating of Coton, in Milwich parish, Mary's new husband, to renounce his claims for £2.2.0. (SRO D917/11/1).

Muggletonians *Where God made his last revelation to man.* Milwich, being identified with Muggleton, the place where Muggletonians (a sect founded by John Reeve and Lodowick Muggleton (1609-98) claim God made his last revelation to man; Ilam has the same claim (ESH p31) (ZSB).

Place-name Milwich first appears in Domesday Book, 1086, and means 'mill wic' (PNSZ p390).

Quote *Choicest.* Rev Joseph White, curate of Milwich 1836-42. In a letter 1849 Rev White remembers his past Milwich curacy with fondness 'I have ministered in many parts of England.... But nowhere have I experienced such universal kindness and real regard as at Milwich and such as I cannot forget' (NSFCT 1980-1 p18).

Poorest Milwich parish entered into agreements to house its poor in Ipstones workhouse 1793 (D917/6/23), and Leigh workhouse 1800 (D917/6/24). After 1838 Milwich poor, unable to support themselves, went to Stone Union workhouse.

Population Milwich was 94th most populated Staffordshire parish in 1801 with 497 people; 91st in 1811 with 563; 101st in 1821 with 567; 102nd in 1831 with 551; 101th in 1841 with 563; 99th in 1851 with 591; 102nd in 1861 with 567; 101st in 1871 with 567; 98th in 1881 with 575; 103rd in 1891 with 515; 108th= in 1901 with 436. Milwich could be ranked 120th= worst affected Staffordshire parish for loss of men in WW1, with four lives lost.

Pubs *Staffordshire CAMRA Pub of the Year winner 2006.* Green Man Inn, Milwich (Sentinel Sunday Sept 10 2006 p21).

Shaw, James *Milwich's longest-serving vicar.* He served 62 years, 1610-1672.

Shirley, Sophia Caroline *Milwich's most famous old worthy and kindest.* (1779-1849). Titular Milwich resident and benefactress. Daughter of Nathaniel Curzon, 2nd Baron Scarsdale of Kedleston Hall, Derbyshire. In 1800 she married Robert Sewallis Shirley, Viscount Tamworth, who died in 1824 before he could succeed his father. From 1825 to her death she lived at Coton House. "She played a prominent part in local activities, particularly in supporting the village school. The local celebrations to mark the coronations of William IV and Queen Victoria were both held at her home. ...There still exists in the parish a table made from the six hundred year old Kedleston Oak inscribed to her memory and presented by her brother, to whom she had always been very close. He maintained links with the parish after her death and contributed £20 towards the re-building of the vicarage." Randle Knight in the North Staffordshire Field Club Transactions 1993.

Wesleyan Methodist chapel Opened 1936 on land at Garshall Green given by Mr E Halden; several farmers lent their teams to draw the materials (SA Feb 8 1936 p9 col 4).

Moddershall See Stone.

Mow Cop See Wolstanton.

Mucklestone Mucklestone was Staffordshire's 62nd largest parish, consisting of 4,252 acres; 80th farthest parish away from the county town, 13.6m NW; extremist length 2.6m; extremist width 3.1m. The parish's chief settlement is Mucklestone, a very small village. The parish is famous for The Devil's Ring and Finger, remnants of a megalithic chambered tomb, and an anvil with Queen Margaret of Anjou associations.

Alstonys, Richard *Mucklestone' person with the earliest-surviving will.* It is dated June 22 1522.

Altitudes The highest point is 725 feet to the E of Mucklestone Wood Farm. The lowest point is 280 feet by the Tern S of Oakley.

Aston, Edward *Earliest person recorded in the parish register.* For his baptism on May 13 1555. He was the son of Robert Aston.

Bourne, Thomas *First winner of 'Staffordshire Advertiser' Root Crop Competition cup, 'one of the best known progressive farmers of the younger generation in the north of the county' 1934.* Of Arbour Farm in 1934, son of JE Bourne (d1925), regarded in his day as 'one of the most prominent agriculturalists in the county'. The cup could be kept by a winner if won three times, not necessarily in succession (SA Oct 27 1934 p7p).

Brook House *Largest fireplace hood in Staffordshire.* Possibly the one 12 feet square at Brook House, Knighton (the house was moved from Bucknall).

Chetwode, Major-General Sir Philip *Staffordshire's highest ranking officer of WW1.* DSO. Of Oakley Hall, who had by late 1915 commanded the 5th Cavalry Brigade - the Scots Greys, the 12th Lancers and 20th Hussars - whose charge went through the German cavalry at Le Cateau. The county's other Major-General was Sir Walter Congreve of Chartley Hall, Stowe-by-Chartley (CL Nov 13 1915 p645).

Church *St Mary* is one of 23 such county dedications (most common dedication in the county); 81st= oldest AP county church dating from 1300. *Fancy that!* Before the mechanism of the clock in the tower was electrified it used to be weighted (duckers) with unusually stones (instead of caste iron weights) in leather buckets (info John Griffiths) (English Church Clocks 1280-1850. CFC Beeson. 1977. p150p). *In the churchyard.* From the road to the left of the anvil (see folklore) Mary Skelhorn school mistress d1876, who could be a descendent of the famous blacksmith William Skelhorn?

Florence, Henry *Mucklestone's villain.* When aged 26, he feloniously and violently assaulted Thomas Smith on Oct 26 1847 at Knighton tollgate, kept by Mr Smith. He was found guilty at the Lent Assizes 1850 and sentenced to death (SA March 16 1850 p7 col 2).

Folklore *Mucklestone's best.* Queen Margaret of Anjou watched the defeat of her forces at the battle of Blore Heath on Sept 23 1459 from the top of the church tower. She escaped on a horse, whose shoes were reversed, to mislead her pursuers, by a Mucklestone blacksmith called William Skelhorn. An anvil purporting to be the anvil he used remains in the churchyard. An inscription on a house opposite the church claims the house stands on the site of the smithy.

Queen Margaret of Anjou and her retinue observe the Battle of Blore Heath from Mucklestone church tower, 1459

The anvil in the church-yard on which blacksmith Skelhorn is said to have reversed the Queen's horse shoes to aid her escape from the scene

Geology The Drayton Spinney area is Keuper Red Marls; Mucklestone village (W), Oakley, Napley, Knightley and Aston areas is Bunter; Willoughbridge, Lunts Farm, Mucklestone village (E) and The Forty Acres is Upper Coal Measures.

Harrison, Miss Bertha *She had an extraordinary school attendance record.* She never missed a single day 1902-1913 during her time at Mucklestone School as Supplementary Teacher. When she left to become Assistant Teacher at St Mary's School, Stafford, March 15 1913, Mucklestone School manager's presented her with a written testimonial, clock and leather writing case (Mucklestone School Managers' Committee Minute book in SRO with newspaper cutting about Miss Harrison's achievement).

Hinchliffe, Sir (Albert) Henry *One of the original members of the board of directors of the Independent Television Association.* Born 1893. Manchester businessman, of Mucklestone Old Rectory, in 1954-59; Sheriff of Staffs 1944; President of the Association of British Chamber of Commerce 1950-52 (Who's Who) (SA Aug 13 1954 p2 col 6).

Laistre, Louis Martin de *First legal Catholic emigre priest to settle in Staffordshire.* He came to tutor the children of the rector of Mucklestone in c1794 (VCH vol 3 p112).

Lawrence, Sarah *Mucklestone's villainess.* She stole 14 lbs weight of bread, the property of James Key at Mucklestone, and was sentenced to six months prison at the Len Assizes 1847 (SA March 20 1847 p7 col 2).

Lee, Thomas *Mucklestone's longest-serving vicar.* MA. He served for 53 years, 1577-1630.

Lea Head Manor *Earliest replication of pineapples in Britain.* Perhaps the stone finials on gate piers at Lea Head Manor, which are late C17; pineapples were only introduced to this country in 1660 (DoE).

Natural history *Only weeping larch in England* was perhaps that on the lawn at Mucklestone Rectory, with a coverage of 100 yards (BPS p166).

Place-name Earliest record of the name Domesday Book, 1086. *Unique derivation for a surname.* Mucklestone will be from Mucklestone in this parish (PDS).

Poorest Mucklestone vestry minutes book (D5725/3/3) refer to a workhouse in 1819. In its churchwardens' accounts Easter 1826 to Easter 1827 it is recorded 'Spent at a Meeting concerning exchanging the Poors Building £0, 1s, 6d' (D5725/3/1). After 1836 Mucklestone poor, unable to support themselves, went to Market Drayton Union workhouse in Shropshire Street.

Population Mucklestone was 77th most-populated Staffordshire parish in 1801 with 683 people; 73rd in 1811 with 772; 70th in 1821 with 924; 71st in 1831 with 964; 78th in 1841 with 879; 81st= in 1851 with 876; 86th in 1861 with 827; 90th in 1871 with 755; 88th in 1881 with 763; 89th in 1891 with 709; 86th in 1901 with 727. Mucklestone could be ranked 104th= worst affected Staffordshire parish for loss of men in WW1 with 7 lives lost.

Quote *Choicest.* Weston E Vernon-Yonge in his quirky Bye-paths of Staffordshire, 1911, says 'Anyway, Winnington Glen is a fair valley, picturesque enough to repay those who may not know of it. And under the fostering care of the Meynell Family it is never likely to lose its charms of tree and shrub, of bud and blossom.'

Smith, William and his sister *Mucklestone's cruellest.* Of Mucklestone Wood Farm. In the early C19 they kept their brother, George (b c1781), an alleged lunatic, shut up in the attic half starved and in appalling conditions, so that they could receive £50 a year for keeping him. In 1826 news of his incarceration came to the attention of the local justices who set about freeing him. George was found naked, filthy and emaciated. On his way to Stafford lunatic asylum a pencil drawing was made of him at Eccleshall. An enquiry was made into the case by a commission set up by the Lord Chancellor. After his at the asylum in 1829, his body was returned to the same relations at their request. But in 1883, a workman accidentally struck a pick through Smith's coffin in Mucklestone churchyard and it was found to have never contained a body.

William Timmins - Staffordshire's tallest boy ever?

Stanley (nee Edwards),

Jessie *Staffordshire's best female naturalist (arguably).* (1893-1987). Farmer's daughter of Eccleshall Road Farm c1905-29, whose countrylore and farming articles were published by The Daily News, Farmer and Stockbreeder, and other journals in the late 1920s and early 1930s. She is buried in the churchyard. Her pen name was Jessie Frederick.

Timmins, William *Staffordshire's tallest boy ever (perhaps).* The parish register says of him 'The said William Timmins wanted not about 3 days of being 11 years old and was 6 feet high.' He was buried 23 June 1781 and was the son of Robert and Elizabeth Timmins of Napley Heath.

N-O

Newcastle under Lyme Newcastle was Staffordshire's 157th largest parish, consisting of 554 acres; 70th= farthest parish away from the county town, 14.5m NNW; extremist length 1m, making it 12th shortest parish in Staffordshire; extremist width 1.2m, making it 12th= narrowest parish in the county. The parish's chief settlement is the ancient corporate borough market town of Newcastle. The parish is famous for its pride and refusal to be associated with the nearby Potteries, a street market, Guildhall, hats and clay pipes.

Altitudes The highest point is 502 feet at The Brampton. The lowest point is 361 feet by Lyme Brook on the south boundary.

Philip Astley - 'Father of the Circus'

Astley, Philip *'Father of the Circus', Newcastle-under-Lyme's most famous old worthy.* (1742-1814). Theatrical manager and equestrian. Born Newcastle-under-Lyme the son of a cabinet maker, to which trade he served apprenticeship. He ran away from home and joined the army (Eliot's Light Horse), 1759. In 1770 he started a circus at Lambeth, and built Astley's Amphitheatre (1798), also establishing 19 amphitheatres all over Europe. Buried Cemetery of Pere la Chaise (TB Aug 1995 p36il).

Athletics *International Boys' 4 x 100m relay winner 1976, European Junior Games 4 x 400m relay bronze medalist 1978.* Melvin Fowell (b1960), of Newcastle Athletics Club. The first race was with The English Schools Athletic Association. In 1980 he was in the reserve British relay team at the Olympics (ES June 21 2008 pp58-59ps). *UK Fire Service Cross Country championships women's team trophy 6km race winner 2008.* Jacqui Slack, of Staffordshire Fire Service, of Newcastle-u-Lyme (E&S Oct 29 2008 p12pc).

Bell, Samuel *Inventor of a certain type of red glazed ware (reputedly).* Of Bell's Pottery, Lower St, early C18 (Trans. Eng. Ceramic Circle. iv, pts, 1 and 2) (VCH vol 8 p52). (NUL p90) (ROS vol i p32).

Beresford, Robert *Inventor of a motor car tyre rim.* (1880-1936), motor car pioneer, JP, thrice mayor of Newcastle, 1927, 28, 29. Patented improvements to bicycle gears 1896; rode his own patent freewheel bicycle from London to Newcastle in 11 and half hours, c1898; one of the first tradesmen in North Staffordshire to sell motor cars. With his patent rim - in general usage 1936 - however, he lacked finance to market it and was unable to reap the financial benefits (SA Dec 5 1936 p10p).

Borough, The *First recorded mock mayor* is Jatty Mayson, chosen Oct 1792.

Newcastle's youngest mayor was Malcolm Clarke in 1974, aged 27 (ES Your Week May 27 2006 p11); *first female mayor* was Miss Ethel Shaw 1954-55 (SA May 28 1954 p5). *'Historically, the most interesting mock mayoralty' (in the country).* Newcastle-under-Lyme's (SA Nov 21 1908 p4 col 4). *Longest serving member of Newcastle council 1984, and elected mayor most times* is William 'Bill' Welsby (d1984) (Labour) who served a record four times 1957-60, and for the 4th time (for the enlarged Newcastle borough) in 1975 (ES April 9 1975. Your Week. June 3 2006 p11p). *Last town council held at the Guildhall* was in Sept 1967, before moving to newly-built Civic Offices in Merrial Street (ES Your Week Feb 3 2007

Largest Union Jack ever flown from Newcastle-under-Lyme Civic Offices

p9). *Largest flag (or Union Jack) flown from a public building in Britain by 1980* was a union flag measuring 40 feet by 20 feet flown from the Civic Offices at Newcastle Carnival for ten minutes, on April 21 1977 (ES Dec 8 1976. April 21 1977) (GBR 1980 p166). *Fancy that!* Bungling officials in the Government Department of Communities mixed up their Newcastles in 2006-8, giving £2.7million meant for Newcastle-upon-Tyne to Newcastle-under-Lyme. The cash had come from funds to be given back to councils that had increased the amount they took in business rates. By early 2008 Newcastle-under-Lyme was refusing to return the money (Daily Telegraph Feb 14 2008 p1).

Bowls *Highest table skittle score in 24 hours* was 116,047 skittles, set on April 15-16 1990 by 12 players at the Castle Mona, Newcastle (GBR 1995 p290).

Brownsword, Miss Rose *Newcastle's first beauty 'Queen'.* Of Ashfield Road, a book keeper at Messrs A & G Murray's Cotton Mills, Cross Heath. She was chosen and crowned by the Mayor's Charity Committee at the Municipal Hall on Jan 27 1934 (SA Feb 3 1934 p9 col 4p).

Built environment *'one of the first purpose-built brick buildings in the borough'.* The Parsonage (later known as Rectory), south side of Lower Ironmarket, built

1698. The building was radically altered in 1926 when converted into shops (Andrew Dobraszczyc, 2008). *First purpose-built office block in North Staffordshire.* A three bay, two storey house adjoining John Sparrow's house on the north side of Ironmarket, built 1784 (Andrew Dobraszczyc, 2009). *Newcastle's first statue.* A bronze figure of Queen Victoria on a granite plinth in Nelson Place, unveiled in late 1903; presented by Sir AS Haslam, MP, as a memorial of Edward VIII's coronation (SA Oct 10 1903. Oct 6 1953 p2 col 3). *'Britain's ugliest building'*, the *'Rubik's Cube'*. Fine Fare supermarket with orange and green-panelling, Stafford Street, 1980s, so conspicuous pilots used it as a sighting guide into Manchester Airport (ES July 21 1993 p8p. April 17 1998 p3p. July 7 1999 p11p). (John Pedrazzini, 2008).

Fine Fare supermarket - 'Britain's ugliest building'

Butterworth, Frederick *First owner of a motor car in North Staffordshire (possibly).* Of Newcastle (source?). Harold Keates Hales of Burslem (see) had a motor car as early as 1897; the law requiring a motor car to be preceded by a man carrying a red flag was repealed in 1896 (POTP p109).

Church *St Giles* is one of 4 such county dedications (of AP churches); 61st= oldest AP county church dating from the C13 or roughly 1250. *In the churchyard* an cast-iron gravestone to John Smith, died 1614, aged 20, erected by his father, also John Smith (see). Originally it was in the chancel until moved to the churchyard when the church was rebuilt in George I's reign. In 1874 it was sold to a foundry at Etruria as scrap iron, but fortunately rescued and returned to the churchyard in 1911. It is some six feet long by two feet wide. The epitaph is raised in relief and occupies only the upper half of the slab. is unique in this area, although examples exist in the Forest of Dean; while many are to be found in the immediate market areas of past Sussex ironworks (NSFCT 1919 pp90-91) (STMSM Dec 1972 p27p).

Cliff, John *Fancy that!* According to the Wolverhampton Chronicle April 9 1823 p3 col 1:- 'John Cliff, hatter, Newcastle, drank 38 half-pints of ale, at the Boat and Horses, on Wednesday the 25th ult, at one sitting - This shocking excess produced immediate indisposition; for a day or two, however, he seemed to recover from his debauch, but on the Monday following he died'.

Cowdall, Stefanus *Earliest person recorded in the parish register.* For his baptism on July 10 1563. He was the son of William and Margaret Cowdall.

Douglas, Henry Pelham Archibald *Granted by Royal Warrant the privilege of providing a glove at Coronations by virtue of the tenure of the manor of Worksop, Notts.* Duke of Newcastle-under-Lyme. This grant was for the coronation of George VI; if invited by the King the glove was to be placed on his right hand, and the Duke could support his Majesty's right arm while he is holding the Sceptre (SA Nov 28 1936 p6 col 8).

Emery, Annie *Newcastle's saddest.* Born c1897, daughter of a brickworker of Rope Street. On July 12 1905 she was sent to fetch a spool of cotton, and was returning with it when it would seem she dropped it on the corner of Shelton New Road and Rope Street. At any rate something caused her just as she had safely gained the pavement to turn round and stoop forward into the street to pick something up. Just at this moment a motor car passed and struck her, fracturing her skull. She shortly died on the way to receiving medical treatment. All the circumstances were most unfortunate. Motor cars were then a rarity; the occupants were strangers to the area, lost and had taken a wrong turn; and the vehicle was only forced to travel near the pavement because a tramcar was travelling behind it. Annie's mother had only just risen from a sick bed, and when the 'sad news was broken to her by the girls' school teacher a little later in the morning, she fainted away.' (The Stone Weekly News July 15 1904 p5 col 3).

Folklore *Newcastle's best.* Two Newcastle pubs are allegedly haunted: The Bull's Head Inn, Lad Lane, believed to be up to 500 years old, is said to be haunted by the soldier Henry Knight, billeted there in 1842 (ES March 20 1996 p13p). Whilst the Gardners Arms Inn, Liverpool Road, was thought to be haunted by the ghost of a former publican's wife, Muriel Humpage (d1983), in 1992, by which time the inn had been renamed the Ale House (ES July

29 1997 p7).

Francks, Naomi *She was the first recorded birth of a Jewish person in North Staffordshire.* Born Newcastle in 1815, daughter of Abraham Francks, optician in Hick Street. Died 1879 (info Pauline Moreland. Jack Leighton Seminar, Keele University. 2009).

Freemasonry *First Freemason Grand Lodge in the Midlands.* Staffordshire Lodge, No. 88, founded by Grand Master John Ward, MP for Newcastle-u-Lyme, later Viscount Dudley and Ward, in 1730. He was initiated into the Grand Lodge in London in 1720. The Lodge predates lodges in Derbys, Shrops, Leics and Worcs (SA Dec 29 1917 p7 col 7). The 'Ancient' or 'Athol' Lodge of Newcastle was founded 1763. In 1767 the 'Moderns' Lodge of Newcastle was founded (SA Dec 29 1917 p7 col 7).

Geology Newcastle ancient borough is barren Coal Measures let down by the Apedale Fault; the rest of the borough is Upper Coal Measures.

Golding, John *He made the longest speech in committee in parliament.* When Labour MP for Newcastle at the committee on small amendments to the British Telecommunication's Bill on Feb 8-9 1983 lasting 11 hours 15 minutes (GBR 1996 p183).

Golf *Dutch Open Golf Tournament winner 2004.* David Lynn (b1974) of Newcastle, by three strokes; this was his first ever victory on the European tour (BBC news Aug 9 2004).

Harrison, Mr AW *'first man to produce X-ray photographs successfully in Britain'.* Of Liverpool Road, Newcastle. Harrison could claim this. Shortly after Prof Rontgen discovered that his rays had an effect on photographic plates which enabled objects to be seen through in the 1890s, two outfits were made by a German firm of electricians in London. One outfit was acquired by Guy's Hospital, London, and Mr Harrison bought the other. It appears Guy's did not at this time have a trained photographer-operator, but Mr Harrison, who held commissions from the old London and North Western Railway Company for carriage photographs, was an expert photographer (SA May 29 1953 p4 col 7-8) (VCH vol 8 p8).

Harrison, Thomas *Most eminent figure in the Fifth Monarchy movement.* Parliamentarian commander, born 1616 on the west side of Newcastle High Street. Son of Richard who kept a butcher's shop, and was mayor of Newcastle in 1626, 1633,

Thomas Harrison.

1643 and 1648. Thomas was one of the 59 signatories who signed the death warrant of Charles I. He was arrested in Merrial St, hung, drawn and quartered in London, 1660. Pepys was present at his disembowelling (POP pp169-170) (NSFCT 1943 p74) (SOSH p204) (NUL p58).

Hassall, Dr Eric *Youngest ever colliery surveyor in National Coal Board's history.* Born Lancashire c1930. Joined the NCB as apprentice mining surveyor 1947. When acclaimed as the above he covered the area from Carlisle to Birmingham. In 1972 he joined K Wardell & Partners in Newcastle, where he was involved in projects including the largest underground coal mine in the world in Brazil. In 1982 he led the merger of Wardells with William Armstrong & Sons of Newcastle upon Tyne; chairman of the British Geological Survey 1994-2001; CBE 1999 (ES March 24 2010 p3pc).

Hemmings, Ann *The Cherry Orchard miser.* She was found starving, unconscious and on the point of death alone in her cottage in the Cherry Orchard area of Newcastle in summer 1896, with 38 sovereigns stitched into the body of her skirt. She was taken to the workhouse infirmary, nourished and attended to, but nevertheless died some days later (SA July 11 1896 p4 col 7. July 18 1896 p5 col 2).

Holland, John *One of only two frying-pan makers in the country 1686.* When the flat-work was finished at Keele Forge the iron plates were brought to John Holland's other forge at Newcastle and worked into shape. He married 1654, and died 1690. The other works was at Wandsworth, Surrey (NHS p335) (NSFCT 1954 pp42-43) (POP p159).

Ives, Peter *George III's favourite coachman.* He served the royal family for some 50 years. His wife, Sarah, outlived him and died after a lingering illness in her 60th year at Newcastle-under-Lyme in late 1812 (SA Jan 4 1913 p5).

Kennedy, Jonathan *Strange but true!* Of Newcastle, aged 2, was summoned to serve on jury service at Hanley Crown Court, 1982 (ES Your Week Feb 2 2007 p6).

Kite, Sgt Fred alias 'Buck' *Newcastle's hero, only British soldier to win the* M.M. thrice in WW2. (1920-94). Born Newcastle; attended Hassell Street School. In WW2 he joined the 3rd Royal Tank Regt. His first Military Medal was won in North Africa in 1943; his 2nd in Normandy in 1944; his 3rd a month later when he scored five direct hits on enemy tanks before being wounded. There is a portrait of him in the officers' mess of a modern tank regt called 2RTR, as well as a building named after him at his old regiment's cadet college in Harrogate (ES Your Week May 12 2007 p9p).

Sgt Fred Kite - The only British soldier in WW2 to win the M.M. thrice.

Libraries *North Staffordshire's first-known book club.* A sort of circulating library of John Swan of Newcastle, 1745 (Andrew Dobraszczyc, 2006).

Military defence *First meeting of the Newcastle Rifle Volunteers* took place on Dec 19 1859 (SA Jan 14 1860 p5 col 4).

Miller, William Henry *'One of the most famous of book collectors'.* Conservative MP for Newcastle-under-Lyme, 1830-41. Died 1848 (SA Jan 10 1948 p7).

Morris, Eva *Possibly world's oldest person 2000, Britain's oldest person 1999, 2nd oldest woman in Britain 1998, Staffordshire's 8th oldest woman ever.* Born 1885. She grew up in Lower Street, Newcastle, lived her adult life at Crewe, Stafford and finally Autumn House nursing home, Stone, where she died aged 114, a week short of her 115th birthday (SN Nov 9 2000 p25p).

Eva Morris towards the end of her life.

Natural history *Strange but true!* A cabbage with eleven distinct formed hearts, planted in spring 1840, was grown in the garden of Alexander Hooks at the Pool Head, and called by the Staffordshire Advertiser 'a great vegetable curiosity' (SA Aug 22 1840 p3 col 4). *'Charles Dickens'.* A celebrated Dalmatian dog belonging to Mr HM Mercer, tobacconist, in Merrial Street. 'Charles Dickens' had by 1893 won a number of gold medals at the prin-

'Charles Dickens' - the celebrated Dalmatian dog.

cipal shows viz., Crystal Palace, Birmingham, Manchester, Liverpool, etc (Graphic Description: Newcastle-under-Lyme (Authentic and Interesting. 1893)).

Parton, David 'Des' *He wrote the number 1 hit single 'Sad Sweet Dreamer'.* Of Whitehouse Road, Cross Heath, born c1944. His hit single reached number 1 in the UK charts in Oct 1974, when Parton was employed by M and M Music, London - the company whose directors were Tony Hatch and Jackie Trent (ES Oct 11 1974. Oct 19 1976).

Pedestrianism *Man who tried to walk 1,750 miles in 1,000 successive hours.* Manks, the pedestrian, from Tuesday May 26 1852 at the Noah's Ark Bowling Green, Newcastle, taking him six weeks, day and night to complete (SA May 29 1852. May 30 1952 p5 col 6).

Place-name Newcastle-under-Lyme first appears as Nouu Oppidu cu soca sub Lima in 1166, and means 'New Castle with its jurisdiction under the Lyme'; there is possibly an even earlier reference of c1142 - novum castellum de Staffordshira (PNSZ p408).

Poorest Property in Higherland, Newcastle, served as a workhouse from 1731. In 1838-9 Newcastle Union workhouse, in Keele Road, Thistleberry, was built. It was demolished in 1938 (VCH vol 8 p31,33).

Population Newcastle was 14th most populated Staffordshire parish in 1801 with 4,604 people; 12th in 1811 with 6,175; 12th in 1821 with 7,031; 13th in 1831 with 8,192; 14th in 1841 with 9,838; 16th in 1851 with 10,290; 17th in 1861 with 12,638; 16th in 1871 with 15,538; 17th in 1881 with 16,838; 17th in 1891 with 17,805; 17th in 1901 with 19,147. Newcastle could be ranked 6th worst affected Staffordshire parish for loss of men in WW1, with 745 lives lost.

Public services *The spring which supplied Newcastle with its first piped water.* Browning's Well (W p302). *One of the first provincial towns to institute communal street lighting.* Newcastle 1799 (VCH vol 8 p36). *One of the first municipal public baths in Staffordshire.* Newcastle, opened 1852 (County Museum, Shugborough). *Last independent borough police force to amalgamate with Staffordshire Police*

Force. Newcastle which was separate force between 1834-1947 (Staffordshire Police 150th Anniversary Commemorative Issue. 1992).

Pubs *Newcastle's oldest pub.* The Star, Ironmarket, recorded as an inn in 1734 and originally was a medieval domestic structure involving four cottages. From 1966 the inn was called 'Super Star'. In 1965 it was discovered the pub had more medieval timber framing than any other building in Newcastle (ES Nov 21 1974). *Hon John Byng's (5th Viscount Torrington) most 'savage, dirty, ale house' he ever entered.* Roebuck Inn, Newcastle, 1792 (The Torrington Diaries 1781-94, vol 3 p127).

Punkie, Billy *Newcastle's villain.* He features in the Mock Mayor painting and was reckoned to be a notorious footpad in London, c1843 (NUL p123 il).

Quotes *Choicest.* Neville Malkin in his A Grand Tour, 1976, said 'The dignified, red brick and stone Guildhall in the High Street has presided over the busy marketplace for more than 200 years and provides a fitting expression of the growth of Newcastle.' Newcastle is mentioned in the T.V. comedy series 'Porridge' in the episode about Fletcher (Ronnie Barker) having to share his cell with Justice Stephen Rawley (Maurice Denham) who sentenced him to prison. Fletcher refers to a former inmate, a native of Newcastle-under-Lyme, who went home to bury his relations '.. under lime' (Porridge, Series 3, Poetic Justice episode, first transmitted 25th February 1977).

Religion *Staffordshire's first registrations under the Toleration Act 1689.* Four Protestant meeting houses in Newcastle, 1689 (HOS 1998 p68).

Schools *One of the earliest Sunday schools in Staffordshire.* That founded by John Whitridge, congregational minister at Newcastle in the 1780s (NUL p64). *First headmaster of Newcastle High School.* Francis Elliott Kitchener from 1876, cousin of Lord Kitchener of Khartoum (ES Staying In Nov 24 2007 p13). *Most assisted places in UK for an independent school.* In the final years of the Government assisted places scheme Newcastle under Lyme School had 60 assisted places per annum (info Newcastle under Lyme School). *First special school in the country to use the 'Light-Writer'.* Blackfriars School in 1974. This revolutionary new machine helped deaf children. It involved a speed typewriter with an attached screen. The child using it was able to tap out letters which were flashed onto the screen. It had been at the Design Centre exhibition earlier in 1974 (ES Oct 23 1974). *One of the first Beacon Schools in Staffordshire.* Blackfriars School (see also Berkswich) (BBC Midlands Today July 7 1998).

Shopping and banking *'The best shop in Newcastle'* in the C18. William Watkiss's general store, upper Ironmarket. Watkiss sold it in the early C19. In the early C21 the building was Yates' wine bar (Andrew Dobraszczyc, 2008). *North Staffordshire's first major shopping development.* The Guild Hall shops, built c1718-19 by the Levesons of Trentham Hall. It included the Fletcher shop. Lancaster Buildings now stand on the site (Andrew Dobraszczyc, 2008). *Newcastle's first bank.* Kinnersley's, 1780 (Andrew Dobraszczyc, 2008).

The Guildhall in the High Street

Shops lining the High Street in 1839

Shows *Staffordshire's first art exhibition* was held at Mr Sheppard's Repository of Arts, High Street, Newcastle, 1842. It comprised some 80 pictures, sculptures and architectural drawings. Apart from works by local artists and amateurs, paintings by David Cox, Henry Bright and JMW Turner, were also included. James Astley Hammersley, born Burslem 1815, appears to have been the moving spirit of the venture, and he became joint-secretary with R. Sheppard (SLM Feb 1948 p75); an

earlier art exhibition occurred at Shelton c1820 (Andrew Dobraszczyc, 2008). *First Newcastle Music Festival* was in 1932; the adjudicator was Granville Bantock (ES Oct 4 2008 p29). *'The floral town'* Newcastle-under-Lyme (Staffordshire Breaks 2006. Staffordshire Tourism).

Shufflebotham, Frank *World Town Crier champion 1979.* Former Newcastle town crier (ES May 24 2008 p31).

Simms, Rupert *'One of the best known residents of Newcastle' 1937.* (1853-1937). Second-hand bookseller in Newcastle, who published the 'Bibliotheca Staffordiensis' 1894 (SA Aug 7 1937 p11 col 6).

Skerratt, General *Newcastle's Napoleonic War hero.* Native of Newcastle, died Bergen-op-Zoom, Holland, March 10 1814, in the build up to General Thomas Graham's (later Lord Lynedoch) bold and daring attack upon the almost impregnable fortress there, March 18 1814. Acting on information that the ice in the trenches was sufficiently strong to bear his troops Gen. Graham captured the town to find Gen Skerratt's body surrounded by the mangled corpses of his comrades in one of the public squares. A memorial was set up to his memory in St Paul's Cathedral; he left a fiance, Hannah Eliza Caldwell (b1785) (Hannah Roscoe (nee Caldwell) website, 2008) (Weekly Sentinel Oct 13 1928).

Smith, Mrs A Berks *Newcastle's oldest resident 1896.* Born March 20 1794. She died aged 102 retaining all her faculties, save her hearing which was defective (SA March 28 1896 p5 col 2).

Smith, John *He erected the first blast furnace in Wales for production of iron, 'the first local ironmaster of whom a good deal is known'.* Ironmaster with a forge at Heath End (now part of Silverdale), Keele parish. Capital burgess of Newcastle-under-Lyme from 1596, mayor in 1598, 1604, 1616. The Welsh furnace was at Nannau, Merionethshire, erected 1597. Died 1620 (STMSM Dec 1972 p27p).

Social care *'Largest social landlord in Staffordshire'.* Aspire Housing Kingsley, The Brampton, with just under 9,000 homes for rent (Staffordshire County Guide 2006/7 p114, advert). *National home (2002) of the British Association for Service to the Elderly (1974).* Hassall St, Newcastle.

Sport See Athletics, Bowls, Golf, Pedstrianism, Swimming, Volleyball.

Stanton, George *Boy killed by an elephant belonging to Messrs.Bostock and Wombwell's menagerie.* Son of Jesse Stanton, cratemaker, of Newcastle. On April 20 1872 he was with other children in a passage leading to the Angel Inn, Hanley, feeding a female 12-year old elephant with nuts and bread. In the absence of supervision the animal squeezed George against a wall, then took him with its trunk - the returned keeper shouting at it - threw the boy against a wall, possibly with its trunk. George was taken back to Newcastle and died the following evening. At an inquest the jury passed a verdict that the boy died from having been crushed by an elephant ('Orrible Murders: An Anthology of Victorian Crime and Passion Compiled from Police News. Leonard De Vries. 1971. p52).

George Stanton is tossed against a wall by an elephant, as depicted in 'Orrible Murders: An Anthology of Victorian Crime and Passion Compiled from Police News

Swimming *'one of the foremost of the Midlands clubs' (women's swimming).* Newcastle Ladies Amateur Swimming Club in 1950 with a membership of 250 (SLM Feb 1950 p95).

Theatre and cinema *Last production staged at the Municipal Hall.* Carousel by Newcastle Amateur Operatic Society in 1965; the building was demolished in 1967 (ES Staying In Nov 24 2007 p13). *Alan Ayckbourn's first play.* The Square Cat, was performed at the old Municipal Hall in 1959 (ES Feb 2 2008 Staying In

p12). *Newcastle's first electric cinema.* Newcastle Cinema Theatre (formerly The Theatre Royal) 1920s (SP-t).

Trade *4th in country for the manufacture of clay pipes in C17.* Newcastle (ES Your Week March 17 2007 p9). *'The Hatteries'.* What Newcastle could have become known as, considering the town's principal trade was hatting C16-C18, considering Stoke-upon-Trent became known as 'The Potteries' (Andrew Dobraszczyc, 2008). *Retailer of the Year 1995.* Boots Herbal Store, Merrial St, Newcastle, as awarded by Realfare, health food suppliers (ES Dec 6 1995 advertisement feature).

Volleyball *Volleyball English under-16 champions 1982, 2009.* Newcastle (ES April 22 2009 p47). *First recipient of a national leadership award.* Colin Roberts, chairman of Newcastle-under-Lyme Volleyball Club, aged 60, as granted by the Institute of Sport, Parks and Leisure, in July 2009; the award reflected the club's growing national profile, particularly in youth development (ES July 20 2009 p40pc).

Walker, Jane *Only woman in Staffordshire charged with publishing and distributing seditious material in the early C19.* Of Newcastle; she was subsequently discharged (LOU p211).

Wedgwood, Joseph *'The Last of the Radicals'.* (1872-1943). Long-serving MP for Newcastle. This was the title for his biography by Veronica Wedgwood (SLM Feb 1952 p19p).

Newchapel See Wolstanton.

Normacot See Stone.

Norton Bridge See Chebsey.

Onneley See Madeley.

Oulton See Stone.

P-R

Penkhull See Stoke-upon-Trent.

The Potteries An undefined district roughly covering the former earthenware manufacturing district of North Staffordshire, certainly covering Burslem and Stoke-upon-Trent parishes, together with Tunstall in Wolstanton. The expression 'The Potteries' was in use during the latter half of the C18, and according to the OED it it first recorded in 1825; although there is an example of 1794, see *Barlaston*

Church.

Artist of the Potteries. Reginald Haggar (1905-88), born Suffolk, coming to the Potteries in 1929. Art director of Mintons -1935; Head of Stoke School of Art 1935-41; Head of Burslem School of Art 1941-55. He devoted much of his life to recording visually the changing landscape of the Potteries (ES May 29 2010 p27p).

Books For the first bookseller see *S-u-T* Libraries and bookseller. For the last town to get a library see *S-u-T* Fenton.

Buildings For the oldest terraces in the Potteries see *Burslem* Housing. For the smallest occupied dwellings see *Burslem* Housing.

Cars First Automobile Association base see *S-u-T* Cars. First car in the Potteries see *S-u-T* Cars. First registered car in the Potteries see *S-u-T* Cars. First garage in the Potteries see *Burslem* Transport. First motorised funeral procession *S-u-T* Cars. For the first purpose-built bus station see *S-u-T* Trams and buses.

Cartoonist of the Potteries. Dave Follows (1941-2003), born Stafford, whose popular cartoon 'May un Mar Lady' appeared in The Sentinel from July 8 1985 to Oct 3 2003. His first published cartoon appeared in SA in 1971.

Cathedral of the Potteries see *S-u-T* Methodism.

Catherine Cookson of the Potteries see *S-u-T* Margaret Kaine.

Cinema For the first Potteries showing of moving pictures see *S-u-T* Cinemas. For the first Potteries cinema See *Wolstanton* Cinemas. For the Potteries' biggest cinema see *S-u-T* cinemas. For the last small independent cinema see *S-u-T* Cinemas.

Reginald Haggar - Artist of the Potteries.

Dialect *Earliest evidence of Potteries dialect.* A conversation of 1810 as quoted by John Ward, author of *History of the Borough of Stoke-on-Trent* (1843) (Fred Leigh publication) (ES Oct 13 2007 staying in p17). *John Abberley's most memorable practitioner of Potteries-speak.* Dr Arnold Green, ceramic research scientist (ES Oct 13 2007 staying in p17). *Greatest writer in the Potteries dialect.* Dr Wilfred Bloor (1915-93) of Audley. His first 'Jabez' story appeared in the Evening Sentinel in Sept 1968 under the pseudonym A. Scott. 'Jabez' is a composite character, reflecting memories of Bloor's childhood in the village of Scot Hay (hence the pseudonym). With a few breaks the stories appeared every week in ES from 1968 to his death. 'Jabez Album' and 'Jabez Stories' appeared in 1980 and 1988, respectively. There is a Wilfred Bloor Collection at Keele University Special Collections. *Academic of the Potteries dialect* could be said to be John Levitt (c1923-2005),

English Literature lecturer and Head of Adult Education at Keele University (The Guardian Sept 22 2005).

Father of the Potteries see *Burslem* Enoch Wood, and *S-u-T* Josiah Wedgwood.

Father of The Mother of the Potteries *Burslem* Enoch Wood.

Industry For the most ambitious and comprehensive display of local products ever staged see *S-u-T* Industry.

Lowry of the Potteries see *Norton-in-the-Moors* (DYKT2) Arthur Berry.

Mother of the Potteries see *Burslem* Pottery.

Novelist of the Potteries see *Burslem* Arnold Bennett.

Paradise of the Potteries see *Audley* Clough Hall.

Parks For the first public park see *S-u-T* Parks. For the finest work in wrought iron (excepting Trentham Hall gates) *Wolstanton* Tunstall.

Pastimes For the last recorded instance of bull-baiting see *S-u-T* Bull baiting. For the first pub saved by the Pub Preservation Group pub saved see *Wolstanton* Pubs and hotels.

People For the oldest inhabitant of The Potteries see *S-u-T* Mrs Catherine Ryder. For the recipient of the V.C. in the Potteries see *S-u-T* Pte James Grundy. For one of the first women to graduate from university see *S-u-T* Gertrude Barlow. For the Potteries' greatest drunk see *Burslem* Vincent Riley.

Photographer of the Potteries. Ernest JD Warrilow (1909-2000). Born in Etruria. He bought his first camera, a No. 2 Box Brownie, in 1920. In 1927 he joined ES as a junior press photographer. He stayed with the paper until 1974. MBE 1964 for service to the city of Stoke-on-Trent. The Warrilow Collection at Keele University Special Collections comprise over 1,800 photographs of the Potteries 1870s-1970s.

Pleasantest village in the Potteries in 1795 was said to be Tunstall see *Wolstanton* Tunstall.

Politics For the first Labour Party candidate see *Burslem* Samuel Finney. For the first wearing an Oswald Moseley black shirt see *S-u-T* Sam Dunn.

'The Potteries county' was the name proposed in jest in 1888 for a unitary authority covering the Potteries (SA July 28 1888 p4 col 5).

The Potteries Poet *Trentham* Frank Smith.

The Potteries Prodigy see *S-u-T* Pottery Industry: People (Evelyn Bailey).

Pottery industry For the first works bell see *Burslem* Pottery. For the first female employed as a transferrer of the impressions from copper plates to pottery see *S-u-T* Pottery Industry: People. For the tallest potbank chimney see *S-u-T* Pottery Industry: Buildings. For the largest bottle ovens see *S-u-T* Pottery Industry: Buildings. For the last firing of a bottle oven for commercial purposes see *S-u-T* Pottery Industry: Buildings.

Religion For the first New Connexion chapel in the Potteries see *S-u-T* Methodism. For the first Sunday school in the Potteries see *S-u-T* Methodism. For one of the nicest churches for its architecture 1959 see Burslem Churches: Holy Trinity. For the 2nd only complete peal in any scientific campanological method ever see *S-u-T* Churches.For the last synagogue in The Potteries see *S-u-T* Judaism.

School For the Potteries' one famous in educational circles see *S-u-T* Schools.

Sport For the first marathon in the Potteries see *S-u-T* Athletics: Distance running.

Pershall See Eccleshall.

Rough Close See Barlaston/ Stone.

S

Sandon Sandon was Staffordshire's 77th largest parish, consisting of 3,574 acres; 19th= closest parish to the county town, 3.8m NE; extremist length 3.4m; extremist width 2.6m. The parish's chief settlement is Sandon, a small estate village intersected by the Lichfield-Stone road; the church is at some distance away on a hill, overlooking the lost medieval village of Sandon. The parish is famous for the great tomb and wall paintings in the church of Sampson Erdeswick.

Altitudes The highest point is 623 feet at Warren Farm. The lowest point is 269 feet near the Trent below Pitt's Column.

Beck, Colour Qmr-Sergt JH *Sandon's WW1 hero.* Born 1895. Of Sandon Farm, of King's Shropshire Light Infantry, awarded the Meritorious Service Medal for service in WW1 (SA July 6 1918 p7 col 1).

Church *All Saints* is one of 19 such county dedications (of AP churches); 5th= oldest county church dating from 1090. *Church with the 2nd most hatchments in Staffordshire.* Sandon with 7; there are 78 known hatchments in the county (Hatchments in Britain No. 8 p147). *Most interesting thing.* The Erdeswick family tree fresco painted on both sides of the chancel commissioned by Sampson Erdeswick a little before his death in 1603. They were rediscovered during a church restoration in 1929. Nearby, on the north wall of the chancel stands a huge coloured monument built for himself in 1601. It is sculpted by Joseph Hollemans of Burton, and has his recumbent effigy, and the kneeling figures of his first wife Elizabeth Dikesswell and his second wife Mary Neale, in recesses above. The recesses are surrounded by coats of arms. Charles Masefield in his Little Guide to Staffordshire called it 'sumptuous'. In addition, the chancel has three more Erdeswick monuments, all table tombs (SOS pxxxvi, il, pxli, ppxlii, xliii) (SMC p172) (W p403) (PS p56) (LGS pp208,264) (VCH vol 2 p202) (BAST vol 71 pp5-6,7 pl 3a) (NSFCT 1929 p172) (SOSH p159) (SH pp22-36,35) (CHMS p48).

Engineering *Staffordshire's only bridge built of precast re-inforced concrete units by 1948.* The three span one at Sandon over the Trent, costing £30,000. It replaced the bridge washed away in floods in Feb 1946 (SA Nov 8 1947 p2 cols 5-6p).

Erdeswick, Hugh. *Sandon's villain.* Lord of Sandon. With his three brothers he terrorised Staffordshire between 1407-14, during a period when the representatives of the great houses of the county - the Staffords, Audleys, Dudleys, who usually kept check on lesser gentry - were all represented by minors; they harangued Sir John Bagot seeking to kill him 1407; besieged Sir John Blount, constable of the Duchy of Lancaster, at Rocester 1409; attacked Edmund, Lord Ferrers, at Chartley 1413; had allies in the Mynors, Gresleys, Giffards and Sir William Newport; later reconciled to the Duchy, and adhered

under Henry V; reformed Hugh became
a Commissioner of the Peace for Staffs
1415-24; JP 1415-7, 1420-4; sheriff 1423-
4; MP for Staffs 1421, 1433 (SHC 1912
pp281, 313, 315. 1917-8 pp177-9) (NS-
FCT 1912 p183).
   Erdeswick, Sampson *Sandon's most
famous old worthy, he compiled the 3rd
earliest county history, 1st history of
Staffordshire.* Antiquarian of Sandon
Old Hall. He much embellished the parish church (see) before he died in 1603.
The claims relate to his history of Staffordshire 'A View of Staffordshire' written 1593-1602, but first published in
1717. Nationally, the book appears to be
only preceded by Carew's The Survey of
Cornwall, 1570s-80s, and Lambarde's A
Perambulation of Kent, 1570 (The Shell
Country Alphabet. Geoffrey Grigson.
1966 p108). *George Tollet's most errone-
ous and defective book.* The first editions
of Sampson Erdeswicke's history, 'A Survey of Staffordshire' (1717, 1723).

The
magnificent
tomb which
Sampson
Erdeswick
(d1603)
had erected
for himself
in Sandon
church.

   **Fisher, Pilot Officer Geoffrey Wilson
O'Neil** *Sandon's WW2 hero, he flew on
the first raid over Berlin.* Son of Rev WF
O'Neil Fisher, vicar of Sandon 1920-27.
He took part in the daring air raid on Berlin on Aug 25-26 1940, that was to change
the outcome of the Battle of Britain, and
perhaps that of the war itself. On leaving Yarlet Hall Prep School he entered
the Royal Navy serving on board HMS
Worcester, transferring to the RAF in
June 1939. In the London Gazette for Feb
1941 he was awarded the Distinguished
Flying for 'gallantry and Devotion to
Duty' in bombing raids over hostile territory', including five missions over Berlin (Stafford At War. an SN publication.

1995. p6).
   Folklore *Sandon's best.* That the Dog and
Doublet Inn, a former inn on the main road
farther north than the present inn (built in
1905) in Sandon, reputedly, received its
name after a dog brought a blooded doublet of a murdered man to the pub and so
alerted the neighbourhood to the murder
(IOM p63) (SSBOP p55) (SPN p103).

A murder at Sandon was brought to
the attention of villagers by a dog
carrying a blooded doublet.

   Franklin, Neil *Played 25 consecutive matches for England, 'generally regarded as the country's best centre-half',
first professional footballer to play for a
foreign club.* (1922-96). Born Shelton,
Stoke-upon-Trent. He obtained 27 full
England caps (25 consecutively in 1948),
when playing for Stoke City FC 1939-50.
For the summer season 1950 he moved
to Independiente Santa Fe of Bogota,
Colombia. In Feb 1951
he returned to England
to play for Hull City
and other clubs, retiring
from football to run the
Dog and Doublet Inn in
Sandon. In 1998 Billy
Wright selected him for
his Dream Team for the
50th Anniversary of the
Footballer of the Year.
The first claim is from
ES Your Week Sept 2
2006 p5; the second
claim and information is
from Wikipedia, 2009;
the third claim is by
Alan Walker.

Neil Franklin,
former England
footballer, who ran
the Dog and Dou-
blet Inn, Sandon
in the 1950s.

   Gardening *Unique deep-bed kitchen
garden* was claimed by John and Marie
Lowe of their Romer Farm garden (National Gardens Scheme (Staffordshire)
guide 2006).
   Geology Hardiwick and SW fringe
is Keuper Red Marls; Sandon village,
church, Sandon road is Bunter; Sandon
Hall is Keuper Sandstones; the east side
of the parish is Keuper Red Marls.
   Henley, Miss Frances E *First member
of the Staffordshire Land Army awarded*

the Distinguished Service Bar. Of Coventry. She was employed by a Mr Wright of Sandon Farm, who on Sept 2 1919 when all the farm labourers were on strike, rescued a cow stuck in the mud banks of the Trent. The Distinguished Service Bar is the Land Army's V.C. (SA Nov 15 1919 p2 col 4p).

Place-name Sandon first appears in Domesday Book, 1086, and means 'sandhill' (PNSZ p475).

Poorest Sandon parish used Leigh workhouse by an agreement of 1799 (D1048/3/3) (D22/A/PO/121). After 1838 Sandon poor, unable to support themselves, went to Stone Union workhouse.

Population Sandon was 93rd most populated Staffordshire parish in 1801 with 516 people; 104th in 1811 with 480; 105th in 1821 with 513; 101st in 1831 with 558; 100th in 1841 with 586; 102nd in 1851 with 556; 101st in 1861 with 590; 100th in 1871 with 576; 103rd in 1881 with 513; 106th in 1891 with 472; 106th in 1901 with 458. Sandon could be ranked 68th= worst affected Staffordshire parish for loss of men in WW1, with 23 lives lost.

Quote *Choicest.* John Darlington, Stafford Borough archaeologist in his Stafford Past, 1994, well evokes Sandon's medieval past 'If you drive up the narrow lane leading off the A51 at Sandon, north-east of Stafford and head towards All Saints Church you will quickly find yourself transported away from the hubbub of the 20th century back over 600 years. For in this quiet backwater of Staffordshire can be found wonderfully preserved evidence of the medieval landscape.'

Ryder, Lady Susan Georgina *She was slightly acquainted with Lord Byron,* having met him at London parties given by her parents and their friends. Daughter of 2nd Earl of Harrowby (d1847). Died 1860 (Aspects of the Black Country. Charles JL Elwell. 1991 p155).

Ryder, Sir Alfred Phillips *Admiral who drowned falling off a pier.* KCB. Of Torquay (1820-88), 7th son of Henry Ryder, Bishop of Lichfield and Coventry, 3rd son of Nathaniel Ryder. He was in indifferent health and decided to take a trip on the Thames believing it would do him good. He was on Vauxhall pier when a big craft came up the river creating a large wave and swept him off (SA May 5 1888 p6 col 5)

Ryder, Henry Dudley *4th President of the British & Foreign Bible Society.*

(1836-1900). 4th Earl of Harrowby. Of Sandon Hall. He served Feb 1886 to his death (info Rosemary Matthew).

Ryder, John Herbert Dudley *He was impressed with German 'National Socialist mentality', died just three days after his wife.* (1867-1956), 5th Earl of Harrowby. Of Sandon Hall. Son of Henry Dudley Ryder, 4th Earl. His wife, the Countess, Hon Dame Mabel Smith, died on March 27, and the Earl passed away on March 30 1956; they were buried on the same day, March 31 1956; a brass was erected in Sandon church to their memory in 1960. In 1937 he visited Germany to see their Small Holdings and Allotments programmes, as well as Labour and Hitler Youth Camps, and reported glowingly about his trip in the Staffordshire Advertiser (SA Aug 21 1937 p6 col 3. SA & Chron April 5 1956 p1. April 7 1960 p11).

Ryder, Dudley *Longest serving Deputy Lieutenant of Staffordshire, the Earl who banned bingo at the village club.* (1892-1987), 6th Earl of Harrowby. Of Sandon Hall. Author of 'Geography of Everyday Things' and 'England at Worship'. In 1962 villagers thought of trying Bingo nights to raise funds for re-roofing the village club. But the Earl, in his capacity as owner of the club, banned it on the grounds of being 'undesirable' and that it was 'an unsuitable and dangerous innovation in a small village community'. As a result all but one of the club committee - Major AT Targett, an estate manager - resigned (SA & Chron Oct 11 1962 p15).

Sandon Hall *'one of the few great Staffordshire houses still lived in by the family who built it'.* Sandon Hall, built by the Harrowbys in 1852 (Historic Houses & Gardens. Trevor Fisher. 1996. p76). *A unique collection of WW1 posters* are housed at Sandon Hall (Historic Houses & Gardens. Trevor Fisher. 1996. p77). *'largest gathering of Staffordshire service men since the war (WW1)' 1936.* The drumhead service in Sandon Park on Sunday afternoon, May 17 1936, arranged by the North and South County Committees of the British Legion in connection with the fraternal visit to England of representatives of ex-Service men's organisations in 14 countries. This included a German delegation to the Park with their swastika banner (SA May 23 1936 p11ps). *Only shrine to only assassinated British Prime Minister.* There is a hillside alcove to Spencer Perceval in

Sandon Hall grounds. He was shot dead in the lobby of the House of Commons in 1812 by John Bellingham. *700th couple to marry at Sandon Hall.* Kate Cross and Mark Fletcher of Tithe Barn Road, Stafford, in Oct 2011 (E&S March 10 2010 p1pc). *One of the first Staffordshire gardens to open in the National Garden Scheme.* Sandon Hall, see Whittington, near Lichfield (DYKT4).

WW1 *Earliest executed WW1 memorial for a Staffordshire estate, 'one of the most beautiful memorials in the county'.* Perhaps that for the Sandon estate at the crossroads of the Lichfield, Stafford and Stone roads which by mid Nov 1919 was to be a pedestal of stone 16 feet 6 inches high, topped with a bronze figure made by the 'well-known' Staffordshire sculptor Albert Toft, officially unveiled in May 1921, when described as in the above quote (SA Nov 15 1919 p8. May 14 1921 p9ps).

Wright, John *The 'Grand Old Man of Sandon'.* (1850-1952). Born Cauldon, Alton. In 1881, after a time at Derby and Chartley, he moved to Sandon and took over Yew Tree Farm. He retired, firstly, to Burston Cottage then Prospect House in the village. Clerk to Sandon PC for a number of years, and he married for the second time in 1931 (SA Jan 18 1952 p4p).

Yates, George Deley *Sandon's saddest.* When aged 45, of Sandy Lees Farm, he so bitterly regretted leaving his father's farm at Rushton, Leek, after his death, and taking on this farm, bigger than he could cope with, he committed suicide by drowning in a marl pit near the farmhouse on April 3 1937. It remains unclear why his wife, Gladys, who discovered his body and raised the alarm, herself had a cut across her throat (SA April 10 1937 p11 col 3. May 8 1937 p10 col 1).

Seabridge See Stoke-upon-Trent.
Shelton See Stoke-upon-Trent.
Silverdale See Wolstanton.
Slindon See Eccleshall.
Stallington See Stone.
Standon Standon was Staffordshire's 102nd largest parish, consisting of 2,620 acres; 47th closest parish to the county town, 8.6m NW; extremist length 3.2m; extremist width 1.9m. The parish's chief settlement is Standon, a small village that rambles sporadically along lanes. It is famous for the breakout from a Child reformatory at Bowers which resulted in a murder. *1st= parish registers transcribed*

and published by Staffordshire Register Society. Standon, 1902.

Altitudes The highest point 532 feet ENE of Shortwood Farm. The lowest point is 312 feet by the Meece near Walford.

Bacon, William *Standon's longest-serving vicar.* He served for 44 years, 1526-70.

Child reformatory *The Standon Boys' Home hero.* Joseph Moore of Stafford was an inmate 1886-88 but served his country as a private in the Boer War with the North Staffs Mounted Infantry and lost his life at Driefontein on May 30 1900 (SA June 9 1900 p4 col 6). *First headmaster of Standon Residential School.* Reginald W Beeston of Stafford, former Stafford Rangers player for the season 1911-12, appointed 1948 (SA Jan 24 1948 p5 col 2p).

Church *All Saints* is one of 19 such county dedications (of AP churches); 13th= oldest county church dating from 1120. *Note* a child's stone coffin, perhaps of Norman origin, with a clearly defined line for the body and head. It was built into the wall of the church and found at the time of the church restoration, 1846-7 (HOPS pp148,149). Also the table tomb with incised effigies of Francis Ross/Rose/Roos (d1500), lord of Laxton, Notts, and Weston, Staffs, and his wife Elizabeth (nee Skrimshire), and their ten children (GNHS p118) (HOPS pp159,160) (LGS p219). *Rare book.* There was a chained copy of 'Foxe's Martyrs' (an edition dated 1583), discovered, or present, at the time of the restoration of the church, 1846-7, chained to the pulpit. It was given by William Lovatt, churchwarden in 1685; Sir G Trevalyan's 'Life of Lord Macaulay' vol ii, p319, mentions a chained copy at Cheddar in Somerset (HOPS pp167,168). *First time Standon was without a vicar since 1100.* The incumbent left in 1979 with no replacement. In the interim Rev John Deakin of Cotes Heath helped out (SN Feb 26 2009 p6).

Civil defence *First Staffordshire people to take part in 'Operation Exodus'.* This was a major Civil Defence training exercise in which 2,000 volunteers from Standon, Wetwood, Ashley and Maer, as well as Audley would act out evacuation in the event of their area being heavily contaminated by radioactive fall out in a nuclear war. The first batch of people in the exercise were some inhabitants of Standon and Wetwood taken on Sunday May 10 1959 to a reception centre at Stafford (SA

& Chron May 7 1959 p1 cols 2-3).

Farming *Staffordshire County Show Best Farm 1948 (80-200 acre category), 1949.* Standon House farm, belonging to Joseph Timmis; 1948 was the first year of this prize (SA July 24 1948 p5 col 7) (SLM Sept 1949 p16ps). *Patented his own potato picker.* Joseph Timmis of Weston House Farm, by Sept 1956 (SA & Chron Sept 27 1956 p7 cols 8-9).

Folklore *Standon's best.* Traditionally All Saints was built of stones brought by angels at night from a hill above the village (HOPS p145).

The legend of Standon church being carried away by angels at night.

Geology Most of the parish and the west is Keuper Marls; Standon and Bower village areas are Keuper Sandstones; Meece valley is Bunter.

Cawley, Gerald, Edward Gittings, Henry Jacobs, and **William Harry Smith** *Standon's villains.* These were the four boys convicted of the murder of Peter Fieldhouse, a much-respected assistant instructor in gardening at Standon Farm Approved School, which they attended, on the afternoon of Feb 15 1947 with air rifles. The fatal shots occurred in the bathroom fired by Cawley, with the other three present. They were sentenced to be detained at his Majesty's pleasure. It was a plot to kill Thomas Dawson, the headmaster, but Mr Fielding had got in the way. The boys were apprehended on the railway line between Madeley and Crewe later that day. Ten boys were charged in all, and all were aged between 15 and 16. In addition five of the remaining boys - Sidney Lyons, James Edward Hooton, Leslie Johnson, Brian Francis Turner, Mitchell Badger - pleaded guilty to conspiring to murder the headmaster, and they all received varying sentences (SA March 15 1947 p5).

Housing *One of Staffordshire's few Swedish timber type houses built to curb the post-WW2 housing shortage.* At Bowers, Standon, built 1946 (manufactured in Sweden); Stone and Lichfield rural dis-

trict councils were the only Staffordshire authorities to secure these types of houses (SA Jan 25 1947 p5p).

Jorden, Rev William *Dr Johnson said to him 'Sir, you have sconced me two pence for non-attendance at a lecture not worth a penny', Standon's most famous old worthy.* (1686-1738). Rector of Standon 1729-1733. He was Dr Johnson's tutor at Pembroke College, Oxford. Johnson abhorred his lectures and is reputed to have said of him on being fined for non-attendance. Jorden was perhaps the son of Humphrey Jorden of Newland, Gloucestershire. Rector of Standon from 1729, which he resigned in 1733, but continued at Seighford where he died.

Lewis, Jacquie *Standon's bravest.* Of Standon old Post Office. She died in 1975 of cancer; her 'Let me tell you how I live with cancer' was published posthumously in 1977.

Lou'at, Ann *Earliest person recorded in the parish register.* For her burial on Dec 20 1558.

Place-name Standon first appears in Domesday Book, 1086, and means 'tun on stony ground' or possibly 'tun at the stone' or 'the tun at the stoney outcrop' (PNSZ p507).

Poorest There is no evidence for a Standon workhouse. After 1838 the poor, unable to support themselves, went to Stone Union workhouse.

Population Standon was 119th in 1801 with 332 people; 111th in 1811 with 420; 118th in 1821 with 415; 119th in 1831 with 420; 120th in 1841 with 382; 122nd in 1851 with 373; 122nd in 1861 with 347; 125th in 1871 with 329; 121st in 1881 with 359; 112nd in 1891 with 404; 110th in 1901 with 418. Standon could be ranked 114th= worst affected Staffordshire parish for loss of men in WW1, with five lives lost.

Quote *Choicest.* Michael Raven in his Staffordshire and the Black Country, 1988, wrote 'The village straggles up the hill from Cotes Heath and the ugly gantries of the electrified main line railway.'

Railways *Staffordshire's first railway accident* occurred in the late hours of Aug 24 1837 about 2.5 miles south of Whitmore going from Liverpool to Birmingham when the axle of one of the fore wheels of the engine, the 'Eagle', broke, with the effect of throwing the engine off the rails, passengers were detained many hours, but no one was hurt (SA Aug 26 1837 p3 col 2).

This illustration shows the first trains from Liverpool to pass through Stafford on their way to Wednesfield using the Grand Junction Railway. The line opened to passengers on July 4 1837. The 'Eagle' engine, involved in the accident, could be pulling one of them. Incidentally, the trains drawings were the first news illustrations to appear in the Staffordshire Advertiser, on June 3 1837.

Travis, Mrs Jane *Standon's saddest.* When aged 81, she and her sister Miss Mary Thompson, 78, burnt to death at their home at Rock Cottage, Standon, on March 17 1937. They lived alone, in the cottage built into the sandstone rock, until 1936, when due to failing health a housekeeper, Miss Theresa Spooner, was employed. In addition, at the time of the fire, a neighbour lived-in during Miss Spooner's temporary illness. Alerted by the cries of 'Fire!' Miss Spooner found the sisters in their room in a pathetic scene: Miss Thompson lying on the floor by the side of the bed with her nightdress burnt away. Standing over her was her sister attempting to smother the flames with coverings from the bed, and in this way her own nightdress caught fire. The Thompsons were a well-known Standon family residing at Ivy House Farm (SA March 20 1937 p6p. March 27 1937 p10 col 7).

Stoke-on-Trent A former county borough (1910), city (1925), and now independent unitary authority (1997), covering most of Burslem, Stoke-upon-Trent, and some of Norton-in-the-Moors, Trentham and Wolstanton, and a little of Barlaston, Caverswall and Stone ancient parishes.

Civil life and Federation *Largest experiment of its kind in municipal history.* The federation of the Pottery towns to form Stoke-on-Trent (Burrow's Reference Map of Stoke-on-Trent 2nd ed 1970 p4). *First meeting of the newly-created Stoke-on-Trent county borough.* At 12 noon on March 31 1910 at the North Stafford Hotel, Stoke (SA April 2 1910 p6 col 1). *Only English city without a cathedral in 1930s.* Stoke-on-Trent (ES Your Week July 8 2006 p11). *Only council of its kind in England not improving adequately 2007.* Stoke-on-Trent city (ES Feb 22 2007 p1).

Policing *Last chief constable of Stoke-*

on-Trent City Police. William Edward Watson (d1994 at Hanchurch) from June 1 1955. On amalgamation of city and county forces on 1 Jan 1968 he became Deputy Chief Constable of Staffs and Stoke-on-Trent Constabulary (Policing The Potteries. Alf Tunstall, Jeff Cowdell. 2002. p237).

Demography *Least affluent place in Britain.* Only 0.3% of constituents of Stoke-on-Trent South earn more than £60,000 a year (BBC Midlands Today Aug 14 2002). *Local authority with most derelict areas 1969.* Stoke-on-Trent, with highest percentage of derelict land (VB p191). *13th largest city in England and Wales 1970.* Stoke-on-Trent (Burrow's Reference Map of Stoke-on-Trent 2nd ed 1970 p4). *One of only five areas in Britain chosen for a test of the 2011 census.* Stoke-on-Trent in May 2007 (ES May 2 2006 p11).

Freemen *First woman made freeman.* Lucy Wedgwood (nee Gibson), wife of Cecil (d1916) (ES April 9 2005 p11). *Stoke-on-Trent's 50th honorary freeman.* John Forrester (1924-2007), Labour MP for Stoke North 1966-87, made freeman in 1992 (ES Nov 24 2007 p12p). *Stoke-on-Trent's first citizens.* John 'Jack' Dimmock (b1932) of the Nook, Longton, and his wife Joan, in 1984 (ES Feb 23 2008 p13).

Hospitality *Best Show Award for the 2005 Strength Calendar.* Stoke on Trent which hosted the finals of England's Strongest Man competition at Hanley Park, 2005 (ES May 10 2006 p12). *Best UK Convention Bureau 2006.* The Staffordshire Stoke-on-Trent Conference Bureau in the Meetings and Incentives Travel Awards - the second time of winning (ES May 8 2006 p22).

Huntbach, Gerald *First Stoke-on-Trent city coroner.* Served 1942-59, and died the day after he retired. Died 1959 (ES Dec 1 2007 Staying In p13).

Living conditions *Worst place to live in England 2001.* Stoke-on-Trent city as placed by Experian, a global information solutions consultant on behalf of The Sunday Times, in a quality of life league table covering 376 local authorities. With 2,421 points Stoke-on-Trent came bottom, suffering from relatively high unemployment, high crime rates and being densely populated; Staffordshire Moorlands was 70th, Stafford 139th, Newcastle-under-Lyme 251st; Sandwell 375th (ES Sept 25 2001 pp1-3). *5th filthi-*

est place in England. Stoke-on-Trent city, based on figures for 2004/5 (ES May 11 2006 p1). *10th noisiest place in UK.* Stoke-on-Trent (BBC 1 Midlands Today Feb 2 2007). *13th worst place to live in Britain 2007.* Stoke-on-Trent, according to a survey for Channel 4's programme Location, Location, Location (ES Oct 16 2007 p6). *15th lowest value postcode in Britain 2008.* The ST1 postcode according to property website Zoopla! which also estimates Stoke-on-Trent has 5th highest number of streets where houses are worth less than £100,000, at 1,355 (ES Aug 4 2008 p19). *Worst postal service in Britain 2007-8.* The postcode region ST, Stoke-on-Trent, with only 79.4% of first class mail delivered the day after posting, according to regulator Postcomm (ES May 31 2008 p6). *Britain's least lonely area 1971-2001.* The BBC Radio Stoke-on-Trent area with the strongest sense of community, registering 22.4% loneliness (Edinburgh with 33.1% came out as most lonely area), according to 'Changing UK, The Way We Live Now', by Prof Dorling of Sheffield University based on census returns 1971-2001. The study was commissioned by the BBC (The Daily Telegraph. Dec 2 2008 p11).

MAYORALTY The old boroughs. *1st mayor of Hanley* was John Ridgway (1785-1860), on its incorpoation in 1857, and was first chief magistrate of any of the Pottery towns. He was potter to Queen Victoria (OTP pp173-4) (POTP p180il); *of Stoke* was William Keary (1815/16-86), solicitor, on its incorporation in 1874 (POTP p132) (SA Nov 27 1886) (DNB) (SK p180).

The county borough (after Federation). *1st mayor, 'One of England's Best'.* Major Cecil Wedgwood (1863-1916), in 1910; the tribute was written on the cross over his makeshift grave on the Western Front; according to legend his last words were 'Carry on the Potters!' (ES Your Week July 1 2006 p16. Feb 9 2009 p18). *1st R.C. mayor.* Henry Beresford, a Burslem publican, in 1947-48 (ES Your Week July 29 2006 p9) (TWWW Nov 1 2008 p3). *1st ordained mayor.* Arthur Perry, vicar of Penkhull, in 1957-58 (TWWW Nov 1 2008 p3). *'Stoke-on-Trent's Queen Mother'.* Doris Robinson (c1901-2000), former mayor (ES Jan 16 2010 p25). *Youngest mayoress.* Sophia Ali, aged 21, consort to her father Mayor Bagh Ali 2007 (SLM Nov 2007 pp28-29pc; article alleges she is Britain's Youngest ever Lady Mayor-

ess, but see Walsall, DYKT No. 5). *Most Lord Mayors of Great Britain assembled together by 1929.* Perhaps when nine mayors gathered for a unique ceremony at the Town Hall, Stoke-on-Trent, on Sept 24 1929. The occasion was the presentation and first use of the Civic Pottery Service, plate worth £1,500, initiated by Sir Francis Joseph, CBE, President of North Staffs Chamber of Commerce. In attendance were the mayors and mayoresses of London, Birmingham, Leicester, Hull, Liverpool, Manchester, Nottingham, Newcastle-upon-Tyne, as well as that for Stoke-on-Trent; the mayor of Newcastle-under-Lyme was unable to attend due to a prior engagement. At luncheon Sir Francis declared that if London was the first city in the land, then Stoke could boast being the central city of England (SA Sept 28 1929 p5ps).

Nomenclature *'Soul on Trent'.* What Stoke-on-Trent has been dubbed because it was a centre of the Northern Soul music movement in the late 1960s and early 1970s. Having begun at Manchester's Twisted Wheel venue it spread to places such as the Golden Torch, Tunstall. A film about Northern Soul, set in the city in 1974, was being shot in Stoke-on-Trent in 2008 (ES June 18 2008 p10). *'Smoke-on-Trent', 'Joke-on-Trent'.* What Stoke-on-Trent was dubbed, being the only English local authority which failed to get its enforcement powers approved by city councillors for the smoking ban from July 1 2007, leaving enforcement officers unable to fine smokers flouting the law, until approval was passed by Aug 2. The Smithfield Bar and Restaurant, Hanley, was one pub which allowed its customers to smoke until the ban was enforceable (Daily Mirror July 10 2007 p1) (ES July 11 2007 p7. July 12 2007 pp8,9).

Society *Britain's Sexiest City.* Stoke-on-Trent was nominated as one of the sexiest of UK destinations by 18-25 year olds with a Young Persons Railcard (BBC Midlands Today July 22 2005). *More massage parlours per head than anywhere else in UK.* Stoke-on-Trent with 17 in 2006 (BBC Midlands Dec 4 2006). *Britain's 9th, 48th, and 49th most influential gay politicians.* Michael Cashman (Lab), West Midlands MEP 1999-2009, Mark Meredith (Lab), Mayor of Stoke-on-Trent 2005-, Mike Wolf (Ind), Mayor of Stoke-on-Trent 2002-05, respectively, according to a Pink News survey Jan 2008 (ES Jan 7 2008 p5pc).

Stoke-upon-Trent Stoke-upon-Trent was Staffordshire's 8th largest parish, consisting of 12,406 acres; 80th closest parish to the county town, 12.5m NNW; extremist length 7.3m, making it 8th longest parish in the county; extremist width 8m, making it 3rd widest parish in Staffordshire. The ancient parish's chief settlements are really three of the famous five towns of The Potteries - Hanley (the commericial centre), Longton (a lesser commericial centre), and Stoke (the municipal centre). In addition, there is also Fenton. The parish is famous for Pottery making.

Adams, Dorothy *Earliest recorded person in Bucknall parish register.* For her baptism on Sept 29 1762. She was the daughter of William and Ellen Adams.

Aircraft *Staffordshire's first balloon ascent* was when Mr Green went up in a balloon from Shelton on Oct 3 1826 accompanied by Rev B Vale, perpetual curate of Stoke-on-Trent, at 4pm. The balloon passed over Hanley, Lane End, Werrington windmill (4.15pm, when half a mile high), Consall Woods (4.20pm), Belmont House, landing between Ipstones and Kingsley (4.50pm) (SA Oct 7 1826 p4). *First parachute from a balloon in Staffordshire* was in 1902 when two women were advertised to do this, ascending from Longton Fete, Queen's Park (SA May 16 1952 p5 col 7). In 1908 Misses Dolly Shepherd and Louie May attempted a similar feat which resulted in the world's first mid-air parachute rescue over Leigh (see DYKT2). *Staffordshire's earliest flying club (probably).* Stoke and District Flying Club which existed by 1907. It was then holding meetings at the Red Lion Hotel, Church Street, Stoke. The President and Treasurer was W. Bosworth of the Blacksmiths' Arms, Longport (The Potteries, Newcastle and District Directory. Staffordshire Sentinel Ltd. 1907. p695) (source found by A. Dobraszczyc). *Stoke-on-Trent's other great aircraft designer, designed the first all-steel aircraft to be produced in Britain.* John 'Jimmy' Lloyd (b1887), aircraft designer, brought up in Etruria. This was the all steel version of the Siskin in 1924; the Siskin first appeared in 1918 (ES May 20 1976).

Allbut, Cpl Stephen *Staffordshire's 1st= fatality of the Iraq War.* Of Stoke-on-Trent. When aged 35 killed in 'friendly fire' in Basra on March 24 2003. He was in the Queen's Royal Lancers. Trooper David Clarke, 19, of Bedworth Ave, Lit-

tleworth was also killed in the same Challenger 2 tank (E&S March 26 2003 pp1,7. March 20 2008 p24).

Allen, Frederick *Strange but true!* Of Penkhull. In Feb 2008 he received a hospital appointment in the post for a check-up at the Central Outpatients unit, University Hospital of North Staffordshire, nearly 40 years after his death on Nov 29 1968 (ES Feb 5 2008 p11).

Allen, Hannah *Testatrix with Staffordshire's last will proved in the bishop's consistory court.* Of Longton. Her will - together with three others at Leek and Burslem - was proved on Jan 9 1858. Wills on and from Jan 12 1858 were proved in a civil District Probate Registry.

Allnut, Alice *Stoke's villainess.* Alias Alice Moore. When on bail, attempted to extort money blackmailing Abraham Boothroyd with rape at Stoke-upon-Trent, 1840. She was found guilty and sentenced to 15 years transportation, which was reduced to 12 months imprisonment with hard labour on grounds of leniency. She was described as a 'good-looking female, respectably dressed in mourning, seemed to be under thirty years of age' (SA Oct 31 1840 p4).

Altitudes The highest point is 817 feet on Caverswall boundary in Park Hall Country Park; alternatively on Baddeley Edge Greenway Hall, Bagnall (W p401) (ONST 1951 p158). The lowest point is 312 feet at Trent and Lyme Brook confluence.

Alvarez, Mariasela *The Miss World who came to Stoke.* When reigning Miss World and Miss Dominican Republic, aged 22, she was booked to appear as a publicity stunt for Bourne Sports shop in Stoke in late Nov 1982 (ES Nov 19 1982 p1p. Nov 25 1982 p1p).

Astbury, William Thomas *First to give an hypothetical structure for DNA.* Born Longton 1889. He achieved this scientific feat with Florence Bell, in 1938. Died 1961 (Cambridge Biographical Encyclopedia. 1994).

Aston, Rev Vernon Gladstone *'Rhymester'.* Vicar of Penkhull in 1946. His 'A Vicar's Anthology of Verse' appeared in 1946 (SA June 15 1946 p8 col 6).

ATHLETICS Track *Women's English sprint relay champions 1960.* Ann Pover, Rosemary Wilshaw, Kathleen Degg and Dorothy Window (nee Hindmarsh) of City of Stoke AC; in 1962 Dorothy was the first North Staffordshire female to compete in the European Games (ES July 4 2009 p28p). *Record crowd at Michelin*

Athletic Club was 10,000 on their gala day at the Clayton Wood site, 1981, due to fears over job security at the works (ES Your Week July 29 2006 p6). *Reebok Cross Challenge under-17s winner 2004-05, Schools Inter-Counties under-17s 3000m champion 2005.* Alex Derricott (b1988) of Berry Hill, City of Stoke AC & Staffordshire Moorlands AC (ES Oct 22 2008 p40pc). *European Junior Championship 2007 200m gold medalist, 4x100m relay silver medalist, World Trial and UK Championships 2007 200m silver medalist.* Alex Nelson

Joe Deakin.

(b1988), of Birches Head, brother of below (ES Aug 5 2008 ppvi-v pcs). *British Junior record holder for 100m 2005, World Youth Championship 2007 100m bronze medalist.* Ashlee Nelson (b1991), of Birches Head, sister of the above. The Games took place in the Czech Republic (ES July 13 2007 p56pc. Aug 5 2008 ppvi-vii pc).

Distance running *Swiftest man in England c1825* was James Wantling, artist and painter with the New Hall Pottery, Shelton, who could run 100 yards in 9 seconds, 200 yards in 19 seconds, and 300 yards in 30 seconds; feats never before equalled (OTP pp164-5). *Olympic 3 mile Gold medalist 1908* was Joe Deakin (c1880-1972), born Wellesley St, Shelton, veteran of the 2nd Boer War, in 14 mins, 39.6 secs. Although he is said to have achieved a faster than this time, but British timekeepers had forgotten to stop their watches in the excitement of his victory. Aged 90 he could still run a mile in under 10 mins (ES Your Week Dec 5 2006 p9. May 13 2010 p2p). *Man who broke record running from Stoke-on-Trent to Sydney.* Kelvin Bowers, born Fenton. He covered 10,500 miles from Stoke-on-Trent to Sydney, Australia, in record time, April 1974 to Sept 1975. He was residing in Cornwall by 2010 (ES Jan 2 2008 p26p. Feb 6 2010 p20p). *First Potteries Marathon.* 1982. A record for the course was set in 1985 by Harry Clague (St Helens AC) with 2 hours 19 minutes 5 seconds (SN June 19 2008 p81). *Toughest Potteries Marathon in history* was on June 17 2000 when dozens of runners fell victim to the searing heat and failed to complete the course (Sentinel Photographers' exhibi-

tion, Potteries Museum, 2008).

Barber, Lydia *Staffordshire's 14th= oldest woman ever.* Of Longton, aged 107 (STM Sept 1964 p39).

Barlow, Gertrude *One of the first women in the Potteries to graduate from university.* Of Hanley. She died 1914 (POTP p30).

Beetlestone, Colin *Hanley's boy hero.* When aged 13 of 80 Rose Street, Northwood, he saved the life of Edward Beadmore, aged 6, of the same street, from drowning in the canal, by diving in fully-clothed. He was presented with gifts to mark his gallantry at his school, the Grove School, in July 1937 (SA July 10 1937 p5 col 7).

Bennett, Sir Albert *Stoke-on-Trent's most influential local politician of the 20th Century'.* (1901-1972), former city council leader (Lab), a leading figure in post-war reconstruction and land reclamation; the Bennett Precinct (1965), Longton (see Shopping), was named after him, since renamed Longton Exchange (ES Staying In Dec 22 2007 p15).

Bennett, R and others *Hanley's heroes.* Mine manager, who with colleagues, W Hough, A Hill, J Brearley, W Winkle, A Beck, and A Maley, all risked their lives rescuing a fellow miner, John Harrison, from beneath a fall of roof in Hanley Deep Pit on the conveyor face of the Cockshed Seam. They received all certificates for their heroism from the Carnegie Hero Fund Trustees in 1935 (SA Dec 14 1935 p9 col 1).

Billiards *World No. 19 Snooker player 2008/9* was Jamie Cope (b1985) of Longton, nicknamed 'Shotgun' due to his speed around the table and aggressive playing style. He was only the third player to achieve a 147 break in the history of the Grand Prix tournament, in 2006 (Wikipedia, 2009) (ES April 22 2009 p48pc).

Boswell, Lawrence 'Lol' *Strange but true!* Celebrated Romany of Hartshill. When he died in 1977 all the clocks curiously stopped at 5.45 in his bungalow (ES Your Week Dec 5 2006 p9p).

Bowls *Highest table skittle score in 24 hours.* 90,446 skittles by 12 players at the Finney Gardens Hotel, Hanley, Dec 27-28 1980 (GBR 1989 p287).

Boxing *The 'home of boxing in Staffordshire' 1920s-30s* was the Palais de Danse (later Palace Cinema), Hanley (ES Your Week July 8 2006 p11). *European bantamweight champion 1921.* Tommy Harrison, Potteries boxer (ES Your Week

Sept 29 2007 p6). *'The first heavyweight champion in the world to visit the Potteries'.* Lee Savold, as he was billed to promote the Lightweight Champion of Great Britain championships staged at Hanley Stadium on July 11 1950. He opened the event boxing three exhibition rounds with Charles Henry Croydon (SA July 15 1950 p5). *When the NUM Boxing Championships were held at Hanley.* Victoria Hall in 1953, and 1954 (SA May 14 1954 p5 col 7). *He once drew with world champion Jackie Brown.* Potteries boxer Benny Jones; in two other contests against him he lost (ES March 14 2009 p25). *'he fought eight professional fights in 12 days, winning by a knockout in each fight'.* According to legend this was John Thomas 'Tut' Whalley, flyweight, who was taught boxing at The Black Boy Inn, Cobridge Road, Etruria. His career consisted of 150 contests, losing only two (ES May 25 2009 p14p). *British super-flyweight champion Dec 2007-March 2008, British flyweight champion Jan 2009-, Commonwealth flyweight champion 2009-.* Chris Edwards (b1976) of Fenton. On his succession to the super-flyweight title he became the first Potteries boxer to win a British title in 85 years (ES Nov 15 2008 p52pc. Jan 26 2009 p40pc).

Bradshaw, Trooper Harold *Died in the last recorded cavalry charge by a British regiment.* Of Stoke; killed at the Battle of Omdurman in the Sudan, 1898 (ES Nov 15 2008 p27).

Buildings *'Most advanced building of its kind in the UK'.* The proposed ProLogis warehouse of 500,000 square feet at Radial Park in Sideway, if approved, 2007, using state-of-the-art technology to minimise the environmental impact of the building (ES June 9 2007 p14). *Largest private photographic collection of North Staffordshire buildings due for demolition* was kept by and taken by Angie Stevenson of Longton (ES April 14 2006 p21). *Tallest building in North Staffordshire.* Unity House, Hanley, built 1973-74, nineteen storeys high, providing 116,000 square feet of office. Demolished 2005-6 (Environment journal. July 1974 p3p) (ES April 14 2006 p21).

Bull baiting *Last recorded instance of bull-baiting in the Potteries* was on a meadow opposite the Red Lion Inn, Hartshill (Collecting Staffordshire Pottery. Louis T Stanley. 1963 p23).

Burndred, William George *First Fitzwygram prizeman.* Of Hanley, veterinary surgeon, 1900 (POTP p54).

Camm, Doug *Oldest surviving fairground showman in the country 2006.* Of Clayton, when aged 88 (ES May 20 2006 p7).

Cars *Potteries' first car* was possibly a Victoria belonging Messrs A Chew & Co. of Hanley. It was bought at Norwich, made by Arnold Manufacturing Co., Peckham, Kent, and driven back through Leicester, Uttoxeter, and Longton, arriving in Hanley on Feb 5 1897 (SA Feb 6 1897 p5 col 3). *Potteries' first registered car* was that privately owned at Etruria Hall in 1903, with a number plate 'EH 1' (SHST p103). *Potteries' first motorised funeral procession* was for Miss Lily Twigge between Stoke and Thorpe Cloud 1910 (SHST p441). *First Potteries base of the Automobile Association.* Normeir Buildings, Hartshill Road, Stoke, 1959 (ES Your Week March 11 2006 p11). *First motor hotel built in a designated green belt area.* The (Staffordshire) Post House, Clayton Rd, Clayton, officially opened on Oct 2 1967 (Newcastle Times Sept 27 1967) (ES). *Stoke-on-Trent's first paying carpark* was one on the former Port Vale football ground in Hanley, early 1950s, tickets cost 1s a day (ES Your Week June 24 2006 p11).

CHURCHES St Peter Ad Vincula is the only such county dedication (for AP churches); 25th= last AP county church built dating from 1826. *2nd only complete peal in any scientific campanological method ever in the Potteries, 1st upon Stoke bells, 1st in Potteries by a local band of rings.* St Peter's Association of Change Ringers on the old church bells on Jan 10 1888 in three hours 3 mins ringing 'Holt's Original' peal of grandsire triples consisting of 5,040 changes (SA Jan 14 1888 p5 col 3). *In the churchyard* as well as the remains of the old church, the *earliest example of the 'Staffordshire Knot'.* It can be seen in the carving on the Saxon cross, dating from c800 AD (www. thepotteries.org, 2008). *Note* the graves of the Clark(e) twins; John Fenton (d1694) and his wife Catherine (epitaph is by their son the famous poet Elijah Fenton); Robert Garner (d1789) and daughter-in-law Lucy (d1844) and her son Henry Fletcher Garner (d1837 aged 5 months) (the father, wife and son of author Robert Garner); Thomas Chatterley engraver of Shelton (d1818); pottery artists - Henry Lark Pratt (d1873) and son Henry Lark Pratt (d1875 aged 36); Herbert Stansfield (see Folklore); various members the potting families of Adams, Spode, and Whieldon.

Holy Trinity at Northwood, near Hanley, built 1848-49. *Staffordshire's only Neo-Norman Commissioners' church* and first in an acceptable Camdenian Gothic (BOE pp34,40).

Holy Trinity at Hartshill. *Church renowned throughout the world for its Minton tiles, high glaze and encaustic and huge variation in design, Staffordshire's 1st church to have electrically recorded chimes.* The tile claim is from Christine Glover in The Sentinel. The chimes were donated, and officially switched on, by Mrs Enoch Haughton of Stoke-on-Trent on April 29 1937, and consisted of a gramophone in the baptistry, connected to four amplifiers in the belfry (SA May 1 1937 p9 col 6) (ES July 5 2008 p30).

St John the Evangelist at Hanley. The *first minister* was Rev John Middleton (1714-1802), he served for 64 years (ROS vol ii pp63-100). *In the churchyard* there are two interesting epitaphs on gravestones. The first is in memory of William Adams, a blacksmith, of Hanley, and lies at the south side of the church. It runs as follows

> 'In memory of William Adams, who departed this life December 27th, 1786, aged 69.
> My sledge and hammer lies declined,
> My bellows too have lost their wind;
> My song extinct, my forge decay'd,
> And in the dust my voice is laid.
> My life is spent, my irons gone,
> My sails are drawn, my work is done.'

The second is in memory of Richard Poole, a publican, of Hanley, whose license was taken from him through false reports, and is thus recorded on his tombstone:-

> 'Sacred to the memory of Richard Poole, who died October 21st, 1788, aged 62.
> Unto strange teachers they gave hear,
> Which led my heart into a snare.
> But they from me my bread did take,
> Which almost made my heart to break,
> But they restored it me again,
> Alas, alas, but all in vain.'

(ROS vol ii p100).

St Mary at Bucknall, was built in 1754-6. *First 'silent peal' rung in Britain* was accomplished in the church on April 6 1897; the six bell ringers rang in silence without a caller counting on the ropes (Plaque inside the church tower) (TWWW April 1997 p2).

Cinemas *First Potteries showing of moving pictures* was Empire Music Hall (which became The Capitol), Hanley, 1896. *Longest-running film at the Odeon Cinema* was 'The Sound of Music' 1965-66 (ES Oct 11 2008 p27). *First Potteries showing of 3-D films* was at The Capitol, 1953 (ES Your Week Sept 30 2006 p9). *Midlands' largest cinema screen, Potteries' biggest cinema*. Essoldo (formerly the Palace, and before that Palais de Danse, a boxing venue), corner of Stafford St and Albion Sq, Hanley. The building was demolished in 1962; Wilkinson store now stands on the site. It was 157 feet (twice that of a normal cinema), seating 2,500 people in the 1950s (ES Your Week Sept 30 2006 p5). *'The Smallest Show On Earth'*. Some of the scenes for this 1957 film starring Peter Sellers and Virginia Mayo were filmed at Longton (ES April 11 2009 p27). *Last small independent cinema in The Potteries* was The Plaza, Fenton, closed 1982 (ES Oct 18 2008 p34p).

Clark(e), Henry and **Sibil** *Staffordshire's 10th= oldest man ever, and 9th= oldest woman ever*. Reputed twins, they share a grave in St Peter's churchyard, Stoke-upon-Trent, with a stout gravestone. It alleges they were both aged 112 when they died in 1684. Some say they were gipsies from Mow Cop or the Moorlands brought here to be buried; that they might have been man or wife, or brother and sister; that the stone mason might have placed an extra '1' in front of the '12' (HSP pp51,130, 131) (SMC p187) (SFH p22) (CAST p46) (ES May 8 1995 p8p).

Clowes, Sam *First pottery worker to sit in Parliament*. MP for Hanley 1924-28 (ES Your Week Sept 2006 p9).

Cook, Rosamond *Staffordshire's 4th oldest woman ever*. Of Longton. She died in 1774, aged 124.

Cooper, Karen *Queen's Award recipient*. Leader of the 7th Hanley Brownies and Guides, in 2010. The award is the highest in the Guiding Movement, rarely awarded (about six current holders in Staffordshire), and requires three years of task-passing (ES March 27 2010 p11pc).

Copestake, Harry *Strange but true!* Of 149 Goddard Street, East Vale. Died aged 13 on Dec 27 1941, whilst riding his bicycle in Maple Place, Meir; he was found to have weighed only 4 stone 5lb (SA Jan 3 1942 p3 col 5).

Council housing *Europe's largest coun-*

cil housing estate. Bentilee, built 1952-55. In the 1950s it consisted of 3,580 dwellings at a density of 10 dwellings per acre and a population of 14,700, covering well over 255.978 acres. In 1989 there were 4,372 households living on the estate (Ubberley Farm & Bentilee Farm Housing Estates, Stoke-on-Trent City plan, c1953. SM29c) (Herbert and Rodgers. 1965) (Community Profile of Bentilee. M.I. Tinkler. 1989 p5) (ES March 10 2000 p15). *First sale of council house to tenant*. 1981 (ES Your Week March 11 2006 p8).

Cowley, Gertrude *First female police officer in Staffordshire*. She and Lily Broadhead could both make this claim becoming police officers with Stoke-on-Trent Borough Police in 1921; however, the first female constables for the Staffordshire Police Force were not appointed until 1944 (Staffordshire Police 150th Anniversary Commemorative Issue. 1992).

Crick, Rev Douglas Henry *Tallest Anglican clergyman in England*. Rector of Stoke-upon-Trent 1924- (bishop of Chester 1939-55), at 6 foot 4.5 inches high (CAST pp27-31).

Cricket *'One of (North) Staffordshire's Best (cricketers)'* 1934. Alfred Smith of Longton CC, who retired from league cricket in 1934, described as a deadly accurate bowler. In a local 'Derby' at Caverswall he achieved the extraordinary feat of all 7's. Having made 77 with the bat, he proceeded to take seven wickets for seven runs; and at Kynpersley, after J Gibson had hit a beautiful 101 for the home team, Smith went one better for Longton and took his bat for 109 (SA May 2 1936 p3 cols 2-4). *Staffordshire Cricket's only international cricket fixture* was against the United States at Longton in 1968, but the match was rained off without a ball being bowled (ES Aug 9 2008 p27).

Tommy Godwin at the World Championships, Paris, 1947.

Cycling Holder of the world m i l e a g e endurance record over the twelve m o n t h s . T o m m y G o d w i n (1912-75), native of Fenton, who cycled 75,065 miles in one year (Jan 1-Dec 31 1939), then went on to May 1940 to cycle 100,000 miles (500 days - fastest ever completion

of 100,000 miles), a feat unsurpassed, and recognised by GBR as his in perpetuity. He died returning from a ride with friends to Tutbury Castle; his name is entered into the Golden Book of Cycling, and a plaque was erected to him on a pillar at Fenton Manor Sports Centre in 2005 (ES Nov 1 2008 p25ps). *Cycling record for over 26 miles in an hour*. Les West (b1944), born Hanley, in 1964 at Lyme Valley. *Milk Race winner 1965 and 1967* was Les West. *Record for London to Brighton and back cycle ride 1970* was Les West. *National half-mile sprint (cycle) title 1956* winner was Roy Swinnerton (b1925) of Fenton. *British women's sprint (cycle) winner 1967, silver medallist in women's road race championship at Brno 1969*. Bernadette Swinnerton (b1951) of Fenton (ES March 29 2003 p25p. Your Week July 24 2004 p7).

Darts *Britain's first darts club*. In 1984 Eric Bristow was trying to open Britain's first darts club in Stoke-on-Trent (ES Feb 21 2009 p26).

Dodd, Edwin *One of the first football pool (Littleworths) winners*. (1913-c1995). Factory worker of Longton winning £1,000, 1934 (ES Dec 27 2003 p12p).

Drakford, Walter *Staffordshire's first casualty due to WW2 blackout regulations*. When aged 55, labourer of New Street, Longton, he walked out into the path of a bus travelling at 6 mph in Stafford Street near Clayton Street on Sept 7 1939. A verdict of accidental death was recorded (SA Sept 16 1939 p10 col 4) (ES Aug 30 2008 p28).

Dunn, Sam *First in Potteries to wear an Oswald Moseley black shirt*. Bus driver. The Public Order Act 1936 banned the wearing of the black shirt. He died in about 1975 (Archive Hour: Potteries Fascists. BBC Radio 4. June 24 2006).

Evans, Andrew *Britain's longest serving prisoner for a miscarriage of justice*. Of Longton. Imprisoned for the murder of Judith Roberts of Tamworth, aged 14, 1972-1997 (MCS pp111-120) (ES June 9 2000 p5).

Fenton *Last Potteries town to get a library*. Fenton in 1906 (ES March 14 2006). *The town Arnold Bennett forgot, The town covering the largest area, The 'Enemy's Town'*. Fenton (ES May 20 2006 p18). *"I like Fenton as a whole, and what a hole it is!"* Wilfred Pickles, broadcaster and comedian, at Fenton Town Hall c1947 (ES Your Week Sept 4 2004 p7).

Folklore *Bucknall and Hanley's best.* The story of Sauntering Ned, pot journeyman, who resided in Parliament Row (formerly Saggar Row), Hanley. According to legend he dressed his donkey up with horns to look like the Devil, and so by succeeded in scaring off body-snatchers at work in Bucknall churchyard. *Clayton's best.* The ghost of a cowled figure haunts Clayton Lane and Springfields and

Sauntering Ned's donkey makes body-snatchers take fright.

has been seen by every member of a certain family (SFH pp19,21). *Fenton's best.* The battle of Fethanleag 584 AD in which the British were defeated by the Angles may have taken place at Fenton Culvert in the vicinity of the field called Groaning Meadows. Tradition says the dying lay here groaning for days and nights after the battle (RHPS pp21-22). *Longton's best.* Longton Hall (demolished 1939) had several ghosts associated with it: A girl in white seen close to the hall site, and (only on New Year's eves) a cloak and a feathered hat-dressed lady, believed to be the wife of a previous owner of the hall, murdered on New Year's eve. *Penkhull's best.* The Greyhound Inn, Manor Court Road, former manorial court house, has the tradition of lodging Charles II. *Shelton's best.* The legend that the miller of Bell's Mill in Shelton was given freehold tenure of his property by Henry VII as a reward for feeding his troops on their way to the battle of Bosworth Field in 1485 was disproved in the early 1960s. *Stoke-upon-Trent's best.* Local boys knew the grave of Herbert Stansfield, a freemason, in Stoke-upon-Trent churchyard as the Devil's Grave because of the figures of death which are on it, and threw stones at it (CAST p45). *Stoke's most haunted place 2009.* The Red Lion Inn, Bucknall. The property used to be a court house, and was also used for public hangings. Said to be haunted by the ghost of George Alfred Metcalfe, a hangman, himself hung for a crime he did not commit (ES Feb 7 2009 p6).

Football *English Ladies' FA Cup win-*

ners 1922. Stoke Ladies, who played at the old Port Vale ground in Cobridge, who at sometime in their history remained unbeaten for five years; the English Ladies' FA, only existed briefly 1921-22 (ES Feb 5 2007 p9 - letter. Oct 25 2008 p29). *LMR Challenge Cup winners 1949, & late 1950s* were Stoke Loco Football Club (ES Your Week Nov 18 2006 p5). *English Schools Shield winners.* Stoke-on-Trent schools, on two occasions in the 1960s (ES Sept 27 2008 p30). *First black chairman of the Professional Footballers' Association 1988-90.* Garth Anthony Crooks, OBE, retired football striker (Tottenham Hotspur 1980-90, with loans) of Jamaican ancestry, and BBC broadcast journalist, born Stoke-on-Trent 1958 (Wikipedia, 2009).

Forrester, William *Stoke's bravest.* Driver of a tramcar which derailed coming down Hartshill Bank in Feb 1924. He remained at his post in a vain effort to bring the car to a standstill. Still suffering from the effects of the accident and unable to return to work Mr Forrester was award the 'Daily Herald' Order of Industrial Heroism in recognition of his bravery at Hanley in Jan 1925 (SA Jan 24 1925 p11 col 4).

Freemasonry *Largest gathering of Freemasons ever held in Staffordshire* was on May 24 1937 when the Earl of Harewood, KG, as Prov. Grand Master of the United Grand Lodge of England, and First Prov. Grand Principal of the Royal Arch degree, came to install Walton Stanley as the new Provincial Grand Master of Staffordshire (succeeding Lord Dartmouth, installed 1893), and Mr HD Austerberry as his deputy at the King's Hall, Stoke, and also install Major TJ Richardson as Grand Superintendent of the Province of Staffordshire in the Royal Arch degree at the Masonic Temple, Shelton (SA May 29 1937 p9ps).

Further education *One of the earliest local scientific and learned societies formed in Britain.* North Staffordshire Naturalists Field Club (The North Staffordshire Field Club), 1865, at the North Staffordshire Infirmary, Etruria Vale. *First WEA, University tutorial class in England.* The Longton Tutorial Class of 1908 under the guidance of RH Tawney, which met at the Sutherland Institute, Longton. Mr ES Cartwright who led the original 1908 Longton classes has been described as 'The Apostle of Adult Education' (SA Dec 7 1946 p5 col 7). *England's first pur-*

pose-built sixth form college was the Sixth Form College at Fenton, opened 1970 (ES March 24 2005 p6). *Leader of most local history walks in Staffordshire* is Andrew Dobraszczyc, Stoke-upon-Trent resident, whose Social History Walks (mainly round the Potteries) for WEA, Keele University, and independently, began with one at Stoke church, 1985; by 2009 he had devised, led and delivered twice some 150 separate walks. *National home of Association of Teachers of Lipreading to Adults (1976)* was Hanley in 2002.

Gay rights *One of the first gay couples to get married.* Craig and Kevin Ashdown of Hanley, entered into one of the new legal civil partnerships on Dec 21 2005 (BBC Midlands Today Aug 9 2005, Dec 22 2005).

Gebremussie, Ruta *First person in Stoke-on-Trent prosecuted under anti-smoking laws.* She was found guilty in 2009 of two charges of failing to stop a person smoking at the Shisha Lounge in Bryan St, Hanley, which she managed, on July 23 2008, under anti-smoking laws, introduced in 2007 (ES April 1 2009 p11pc).

Geology Bagnall is Carboniferous Limestone (Pendleside Series) (N and NE), Millstone Grit (Bagnall village, central bands from NW-SE), Middle Coal Measures (S fringe); Bucknall is Middle Coal Measures (all); Fenton is Upper Coal Measures (all); Longton is Middle Coal Measures (E), Upper Coal Measures (W); Stoke is Upper Coal Measures (all).

Godwin, Len *The man who started meals-on-wheels.* Stoke businessman; in 1946 or 1947 (ES Your Week May 20 2006 p11. July 5 2008 p29p).

Golf *England's captain for handicapped golf.* Fred Berrisford (1918-90), who lost a leg and a hand in WW2; he owned a chain of bookmakers in the Potteries (ES Your Week Oct 7 2006 p9p).

Goss, W. H. *Fancy that!* Pottery owner on London Road, Stoke-upon-Trent. In the Great Depression of the 1930s his business got into trouble. According to a manservant, Goss's circumstances had grown so straightened he lived on baked beans throughout the period; the fact that he could afford to surround himself with domestic servants remains something of a conundrum (this claim was made by Staffordshire Housing Association on a billboard in Corporation Road, Stoke-upon-Trent, to promote West End Village, 2009) (Sandra Barber, Staffs Housing

Ass. Communications Manager) (ES Aug 1 2009 p3pc). W.H. Goss was most likely William Huntley Goss (1867-1947), son of William Henry Goss (d1906). He sold the firm of WH Goss in 1930, staying on for a while as manager (William Henry Goss. Lynda & Nicholas Pine. 1987. p213).

Gregory, Rev Ian *The politest man.* Congregational minster of Hartshill, who founded The Polite Society, 1986, re-launched as the Campaign for Courtesy, 1996; another of Gregory's initiatives is based at Cheadle, Staffs. When Stoneyfield house on Etruria Rd, Basford, became an inn it was called the Polite Vicar Inn after him (BBC, and other websites, 2006).

Griffiths, Dorothy *Hartshill's heroine.* (1946-2010). Diagnosed with terminal breast cancer in 1999 and given months to live. Led a long national campaign for women to be treated with the unlicensed drug Herceptin, launching with others in 2005 the Women Fighting For Herceptin. It forced primary health trusts to fund the use of the new drug; Dorothy 'Dot' coordinating the campaign from her hospital bed. North Staffs Citizen Of The Year 2005 (ES April 26 2010 pp1,15pcs).

Grundy, Pte James *Fenton's war hero, Potteries' first recipient of the V.C.* Of Mount Pleasant, Fenton, of the Grenadier Guards for going over-the-top into open ground under enemy fire to mend a telephone wire on April 19-20 1916 (SA May 13 1916 p5p).

Hall, Eric *Man who cycled to the Llandudno Music Festival and won its pianoforte trophy (over 18 section).* Born 1931. Of Church St, Hanley, in 1950 with his playing of the Brahms Rhapsody in G Minor. He also gained second place in the Chopin class and third place in the Beethoven class. The Festival Chairman afterwards announced that a fund would be opened to enable Hall to make a full time study of music (SCP Nov 1950 p16).

Hanley *Out of the six towns, largest from c1850 is Hanley. One of the first to receive the freedom of Hanley borough* was George Howson (1818-96), sanitary ware manufacturer in Hanley (POTP p127). *First recorder of Hanley* was John Beavis Brindley, barrister-at-law of Newcastle-under-Lyme (1827-90); there is a window to his memory by Burne-Jones in Kingsley church (Kingsley PR). *Largest Citizens Advice Bureau in UK.* Cheapside branch, Hanley, by Summer 2008, with

80 staff (info CAB employee, 2008).

Hartill, Venerable Percy *Clergyman who banned a Battle of Britain memorial service.* Archdeacon of Stoke-on-Trent, at St Peter's, Sept 1949, because of his pacifist sympathies, outraging ex-servicemen (ES Your Week Feb 11 2006 p11, Dec 5 2006 p9).

Health *Biggest-publicly-funded NHS scheme in UK.* The new University Hospital of North Staffordshire, due to open in Spring 2009, costing £60 million (ES April 21 2007 p1). *5th biggest hospital in the country 2008.* University Hospital of North Staffordshire, with 6,500 staff, treating as many as 400,000 patients a year, serving a population of nearly 500,000 (ES July 5 2008 p27). *Safest place in Britain for elderly people to have a thigh operation 2008.* University Hospital of North Staffordshire, due to the work of consultant Dr Philip Roberts (ES Sept 24 2008 p5pc). *Unique superbug.* The 'Stoke Strain' of the Klebsiella pneumoniae bacteria, from a family of bugs called Extended Spectrum Beta-Lactamases. It is unique to Stoke-on-Trent, affecting patients on Ward 29 at the University Hospital of North Staffordshire. By April 2010 eight patients had been infected, and one had died (ES April 1 2010 p3).

Higginson, Fanny *Britain's longest-serving spiritualist medium.* Born 1890. Of Longton, when she died in 1978 (ES March 29 2003 p25).

Hilton, William and **Catherina Sale.** *Earliest persons recorded in Stoke-upon-Trent parish register.* For their marriage on Feb 28 1630. See also Lawson, and Walklate.

Hobson, Dorothy *Etruria's saddest.* Daughter of Ephraim Hobson who was stolen by gypsies. She was eventually rescued, and grew up to be a beautiful girl later marrying Rev Joseph Jones, a young missionary in 1824. They settled on the island of Antigua but Rev Jones disappeared in a disaster at sea. She returned to Etruria and died of a broken heart in 1847 (HOE p126).

Horticulture *The nursery 'second to none'* was Martin's Hill Nurseries, south of Bagnall, whose plants have a national reputation for quality, 'second to none' (MR2 p28). *'Britain's most expensive single garden' vendor.* John Ravenscroft born Longton 1936, and raised in Bagnall, who sold his Bridgemere Garden World, Cheshire, for £15 million to Wyevale Garden Centres in 2006 (ES Nov 10 2006

pp1,2). *Only garden created by a surgeon whilst on call for kidney transplantation in UK.* Possibly Barn House garden by Mike French, Clayton Road, Great Clayton (National Gardens Scheme (Staffordshire) guide 2006).

Industry (other than pottery) *Site of the first Fourdrinier paper machine* was by London Road, south east of Stoke Union Workhouse, south of Newcastle-u-Lyme, 1818 (Andrew Dobraszczyc, 2008). *Works record for a first cast on a new plant.* Shelton Iron & Steel Ltd on their Continuous Casting Plant at their new Shelton Steelworks (in full operation by late 1964), in summer 1964 when it cast 35 tons of steel in a bloom size of 16.25 inches by 9 inches (SA & Chron July 16 1964 p12p). *One of the biggest suppliers of bricks in the Midlands* was the Berryhill Birckworks, in the 1930s. The firm had closed by 1971 (ES July 18 2009 p25). *First North Staffordshire space craft equipment* produced was Atom-thin surface coating testing apparatus used on the European Space Agency's Aeolus Satellite. Developed by the Centre for Surface and Materials Analysis (part of Ceram) at Queens Rd, Penkhull, 2007 (ES May 23 2006 p3). *Only combined painters and plumbers association in the country.* The North Staffordshire Master Painters and Plumbers Association 1942-2007, which strove for quality in workmanship; it met every first Thursday in the month at Hanley Town Hall (ES Jan 5 2007 p19). *Most ambitious and comprehensive display of local products ever staged in the area.* The North Staffordshire Industries Fair on old Port Vale football ground, Hanley, as part of the Festival of Britain, 1951 (ES Your Week July 22 2006 p5). See also Tyre manufacturing.

Jones, Ivor *Britain's smallest working page boy late 1940s (reputedly).* Of Cobridge (died c1999). When aged 17 he stood just 3 feet 11 inches. He was a concierge at the old Odeon in Hanley in the late 1940s (ES June 9 2001 p21p).

Judaism *Last synagogue in the Potteries.* Birch Terrace, Hanley, closed 2006; it opened in 1923 (ES March 30 2006 p3). *Finest Torah scroll in the country* was that presented to Hanover Street Synagogue, Hanley, consecrated 1875, by Rabbi Zebi Hirsh Wlosin of Wilna or Vilna (info Pauline Moreland. Jack Leighton Seminar, Keele University. 2009).

Kaine, Margaret *Catherine Cookson of the Potteries, Of Love and Life New Writ-*

er's Award holder 2002, Sagittarius Prize winner 2002. Born 1939. Novelist. The awards were for her first novel, Ring of Clay (2002, set in the Potteries). The first award is made by the Romantic Novelists' Association and Reader's Digest, the

Margaret Kaine

second award by Society of Authors. Her other romance novels include Rosemary (2003, set in the Potteries), A Girl of Her Time (2004), Friends and Families (2005, based in Dresden, Longton), Roses for Rebecca (2007, based in Hanley), Ribbon of Moonlight (2008, based in Stone). She grew up in Meir, but moved away from the Potteries in 1960 (The North Staffordshire Magazine Jan 2008 pp90-91pcs).

Kenealy, Dr Edward *First M.P. unable to be formally 'introduced' in the House of Commons.* Independent member for Stoke-upon-Trent 1874-80, as no member could be found to present him; this brought about the ending the ceremony of being 'introduced' (POTP p134) (William Henry Goss. Lynda and Nicholas Pine. 1987 p64p cartoon).

Lawson, Richard *Earliest recorded person in Stoke-upon-Trent parish register.* For his burial on Feb 28 1630. See also Hilton, and Walklate.

Lee, William *'oldest surviving British World War One veteran' 2000, Oldest Man in UK 2000.* Born Hanley Jan 1892. Royal Engineer sapper. Awarded Chevalier de la Legion d'Honneur. He was still living (at Shelton) independently aged 100; died Oct

William Lee

2000, aged 108 (GBR) (ES Aug 31 2000 p3. April 12 2005 p13).

Legand, Mrs Elizabeth *North Staffordshire's oldest woman 1929.* She died aged 102 in Newcastle Poor Law Institute. Only a short time before she died she complained of feeling a little unwell. She was born in Sept 1827 and lived with her husband a miner and then a cooper at Shelton for 54 years until he died c1889 (Staffordshire Weekly Sentinel. April 20 1929 p10p).

Libraries and bookseller *First bookseller in the Potteries.* John Strahan, 1786 (POTP p18).

Lloyd, John *'one of the 20th century's leading aeronautical engineers'.* (1888-1978). Of Etruria. This claim was made by Sir Morien Morgan, Director of the Royal Aircraft Establishment, Farnborough, 1969-72. Lloyd attended Cavour Street School, Etruria, Hanley High School, and Stoke Technical School, going on to design the Whitworth Whitley bomber, used in WW2 until 1942; in 1950s he developed the Sea Slug missile for the Royal Navy (ES Oct 21 2008 pp8-9 - correspondence of Betty Cooper).

Lodge, Eleanor Constance *First woman recipient of a D. Litt by the University of Oxford 1928.* (1869-1936). Born Hanley. Sister of Sir Oliver and Sir Richard. The D. Litt was awarded to her work in the field of modern history; Vice-Principal of Lady Margaret Hall, Ox 1890-1921; Principal of Westfield College, Hampstead, University of London, 1921-31 (Wikipedia, 2009).

Lodge, Sir Oliver *1st Principal of University College, Birmingham, first man to transmit a message by radio telegraphy.* Scientist. Born The Views, Penkhull, 1851. The transmission was at a British Association meeting in Oxford, on 14 Aug 1894. He held the position of Principal from 1900. Died 1940 (POTP p142).

Sir Oliver Lodge

Lodge, Sir Richard *'one of the greatest historians the county has ever produced'.* (1855-1936). Of Penkhull. Older brother of Oliver Lodge (SA Aug 15 1936 p10 col 7) (ES July 18 2009 p27).

Longton *China Town, poorest and most insanitary (of the Pottery towns) in C19.* Longton ('China Town' is a chapter heading in JHY Briggs' A History of Longton). *Most fashionable clothing from Staffordshire* is the Belstaff motor bikers leather jacket; the company formed in Longton in 1924 and started developing leather jackets in 1930s (BBC internet site: Stoke & Staffordshire).

Machin, Arnold *'created the world's most reproduced work of art', 'one of the country's finest sculptors'.* (1912-99).

Arnold Machin.

Sculptor. Born Oakhill, with his classic sculpture of the Queen for postage stamps in 1967, described as 'one of the most enduring and instantly recognisable designs of the 20th century' by Royal Mail. The first time a stamp designer has ever appeared on a stamp was when a portrait of Machin appeared on a £1 ruby red 'Machin', to mark the ruby anniversary of the introduction of his stamps, 2007 (ES June 11 2002 p10p. June 9 2007 p3).

Mainwaring, John *Stoke-upon-Trent's longest-serving vicar.* He served for 59 years, 1633-92.

Martial Arts *European team weapons Junior? (Karate) champions 2009.* Jay Ricardo Vieira, aged 11, and Ben Saville, aged 13, both of Longton National Karate Association, Edensor Road, Longton (ES Jan 11 2010 p44).

Martindale, Hilda *First female factory inspector in the pottery industry.* She started this role in 1906 (ES Your Week March 17 2007 p9).

Maternity hospitals *First and last babies born at the North Staffordshire Maternity Hospital.* Robert Bell on March 31 1968, and Ellie Grace Johal of Trentham at 6.34pm on April 25 2009 (ES April 29 2009 p5pc). *First baby born at the 'new' Maternity Centre of the University Hospital of North Staffordshire.* Ruby Wynne of Bradwell, at 10.23pm on April 25 2009, just 10 hours after the Centre opened (ES April 29 2009 p5pc).

Stanley Matthews.

STANLEY MATTHEWS: General *'Staffordshire's best-loved son' 1955* (SA & Chron Oct 6 1955 p4 col 5), *oldest player to score in the FA Cup* was in 1964 when aged 49, *'the wizard of dribble', first footballer knighted while still a player* (HOS 1998 p22), *Footballer of the Year 1948, 1956 and 1963, European Footballer of the Year 1957,* being the inaugural winner of the title in 1948 (it was created by the Football Writers' Association). *The 'Matthews Final' was* the FA Cup Final 1953 owing to Stanley

Matthews turning the game around for Blackpool. *Matthews' first appearance for England* was against Wales at Cardiff on Sept 29 1934; an honour he coincidentally shared with another Staffordshire player, Ray Westwood of Brierley Hill (BCM Summer 2005 p80). *Matthews' final appearance for England* was when England played Denmark at Copenhagen, 1957 (ES Your Week Nov 4 2006 p9). *Matthew's hotel in Blackpool* the Romford Private Hotel at Blackpool South Shore in the late 1940s (ES March 14 2009 p25). *Matthews' first autobiography* is called Feet First, 1948 (ES Your Week Aug 5 2006 p9). *Matthews' last home* was The Views, Penkhull (ES Your Week June 11 2005 p11). *Man who claimed he was Stanley Matthews* was Daniel Thornhill, aged 34, labourer of Tunstall, who was sentenced to one year hard labour for thief at the Autumn Staffordshire Quarter Sessions 1938. After the theft at Stockton Brook Thornhill went to London where he claimed at the Belle Vue Club, Tottenham Street, to be Stanley Matthews. There was laughter in Court when Justice Wrottesley, who presided, inquired: "there is a footballer named Stanley Matthews, is there?" (SA Oct 8 1938 p5 col 4).

Legacy *Citizen Of The Century 1910-2010.* Stanley Matthews, as voted by The Sentinel readers to mark the centenary of the Federation of the Potteries in 1910 (ES April 1 2010 p6). *Man who bought his 1953 FA Cup boots back to Stoke.* Paul Totterdell of Hanley, 59, former Indesit worker, Blythe Bridge, who paid almost £40,000 of his redundancy money to buy Matthews' boots at auction in 2010 (ES March 27 2010 p5pc).

Mellor, Joseph *2nd ever ceramicist elected to the Fellowship of the Royal Society.* (1869-1939). Scientist, born Huddersfield; chemistry teacher at Newcastle High School. Produced a 16-volume encyclopaedia 'A Comprehensive Treatise on Inorganic and Theoretical Chemistry' (1921-37). Resided at The Villas, London Rd, Stoke. Mellor was elected to the Royal Society in 1927; their first ceramicist was Josiah Wedgwood I (POTP pp151p-152).

Methodism *One of John Wesley's last sermons occurred at Old Foley Pottery,* The Foley, Fenton, March 28 1790 (POP p120) (MR p151). *First Sunday school in the Potteries.* The Tabernacle Sunday Schools, Hanley, founded by the current minister Rev J Boden, 1785 (SA Sept 19

1835. Sept 21 1935 p9 col 2). *First Boys'* *Brigade Company* was that formed 1891 at Hanley Trinity Presbyterian Church, founded by William Mackie, former Sentinel editor (ES Your Week Oct 21 2006 p9. Oct 11 2008 p27). *Stoke-on-Trent's first ever road safety service* was held on Sunday Sept 23 1951 at the Central Methodist Hall, Longton, to a congregation of 600, with lessons about road safety read by Mr GEY Ingley, assistant education officer for Stoke-on-Trent, and Police Inspector CH Holland, city traffic and communications officer (SA Sept 28 1951 p4 col 4). *The 'doctors' church'* is Hanley Trinity Presbyterian, after c1900, on account of the relatively large number of Scottish physicians in the congregation (TWWW Nov 1 2008 p3p). *First New Connexion chapel in the Potteries* (HOS 1998 p69), *Cathedral of the Potteries, once 'largest Methodist chapel outside London'* (BBC Midlands Today Aug 28 2007) Bethesda chapel, Albion Street, Hanley, opened in 1798. Pentecostal church, Franklin St, Penkhull, is a Nissen hut (MR2 p245).

Military defence *First meeting of the Longton Rifle Volunteers* took place on May 27 1859; the first meeting of the Hanley Rifle Volunteers took place on May 30 1859, and the first for Stoke-upon-Trent Rifle Volunteers on Nov 25 1859 (SA Jan 14 1860 p5 col 4).

Mining *Deepest pit in North Staffordshire 1869, 'the deepest pit working in the country' 1935, only working colliery in Hanley from c1937.* Hanley Deep Pit (VCH vol 8 p169) (SA Dec 14 1935 p9 col 1). *Deepest colliery in the country 1960* was Stafford Colliery, Great Fenton, at 3,318 feet, with still deeper seams below the existing workings (HOS 1998 p103). *Country's first colliery for trainee miners.* Kemball Pit, Fenton, opened 1943 (ES Your Week June 3 2006 p11). *Strange but true!* An orange was found in the treacle-tin lunchbox of miner Joseph Roberts, who was killed in an explosion at the Racecourse Colliery, Etruria, in 1891 and put on display at the Potteries Museum in 2007 (The Daily Telegraph Oct 31 2007 p14).

Moor, Andy *'one of the world's most credited trance and progressive producer-DJs', 30th top world producer DJ 2005, 2006, 18th top world producer DJ 2009.* Born Andrew Beardmore in Stoke-on-Trent, 1980. Disc jockey and record mixer, alias 'Dub Disorder,' 'Dwight van Man,' 'Sworn'. The first quote was made by Wikipedia, 2009; the DJ rankings were compiled by DJ Magazine.

Morse, Denise *First bone-marrow transplant patient in North Staffordshire, 'Mother Courage'.* (1956/7-1989). Of Penkhull. National inspiration to other leukaemia sufferers; her campaign to help others with the disease raised an estimated £250,000 in North Staffordshire, alone (ES Your Week March 3 2007 p9p).

Museums *First new museum opened in England after WW2.* City Museum and Art Gallery, corner of Broad and Bethesda Streets, 1956. *Museum of the Year winner 1972, 1976* Gladstone Pottery Museum.

Music and musicals *Midland Area Mixed Voice Choir Championship winners 1952* was Etruscan Choir (SA June 13 1952 p8 col 3). *Musical play which ran for record number of performances at Old Victoria Theatre, Hartshill.* The Knotty, a railway documentary, 1966-78 (ES Your Week Oct 7 2006 p9). *UK's longest-running record fair 2009.* A monthly Potteries record fair, launched at Hanley YMCA in 1977 and still running at Cobridge community centre in 2009, a leading light in it was Chris Savoy (c1947-2009), broadcaster and record collector (ES Sept 5 2009 p12).

Myatt, Gareth *First child to die while being restrained in custody.* (1989-2004). Former Birches Head High School pupil, Hanley. He died in the seated double embrace restraint (since banned because of this case) in Rainsbrook Secure Training Centre, Rugby, only three days into a custodial sentence for assault and theft (ES June 29 2007 p6). In Feb 2007 an inquest into his death started and was by June 2007 the longest inquest into a death in custody (BBC Midland Today June 29 2007).

National Garden Festival *Largest industrial wasteland in the North Midlands 1985* was the Shelton Iron and Steel Works site of 125 hectares. This was an industrial site between 1841 and 1979. *3rd most popular paying visitor site in the UK* was the Etruria Valley, when it hosted the 1986 Garden Festival (ES May 9 2006 p6). *Most visited new attraction of 1986, The Greatest Day out in Europe in 1986, The Greatest show of '86, Britain's biggest ever garden festival* was the Festival (contemporary publicity material). *The Festival's official mascot* was Sergeant Freddie Stilton of the Royal Mousegards - the cartoon adventures of 'Freddie and the Volunteers' by Sheila and Francis Wainwright first appeared in The Evening Sentinel during the 12 months leading up to the Festival. *UK's biggest sculpture display since 1951* was The Festival. *Largest cable car system in the UK* was at The Festival. *Biggest flower shop in the UK* was at the Festival. There were also 87 themed gardens and three major event areas.

Natural history *Rare plant*. A bee orchid of five-inch tall discovered by children in Berry Hill Fields, July 1997 (ES July 9 1997 p1pc. July 10 1997 p1pc).

Newspapers *First Evening Sentinel produced entirely by new electronic system*. Early July 1981 (ES Your Week July 8 2006 p8). *'a paper which deserves to be read throughout Britain, if not the world'*. The Sentinel, formerly The Evening Sentinel, in the opinion of Punch editor (1957-) and native of Burslem Bernard Hollowood (d1981) (ES Your Week June 9 2007 p9). *Europe's Best Designed Newspaper 2004* was Sentinel Sunday (ES Aug 4 2006 p2).

Nightlife *One of the first disco night clubs in Britain* was The Place, Bryan St, Hanley, which opened in the 1970s. *Europe's largest disco* was Romeo and Juliets night club in Hanley, which closed in 1979 (ES Your Week May 29 2004 p8). *First winebar in the Potteries* was Heath's Wine Bar, corner of Albion and Bethesda Streets, Hanley 1980s? (Andrew Dobraszczyc on a social history walk, May 2007). *One of the best B&Bs in Britain*. The Corrie Guest House, 13 Newton St, Basford (The Good Bed and Breakfast Guide: Over 1000 of the best B&Bs in Britain. 1990. p313).

Parks *First public park in the Potteries*. Queen's Park, Longton, opened July 25-26 1888 causing one proud Stafford

Street shopkeeper, Longton, to place a motto in his shop front "Longton leads: who's next?" (SA July 28 1888 p4 col 5). *Largest and most original skateplaza in Europe*. Perhaps Central Forest Park, Hanley; 34,000 square feet and based on city squares and streets; cost £500,000 (BBC Midlands Today Oct 28 2005). *'UK's No. 1 aqua park'*. Waterworld, Festival Park, Etruria (Staffordshire Breaks 2006. Staffordshire Tourism).

Perkin, Harold *First lecturer, and then professor of Social History in a British university.* (1926-2004). Born Hanley, attended Hanley High School from 1938, at sometime resident at Burslem; Lecturer in Social History, Manchester University 1951-65; Senior Lecturer in Social History, Lancaster University 1965-67, Professor 1967-84, Director, Centre for Social History 1974-97 (Emeritus), 'one of the most visionary, gifted and dynamic historians of his generation'; he launched the Studies in Social History series at Routledge; initiated the foundation of the Social History Society, 1976, chairing it for 10 years; author of the trilogy of works 'The Origins of Modern English Society' (1969), 'The Rise of Professional Society' (1989), and 'The Third Revolution' (1996) (David Cannadine in The Guardian Oct 23 2004) (website, 2009).

Perkins, Syd *World amateur ballroom champion 1948, Carl-Alan award winner 1965 (for being the most outstanding dance teacher in the country).* Of Hanley (ES Your Week Aug 12 2006 p9p).

Syd Perkins and his dancing partner Edna Duffield. The couple were regularly seen on the BBC's 'Come Dancing' programme. Syd taught thousands of pupils at studios in Silverdale, Newcastle and Sandbach.

Place-names Stoke first appears in Domesday Book, 1086, and means 'place', probably here meaning 'dependant settlement'; Stoke under Lyme appears in 1305, and Stoke-upon-Trent in 1686. Fenton first appears in Domesday Book, and means 'the fen, marsh tun'; Hanley in 1212, and means '(Place) at the high leah'; Longton in 1242, and means 'long tun' (PNSZ).

Pole vaulting *Britain Junior champion 2004, Commonwealth bronze 2006, European bronze 2008.* Steven Lewis (b1986), pole vaulter of Light Oaks, Bagnall. The 2008 title was at the Spar European Cup, France, 2008 (ES June 23 2008 pp42,48pc. Aug 5 2008 ppiv-v pc).

Policing *2nd oldest institution of its kind in the country 1953.* The Hanley Association for the Prosecution of Felons, founded 1792, still holding annual dinners in 1953 (SA March 6 1953 p3 col 1); indeed they still (2009) hold dinners. *Country's first police surgery in a supermarket* was held by PC Neil Russell at Tesco supermarket, Newcastle Road, Springfields, on Oct 2 1998 between 9.00am and 11.00am (ES Oct 1 1998 p3p) (BBC Radio 4. You and Yours. Oct 2 1998).

Poorest Stoke-upon-Trent parish workhouse reputedly built 1735 stood at the corner of Trent Valley Road and Manor Court Street, Penkhull (WITP p5). Stoke-upon-Trent and all its townships formed Stoke-upon-Trent Union from 1836 using the Spittles Workhouse, built 1832-3, with hospital of 1842 and later ancillary buildings; these went on to form part of City General Hospital, Penkhull. The union merged with Wolstanton in 1922.

Population Stoke-upon-Trent was 2nd most populated Staffordshire parish in 1801 with 16,414 people; 2nd in 1811 with 22,495; 2nd in 1821 with 29,223; 2nd in 1831 with 37,220; 2nd in 1841 with 47,951; 2nd in 1851 with 57,942; 2nd in 1861 with 71,308; 2nd in 1871 with 89,262; 2nd in 1881 with 104,968; 2nd in 1891 with 122,101; 2nd in 1901 with 140,335. Stoke-upon-Trent (includes Tunstall)could be ranked 1st in Staffordshire for loss of men in WW1, with 2,383 lives lost.

POTTERY INDUSTRY Buildings *Largest earthenware manufacturer in the world.* Johnsons during the directorship of Sir Ernest Johnson (d1962) (Salute to the Potters. John Abberley 2005? p123). *Largest pottery/ sanitary ware factory in*

A typical Pot Bank scene in the 19th Century

Staffordshire was that of Thomas Twyford at Cliff Vale, Shelton, when it opened 1877 (ES Your Week June 17 2006 p11. ES July 4 2006 p7). *Potteries largest bottle ovens* were at Bedford Works of Ridgway Pottery, Shelton, built C19, 80 feet high, demolished 1960s (Salute to the Potters. John Abberley 2005? p29) (ES Your Week June 17 2006 p11). *Potteries tallest potbank chimney* was Harvey's Chimney, Forrester Brothers, by Eagle Inn in Times Square, Longton (ES Your Week April 7 2007 p8). *Britain's sole surviving steam powered potters mill.* Etruria Industrial Museum, Lower Bedford Street, Etruria (Staffordshire County Guide 2006/7 p110). *Last firing of a bottle oven in the Potteries for commercial purposes* was at the old Hudson Middleton Works, behind the Gladstone Pot Works, Longton, on Aug 26 1968; Frank Collis of Stone made a watercolour painting of the event (ES Aug 8 2009 p36 il. Aug 22 2009 p29. Sept 5 2009 p26). *Very last firing of a bottle oven in the Potteries* was at Gladstone Pottery Museum (formerly Gladstone Potworks) in 1978, having gained permission to coal fire a kiln full of ware, for show purposes (SPT Nov 2006). *Man who walked a circuit of the last remaining 45 bottle ovens, 2009.* Keith Meeson, aged 63, retired miner, of Stanley, near Bagnall, on Sunday, Sept 20, to raise funds for the Donna Louise Children's Hospice Trust. The circuit of 15 miles began at Moorland Pottery, Burslem, and ended at Minkstone Products, Normacot Road, Longton (ES Sept 21 2009 p4pc).

General *England's oldest industry* is pottery (SA May 1926, advert for Stoke-on-Trent Civic Week). *First pottery works in Longton* was the Longton Hall Works from c1749 (VCH vol 8 p239). *First royal visit to a potbank* was when the Prince of Wales (later George IV) and his brother the Duke of Clarence (afterwards William IV) visited Davenport's at Longport and Spode's at Stoke when staying with the Marquis of Stafford at Trentham Hall in 1806 (SA May 29 1953 p4 col 4). *Potter to the Queen.* Paragon China, Longton, 1933- (ES Your Week Nov 18 2006 p9). *Oldest surviving family business in the ceramic tableware industry 2000* was Dudson (Dudson Centre notice board c2000). *'One of the best ceramics collections in the world'* is Potteries Museum and Art Gallery, Bethesda Street, Hanley (Staffordshire County Guide 2006/7 p111). *'The Worst Jobs In History' relating to* *the Pottery industry.* In the episode on Industrial Britain for this T.V. series Tony Robinson, identified the Bone scrappers (preparing bone for the china), and the mould pressers, alias 'the Jumpers' (The Worst Jobs In History. Channel 4. July 7 2007 repeat). *National home of the Clay Roof Tile Council (CRTC)* was based at Federation House, Station Road, Stoke, in 2008.

Individual ware *First free-standing water closet* was designed at Cliffe Vale works (ES July 4 2006 p7). *First pottery firm to make a ceramic doll's head* was Willow Pottery at Longton, 1914 (ES Your Week July 1 2006 p11). *First use of Royal Arms on pottery for general public.* The Edward VIII coronation mug designed by Dame Laura Knight, artist, and made in the Potteries (SA Aug 15 1936 p9 col 2). *Blue Riband of the Atlantic trophy for fastest liner crossing* was made by Pidduck and Sons of Hanley, 1935 (ES Your Week July 22 2006 p9). *World record for sale of a Stubbs-Wedgwood painted plaque* was one the painted plaques painted by George Stubbs (1724-1806), sold for £300,000 in 2003 (ES Your Week May 12 2007 p9). *One of Henry Sandon's most thrilling finds.* Ozzy the Owl, a C17 brown and black Staffordshire slipware owl jug which came to the attention of antique ceramics expert, Henry Sandon, on a BBC 'Antiques Road Show' at Northampton, and was bought 1990 by the Potteries Museum for £20,900. 'Seldom has the touring antiques show turned up such a remarkable piece' (ES Sept 27 2008 p25p).

People *'Father of The Pottery'* John Proudlove, fl1784, since he was the best mould maker and tureen maker in the Potteries in the later part of C18. He was hired by Mr E Wood for three years, at 12 shillings per week (HSP p223). *Potteries' first female employed as a transferrer of the impressions from copper plates to pottery.* Mary Broad, who died at Penkhull in 1828 (HSP p65). *'Pottery George'* alias of George Shaw, notori-

ous thief, sentenced to 10 years penal servitude at the Spring Assizes 1878, for housebreaking and burglary, after numerous previous convictions (SA March 23 1878 p4 col 5). *Potter who appeared in breaks between programmes on T.V. in 1950s* was Fred Halfpenny, head potter at Wedgwood Pottery (ES Feb 21 2009 p27). *'Father of British Bathrooms'* was the sobriquet of Thomas William Twyford (1849-1921) (ES July 4 2006 p7). *World record for making 3,591 bowls in 72 hours* was set by Kevin Millward at Gladstone Museum, 1979 (ES Your Week Aug 28 2004 p8). *Strange but true!* In the early hours of Sunday morning Feb 8 1885 two of the best-known and most generally-esteemed Pottery manufacturers of the time, Colin Minton Campbell and James Meakin, died within a few minutes of each other; Campbell of a protracted illness, but Meakin was in excellent health (SA Feb 14 1885). *The Potteries Prodigy* was Evelyn Bailey of 52 Church Street, Hanley, aged 13, in 1930 when she had a remarkable talent for throwing pots (Salute to the Potters. John Abberley 2005? p128p) (ES Oct 3 2009 p30p). *First 'Pottery Queen of Britain'* was Miss Annie Sheppard of Charles St, Hanley, in 1934. She was employed at Messrs George Jones & Sons, Crescent Potteries, Stoke (SA July 14 1934 p11p).

Processes *Staffordshire's first porcelain factory.* Longton Hall, 1750 (ES Your Week June 3 2006 p11). *Last salt-glaze potter in Staffordshire* was Samuel Spode (1758-1817) at Foley Pottery, south side of King Street, Fenton. *First to perfect the method of multi-colour or polychrome printing* was the firm of F&R Pratt of Fenton, c1840 (later the Rialto Pottery) (VCH vol 8 p220) (POP p108). *First Staffordshire pottery to use Cornish clay in the manufacture of true 'hard paste' porcelain* was Shelton New Hall Works, Newhall and Marsh Streets, Hanley (OTP p184). *First to use mechanical firing com-*

A placer lifting a sagger (which contained the wares for firing) into the correct place in the kiln. It was the sagger-maker bottom knocker (usually a young lad) who made the bottom of the sagger; saggers had a lifespan of about 40 times in the kiln.

Evelyn Bailey: The Potteries Prodigy.

mercially in bone china manufacture, the Wilds at St Mary's Works Uttoxeter Rd, Longton, c1906 (VCH vol 8 p243). *Potter who created a mixture for flambe ware* was George Moore c1900; flambe ware was made by Royal Doulton (ES Dec 1 2007 Staying In p13). *World's largest collection of open stock transfers 1977.* KH Bailey & Sons Ltd, Marsh St, Hanley, transfer manufacturers (Advert in The City of Stoke-on-Trent Official Handbook, 1977).

Sales *First pottery export to the U.S.* was when a consignment of 500 Royal Doulton figurines was sent to the United States in 1949 (ES Your Week May 12 2007 p9). *Queen's Award for Export Achievement 1987* John Tams; *1988, 1993* Churchill Tableware (Salute to the Potters. John Abberley 2005?) (Churchill China. Rodney Hampson. 1994 pp121, 133). *'one of the biggest factory shops in Britain'* was that proposed by Royal Doulton, to be opened in a 10,000 square foot building at Etruria Valley in Aug 2001; the store will sell a wide range of household wares as well as pottery (ES July 16 2001 p9).

Powell, Jeffrey *Fenton's bravest.* Of Fenton. He received the Royal Humane Society Award for bravery in 2004. He tried to save a woman who had set herself alit with turpentine and whom he heard screaming whilst he was fishing at a pool in Trent Vale. Powell tried to stop the flames with his bare hands, managed to remove clothes and cover her with a water-soaked blanket. But the woman died in hospital three days later (BBC news Sept 17 2004).

Public art *'The Man of Fire'* is a 35-feet tall aluminium statue of a man erected over the entrance to John Lewis's store, Stafford Street, Hanley, erected 1963, by sculptor David Wynne. Variously known as the Man of Ice, or Icicles, Jack Frost, and Spikey Man. Restored 2003-08 (ES July 26 2008 p27p). *'The Man of Iron'* Statue of an ironworker stands outside the Potteries Museum, Hanley. The man who was the model for it was Allen Fawcett (ES Aug 10 2007 p9p).

Pubs *One of the 12 most haunted pubs in England.* Albion Inn at No. 64 Uttoxeter Rd, Longton (Real Ale in and around the Potteries. CAMRA p49) (John Timpson's England. 1987) (HPG pp174,177). *Potteries Community Pub 1998, 1999, 2001, 2003, 2006, and 2007.* Respectively, Golden Cup Inn, Hanley; Greyhound Inn, Penkhull; Greyhound and Beehive

Inns, Penkhull; Unicorn and Coachmakers Arms Inns, Hanley. The Potteries Pub Preservation Group, who run the Award, present each winner with the Titanic (Brewery) Trophy. *'one of the smallest pub rooms in the UK'.* The snug at the Coachmaker's Arms Inn, Lichfield St, Hanley, dating from 1860, which is no bigger than an old railway carriage (ES May 31 2007 p5). *First bar in the country to win the official backing of the All Party Parliamentary Save the Pub Group.* Coachmakers' Arms Inn, Lichfield St, Hanley, which was under threat of demolition in 2009 for site clearance to build the East West Centre (ES June 10 2009 p11).

Quotes *'Dear Stoke-on-Trent. By far the dirtiest place I walked through and by far the friendliest'* said John Hillaby in his Journey through Britain. Paladin. 1968, p124. *Choicest for Stoke-on-Trent.* JB Priestley in English Journey, 1933, said 'May Stoke-on-Trent, a real city, spacious and gay, fit for good craftsmen to live in, rise high and white; and may the blanket of smoke, the sooty dolls' houses, the blackened fields, soon be nothing but a memory, a tale of the old pioneers.'

Racket sports *First female squash player in the world to turn professional, Squash hat-trick winner.* Angela Smith (b1953), brought up in Bucknall, learnt squash at Northwood Stadium. Became a professional squash player in 1979. Ranked one the world's squash players 1979-90. Won the British Open, the British Closed and the World Championship 1989 (FWNS pp81-83ps) (Wikipedia 2008). *Tennis under-21s Singles Champion of Great Britain 1964.* Keith Wooldridge of Longton (A Souvenir Publication Commemorating The Centenary of the Staffordshire Lawn Tennis Association 1893-1993 p9).

Radio *First BBC radio station in Stoke-on-Trent* was 6ST at the Majestic Cinema, Stoke upon Trent, 1920s (ES Your Week May 27 2006 p11). *First person on BBC Radio Stoke* was John Snagge in 1968 (ES Your Week Sept 29 2007 p6).

Railways *One of only two UK private railway companies to have exclusive rights over a coalfield.* North Staffordshire Railway (formed 1847); the other was the Northern Railway in the NE of England (Jack Leighton Seminar, March 5 2008). *Britain's only crane tank railway engine.* Dubsey, made by Dubs and Co. of Glasgow, owned by Shelton Steelworks 1901-73 (ES Your Week Aug 19 2006 p5p). *Staffordshire's best example of Neo-Jacobean architecture* is Stoke Railway Station and the Station Hotel (later North Staffordshire Hotel), 1847-48 (BOE p35). *Largest 'stable' in the country 1848* was the Round House railway engine shed at Whieldon's Grove, Fenton (SA April 22 1848) (W) (POP p100). *Last steam locomotive driven out of Stoke Shed* was a Class 4 freight engine (a Crab), Aug 1967; the Shed was situated behind a row of cottages off City Road, Fenton (ES Your Week July 15 2006 p7).

Roman Catholicism *First Dominican house in Staffordshire after the Reformation* was a convent at Foley, Longton, by Mother Margaret Hallahan, in 1852 (HOS 1998 p60).

Rushton, Joseph *Testator with Staffordshire's last will administered by the bishop's consistory court.* Of Stoke-upon-Trent. His will - with others from Pensnett, West Bromwich, and Wolverhampton - was proved on Dec 31 1860. This was after the Probate Court Act (1857) became law from Jan 12 1858, replacing ecclesiastical courts with civil District Probate Registries.

Ryder, Mrs Catherine *'oldest inhabitant of the Potteries' 1954.* Born 1852. Of King Street, Fenton; pottery paintress, who reached her 102nd birthday in 1954 (SA March 12 1954 p1 col 6).

Sailing *Man who inaugurated the Blue Riband of the Atlantic trophy.* Harold Hales of Hanley. The trophy is for vessels making the fastest trip across the Atlantic. Hales personally presented the Riband to Mussolini when it was won by the Italian liner 'Rex' (Staffs Illustrated. Oct 1969. Staffs Scene. Feb 1970. photo).

Schools *Potteries school that was famous in educational circles.* Longton High School during the headship of Dr Walter Harris (1866-1954), esteemed educationalist, 1902-31; he was the author of several books on science (SA April 2 1954 p2 col 6). *Worst funded high schools of any UK unitary authority 1998.* Stoke-on-Trent (ES July 4 1998). *Only Voluntary Aided Church of England High School in North Staffordshire.* St Peter's, Queen's Rd, Penkhull. *One of the first schools in England to get a perfect score in an Ofsted inspection.* Our Lady and St Werburgh's RC primary school, Seabridge Lane, Clayton, which achieved grade ones for every single judgement, achieving 27 marks (ES Dec 4 2006 p5). *Fancy that!* Kingsland Primary School,

Bucknall, bought a 60-foot former S-360, 40-seater commercial aircraft (minus wings) for an outdoor classroom in their school grounds in 2009 (The Guardian (Education supplement) March 24 2009) (ES March 31 2009 p6pc).

Sheard, Trumpeter Arthur *Founder of the Salvation Army bands.* Born 1858. Of Cavour St, Etruria, born Barnsley, came to the Potteries to work at the Shelton Iron and Steel works in 1885. In the later 1870s when General Booth was touring the country Sheard was always in attendance 'trumpeting' the General, and thus he became the first of the Army's bandsman (SA May 21 1938 p5 col 3).

Shopping *'world's last surviving traditional oakcake shop'.* Hole In The Wall, Waterloo Street, Hanley, under threat of demolition in 2008 due to regeneration of the area; customers are served through a window in the external wall. The shop appears in a mural in the Potteries Shopping Centre (ES Jan 14 2008 p5pc). *Staffordshire's (post-1974) largest shopping mall, 'biggest commercial development in Stoke-on-Trent since the war'.* The Potteries Shopping Centre, Hanley, opened June 1 1988. The quote is from a Sentinel report during its construction (Stafford-

The Bennett Precinct, Longton.

shire Breaks 2006. Staffordshire Tourism) (ES Dec 1 2007 Staying In p15p). *2nd shopping precinct of its kind in the country.* Bennett Precinct, Longton, opened March 1965. It is named after the man who championed it Alderman Albert Bennett (see) (Staffs Weekly Sentinel. March 5 1965 p10p) (STM May 1965 p57ps) (ES Your Week Aug 7 2004 p7). *Amongst first in the country awarded a Qualification and Credit Framework (QCF).* 94 staff at Morrisons supermarket in Festival Park, Etruria, in a national trial programme in March 2010. The award was a Level 2 certificate in retail skills, equivalent to five GCSEs. The staff were tested on subjects, including health and safety, dealing with customers and food hygiene, all while carrying out their duties. It is hoped this retail skills award will be rolled out nationwide (ES March 4 2010 p5).

Simmonds, Gunner Thomas *Stoke's war hero.* When aged 25, of Garner Street, Cliffe Vale, Royal Marine Artillery he was at the battle of Jutland. He died of wounds sustained while serving on the Vindictive on its raid of Zeebrugge in WW1, and was buried with full military honours in Hartshill Cemetery (SA June 1 1918 p7 col 5).

Slater, Harriet *First woman appointed a government whip.* Labour MP for Stoke North 1955-1966 (ES April 11 2009 p27).

Smith, Ellis *First M.P. to receive the Trades Council officer's silver badge in recognition of service to the trade union movement, 'most sincere man in the House of Commons' 1966.* (1896-1969). MP for Stoke Division of Stoke-on-Trent Parliamentary Borough 1935-50, Stoke-on-Trent South 1950-66, on his retirement in 1966 (ES Oct 18 2008 p29). As early as 1947 he was considered ubiquitous in his sense of duty. He was awarded the silver badge in 1948; only 61 persons had ever previously received this badge (SA June 21 1947 p5 col 2. June 26 1948 p5 col 6).

Speedway *Only time UK hosted midget car speedway league racing* was in 1938 at Sun Street Stadium, Shelton, when Stoke Potters came 2nd (ES Jan 1 2007 p16) (Midget Car Speedway. Derek Bridgett. 2006). The *Stoic of Stoke* alias Dave Anderson, Stoke Potters speedway rider in late 1940s, and briefly in 1960, after winning all his five races in a world championship round at the Sun Street Stadium, in spite of the death of his young wife earlier that day (ES May 8 2010 p34p).

Sport See Athletics (track) and (distance running), Billiards, Bowls, Boxing, Bull baiting, Cricket, Cycling, Darts, Football, Golf, Martial Arts Stanley Matthews, Pole vaulting, Racket sports, Sailing, Speedway, Stoke City FC, Swimming, Wrestling.

Stamer, Sir Lovelace Tomlinson *Stoke's greatest rector and greatest citizen, 'the modern church history of Stoke is the history of the man'.* (1829-1908). Bart. Born York. Rector of Stoke 1853-92. The first claim is according to Archdeacon Hartill. The second is by 'Wayfarer' a columnist in the Staffordshire Advertiser July 26 1947 p5 col 2, who goes on to say Stamer came to Stoke in 1858 and found the ecclesiastical affairs in a very dull state. Besides the parish church and the old school built by Dean Woodhouse in 1815, there

was only one little school in North Street. He determined to remedy this and established what is still (1947) known as the Stamer tradition. By the end of his incumbency there were four flourishing mission churches, three mission rooms, and five schools, 'all bearing high testimony to a record of work unique in the annals of the Lichfield diocese' (CAST) (POTP p199p).

STOKE CITY FOOTBALL CLUB General *Alias.* 'The Potters'. *Country's 2nd oldest football club* is Stoke City, founded 1863. *One of the world's oldest surviving football programmes* is thought to be that for the Stoke City v. Notts County match on Sept 22 1888, found in a house in The Westlands, Newcastle, by 2009. It was published during the Football League's first season. The game was the third played by Stoke in the league, their second at home, and the club's first league win, with a score of 3-0 (ES Feb 17 2009 p7pc). *'Bob McGory's £10 team'* was the squad in the late 1940s, because nearly all the players were local boys who joined the club for a £10 signing-on fee (ES Your Week 26 2006 p9). *'Stoke will win the FA Cup when Hanley is a seaside town'.* Local saying (ES Your Week July 14 2007 p8).

Individual matches *Football team who have played before the greatest crowd that has ever paid to see a league match between two provincial teams by 1950.* Stoke City at Manchester City's Main Road ground, on March 3 1934, to 84,569 spectators, in a sixth-round FA cup-tie ("Ask Me Another" series quiz by RD Woodall) (ES June 14 2008 p31). *'Stoke City's "Waterloo"'* was when a depleted Stoke side went out of the F.A. Cup in 1938. They were decisively beaten 2-1 by Bradford in a re-play. At the close of the match a large crowd of spectators demonstrated in front of the club offices, apparently at management's inability to secure a capable centre-forward to understudy Steele, injured in the first game, instead risking the new inexperienced centre-forward Peppitt (SA Jan 29 1938 p3 col 5). *Feat never previously recorded in the history of the old First Division* was when Stoke won 1-0 at Bolton in Aug 1947, fielding an entire team of locally-born players (ES Feb 7 2009 p27). *Britain's worst sports disaster to 1968* was when

Bolton Wanderers played Stoke away on March 9 1946; 33 were killed after a section of the barriers collapsed (GBR 1968 p258). *Most protracted FA Cup tie* was when Stoke City played Bury culminating with Stoke winning 3-2 in a match on Jan 24 1955, after five meetings and after nine hours 22 minutes of play (GBR 1969 p313. 1974 p270). *First goal scored under the Victoria Ground floodlights* was that by Stoke winger Tim Coleman on Oct 10 1956, against Port Vale, the score was 3-1 to Stoke (ES Feb 21 2009 p27). *Last football special train for Stoke City fans*. It was proposed that it would be the one bound for Aston Villa on Saturday Nov 14 1964; Villa won 3-0 (SA & Chron Nov 19 1964 p5ps). *Last visitors to play Colchester United at Layer Road*. Stoke City on April 26 2008, before the club moved to the Cuckoo Farm stadium for the 2008–09 season. Layer Road been their home since the formation of the club (BBC Midlands Today April 25 2008).

Players *Had international caps by playing for both Northern Ireland and the Irish Republic*. Jimmy McAlinden, signed by Stoke in 1947 (ES Oct 4 2008 p29). *25 consecutive matches for England, 'generally regarded as the country's best centre-half', first professional footballer to play for a foreign club*. Neil Franklin, see Sandon.

Dennis Smith - 'The Most Injured Man in Football'.

Youngest player ever to play for Stoke City was Gerry Bridgewood, aged 16 (SN July 12 2006 p6). *The father and son who both played at wing half* were Harry and John Sellars (ES Your Week Feb 17 2007 p9). *Oldest player to score the winning goal in a cup final at Wembley*. George Eastham when aged 35 scoring Stoke's second goal against Chelsea in a League Cup final in 1972 (ES Your Week Oct 21 2006 p9. Dec 19 2009 p25). *'The Most Injured Man in Football', 'the hardest man in football'* See Denis Smith, under Caverswall. *Most match appearances (1,389)/ record for 1,005 league appearances for various clubs, including 110 for Stoke City (1974-77)*. Peter Shilton, goalkeeper (GBR 2003 p209). *Man who took a photograph from every seat in Britannia Stadium* was Phil Greig who had taken a photograph from all 28,000 seats using a fisheye lens. By June

6 2008 he had taken photographs from 1,200 seats (BBC Midlands Today June 6 2008).

Stoke Town Hall *'largest and most imposing municipal building in the six towns', 'one of the finest buildings in North Staffordshire'*. Glebe Street, Stoke. Built 1834-50 as Stoke-upon-Trent town hall to designs by Henry Ward. After Federation in 1910 the building has adjoined a complex of administrative buildings for the county borough and later the City of Stoke-on-Trent. The first claim is by VCH vol 8 p182. The second claim was made in the Staffs County Handbook c1951 p135. (AGT pp140il,141).

Swimming *'the greatest freestyle swimmer Britain has ever had'*. Norman Wainwright (1915/6-2000), Hanley native, Olympic games (1932, 1936, 1948), and broke 50 records (ES Your Week Dec 23 2006 p9). By 1936 he was the holder of six British native records (SA March 28 1936 p7p), including setting the record for one mile in 21 minutes 45 seconds. *Oldest unbroken Staffordshire swimming record 1955* was Norman Wainwright's 220 yards freestyle in 2 mins 15 secs, achieved c1935 (SA & Chron March 24 1955 p5 col 7). *Great Britain Open Swimming 100 metres winner 1930, 1931*. Bob Leivers (b1914),

Norman Wainwright - Staffordshire's greatest swimmer.

of Longton. Also by 1936 the holder of the British native 800 yards record (SA July 25 1931 p7p. March 28 1936 p7p). *British Olympic swimming team manager 1948* Harry Hoskie of Hanley (ES June 13 2009 p27).

Swinnerton, Frank *'The 'Sandwich King' of Britain'*. Of Hanley. Chairman and Managing Director of Swinnerton (Industrial Canteens) Ltd. In 1946 was making 160,000 sandwiches a week for miners and heavy industrial workers in North Staffordshire; the firm began in 1941 (SA July 20 1946 p5 col 4).

Thackwell, Kevin *World record for most clothes pegs clipped to face and neck*. Of Stoke-on-Trent. He clipped 116 pegs in five minutes at the Horseshoe Inn, Church Lawton, Ches, Sept 27 1999 (GBR 2001 p18).

Theatre *Britain's first purpose-built theatre in the round*. The New Victoria

Theatre, Basford (Staffordshire Breaks 2006. Staffordshire Tourism). *First professional company in Britain to perform permanently in-the-round* was the Victoria Theatre Company at the New Victoria Theatre, Basford, early 1960s (Staffordshire County Guide 2006/7 p53). *First full-length play by a local writer performed at The Victoria Theatre* was 'The Spanish Dancer from Pinnox Street', Arthur Berry (d1994), in 1976 (ES July 6 1994). *Stoke-on-Trent Repertory Theatre's last production at Beresford Street, Shelton*, was 'Journey's End' by RC Sheriff which ran to May 17 1997 (ES May 13 1997 p14).

Tildsley, Spurgeon *Stoke's kindest (perhaps).* (1891-1981). Pawnbroker of Tildsleys (closed 1975) Marsh St, Hanley, noted for his acts of kindness (ES Your Week Sept 9 2006 p9p).

Trams and buses *North Staffordshire's last electric tram* ran on July 11 1928 (ES Your Week May 20 2006 p11). *First Potteries purpose-built bus station.* The Strand (formerly Stafford Street), Longton 1944-64; the site has since become the Bennett shopping precinct (ES Your Week May 6 2006 p11p). *North Staffordshire's longest-surviving independent bus company.* Berresford's, who sold to PMT in 1987 after nearly 70 years (ES Your Week May 6 2006 p7). *Cleanest buses in North Staffordshire* were Baxter's, c1921-1960 (ES Your Week Sept 2 2006 p5). *Stoke-on-Trent's first city ambulance station* was on land of Cauldon Potteries, off Campbell Road, Shelton, 1948-68 (ES Your Week April 29 2006 p11, June 24 2006 p11).

Tyre manufacturing *Michelin Tyre's first British factory* was at Boothen, Stoke-upon-Trent, 1927 (Staffordshire Handbook c1966 p99), and chosen by Michelin as their UK headquarters in preference to Nottingham (ES Oct 18 2008 p28). *World's first radial tyre* was the Michelin X, which went into production at Michelin, Stoke factory in 1952 (ES Oct 18 2008 p28). *Michelin Tyre's first beauty queen* was Cynthia Bate 1957 (ES Staying In Nov 24 2007 p18p).

Variety shows *First show of Buffalo Bill's last UK tour* was at the Old Racecourse at Boothen, involving 800 people and 500 horses, on April 25 1904 (ES Sept 6 2008 p30). *Gertie Gitana's first stage role* was Little Gitana (gypsy) with a troupe called Tomkinson's Royal Gypsy Choir, aged 4 in 1892. This child prodigy

went on to become an acclaimed music hall artist. The song which made her famous was Neldean, after which she named her London home. When she died of cancer in 1957, Frederic Street, Hanley, where she spent her early childhood, was renamed Gitana Street (ES Oct 11 2008 p25p). *'Handsomest and most commodious house of entertainment in the northern part of the county, and indeed in the whole district between Birmingham and Manchester'* was the Grand Theatre of Varieties, Trinity St, Hanley, 1920; rebuilt as Odeon Cinema 1932 (SO&N p37). *'Penkhull Belles'.* A revue written and produced by Rev VG Aston, vicar of Penkhull, first performed in 1932 (SA Jan 6 1934 p2 col 2).

Gertie Gitana.

VICTORIA HALL General. *1st North Staffordshire Musical Festival* was 11-13 October 1888, at the Victoria Hall, Lichfield St, Hanley (SA Oct 13 1888 p3 col 6). *Finest acoustics in the country* this concert hall thought the composer, Thomas Beecham. *Longest symphony ever written* was Symphony No. 2 (the Gothic) by William Havergal Brian (1876-1972) which was performed at the Victoria Hall. After his death Brian was described as *'Britain's forgotten man of music'* (ES April 11 2009 p27). *Choral music heard most at the Victoria Hall in C20* was Handel's oratorio The Messiah (ES Your Week Nov 4 2006 p9). *Gracie Fields' last public performance* was at the Victoria Hall, 1952, aged 54 (ES Staying In Nov 24 2007 p13). *First wedding reception at Victoria Hall* was that of Paul Pike of Birches Head and Susan Dale of Gillow Heath on Nov 26 1982 (ES Nov 27 1982 p1p).

First performances at Victoria Hall: *Elgar's 'King Olaf'* 1896, *Frederick Delius' 'Sea Drift'* 1908 (ES Your Week June 24 2006 p11) (VCH vol 8 p172) (POP p54), *Samuel Coleridge-Taylor's 'Minnehaha'* on Oct 26 1899, commissioned by the North Staffordshire Triennial Musical Festival, and conducted by the composer himself (SA July 28 1934 p7 col 8), *JB Priestley's play 'Dragon's Mouth'* on April 15 1952; Priestley attended (SA April 18 1952 p5 col 5) (ES Oct 4 2008 p29).

Walker, Mr and Mrs John *They lost*

their lives on the Luisitania. Of Etruria. The son and daughter-in-law of William Walker of Fowlea Farm, Etruria. In addition, were victims: Mr WH Crutchley, a sanitary presser of Etruria Vale; Edward Jones of Shelton, musician in the ship's orchestra; Winnie Barker, aged nine, a granddaughter of Mrs Bullock of Mostyn Street, Birches Head, and daughter of a sanitary presser at Trenton, New Jersey. This was a Cunard passenger liner torpedoed by a German submarine off the Irish coast while in transit from New York to Liverpool, May 1915 (SA May 15 1915 p7ps).

Walklate, Joanna *Earliest recorded person in Stoke-upon-Trent parish register.* For her baptism on Feb 28 1630. She was the daughter of Richard Walklate and Margaret. See also Hilton, and Lawson. The earliest recorded person in Longton (St John) parish register is Isaac son of Isack & _____?, baptised on June 4 1764.

Walters, Frederick W *Stoke's boy hero.* Of Bridge Road, Trent Vale, 15, who saved a publican's daughter Mary Ford, 5, from drowning in the canal at the rear of Minton's factory on April 27 1935, and was presented with the Royal Humane Society's Certificate (SA July 20 1935 p12 col 6).

Waterways *Paul Gogarty's 9th best canal of the English Waterways.* Trent and Mersey Canal, especially the stretch from Stoke to Anderton Boat Lift, according to Paul Gogarty author of The Water Road - A Narrowboat Odyssey Through England, 2007 (Daily Telegraph May 25 2007 p16).

Wedgwood Pottery at Etruria *First pottery to be anything other than entirely functional in appearance ever.* Probably the Etruria Works of Josiah Wedgwood. *'One of the finest examples of the potter's art to be found anywhere in the world'.* Josiah Wedgwood's version of the Portland Vase, 1789; the first edition was limited to about 24 copies (Salute to the Potters. John Abberley 2005? p85). *Most interesting ceramic modeller of the C18* was John Voyez (born c1735), of French extraction, who worked for Josiah Wedgwood, 1768-9, and then Humphrey Palmer of Hanley 1769.

Wedgwood, Josiah *'The Prince of Potters,' 'Father of the Potteries,' Stoke-up-on-Trent's most famous old worthy, Greatest West Midlands industrialist, one of the 'Seven sons of Staffordshire'.* (1730-95). Born Churchyard House, Burslem. In-

dustrialised the pottery process; potter to Queen Charlotte, 1762; promoted the Trent & Mersey Canal, 1765; opened new works at Etruria in Stoke upon Trent, building there Etruria Hall, and employing the leading designers of the day; created

Josiah Wedgwood I - 'The Prince of Potters'.

a famous dinner service for the Empress Catherine II of Russia, 1773. He died on 3rd January and despite being a Unitarian was buried in the Anglican churchyard of St Peter's, Stoke-upon-Trent. The first claim comes from the introduction of 'The Wood Family of Burslem' (1912) by Frank Falkner p38, as a tribute to his wonderfully successful artistic and commercial achievements. The Greatest Industrialist claim was made after a poll in a competition for the first Regional Wall of Fame in Birmingham's City Plaza (ES April 7 2006 p15). The 'Seven Sons' attribution appears in Staffordshire Handbook c1966 p26.

Wedgwood, Col Thomas Josiah *Fought at Waterloo.* Born 1797. When in the Guards' Regt, married Miss Allen of Cresseley near Tenby, and has a memorial in Tenby church (SA Jan 27 1934 p5 col 2).

Wedgwood, Thomas *The First Photographer* (Burrow's Reference Map of Stoke-on-Trent 2nd ed 1970 p7), and perhaps *first to think of using light upon silver nitrate to make copies.* (1771-1805). Of Etruria (LHSB G30 pp28-29).

Wild, Mrs Ada *First female Mayor of Stoke-on-Trent* was Mrs Ada Wild, wife of a Longton pottery manufacturer, 1928 (ES Your Week April 8 2006 p11).

Women, claims for See Lydia Barber, Gertrude Barlow, Rosamond Cook, Gertrude Cowley (and Lily Broadhead), Hilda Martindale, Harriet Slater, Mrs Ada Wild.

Women's suffrage *Staffordshire's first women's suffrage society.* Probably the Stoke-on-Trent committee of the London National Society for Women's Suffrage (itself formed July 1867), formed 1871. The secretary was Mrs Ambrose Bevington, 47 Windsor Street, Hanley. In 1872 it associated itself with the Central Committee of the National Society for Women's Suffrage. Earlier, in 1869 a 'working man in the Potteries', William Wood of

Hanley, had collected signatures locally to a petition in favour of women's enfranchisement, perhaps with a view to organising a meeting in Hanley, possibly to be addressed by Millicent Garrett Fawcett (The Women's Suffrage Movement: A Reference Guide 1866-1928. Elizabeth Crawford. p656).

Wrestling *'The Hanley Dwarf'* was Isaac Leech of Hanley, capable of great feats of strength in the 1870s, famed for fighting a bulldog (Daily Telegraph) (English Night-Life. Thomas Burke) (TB Nov 1993 p31). An alleged dog-and-dwarf fight at Hanley in 1874 which caused a local sensation, was said by the end of the year to be fictitious (SA Dec 26 1874 p4 col 5). *'one of the biggest draws of all time*

The legendary Peter Thornley, alias 'Kendo Nagasaki'.

in British wrestling, especially in the mid 1970s to mid 80s period', WWA World Heavyweight Champion 1987, Wrestler of the Millennium trophy holder 2000. Peter Thornley (b1946), native of Stoke-on-Trent, legendary masked British professional wrestler known as Kendo Nagasaki. His first professional contest was again 'Jumping' Jim Hussey at Willenhall Baths, Nov 1964. His 1960s most notable achievement was defeating Crewe's Geoff Condiliffe alias 'Count Bartelli' at the Victoria Hall, Hanley, March 1966; famously unmasked by 'Big Daddy' on TV in Dec 1975 (Wikipedia 2008).

Stone Stone was Staffordshire's 4th largest parish, consisting of 20,509 acres; 21st= closest parish to the county town, 4m NNW; extremist length 7.8m, making it 5th longest parish in the county; extremist width 7.4m, making it 7th= widest parish in the county. The parish's chief settlement is Stone, a growing market town. It is famous for the canal, shoes, restaurants and old people's homes.

A model of 'Star of Stone'.

Aircraft *'Star of Stone'* was a Mark V Spitfire built at the Vickers-Armstrong factory at Castle Bromwich, paid for with funds raised in Stone

in Oct 1941. It did not fly with a fighter squadron of the RAF but was given to 331 Squadron, a unit of Norwegian pilots who had escaped to England during the 'Phoney War' and from the Dunkirk evacuation. It was lost on her first combat mission, a patrol over France on June 9 1942. No trace of it nor its pilot, Norwegian pilot Lieutenant Kaarl Jacobsen were found (Stafford At War. an SN publication. 1995. p6p of model). See also Meir Aerodrome.

Altitudes The highest point is 833 feet at Meir Heath. The lowest point is 272 feet by the Trent S of Burston Hall.

Archery *Staffordshire Junior and Senior champion 2009, West Midlands Junior champion 2009, Compound Under-16 National champion 2009, Youth World Championship 19th 2009, UK top archery cadet 2010.* Stuart Taylor of Stone, member of Stafford Archery Club (ES Jan 7 2010 p40pc). *Ranked top under-18 indoor archer 2009, National Indoor Archery Championship (senior) bronze 2010* Becky Martin (b1996), Sandon Business & Enterprise College pupil, of Meir (ES Feb 23 2010 p49pc).

Art *'reflects perfectly the aura of the age'* was the painting called 'Pauline waiting' (1939) by Sir James Gunn; his model was Pauline Miller, whose family lived in Station Rd, Stone (CL March 30 1995 pp66-67) (local info).

Aston Hall *First house of the Passionists.* Aston Hall, Aston-by-Stone. This branch of Catholicism, English Province of the Congregation of Clerks Regulars of the Passion and Cross of Jesus Christ, or simply Passionists, founded by Father Dominic Barberi or Bardi (1792-1849), had its base at the hall (renamed St Michael's Retreat) from 1842. *'one of the oldest Yew hedges in the country'*. A giant Yew hedge in the north of the grounds of Aston Hall, Stone, measuring some 16 feet in thickness, and 48 feet in length, was thought to be in 1957. In the deeds of the hall it is described as an ancient monument and must not be removed or damaged (SA & Chron Aug 1 1957 p9 col 5).

Athletics *'the finest sports meeting in the country' 1903.* Stone was the venue for a large annual athletics meetings in the early C20, and this was a description of the 1903 meeting. The report goes on '..Such a band of star performers has not been seen in any other place this year'. The highlight was an international 100 yard race between RW Wadsley (England) and AF Duffey (USA). Duffy won (Roy Lewis postcard collection) (Picture Postcard Monthly Oct 2008. No. 354. p24). *Harborne Harriers Road Relay Race record* was when Don Shelley of North Staffordshire and Stone Harriers (a frequent winner in athletes at this time), broke the record for a lap (over 5 miles) in 26 mins 51 secs, breaking the record by 15 secs at Harborne on April 9 1960 (SA & Chron April 7 1960 p18). *European cross-country club championship winners 1967.* North Staffordshire and Stone Harriers, captained by George Rhodes of Biddulph, at Belgium (ES July 4 2009 p28). *Female world record for most marathons in a year.* Rita Banks of Moddershall with 52 in 1993 (SN April 8 2010 p8p).

Ball, Stephen *First in the world fitted with a unique bionic hand.* Born c1957, of Tittensor. In 2001 he was fitted with a prototype prosthetic glove with electronic fingers controlled by electrical impulses from muscles in the palm of his hand invented by David Gow and designed by surgeons at Nottingham City Hospital. His lower leg, thumbs and fingers from his right hand had to be amputated after suffering frostbite in a mountaineering accident in Alaska (ES June 29 2001 p2p).

Bassett, Reg *His band won Melody Maker (music newspaper) dance band championship winner 1946.* Of Tittensor (ES Your Week Oct 28 2006 p9).

Beardmore, Dawn *Staffordshire Coal Queen 1980.* Of Copeland Ave, Tittensor. Her father worked at Florence Colliery (SN April 24 2008 p6p).

Bull baiting *Last bull baiting at Stone wakes* was in c1830 (RHPS pp65,66-67) (SEDG Feb 1988 p9il).

Bullough, Eleanor Ilaria *Granddaughter of legendary Italian actress Eleanora Duse - 'La Duse' (1858-1924).* (1912-2001). Dominican Sister, Sister Mary Mark, headmistress of St Dominic's Priory School, Stone, 1942-87, often using her grandmother's magnificent designer dresses in school plays; her mother was Enrichetta Duse (SN May 24 2001).

Canals *'Stone - Birthplace of the Trent and Mersey Canal'* (sign by canal on entry to Stone), probably on account of Stone being the venue for the *first committee meeting of the Trent & Mersey Canal promoters* which was held at the Crown Inn, High St, Stone, June 10 1766 (SIS p63). *'Canal Town'.* Stone (Down the Trent: Francis Frith's Photographic Memories. Michael Taylor. 2001 p34).

Strange but true! At the opening of the Stone section of the Trent & Mersey Canal, Nov 12 1771, a cannon was repeatedly fired to celebrate the occasion, but the balls so damaged a lock and a bridge, they fell in, leaving boats stranded in the terminating section (SIS p63) (BBC R4 Garden's Question Time from St Michael's First School, Stone, Nov 4 2007). *UK's first/ oldest existing family-run/ private narrowboat hire company, one or one of only two pleasure boat firms operating on the English canal system 1948.* Canal Cruising Company, Crown Street wharf, Stone; by 2006 it was the only remaining such company in UK (BBC 1 Midlands Today May 26 2004) ('Set in Stone' leaflet 2004) (ES Your Week Nov 4 2006 p9) (The Stone & Eccleshall Gazette Nov 2006 p15). *'First people ever to take a narrowboat across the English Channel', first to sail an English narrowboat in the USA.* Terry Darlington (born c1936), his wife Monica (born c1937), originally of Wales, latterly of Oulton Road, Stone, and their whippet, Jim, in their narrowboat 'The Phyllis May'. They achieved the first claim on their voyage from Stone to Carcassonne, France, following canals, in 2003, and the second along the US Intracoastal Waterway from Virginia to Florida in 2007. The first voyage was recalled in their 'Narrow Dog to Carcassonne' (2005) - *Britain's top-selling travel book May 2006*; the second in their 'Narrow Dog to Indian River' (2008). 'The Phyllis May' moored in the Canal Cruising Company wharf, Stone, was destroyed by fire in Nov 2009 (BBC Stoke & Staffordshire website July 25 2007) (ES Nov 25 2009 p2).

The cover of Britain's top-selling travel book in May 2006.

Canoeing *Most successful slalom canoe club in the country 2008.* Stafford & Stone Canoe Club, Westbridge Park, Stone, founded 1975, with recognition as a National Centre of Excellence for canoeing.

Slalom kayak world champion, Richard Fox, an early member of Stafford & Stone Canoe.

To 2008 it has had 16 World Champion-ship Gold medallists, 17 World Silver and Bronze medallists, 30 National Cham-pions (Maria Lund, who came 2nd in British Open 1993), 5 Olympians and 6 World Junior and European Junior (Laura Blakeman, b1981, Gold in 1997) and U-23 national champion (Elizabeth Neave, b1987, in 2006, 2007, 2008) (SN July 4 1980 p61ps. Oct 23 2008 p72pc. Nov 5 2009 p58). *World individual slalom kayak bronze medalist 1979, gold medal-ist 1981, 1983, 1985, greatest ever slalom canoeist and most decorated slalom kay-aker in the history of the sport by 2008, International Whitewater Hall of Fame (Champion Category) inductee 2007.* Ri-chard Fox (b1960), early member of Staf-ford & Stone CC. First to win the world individual kayak championship thrice, consecutively. In addition he helped Brit-ain win team gold in 1979, 1981, 1983. In 1998 he moved to Australia to be National Head Coach for the Sydney Olympics. By 2008 he had won 10 world champion-ship gold medals, including 5 individual titles (websites) (SN June 21 1985 p48). *European Canoe Slalom Championship women's K1 winners 2009.* Laura Blake-man and Elizabeth Neave of Stafford and Stone Canoe Club, along with Louise Donington of Nottingham (ES June 1 2009 p46pc).

Cardboard cutout *Britain's only life-size cardboard cutout company.* 'Card-board Cutout.net' is based in Stone (BBC internet site: Stoke & Staffordshire).

CHURCHES St Michael in Stone is one of 12 such county dedications (of AP churches); 37th last AP county church built dating from 1753. *Note* the badly-worn stone effigies of a priest (an Austin Friar?) and a woman in the west porch (according to Ashmole they used to be in the north wall of the north aisle). The male effigy, of c1250, is similar to the effigy at Gayton. The female effigy, of c1300, is six feet four inches long and 18 inches wide (RHPS il No. 4) (LGS p221) (JME part 1 p19). *6th largest collection of Charles Eamer Kempe glass in the country.* St Michael's with 21 windows of 1897-1924 by the C19's most prolific maker of stained glass; 10 of these have a trademark (The Stone & Eccleshall Ga-zette. Dec 2007 p47, & additional info Helen Holmes). *In the churchyard.* The grave of John Hodson, who lived to the age of 103, from Jan 21 1753 to Sept 22 1856 (RHPS il No. 20).

All Saints at Moddershall, was originally built in 1903, taken down and rebuilt on firmer foundations in 1993. *First married in the church.* The bride was Miss Pamela E Palmer in summer 1950; the church was only licensed for marriages in early 1950 (SCP Sept 1950 p35p).

Christ Church in Radford Street, Stone, was built in 1838-40, and has been added to since. *Oldest surviving gravestone* is that of Jane Kate Barnes (d1698), wife of Gabriel Barnes (RHPS p30).

St Francis at Meir Heath. *First vicar* was Rev GHH Bateman, appointed 1948; former curate of Sedgley (SA May 15 1948 p5 col 9p).

St John the Evangelist at Oulton was built in 1878. *In the churchyard* is the grave of Francis Elliot Kitchener (d1915), cousin of Lord Kitchener of Khartoum. He lived at Oulton Hall, was Assistant Master of Rugby School for 11 years under the redoubtable Dr Arnold, and in 1873 became headmaster of Newcastle High School, introducing there the game of rugby (ES Sept 18 1993 p25p).

St Luke at Tittensor. The foundation stone laying ceremony on June 18 1880 was *unique*, as it was performed in the presence of the Prince of Wales (later Ed-ward VII), staying with the Sutherlands at Trentham Hall at the time; the Duchess of Sutherland laid the stone (SIS p108).

Cock fighting *Last prosecution of cock-fighting heard at Stone* was in c1900 (NS-FCT 1915 p156).

Combat sports *One of the most com-plete boxers of his time.* George Cooper (d1834), pugilist gypsy, born in a caravan by Redhill Lane, on Red Hill in c1791. *National Air Training Corps Champi-onship (Boxing) winner 1962.* Michael Dawson, aged 17, of 72 The Filleybrooks, Walton (SA & Chron March 1 1962 p6p). *Junior Novice National 60kg Class A (boxing) champion 2009.* Liam Berrisford of Meir Park, aged 15, attends Sandon High School (ES Nov 17 2009 p42pc).

Conservation Area *An original Staf-fordshire Conservation Area.* Stone in 1969, one of the first four areas to come before the Subcommittee (of the Town and Country Planning Committee) (BOb Aug 7 1969 p1).

COUNCILS Local board, town, ur-ban district. *Local Government Board medical officer's worst place he had seen in all his experience.* Goodwin's alias Goblin's Hole, a slum below the level of the present Church St, Stone, 1874 (SIS pp124,126 note). *First Stone town clerk* was Sydney Watson, solicitor, with the creation of Stone Urban District in 1895 (The Stone & Eccleshall Gazette. Dec 2007 p47). *First female chairman of Stone UDC* was Mrs Phyl Hawley (Conservative) of Wellington House, Longton Road, Stone, 1960-61. There was an additional aspect to Mrs Hawley's tenure, for with Mrs F Wain of Croxton as chairman of Stone RDC at the same time, Stone had women chairmen on both its councils for the first time (SA & Chron Feb 4 1960 p11. May 26 1960 pp9,13).

Stafford borough council *First presentation of the Freedom of a borough outside the city or main town of the borough*. HMS Collingwood given the Freedom of Stafford borough at Stone on March 31 1979. *First time a council meeting occurred during a church service* at the above presentation to HMS Collingwood.

Cricket *Boy who helped England under-15s cricket team win against England under-16s*. Sam Kelsall of Moddershall CC at Loughborough in a three-match series in 2008, scoring 60, 85, and 54 runs in each match (ES Aug 23 2008 p58).

Crime *The 'Stone Gang'* was a gang of thieves operating in the Stone area, under the leadership of John Higginson of Stone, shoemaker, who was sentenced to transportation for theft of poultry for seven years in 1825 (SA Oct 22 1825 p4). *UK's first use of Taser guns by police as hand-held stun guns to break up a fight* was at a brawl involving 20 people outside The Saracen's Head Inn, Sandon Road, Normacot at 11.25pm Sept 19 2007, used in a 'dive-stun' method on three individuals; the guns had never before been used at close quarters to deal with a violent flare-up in public (ES Sept 20 2007 p1. Sept 22 2007 p11). *'one of the largest thefts from public funds that has been brought to court after a Customs investigation'*. The £138 million tax scam run by Craig Johnson (b1973), employing a gang of 21 fraudsters, enabling him to buy Meaford Hall, costing £1.5 million. The tax racket was the exploitation of the EU VAT system - known as 'carousel' or 'missing trader' fraud. It involved the import of mobile phones from various EU countries VAT free. The goods were then falsely sold on with VAT added, and then exported back to the EU, with the exporter claiming a VAT credit. In 2008 Johnson was jailed for 10 years - 'one of the longest prison sentences for such a VAT-related offence

and one of the largest confiscation orders ever secured' claimed Robert Alder, assistant director of Criminal Investigation for HM Revenue and Customs (HMRC). In Nov 2008 Johnson was served a government repayment order totalling £6m, pending a further 10 years in prison (SN Oct 2 2008 p17) (BBC Midlands Today Nov 21 2008).

Cumberland, William Augustus, Duke of *Worst Briton of the C18*. As polled by BBC History Magazine, late 2005; he came to Stone in 1745 to head off the Jacobite Rebellion.

Darts *First Stone and District Individual (Darts) Championship*. 1958, the winner was Barry Babb. The tournament had 64 entries (SA & Chron Jan 2 1959 p8 col 4).

Day, Miss Brenda *Miss Staffordshire 1947*. When aged 19, a Lotus employee; she was Miss Lotus Stone 1947, and the 10th Miss Staffordshire ever (Stafford Pageant: The Exciting Innovative Years 1901-1952. Gordon Henry Loach. 2007).

De Wint, Peter *'one of the finest water-colour painters of the English school'*. Died 1849 (SA Jan 1 1949 p5); his first works were exhibited at the Royal Academy 1807; this Stone native displayed his pictures including one of Tittensor Common and two views of Trentham Hall (SEDG Nov 1987 pp9-10).

Peter De Wint as a young man, after a miniature by an unknown artist.

Edwards, Mandy *Staffordshire's first female Queen's Scout*. Of Stone, in 1979 (SN March 8 2007 p6).

Farming *Staffordshire's 15th earliest and last commutation of tithes when they were dealt with under a parliamentary enclosure act*. The great and small tithes of Stone, by allotments of land, 1838. *First meeting of the North Staffordshire Agricultural Society* was held at the Crown Inn, High St, Stone, 1844 (The History of Staffordshire Agricultural Society. Brenda Greysmith. c1978). *Prolific ewe* was a ewe sheep of Mr A Malkin of Moddershall, of the celebrated twinning breed of John Shaw, of Moddershall, which in five years to 1851 had given birth to as many as 25 lambs (SA April 5 1851 p4 col 5). *Rare horse gin in mid Staffordshire* existed at Meaford Hall Farm (COS p50p).

'Blakelow Tom' was a Shire stallion of B Fielding of Blakelow, near Stone, foaled in 1898, toured in 1904 to impregnate local mares. He was by 1904 the winner of eight First Prizes at various shows (SA April 23 1904 p8 col 6). *Last cattle market at Stone* was in May 1994 (Stone & Eccleshall Gazette Nov 2006 p43).

Folklore *Aston's best.* That a wooden cross on the wall of an enclosure in the grounds of Aston Hall marks the spot where a monk was struck dead by light-

ning or where Father Dominic Barberi is buried. *Burston and Stone's best.* King Wulfhere of Mercia, who had his palace on Bury Hill, murdered his second son, Rufin, at Burston in c670 for converting to Christianity. By tradition Rufin's Christian mother, Queen Ermenilda, daughter of Egbert, King of Kent, then had a chapel built

Princes Rufin and Wulfad. See Burton and Stone folklore.

on the spot. Alternatively, Wulfhere had both his sons slain at Stone, the other being Wulfad, for the same reason, and their mother, erected a cairn of stones on the site - hence how Stone came to take its name. *Darlaston's best.* A burial mound on Bury Bank is said to be the grave of a giant (SCSF p74), arising possibly out of the belief that a 'giant' among men - a warrior leader - was buried here (SMM p17). *Hilderstone's best.* Phantom white cows and dogs are said to haunt Milwich and Garshall Lanes, respectively (NSFCT 1900 pp145-146) (PHH pp16-17). *Moddershall's best.* 'The Frightning' at Moddershall Oaks is a spot where a man was thrown from his horse, died, and is now haunted by his ghost riding a white horse. *Oulton's best.* Oulton Vicarage is said to be haunted by a miser who died in some tragic way (burnt to death). His ghost returns to the study each month to count his money (NSFCT 1900 p143) (FOS p21). *Tittensor's best.* The tradition that King Wulfhere is buried in Saxons Lowe. *Walton's best.* On the Eccleshall Road at Micklow has been seen a greyhound boggart (NSFCT 1900 p142) (FOS p18).

Food and drink *One of the last Staffordshire pubs to brew its own beer.* Bird In Hand Inn near Hilderstone, whose brewery closed Dec 20 1927 (SP-t Nov 2006). *'The Food & Drink Capital of*

Staffordshire'. Stone (Stone - Calendar of Events 2006 leaflet).

Foulkes, Vincent James *Country's oldest person with a Legion d'Honneur (Chevalier class) 2001.* Born 1899. Formerly of Churchill Road, Stone. The award was made for his services to France, fighting on French territory in WW1 (SN Aug 2 2001 p9p).

Fulton, Peter *Professional Trainer of the Year 2007.* Regional director of abv Training Ltd based in Stone (SLM Feb 2007 p110).

Gallimore, Ralph and **Hannah Bromley** *Earliest persons recorded in Fulford parish register.* For their marriage on Nov 3 1800. They were both of Stone parish.

Geology ASTON area is Keuper Marls (most), Alluvium (Little Aston, Little Stoke villages, Trent valley).
BEECH is Keuper Sandstones (Beech Dale-Long Compton), Keuper Marls (SW), Bunter (E), Upper Coal Measures (N).
DARLASTON is Keuper Marls (S and most), Keuper Sandstones (Burybank).
FULFORD is Keuper Marls (E), Keuper Sandstones (Fulford village and W fringe), Hilderstone is Keuper Marls (Hilderstone village and most), Bunter (SW).
MEAFORD is Upper Coal Measures (Meaford Hall and N), Bunter (S); Moddershall is Upper Coal Measures (Knenhall and NW), Bunter (Moddershall village and N), Keuper Marls (Spot Grange).
NORMACOT is Bunter (Normacot village and most), Coal Measures (NW tip); Keuper Marls (SE).
OULTON is Bunter Sandstones (Oulton village (N) and the N), Keuper Marls (Oulton village (S) and the S), Upper Coal Measures (N fringe).
STALLINGTON is Keuper (most), Bunter (W tip).
TITTENSOR is coal measures (N), Bunter (S).
STONE is Alluvium (Stone town (E)), Bunter Sandstones (Stone town (W)), Keuper Marls (Stonefield and the N).
WALTON is Keuper Marls (W and most), Alluvium (Walton village and Trent valley).

Gooseberries *England's gooseberry growers' society offering the best prizes 1905.* Stone Gooseberry Growers' Society (The Stone Weekly News March 17 1905 p4 col 5). *World's heaviest gooseberry.* A 'London' variety by John Flower, of Little Stoke, in 1852, weighing 37 pennyweights and 7 grains, holding the record for just over 100 years; exhibited at Stone, Cheadle, and Birmingham (The Stone Weekly News March 17 1905 p4 col 5) (info Phillip Leason in Stone Food & Drink Festival 2006 programme; gives date 1842). *Heaviest dozen gooseberries* *ever grown record holders 1860-1901.* Stone Gooseberry Society, with a bunch weighing 15 and a half ozs (SARA May 11 1956).

Grindley Lane works *Second-largest factory of its kind in Europe.* At one point in its history the Creda factory at Blythe Bridge, which produced domestic electrical appliances 1946-2007, producing in the late 1950s 30% of the total electrical cooker production in the UK (ES Staying Inn p15). *a 'miniature Black Country'.* What local residents in Grindley Lane, Blythe Bridge, feared their area might become if Simplex Electric Co. Ltd of Oldbury were allowed to extend their operations at Blythe Bridge infinitely, when a planning restriction period ceased. The remark was made to Stone Rural District Council (SA & Chron Nov 19 1959 p9 cols 1-2).

Hallahan, Mother Margaret *First Mother-Provincial of the English Dominican Tertiaries.* Born 1802. Founder of Stone Convent in 1853 (SA Sept 5 1896 p6 col 4).

Harvey, Joseph *'one of the oldest surviving breeders of shires in the country' 1921, 'one of the best known farmers and shire horse breeders in the county' 1921.* (1838-1921). Of Darlaston Grange. His name appears in the first volume of the English Cart Horse Society, 1880, as the owner of two stallions, Lincolnshire Hero and Waxwork. Waxwork did good service in the Stone district for several years; his sire was a stallion of the same name, by the famous Dack's Matchless, a horse which James Forshaw described as 'the sire of all time' (SA May 7 1921 p11p).

Hilderstone *Staffordshire Best Kept Village County winner (Small Village category) 1970.* Hilderstone. *Last and only pupil at Hilderstone Primary.* Sharon Fairbanks. The school closed in 1981 when Sharon was aged 9 (ES Your Week April 15 2006 p8).

Holt, Joseph *Tittensor's poet.* Born 1802. Of Tittensor, still alive in 1872. In 2000 his great great grandson Norman Holt reproduced some of his poems, which he had transcribed (copy in Stone library).

Horticulture *'The Village that has grown into a Garden'* Moddershall, according to MMB Higham in Staffordshire Life magazine, for 'Nature, in Moddershall, is bountiful' and it had in 1948 the nurseries of John Hill & Sons, and Boulton Brothers (SLM June 1948 pp130-131ps).

Jervis, John *One of the 'Seven sons of Staffordshire,' 17th Admiral of the Fleet, 'he was the greatest Commander that England has produced in the present age', 'Old Oak', Stone's most famous old worthy.* (1734/5-1823). Victorious admiral, born at Meaford Hall; held the position of Admiral of the Fleet 19 July 1821- 28 June 1830 (Staffordshire Handbook c1966 p26). The greatest Commander quote is from an evening paper contemporary at the time of his death (SA Jan 5 1935 p7 col 1), 'Old Oak' was his nickname (SLM Winter 1954 pp9,26). Commanded the Foudroyant, 1782. Awarded for defeating a far superior Spanish fleet off Cape St Vincent in 1797 with the barony and earldom of Jervis. When he became First Lord of the Admiralty, 1801, he received the viscountcy of St Vincent. He retired to Rochetts, Essex, and died there. He had a monument in the crypt of St Paul's cathedral.

Admiral John Jervis - Stone's most famous old worthy - when a Captain, from a painting by Francis Cotes, R.A. in the National Portrait Gallery.

Jervis, John Edward Leveson *Unique British Army distinction (perhaps).* (1850-85), 4th Viscount St Vincent, a descendent of the Jervis' of Meaford Hall for serving in all five of the major colonial campaigns 1879-85 - Zululand 1879, Afghanistan 1880, South Africa 1881, Egypt 1882 and the Sudan 1884-85; it was also strange but true he died of wounds caused by being crushed by a camel on St Vincent's day (22 Jan) (SHCSYB 2006-07 p7).

Jervis, Mary Anne *Stone's kindest.* (Lady Forester) (1812-93). Daughter of the 2nd Viscount St Vincent of Meaford Hall by his second marriage. She married (1) (1840) David Ochterlony Dyre Sombre (declared mad 1842, d1851), heir to the fortune of the Begum of Sirdhanah in Bengal, (2) (1862) George Cecil Weld, later 3rd Lord Forester; with him she won the famous five-year long court case (the Arms Suit) against the East India Company over possession of her first husband's estate 1872; with the fortune purchased Meaford estate 1873; vastly extended Meaford Hall 1874-7. Before and after the acquistion of this wealth she endowed new market and town halls, chancel and organ chamber for St Michael's, Christ Church school in Northesk Street, provided funds for the purchase of land at Oulton Cross for the new Alleyne's School, and at Meaford rebuild the estate cottages, and school (SIS pp120-121).

Joule's Brewery at the STAFFORD COUNTY SHOW...the bar's open.... *Joule's winning beer 1926, 1957.* Stone Ale, a strong, high gravity beer brewed by Joule's Brewery (SA & Chron May 7 1959 p11). *Strange but true!* When Joule's Brewery, High St, closed in 1974 Bill Lewington, their director, claimed he and several others swam around in the fermenting vessel (SN April 10 2008 p6).

Keep fit classes *Staffordshire's first 'keep fit' centre for women (perhaps).* At the senior school, Stone, after a lecture and demonstration arranged by Stone Higher Education Committee on Sept 21 1937, organised under the national 'keep fit' campaign. Classes were to be held twice a week (SA Sept 25 1937 p11 col 6).

Kibblestone Camp *First Scout camp at Kibblestone* was at Easter 1927 (ES March 27 2006 p6). *Record attendance at a Whitsuntide camp* was 500 scouts in 1956 (ES Your Week May 27 2006 p7).

Knight, Kate *Meir Hay's villainess.* Born 1979. She tried to poison her husband, Lee, with curry and red wine laced with antifreeze at their home in Meir Hay in 2005 to cash in on a £130,000 payout from his employers and clear her debts. He was left with acute kidney failure and vision and hearing problems. She was convicted of attempted murder and sentenced to 30 years in prison (ES June 18 2008 p3pc).

Leather working *'leather town', 'The Town of Tanneries'.* Stone, according to the News Shopper (c1970). The paper states the town was once known as 'leather town' long ago, but gives the article the title 'Once known as The Town of Tanneries' (so Stone may never have been known as this) (WSL D323/41/80. Horne's Scrapbook. No. 2. item 182-185). *Stone's last shoe factory.* Lotus in Cross St, Longton Rd, which closed 1975 (Stone & Eccleshall Gazette July-Aug 2006 p50).

Leese, Mrs Jane *Oldest woman in Staffordshire 1929 (perhaps).* Of Hilderstone, who celebrated her 100th birthday on Feb 28 1929 (Staffordshire Weekly Sentinel. March 2 1929 p12p).

Leigh, Mr and **Mrs Arthur** *'famous throughout the country for their culture of sweet pea blooms', strange but true!* Of Strongford, Tittensor. Both died in tragic circumstances within five minutes of each other. He was born Penkhull c1889, she at Rugeley c1891 but brought up in Tittensor. They had been cultivators of sweet peas since 1919. In 1929 he secured no fewer than 14 firsts at leading horticultural shows. He was the possessor of the Llewellyn Trophy, which he won outright for successes at Walsall in 1926-27-28; he also won trophies at Leeds in 1928-9. He died at 4pm on Nov 21 1930 after an illness of about two weeks, in the company of his wife, their son, a sister-in-law and Dr Chandler of Stoke. When Mrs Leigh knew of his death she collapsed, falling on the grate in which a fire was burning, and when Dr Chandler examined her she was dead. Their marriage had been 'ideally happy' (ES Nov 22 1930 p1).

Lutyens, Sir Edward *One of only two buildings by Sir Edward Lutyens in Staffordshire.* Possibly Hillcrest, Airdale Road, Stone (ES July 8 1999 property pages); the other may be an entrance lodge at Haselour.

Magistrates Court *A Maiden Sitting of the Stone Bench* was on March 8 1898 when the sole business before Stone magistrates John Bourne and W Kirkham was the transfer of the license of the Meaford Inn to Mrs Helen Stephens, widow of the late holder; it was believed to be the first time since at least 1880, perhaps ever, no cases had been brought before the court (SA March 12 1898 p7 col 3). *First woman magistrate to sit on Stone Bench* was Miss Ethel Mary Parker-Jervis (d1956), formerly of Darlaston, later of Spring Bank, Barlaston. In 1918 she was decorated with the Medaille de la Reine Elizabeth by the King of the Belgians for her welfare work with a colony of refugees from stricken Belgium towns near the front line in WW1 (SA & Chron Nov 8 1956 p1 cols 2-3) (ES Your Week Nov 4 2006 p6). *Last sitting of the Stone Bench* was in 1991, it then amalgamated with the Stafford Bench of Magistrates (SP-t Nov 2006).

Marriage *First Stone gay marriage* was between David Westwood and Paul

Blount at Stonehouse Hotel July 16 2006 (SN March 30 2006 p27). *First wedding ceremony at Stone station* was on July 22 2006 (SN Aug 3 2006 p5).

Martial Arts *European Grand Prix (Karate) Series champion 2000*. Tony Boltonwood of Normacot, born c1960 (ES Jan 11 2010p 44pc).

May, Alan *First to make a replica of a Gutenberg press (probably)*. Born 1935. Retired lecturer, of Stone, for Wavelength Films documentary-makers in Dec 2006, screened by BBC4 in April 2008. The press was originally invented by Johann Gutenberg in the 1450s (ES April 12 2008 p16pc).

Meaford Power Station *First new power station to come into operation after WW2, first new power station since nationalisation of electricity, 'most up-to-date unit in the Central England scheme of the Central Electricity Board'*. Meaford Power Station as described in early Jan 1947, capable of producing 120,000 kilowatts, initially with twin 240-feet cooling towers, and a chimney stack 350 feet high; the Meaford site was the third to be chosen for the power station, Barlaston having objected to a site closer to its village. Meaford 'A' was officially opened on Oct 20 1947 (SA Jan 4 1947 p5p. March 22 1947 p8 col 1. Oct 25 1947 p5). *Sir Christopher Hinton 'Good House-keeping' Cup winner 1960.* Meaford 'A' in the Central Electricity Generating Board's best-kept power station awards (SA & Chron July 14 1960 p1). *Last generation of electricity at Meaford Power Station* occurred at 1pm on 28 Sept 1990 (SN March 22 2007 p6).

Meaford Power Station cooling towers as they were being blown up on Saturday 7th September 1991. Notice one tower has begun to cave in.

Meir Aerodrome *One of the first aerodrome's in the country* was Meir, used by passengers on route between Speke and London (SP-t). *Staffordshire's 1st military flying unit formed before WW2* was 28 Elementary & Reserve Flying Training School at Meir on Aug 1 1938. The unit was actually civilian run but trained new pilots for the RAF (SAWW2 p18).

Staffordshire's 1st flying school in WW2 was the No. 5 Elementary Flying Training School at Meir from June 17 1940, the 28 E&RFTS having disbanded on the outbreak of hostilities (SAWW2 p19). *The aerodrome's last commercial flights.* Dragon Airways flights to the Channel Islands in 1955 (ES April 25 2009 p23); the *last powered flight* was Fred Holdcroft in Piper Tri-Pacer G-APZL on August 16 1973; Holdcroft was the first pilot to fly a hot-air balloon over Mount Snowdon (ES May 9 2006 p9p). *World's largest producer of coffee mugs later 1960s.* Staffordshire Potteries, on a 38-acres site at Meir Aerodrome, later Meir Park; the company is said to have introduced the coffee mug to the UK (ES Feb 21 2009 p14). *National home of the Federation of Recorded Music Societies (FRMS, 1936).* No. 2 Fulmer Place, Meir Park, in 2008.

Moddershall Valley watermills *One of the last bone mills in North Staffordshire.* Hayes Mill, Nicholls Lane and Longton Rd, Oulton (DoE II). *Prettiest of the Moddershall Valley mills.* Possibly Splashy Mill (MR2 p218). *Inventor of the first machine for making continuous paper, of any size.* George Henry Fourdrinier (1766-1854), with Sealy Fourdrinier (d1847), invented by 1807. He had worked the Coppice Mill in the Moddershall Valley.

Motherhood *Staffordshire's second oldest mother ever.* A woman from Stone in her 57th year, wife of a labourer aged 60, who gave birth to a boy c1798; the couple had not a child in the last 13 years (SA Feb 17 1798 p4).

Motor racing *When a famous racing driver was stopped for speeding at Tittensor.* Charles Joseph Pearson Dodson, of Wineham, Sussex, who exceeded the legal speed of 30 mph when towing (with a racing car in tow, bound for the Isle of Man races) by over 20 mph between Stone and Tittensor. He did not appear at his summons at Stone Police Court on July 14 1937, complaining of tonsillitis, and was fined £3 and his licence endorsed (SA July 17 1937 p10 col 4). *Had 23 out of 25 wins in rally driving 1955.* Geoff Keys, garage proprietor of Auto Services, Newcastle Street, Stone, who in the period 1953-1961 was 1st in class in the Bournemouth Rally; Annual Trophy winner in the Stafford and District Car Club; Regent Trophy winner in Stafford and District CC; 1st in class in Morecombe and Westbrook Trophy, West Hants and Dorset CC (SA March 23 1961 p20p).

Murrell, George *One of the longest serving poppy collectors.* Born 1915. Of Fulford. He raised £50,000 for the Royal British Legion over 30 years (ES April 14 2006 pp16-17).

Nash, Ernest *'Sir Malcolm Sargent's deputy'.* Fellow of the Royal College of Organists, who came to Stone in 1942, and joined the newly-formed Ceramic Choir in Stoke-on-Trent as a chorister. He very quickly became accompanist and later chorus master and it was in that position, deputising for Sir Malcolm Sargent, that he conducted the Ceramic Choir for the Royal concert in honour of the visit to the Potteries by HRH Princess Elizabeth (SCP March-April 1950 pp35-36).

Natural history *Largest boulder in the area* is a block of igneous rock in a field at Groundslow Farm, 1877. *Freak potatoes* appeared at Stone Congregational Church harvest festival 1921 for the Staffordshire Congregational Union Fund. One was shaped like a duck, the other like a stunted, bloated centaur. They were grown by Mr Pass of Newcastle Road, Stone, and purchased by Oliver Dyke, JP. He subsequently exhibited them in Bratt & Dyke store, Hanley (Staffs Weekly Sentinel. Oct 1 1921 p6p). *2nd litter of red and white Irish setters born in Staffordshire* was to a bitch belonging to Mrs Ann Millington of Rose Cottage, Stallington Grange, in Nov 1982. In 1952 there were only seven of these setters in the world; the breed was only introduced into Britain in the 1960s (ES Nov 29 1982 p10p). *'Beast of Blythe Bridge'.* Unknown animal plaguing in Blythe Bridge area in summer 1994. By mid Sept 1994 it was blamed for the deaths of 10 pets and livestock. So called by local residents (ES Sept 15 1994 p1).

Normacot *Smallest house in North Staffordshire* was possibly a tiny one storey property in Uttoxeter Road, Normacot (ES Oct 1 1932 p3p).

Performance *Staffordshire's last Guiser play performance (before modern revivals).* Stone 1897 (Staffordshire and some Neighbouring Records, Historical, Biographical and Pictorial p26). *First singing of the 'Contakion' in England.* This Russian burial anthem was sung at Elizabeth Brisco-Owen's funeral in St Michael's church, on July 17 1899 (RHPS p232). *Carol Ann Duffy's first public reading of her poetry.* Stone when she was aged 17. She confessed this when Poet Laureate (appointed 2009), confessed at a reading of her poetry at the first Stone Literary

Festival, Sept 18-20 2009 (BBC Midlands Today Sept 21 2009). Carol Ann Duffy spent her childhood at Castle Church (see).

Place-name Stone first appears possibly in 1132, certainly 1149-59, and means '(place at or by) the stone or stones' what this stone(s) was is unknown. The most famous theory is folklore (see). Others are that it is derived from a stone bridge, or a megalith, or some topographical feature, or simply stone exposed on the ground (PNSZ p514).

Political gatherings *UK's biggest ever one-day rally of BNP supporters* took place on Saturday Sept 20 2008 when about 400 British National Party supporters gathered on the car park of The Potters Bar Inn, Lysander Road, Normacot, to protest against the leniency of Habib Khan's sentence for the manslaughter of his white neighbour, Keith Brown in Uttoxeter Road, Normacot on June 6 2007 (ES Sept 22 2008 pp6-7).

Poorest A Stone parish workhouse existed by 1735. It was re-thatched in 1743 (SIS p48). After 1838 Stone poor, unable to support themselves, went to Stone Union workhouse, called Trent House, west of Crown Street, built 1792, enlarged 1838. It subsequently became Trent Hospital, and is now flats. The first meeting of the Board of Guardians of the Stone Union occurred on Monday Feb 5 1838 (SA Feb 10 1838. Feb 12 1938 p2 col 2).

Population Stone was 9th most populated Staffordshire parish in 1801 with 5,373 people; 11th in 1811 with 6,270; 11th in 1821 with 7,251; 14th in 1831 with 7,808; 15th in 1841 with 8,349; 18th in 1851 with 8,736; 19th in 1861 with 9,382; 19th in 1871 with 10,387; 20th in 1881 with 13,155; 20th in 1891 with 14,066; 20th in 1901 with 14,233. Stone could be ranked 21st worst affected Staffordshire parish for loss of men in WW1, with 191 lives lost.

Powerlifting *Set British youth female powerlifting records in bench press (60k), squat (120k), and deadlift (140k) 1992, British and European records Female 16-17 years in the 75kg class (squat, bench-press and deadlift categories) 1993.* Marie Jordan; the first records were achieved at the national powerlifting championships at Stone, 1992; her bench press record there was also a new European teenage 67.5k category record (SN July 2 2009 p58. Nov 5 2009 p58).

Quad biking *Off Road Promoters Association British Championship aged 14*

category winner 2008. Jordan Turnock of Little Aston, aged 11, placing him 6th in the Endro British Championship title series 2008 (SN Sept 4 2008 p68pc).

Quickfit and Quartz Ltd *Largest factory in the Commonwealth producing specialised industrial and laboratory chemical glassware 1952, 'world's largest glass pipeline'.* Quickfit and Quartz Ltd. In 1952, extension to the firm's factory at Stone would increase its size still further, and enable the firm to produce the 'world's largest glass pipeline', with a diameter of 18 inches (SA Jan 5 1952 p8 cols 5-6). *World's largest all-glass heat exchanger 1960.* The 18 inch bore exchanger produced by Quickfit and Quartz Ltd of Stone, designed by their associate country Q.V.F. Ltd (SA & Chron May 19 1960 p6). As the firm was sending scientific glassware to every corner of the world, with returned correspondence bearing foreign stamps, this made it something of a philatelists' paradise (SA & Chron March 10 1955 p5 col 6).

Quote *Choicest.* Puritan Survey of the Church in Staffordshire in 1604 (English Historical Revue, vol. 26 (1911) pp38f, and SHC 1915 pp258-262) says 'A great parish (as in large) and market town'.

Rail *First passenger train through Stone* was hauled by 'Dragon' the No. 1 engine of the NSR on April 17 1848 (SA & Chron May 14 1959 p12 col 5). *National home of Permanent Way Institution (PWI, 1884).* No. 11 Caraway Place, Meir Park, in 2008. The Institution deals with the management, construction and maintenance of railway permanent way and works. *First swing bridge* was at Reedham on the Norfolk and Lowestoft Railway c1858 by GP Bidder, resident engineer for the NSR he was living in Stone in 1851 (POTP p36).

Roads *First coaching advertisement* occurs in the Mercurius Politicus of April 9 1657 and mentions Stone (RHPS pp241-242). *First Turnpike Act in North Staffordshire* was for a route between Darlaston and Talke on the London-Carlisle road, 1714 (IANS p16). *Staffordshire's largest single span reinforced concrete bridge 1960.* Darlaston Bridge over the Trent, which opened in May 1960, with a flood relief span 240 feet in length and 33 feet wide, containing 5,000 tons of concrete and 70 tons of reinforced steel (SA & Chron May 26 1960 p9). *Staffordshire's first accident involving a motorcycle.* Perhaps that which occurred at Tittensor Bridge over the Trent on June 11 1898 when the horse of a southbound trap containing George Edwards and his sister Mrs Greenwood, took fright at the sight of a motor bicycle, lost control, was further alarmed by a dog rushing upon it and jumped over the parapet of the bridge, taking the passengers of the trap towards the river, their flight being softened by undergrowth; nobody sustained serious injury (SA June 18 1898 p7 col 7). *Staffordshire's first controlled road crossing for horseriders* was set up by Staffs CC at the junction of Lichfield and Uttoxeter Roads with Copeland Drive at Little Stoke in 2010; horseriders have to obtain an electronic flob from nearby stables to active the crossing (SN April 1 2010 p24pc).

Romans *Staffordshire's largest Roman coin hoard.* 2,500 coins and two silver snake bracelets found at No. 698 Lightwood Rd, 1960.

Roper, Kirsty *2nd runner-up (or 3rd in contest) in Miss World 1988, Miss UK 1988, Sunday Times Rich List 2008-2010 highest ranking female, 6th (2008), 4th (2010) richest person (jointly with husband) in Britain.* Born 1969. Of Oulton Heath near Stone. She married Ernesto Bertarelli in 2000, one of Switzerland's richest men, worth £5.65 billion in 2008; his family own the pharmaceutical company, Serono (Daily Express Aug 25 1988 p4p) (ES Aug 27 1988 p7ps) (The Daily Telegraph. April 25 2008 p2p).

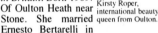

Kirsty Roper, international beauty queen from Oulton.

Sailing *International Sailing Federation World Topper Champion 2009, West Midlands' Young Sailor of the Year 2009.* Andrew Bridgman. Born 1994. Of Stone. The award is made by the Royal Yachting Association (E&S Aug 5 2009 p18pc) (ES Jan 12 2010 p46pc).

Sanders, Morris *Officer's Cross of the Order of Merit medalist.* Of Fulford for services by the RAF in the Warsaw Uprising, 1944; it is Poland's highest civil honour (SN Aug 10 2006 p1pc).

Schools *Staffordshire's first co-educational grammar school.* Alleyne's Grammar School, founded 1558, which accepted girls from Sept 1944, with the closure of Field House, a private school in

Stone offering a secondary education for girls (Alleyne's School, Stone. Cope & Woods. 2008. p61). *Country's 2nd school (Stoke-on-Trent's 1st) rebuild in the Building Schools for the Future programme.* Sandon Business and Enterprise College, Sandon Road, Normacot. The new school was opened in this Government funding initiative programme on Feb 25 2008 and officially on Oct 24 2008, costing £17 million; the old school was built in the 1930s (ES Feb 25 2008 p12. Oct 24 2008 p19). It was also the first school in the programme to fail an Ofsted inspection (BBC Radio 4 Costing the Earth Jan 26 2009). *Britain's first school for chimney sweeps* was to be opened by the National Association of Chimney Association of Chimney Sweeps in Stone, according to a newspaper report in June 2001 (The Sunday Telegraph. June 10 2001 p7).

Shenton, Stephen *2nd child in UK diagnosed with Prader-Willi Syndrome.* (1955-2000), of Spot Acre, Stone; Stephen attended Aynsley Special School, Blythe Bridge, in the early 1960s. This genetic disorder was identifed in 1956 (ES Aug 15 2006 p23pc).

Smith, Richard *Inventor of Hovis bread.* Born at the Old Mill, Mill Street, 1836.

Social care *National home of Re-solv (the Society for the Prevention of Solvent & Volatile Substance Abuse) (Re-solv, 1984).* No. 30A, High Street, Stone, in 2008. This is the only national society dealing with all aspects of solvent and volatile substance abuse. *First Multiple Sclerosis Resource Centre in the country.* Staffordshire Active Multiple Sclerosis Centre at Unit 22 Whitebridge Estate, Stone, opened with funding from the Multiple Sclerosis Resource Centre in 2009; and is MSRC's pilot/ first branch centre; the centre offers physiotherapy and Tai-Chi sessions, and a drop-in cafe (info Liz Gumbley) (Stone & Eccleshall Gazette. Dec 2009. p19).

Sport See Archery, Athletics, Bull baiting, Canoeing, Cock fighting, Combat sports, Cricket, Darts, Motor-racing, Powerlifting, Quad biking, Sailing, Squash, Tennis.
Squash *She ranked third in the UK U-16 list.* Tracey Shenton, squash player of Stone, born c1977, who reached the finals of the British Open U-16 championships in 1992 (SN Jan 10 1992 p56p).

Stafford, William *Stone's villain.* Or William Strefford (SA Jan 2 1892 p6 col

5). (c1866-91). In 1890 he and his wife Mary (born c1864), came from Wellington, Salop, to manage the Falcon Inn, at the south end of High St. After their little girl died the marriage became turbulent; Stafford took to drink; was accused by his wife of being unfaithful. On the night prior to the murder, fearing his temper she sent for his sister for protection, after he had stabbed her in the shoulder. On Feb 17 1891 as the pub closed for the night he shot her dead with a double barrelled shotgun, and then himself through the chin, bisecting his head vertically; not a shred of his face remained intact. The inn subsequently became known as 'The Blood Tub' (DMF pp81-89).

Stanley, Dame Ellen *Stone's person with the earliest-surviving will.* It is dated 1525.

Stone Priory *One of the first Staffordshire religious houses to be suppressed.* Stone Priory, an Augustine religious house, 1536/ spring 1537 (SIS p27).

An Augustinian canon stands beside the cloister of Repton Abbey, which resembles the crypt of Stone Priory. The crypt now forms the cellar of The Priory house in Lichfield Road, Stone.

Sutton, Sergt Major James 'Jim' *First Stone man to have the double distinction of the D.C.M and M.M.* Of King's Ave, Stone, 6th Royal West Kent, a former Joule employee. He was awarded the Distinguished Conduct Medal in the 'Big Push' of March 1918 for capturing 9 Germans and two machine guns, and the Military Medal for action on Nov 9 1918 for gallantry and devotion to duty (SA Dec 21 1918 p5p).

Tennent, Rachael *Miss Worcestershire 2005, Miss Great Britain 2007.* Born 1984. Of Blythe Bridge, nee Davies.

Tennis *Stone Lawn Tennis and Croquet Club's first tournament* was held in early July 1912 (SA July 13 1912 p9

Joan Fry, tennis star, daughter of a Stone doctor.

col 4). *Birdhurst Club Tournament (Croydon) Women's Singles winner 1925*. Miss Joan Fry (b1904), daughter of Dr A Cradock Fry of the Mansion House, Stone, defeating Miss K McKane, Wimbledon Ladies Singles winner 1924 (SA May 9 1925 p4p). *Staffordshire's most successful tennis club at Wimbledon.* Stone Lawn Tennis Club fostering Keith Wooldridge who competed several times in the men's singles, and reached the third round in 1966; Stanley Matthews junior; Jack A Moore, who competed on seven occasions 1939-50 (in 1951 he won Staffordshire County men's single title for the 8th time in succession, first winning the title in 1936), twice reaching the second round; Joan Fry who reached the final of the women's singles 1925 at her first attempt (SA June 1 1951 p4 col 3) (ES Your Week July 10 2004 p11, March 11 2006 p11, July 1 2006 p7).

Thomas, Monsigneur Francis Gerard *9th bishop of R.C. diocese of Northampton*. Born Stone May 20 1930, appointed Aug 27 1982, served to his death Dec 25 1988 (SN Sept 13 2007 p6) (Diocese website).

Tittensor *'most wickedest people, i believe on the face of the earth'* were the old inhabitants of Tittensor, according to Joseph Holt in his unpublished The history of Tittensor, written c1868, especially, he notes, for drunkenness, sabbath breaking and other bad conduct (WSL CB/HOLT/2.2). *Staffordshire's only accommodation for female tuberculosis sufferers.* Groundslow Sanatorium in 1936 (SA Aug 1 1936 p10 col 3). *'one of the bustiest villages in Britain'* Tittensor, as named by The Sun newspaper, in National Cleavage

Two women in brassieres in front of the sign to Tittensor, 2001. The image was made from a Sentinel photograph accompanying the newspaper's story about Tittensor being one of the bustiest villages in Britain.

Week, in 2001, along with Upper Swell, Glous, and Titmore Green, Herts. But the honour was met with moral indignation in the village, as it was felt it was insulting to Tittensor women (ES March 28 2001 p1,5). *'Power cut capital of the Midlands'*. Tittensor as reported by Nick Owen on BBC Midlands Today, Sept 27 2006; the village had suffered weekly power cuts since winter 2004, making the community very fed up. The problem, arising from an expensive electrical fault in the substation in Copeland Avenue, still remained unsolved in late 2009 (local info).

Trade *World's first portable bandstand* was made by Haynes and Sons, wheelwrights, joiners and general contractors, of off Station Road, Stone. It was puchased by Stone UDC, and in use for the Proclamation of the accession to the throne of George V in High St, Stone, May 12 1910. Haynes' patented it, but there was no market, and only about three were ever made (info David Hayes via Chris Copp) (The Stone & Eccleshall Gazette. March 2010 p38p).

Travlos, Louke *UK's Sexiest Sixth-Former runner-up 2004*. When aged 18, of Stone, in a competition run by Cosmo Girl Magazine (BBC Midlands Today Sept 21 2004).

Warrilow, David *Samuel Beckett wrote a play for him*. (1934-95). Existential monologue actor highly acclaimed in New York and Paris, whose voice was 'a perfectly modulated tool'. Born Stone, attended Alleyne's Grammar School. Former journalist, who by the 1970s had turned to acting. He met Beckett whilst performing in his 'The Lost Ones' and in 1980 Beckett wrote 'A Piece of Monologue' for him (The Daily Telegraph Aug 26 1995 p17p).

Wedgwood, Miss Mary *Croce de Guerra recipient, traveller*. Mrs JWP Mosley, formerly Miss Mary Wedgwood, daughter of Godfrey Wedgwood of Idlerocks, awarded the Croce de Guerra by the Italian Government for work in WW1 amongst the British troops in Italy; made a protracted journey through the Congo and down the upper waters of the Zambesi river, whilst visiting her cousin Hon Hugh Wedgwood, at Malo in Kenya (SLM Jan 1952 pp10-11p).

Wenger, Miss Celia *One of the last Staffordshire debutantes presented at court*. Daughter of Mr and Mrs HC Wenger of Aston Hall, Aston-by-Stone, in 1958. There was also three others (see Ingestre) (SA March 20 1958 p1p).

Whiteman, Rod *First warden of the Downs Banks.* Of Swynnerton. Appointed by the National Trust, May 1997 (SN May 30 1997 p5).

William, Phil *Auctioned his services on the internet site eBay.* Of Mount Road, Stone, aged 42, salesman, he was reduced to this very unusual initiative as he was being made redundant from Mica Hardware at Hixon in the Recession, July 2009. Phil started the bidding at £9.99 an hour and said he was looking for an 'honest salary for a hard week's work' (ES July 18 2009 p1pc).

Winsor, Stella *First Stone Citizen of the Year.* In 2005, organiser of Stone Stroke Club at Lotus Court, from c1985. The award, given by Margaret Goodall in memory of her husband Stan (d2004), is run by the Stone & Eccleshall Gazette magazine. The 2nd winners in 2006 were John and Vera Ferrie (Stone & Eccleshall Gazette July-Aug 2005 p5).

Women, accomplishments by See Beardmore, Day, Edwards, Hallahan, Leese, Motherhood, Roper, Wenger, Wright.

Wright, Christine *Britain's oldest female organ donor by 2008.* When aged 81, of Bromfield Court, Stone, who donated her kidney to her son David, 51, of Meir, at Queen Elizabeth Hospital, Birmingham in April 2008. The oldest living transplant donor in the UK is an 83-year old man. In a twist of fate David Wright died in a freak accident whilst returning a trolley at a supermarket on June 11 2008 (The Daily Telegraph. May 1 2008 p12) (SN May 1 2008 p3. June 19 2008 pp1,5).

Wright, Emily *Tittensor's saddest.* Postmaster's daughter, when aged 15, she and Ann Bentley, 16, postmaster's servant, drowned trying to walk on iced-over Trentham Lake from the Tittensor end. They got 30 yards when it broke on March 4 1888. At the time the Marquis and Marchioness of Stafford were walking in the park, and expressed their sympathy with the parents (SA March 10 1888 p7 col 5).

Swynnerton Swynnerton was Staffordshire's 40th largest parish, consisting of 6,481 acres; 34th= closest parish to the county town, 6.4m NW; extremist length 7.7m, making it 6th longest parish in the county; extremist width 5.3m, making it 23rd= widest parish in the county. Both

Swynnerton and Yarnfield villages have some recent residential growth. The parish is famous for the Fitzherbert family of Swynnerton Hall, current Lords Stafford, and youth disturbances at Yarnfield; for Swynnerton Royal Ordnance Factory (excepting the sad story of Miss Sarah Ann Lowe) and 'Swynnerton Roses' see under Eccleshall.

Altitudes The highest point is 718 feet on Hanchurch Heath. The lowest point is 312 feet at Yarnfield.

Church St Mary at Swynnerton is one of 23 such county dedications (most common dedication in the county); 13th= oldest county church dating from 1120. *'The Christ of Swynnerton'* is the local name for a large seated Christ in the south chapel. It is of the period 1260-80, seven feet high, 'of a quality worthy of Westminster Abbey or Lincoln Cathedral' according to Pevsner, and of most uncertain provenance; tradition says that it was formerly the central figure on the west front of Lichfield Cathedral, and saved by the Fitzherberts at the time of the Reformation, buried in their chapel for safety, and dug up in more peaceful times (FS p of facing p72) (LGS p224) (SLM Feb 1950 p101p) (BOE p272). *The 'Old Crusader'* is the local name for an effigy of c1254 in the church of a recumbent cross-legged Knight in the south wall under a moulded arch, perhaps moved from some other part as one of the sedilia, of which only two remain, appears to have been encroached upon to make room for it (SA Nov 17 1849? p3 col 2) (JME part i pp22-23) (CHMS p52). Some think it is to a Knight Templar (SOS p109), or to Sir Roger Swynnerton (HOPS pp45,46), or to Sir John de Swynnerton (d c1254) (LGS p224). The grave beneath was accidentally opened during a restoration in 1856, and found to contain the skeleton of a youngish man six feet two inches tall, still wearing a reddish-brown beard (LGS p224).

Dodsley, Rev Christopher *Swynnerton's villain.* (c1783-1851). Of Willington, Derbys. He apparently purchased the advowson of Swynnerton in the early 1820s. Over-stretched himself financially and got into serious arrears with his rents. In 1831 he probably deliberately absented himself from the village to avoid a notice to quit. It was served on his wife in his absence by Richard Sutton Ford, agent to the Fitzherbert family at Swynnerton Hall, who recorded '.. a

more unpleasant duty I never had to perform....she was approaching fainting'.
Ford loathed him, and makes vitriolic
comments in further correspondence as
to his character. Dodsley's financial position worsened and he was imprisoned
for debt in Feb 1845, July 1846 and April
1849 (at least). His stock and household
furniture were sold at auction in Feb
1844. In 1845 he was accused by the
churchwardens of having pocketed the
alms collection for at least four years.
His estate was sequestered and the rectory in the hands of the sheriffs office in
1838 (SRO D641/5/E(c)/24 12 December 1843) (info Rose Wheat).

Geology The Acton-Swynnerton (W
side) village areas are Bunter; Harley
Thorns-Swynnerton village (E side)
and Pilstones-Yarnfield village (W) is
Dolerite Swynnerton (alias Butterton)
Dyke; Sandyford is Bunter; Shutlane-
head and the north of the parish is Upper Coal Measures; Yarnfield village, the
S stretching N to Sandyford is Keuper
Marls. *First geomagnetic surveys tried
out in Britain* were at Highlows Farm
Quarry, on an exposure of the Butterton Dyke; the survey tried to prove re-
mote sensing could be used to identify
sub-ground geological features (NSFCT
1993 p23).

**Fitzherbert, Evelyn Thomas Francis
Ralph** *Died in a yachting accident in
Egypt.* Born 1928. Grenadier Guards,
younger brother of 14th Baron Stafford,
drowned in a yachting accident on the
Great Bitter Lake in Egypt on March 9
1952 (SA April 25 1952 p3 cols 4-5)

Fitzherbert, Francis *First Sheriff of
Staffordshire to walk the Staffordshire
Way.* Baron Stafford. Of Swynnerton
Hall. He walked the 92 miles over six
separate days from May 2005 to April
2006, raising £9,800 for charity (The
Stone & Eccleshall Gazette magazine
May 2006 p40).

Fitzherbert, Maria Anne *First woman
with whom the future George IV under-
took a wedding ceremony, Swynnerton's
most famous old worthy.* (nee Smythe)
(1756-1837). Roman Catholic of Bram-
bridge, Hampshire. Second wife of Thomas Fitzherbert (1746-81) of Swynnerton Hall. She famously went on to marry
the Prince of Wales, 1785. But the union
was invalid under the Royal Marriages
Act. In 1830 she turned down a title (offered by William IV to recompense her
for past difficulties) replying "she had

borne through life the name of Mrs Fitzherbert; that she had never disgraced it,
and did not wish to change it."

Fitzherbert, Morag Nada Campbell
Junior Skiing Champion of Britain 1950.
Born 1931. Wife of Basil Francis Ni-
cholas Fitzherbert, 14th Baron Stafford
(d1986), whom she married in 1952 (SA
Dec 14 1951 p3p).

Fitzherbert, Capt Thomas Charles
Swynnerton's bravest. (1869-1937). 4th
son of Basil Fitzherbert, of Swynnerton Hall from 1934, awarded the Albert
Medal for gallantry while as a bombing
instructor at Cupar, Fifeshire, in 1916 for
his action in picking up a smoking bomb
and throwing it away, undoubtedly saving many lives (SA Sept 25 1937 p7p).

Henry Wadsworth Longfellow. The photograph
shows the former smithy, later a garage. The
chestnut tree stood to the right, (out of the
picture), to at least 1989, but is no more.

Folklore *Swynnerton's best.* There is a
tradition the chestnut tree opposite the
Fitzherbert Arms Inn is the model for
the chestnut in 'The Village Blacksmith'
by American poet, Henry Wadsworth
Longfellow (1807-1882). Although
Longfellow had been a guest at Swynnerton Hall, the smithy and chestnut, he
alludes to were in Cambridge, Massa-
chusetts.

Heathe, Ales
*Earliest person
recorded in the
parish register.*
For her baptism on
Aug 4 1558. She
was the daughter
of Richard Heathe
and Elsabeth.

Heraldry *One of
the earliest known
instances of the
seal of arms of a*

The arms on a seal of a
Norman member of the
Fitzherbert family, kept
at Swynnerton Hall - one
of the earliest known in-
stances of the seal of arms
of a private gentleman.

private gentleman. Fitzherbert arms, as appearing on a deed of the Norman period, granting possession of the manor Norbury, Derbys. In 1910 it belonged to the 27th lineal descendent of the Fitzherbert family, Basil Fitzherbert of Swynnerton Hall (Forgotten Shrines. Dom Bede Camm. 1910. p2, ils of facing pp2,4).

Lowe, Miss Sarah Ann *Swynnerton's saddest.* Of Hartwell Road, Meir, a 50-year old process worker at Swynnerton Royal Ordnance Factory, instantly killed when a round of 20 mm. ammunition exploded in her hand on June 6 1951. She had been employed at the factory since 1941. Production of this type of ammuniation had only just been restarted at Swynnerton (SA Aug 24 1951 p1).

Motorways *Runner-up motorway service station.* Moto's Stafford Northbound services on M6, awarded by Holiday Which? Magazine in 2006 (The Daily Telegraph. March 7 2006 p12).

Place-name Swynnerton first appears in Domesday Book, 1086, and means (with reservations) 'tun by the pig ford' (PNSZ p526).

Poorest There is no evidence for a Swynnerton parish workhouse. After 1838 Swynnerton poor, who were unable to support themselves, went to Stone Union workhouse in Stone.

Population Swynnerton was 79th most populated Staffordshire parish in 1801 with 648 people ; 65th in 1811 with 893; 79th in 1821 with 832; 81st in 1831 with 791; 71st in 1841 with 961; 75th in 1851 with 946; 81st in 1861 with 880; 80th in 1871 with 876; 84th in 1881 with 778; 79th in 1891 with 880; 81st in 1901 with 811. Swynnerton could be ranked 74th= worst affected Staffordshire parish for loss of men in WW1, with 17 lives lost.

Quote *Choicest.* Staffordshire Federation of Women's Institutes in their The Staffordshire Village Book, 1988, wrote 'Swynnerton typifies the old English village with its stately Hall standing in parkland, the churches, thatched cottages, cricket ground and inn which once incorporated a farm.'

Sweyn *First Danish king of England.* He conquered the Saxons in 1010, and may give his name to the first part of Swynnerton (STM Nov 1966 p30).

Swinnerton, John *Swynnerton's person with the earliest-surviving will.* It is dated 1521.

Village life *First Staffordshire village*

to have a visit from a mobile X-Ray Unit. Swynnerton in Sept 1956, as something of a pilot scheme, part of the county health service fight against tuberculosis; the Unit had already been in towns such as Stone (SA & Chron May 17 1956 p1). *Single biggest court action against anti-social behaviour in UK* occurred when 11 Anti-Social Behaviour Orders were served on members of a teenage gang who had terrorised Yarnfield in July 2004. Thereafter, Yarnfield was known as *The ASBO Capital of Europe*, and *The ASBO Village* (ES July 27 2004 pp1, 3ps) (SN Aug 25 2005 p7) (BBC Midlands Today. Oct 29 2009). *Staffordshire Best Kept Village County winner (Small Village category) 1964, Stafford District (Large Village) winner 1999.* Swynnerton village. *Staffordshire's most controversial inn sign.* Without much doubt that of The Labour in Vain, Yarnfield Lane, Yarnfield. It showed a white couple trying in vain to scrub the blackness from a negro boy in a bath tub, and was removed and replaced by a sign with less racist connotations in 1994, after a complaint by some residents; the new sign shows a farmer sowing seeds being mobbed by birds.

Labour in Vain's controversial old inn sign.

Some villagers complained about the loss of the old sign and it was at length put up in the entrance way, until hung in the beer garden in 2001. Stafford and District Racial Equality Council then requested to have it removed from public view, but this was ignored (ES Jan 8 1994 p7p. March 16 1994 p9p. Sept 14 2009 p5pc).

Watson, George *Yarnfield's saddest.* A 'half-witted man' aged 28, of Yarnfield, employed by Joesph Harvey of Darlaston Grange, mysteriously disappeared on his way to work on Jan 29 1896. After a lengthy search, including dragging in the Trent, his body was found in a pit containing only two feet of water. The pit was fenced round, and the theory was Watson had climbed an overhanging tree, and jumped or fell in. A verdict of suicide whilst suffering from temporary insanity was returned at the inquest (SA Feb 15 1896 p7 col 5).

T-X

Trentham Trentham was Staffordshire's 31st largest parish, consisting of 7,445 acres; 61st= closest parish to the county town, 10.3m NNW; extremist length 2.8m; extremist width 6m, making it 15th= widest parish in Staffordshire. The ancient parish's chief settlement is in Blurton township, now wholly a conurbation of Longton; Trentham and Hanford have also become residential districts. The parish is famous for Trentham Gardens.

Altitudes The highest point of the parish is Hanchurch Heath at 718 feet. The lowest point is 305 feet by the Trent at Strongford.

Anderson, David *UK's Young Volunteer of the Year 2007*. Of Thackeray Drive, Blurton, 18, for his work for the Douglas Macmillan Hospice, as awarded by the Association of Charity Shops (ES July 4 2007 p17pc).

Anderton, Paul *Local History Award holder 2006*. Retired teacher. Of Berne Ave (Clayton Griffith), 71, for services to local history, awarded by the British Association for Local History.

Bould, Margerie *Earliest person recorded in Trentham parish register*. For her baptism on Dec 3 1558. She was the daughter of Thomas Bold.

Burgess, Frank *'Mr Hanford'*. (1929-2010). Former tiler of Oakhill, Stoke, but known as this due to his long association with Hanford Boys' Club in the Staffordshire County (Football) League, formed 1959; refereed the Potteries and District Sunday League 's first cup final, 1964; recieved a City of Stoke-on-Trent Sports Personality of the Year Award 2007 (ES Jan 16 2010 p55pc).

Chaudry, Mo *'The Secret Millionaire'*. Born 1961. Waterworld entrepreneur, Etruria, starred in an episode of the Channel 4 series of this name, in which a millionaire goes undercover to covertly select mostneedy recipients of their money. Prior to screening on Dec 12 2007 Mr Chaudry had a residence in Beechfield Road, Trentham (ES Dec 13 2007 p12pc).

Canoeing *British National J12 Kayak champion 2009, British National J12 Canoe champion 2009*. Paul Sutherland, aged 12, Trentham High School pupil. In 2009 he was promoted to compete in the men's Division One kayaking events - the only under-12 from across the country to do so (ES Jan 26 2010 p54pc).

CHURCHES St Mary and All Saints by the site of Trentham Hall is one of 3 such duel dedications in the county (for AP churches); 41st= oldest county church dating from 1190. *Note* the effigy of a Knight dated to c1215 in the north aisle; Rev JF Challis was in no doubt it is Ranulph de Gernon (d1153) 4th Earl of Chester, probable refounder of Trentham Priory, and a great nephew of Earl Hugh. He was a loyal support of the Empress Maud in the civil war with Stephen. It is said he was poisoned by William Peveril at Gresley Castle. By the late 1950s the effigy was broken and placed in a niche in the north aisle. It would originally be placed on the altar tomb, but had been thrown out of the church and was found in fragments in the churchyard in 1854 (it had been there when Robert Garner saw it - GNHS p20) (LGS p237) (JME part i p22, pl 4 (a)) (CHMS p55) (TTH p22il). *Staffordshire's earliest Royal Arms in a church*. That of Charles I in Blurton church which is inscribed '16 C.R. 29'; one that was at Caverswall might have been earlier (BAST vol 78 1962 p89). *In the churchyard* is the shaft and base of an ancient cross, renovated in 1949. It is thought the cross was a memorial to St Werburgh, and may indicate the sport where her body rested on the journey from Hanbury to Chester in 875 (NSFCT 1949 p109).

Church of the Resurrection in Chaplin Road, Dresden. *'one of the many Staffordshire churches built by "Adam Bede"'*. Consecrated on June 23 1853, was built by William Evans, on whom George Eliot based the character 'Adam Bede' in the novel of the same name; he has been described as 'a man of genius, as a Gothic artist, sculptor and church builder' (SA June 19 1953 p4 col 4).

St Bartholomew at Blurton was built in 1626, enlarged in 1867. *In the churchyard* is the grave of John Brammer (d1841) which records 'The Grave at his feet was thrice opened within 10 months' for his daughters Jane died Sept. 21 1833 aged 16, Eliza died June 19 1834 aged 12 and Hannah died July 5 1834 aged 22.

Earl, Capt Ruth *Trentham's heroine.* Born 1974, originally from Trentham. She spent six months at Camp Bastion in Helmand Province, Afghanistan, commanding more than 150 soldiers. She was also responsible for ensuring equipment and weaponry was fit for purpose. She was awarded an MBE in 2008 (ES May 16 2008 p3pc).

Edwards, Edward Jas. Justinian *Trentham's longest serving vicar.* Prebendary. He served for 45 years, 1841-86.

Farming *'Newstead Royal William'* was a Shire stallion of Newstead Farm, Blurton, foaled in 1899, toured in 1904 to impregnate local mares (SA April 30 1904 p8 col 7). *'Hanchurch Harold'* was a Shire stallion of Toft Farm, Hanchurch, foaled 1905, winner of two first prizes, toured on stud in 1908 (SA May 16 1908 p8 col 7).

White mice spiriting away Trentham church from Hanchurch to its present site.

Folklore *Trentham's best.* Traditionally, St Mary and All Saints' church, was carried from Hanchurch by white oxen, white swans or white mice, (accounts differ as to which), but it was something white; or that Trentham people helped by fairies spirited away the Hanchurch church for their own village. *Trentham's most haunted place 2009.* The Bull's Head Inn, Hanford. A paranormal investigation involving a glass spinning session revealed the first images of an apparition. The vision was caught on film but cannot be easily identified (ES Feb 7 2009 p6).

Football *'the hero of Elland Road'.* Malcolm Heath of Blurton, Football League referee after his common sense interventions at the Leeds ground in a match between Leeds and Newcastle United (in the

2nd Division) on Oct 30 1982; nearly 50 fans were arrested for hooliganism (ES Nov 1 1982 p16).

Geology Blurton township is Upper Coal Measures (most), Bunter (E tip); Butterton township is Upper Coal Measures (most), Dolerite Swynnerton (alias Butterton) Dyke (W fringe); Hanford township is Upper Coal Measures (all); Trentham township is Upper Coal Measures (most), Bunter (W fringe, King's Wood).

Golf *Midland Professional Championship winner 1947, Midland Challenge Bowl winner 1949.* Ken Adwick of Trentham Golf Club (Trentham Golf Club Centenary 1894-1994 pp25,26). *Staffordshire Boy Champion (Golf) 1955, England Golf Captain 1980-83, Great Britain and Ireland Golf Captain 1987-91, only person to have played in, and later captained, a winning Walker Cup team, 1st Staffordshire President of the English Golf Union (1995-).* Geoffrey Marks (b1939), born near Hanley Park, moved to Trentham as a child; County Amateur Championship winner 7 times 1959-69; played 65 times for England (from 1963), 250 times for Staffordshire; Staffordshire Champion 8 times; in the Walker Cup he led Great Britain and Ireland to their first ever victory on American soil in 1989 (Trentham Golf Club Centenary 1894-1994 pp33,40-41ps) (ES Aug 23 2008 pp56-57ps). *Greek Amateur Championship winner 1994.* David Anthony Lynn, born Billinge, Lancs, 1973. Turned professional 1995; member of Trentham Golf Club; has featured in the top 100 on the official World Golf Rankings (Wikipedia, 2009).

Health *First meeting, and public meeting, of the Stoke-on-Trent Primary Care Trust* was at St Paul's church, Blurton, 27 April 2006; the Trust resulted from a merger of the North and South PCTs (ES April 21 2006 p16).

Homes *'Most sought after town in Midlands' 1980.* Trentham with its new executive homes on the Leyfield Park housing estate. The houses on it - considered value for money at £37,500 to £44,000 - were built by Clarke Homes (SN Jan 11 1980 p22p - sort of Clarke Homes advertising feature).

National homes: *Of the National Association of Choirs (NAC, 1920).* No. 612 Lightwood Road, Lightwood; *National & Architectural Ceramics Society (Tile Society, 1981).* Oakhurst, Cocknage Road,

Rough Close, in 2008.

Hutchinson, Rev Preb William *'The oldest clergyman in England' 1910.* (1810-1910). Vicar of Blurton 1865-1910, aged nearly 100 (SA July 9 1910 p5 col 2).

Lawton, Ron *Blurton's WW2 hero.* Born c1926. In the later stages of WW2 he was part of a regiment set up to seize enemy secrets, 5th Kings Regiment/ T-Force; his Company helped oversee the liberation of Denmark, 1945, for which he was awarded a medal by King Christian X. Later, he was an Aynsley Potter worker and newsagent in Fenton; retired to Blurton (ES Jan 11 2010 p16ps).

Leveson, Sir Richard *Identified as the Englishman in 'The Spanish Lady's Love of a Englishman'.* Son of Sir Walter (d1602). Admiral of the English fleet who destroyed the Spanish fleet off Kinsale, Ireland, 1601; MP (SHC 1912 pp325,328. 1922 p32) (HOS 1998 p45). Amassed great debts. The Crown alleged he had illegally taken treasure from a captured ship, the St Valentine, a Portuguese Carrack, in 1602. In 1607 Crown Commissioners came to Trentham Hall attempting to seize a fine imposed on the estate. He died without issue. Eventually, kinsman Sir John Leveson of Haling, Kent (d1615) had to pay £5,000 to placate the Crown. Died 1605. The claim relating to a famous ballad was remade by Hackwood in The Stone Weekly News Feb 2 1906 p9 (D593 C/9/3) (VCH vol 2 p193) (BOE p283) (SHJ autumn 1996 pp6-14) (info Richard Wisker) (DNB 2004).

Leveson, Sir Richard *The Royalist, rebuilt Trentham Hall 1630-9.* (1598-1661). Eldest surviving son of Sir John Leveson of Haling, Kent (d1615), and distant cousin and adopted son of Sir Richard (d1605). He declined to raise troops in Staffs without the King's authority; joined Charles I at Oxford, declared delinquent 1642 and disabled to sit in Parliament; sat in the anti-Parliament at Oxford, Jan 1644; held Dudley Castle for the King Nov 1643- May 1644; taken prisoner at Nantwich 1645; tomb in Lilleshall church (SHC 1912 p331. 1922 pp31-3) (VCH vol 2 p193) (BOE p283) (SHJ autumn 1996 pp6-14).

Leveson, Sir Walter *Appointed to conduct Mary, Queen of Scots to Fotheringhay 1585.* (1550-1602). Of Lilleshall and Trentham Hall (SHC 1912 p324. 1917-8 p404). His second wife, Susan, appears to have lived at Trentham Hall (VCH vol 2 p193) (BOE p283) (SHJ autumn 1996 pp6-14).

Leveson-Gower, George Granville *'a leviathan of wealth'.* (1758-1833), son of Granville (d1803). He amassed much wealth on his marriage (1785) to Elizabeth suo jure Countess of Sutherland, inheriting the vast Bridgwater estates from the last Duke, succeeded to the Marquissette of Stafford, and the lands of Sittenham, Trentham and Lilleshall 1803; MP for Newcastle 1779-80, 1780-4, for Staffs 1787-90, 1790-6, 1796-9; nominally a Whig, he was a member of the Tory Government until 1779; supported the Whigs 1779-83; thereafter connected with Pitt; created Duke of Sutherland 1833; buried Dornoch; statue of him on Tittenson Hill. When he died it was said of him by Charles Greville 'He was a Leviathan of Wealth, I believe a richer individual never died' (SHC 1922 pp297-8) (TOS p29).

Leveson-Gower, Granville *Trentham's most famous old worthy.* (1773-1846). Diplomat. Third and youngest son of Granville, 1st Marquis of Stafford, of Trentham Hall. Lord of the Treasury 1800; Privy Councillor 1804; Secretary for War 1809; Ambassador to St Petersburg 1804-5, 1807, to the Hague 1824, to Paris 1824, 1830; Grand Cross of Bath 1825; Baron of Stone and Earl Granville 1833. Retired 1841 and died after a long illness. He was considered the best whist player of his day and the gambling fraternity in Paris knew him as 'Le Wellington de jouers'.

Leveson-Gower, John *Chief protagonist in the Elibank Plot 1747.* (1694-1754). Son of Sir John (d1709). 2nd Lord Gower of Trentham Hall. Rallied to the Whigs 1744; Lord Privy Seal 1742-3, 1744-54; Earl Gower and Viscount Trentham of Trentham 1746, to reward his loyalty to the Hanoverians in the 1745 Jacobite Rebellion (SHC 1922 p217).

Marriage *First couple to get engaged on Deal Or No Deal.* Eddie Moores, tree surgeon, formerly of Stone Road, Trentham, who appeared on the Channel 4 TV game show on February 22 2010. He proposed on the show to Sarah Mills, also formerly of Trentham, his girlfriend in the audience, a student. They first met in a night club in Hanley, c2007. The proposal was made as a condition of the game show 'Banker' raising his offer to Eddie (ES Feb 22 2010 p5pc).

Masefield, Sir Peter *First Civil Air Attache in the British Embassy in Washington, he introduced the first plane powered* *by gas turbine, and the first passenger helicopter service.* Native of Trentham, he was appointed to the Attache post in July 1944. The introduction of aviation innovations were made when he was chief executive of British European Airways. Died 2006 (ES June 3 2006 p14).

Mining *Staffordshire's deepest pit 1946.* Florence Colliery at 3,000 feet (SA Feb 1 1947 p5 col 2. Feb 8 1947 p5 col 2). *Deepest mine workings in the UK 1969-74.* Hem Heath Colliery's Moss Seam, at 3,300 feet (GBR 1969 p168. 1974 p134). *First North Staffordshire pit into which a royal descended.* Hem Heath by Princess Margaret in 1974 (ES Dec 8 2007 p13). *Oldest miner killed at Florence Colliery.* William Lander, 70, d1953 (ES June 26 2006 p19). *Coal production record* was achieved by miners at Florence and Hem Heath with 1,016,195 tonnes of coal, 1982 (ES April 7 2007 p6). *Youngest miner killed at Florence Colliery* was Charles Parker, 13, d1913 (ES June 26 2006 p19). *Last North Staffordshire mineral railway* was that from Trentham to Florence Colliery closed in 1985 (ES Your Week March 25 2006 p11).

Nomenclature *Trentham Blues.* Buses run by an independent service for the Trentham area (ES Dec 12 2009 p29). *Trentham Boy.* Racehorse trained at Hartwell Stud, Barlaston. Josh Gifford (b1941), jockey, had his first win on him in the Manchester November Handicap 1956 (info Ernest Hawkins).

Place name Trentham first appears in Domesday Book, 1086, and means 'ham or village on the river Trent' or possibly 'meadow, especially a flat low-lying meadow on a stream, a water meadow; an enclosed plot, a close', since the place lies on low ground by the Trent (PNSZ p543).

Pointon, John *Earliest person recorded in the Blurton parish register.* For his baptism on Jan 3 1813.

Poorest Trentham parish workhouse was built 1809-10 on land given by the Duke of Sutherland off Trentham Road in the Splatslade area of Blurton. It housed 56 inmates in 1813; 48 in 1839 (WITP p9 figs 6, 7), the last year it was used before inmates went to Stone Union workhouse in Stone.

Population Trentham was 32nd most populated Staffordshire parish in 1801 with 1,857 people; 33rd in 1811 with 2,120; 35th in 1821 with 2,203; 37th in 1831 with 2,344; 34th in 1841 with

2,567; 34th in 1851 with 2,747; 26th in 1861 with 4,611; 24th in 1871 with 6,371; 24th in 1881 with 8,383; 23rd in 1891 with 10,219; 23rd in 1901 with 12,516. Trentham could be ranked 35th= worst affected Staffordshire parish for loss of men in WW1, with 63 lives lost.

Powerlifting *Powerlifting world champion 1992, 'Best hand-cyclist in Britain' 2008.* Ian Marsden (b1972) of Blurton, microbiologist (ES Sept 6 2008 pp56-57pcs). *UK's Strongest Man 1994.* Thomas Smith (b1960), of Fairfield Avenue, Dresden, alias 'The Tank.'

Roscoe, Geoffrey Lawrence (Pete) *Hanford's bravest.* (1915-42). Born Primrose Hill, Hanford, who was a fighter pilot in the 'Battle of Britain'. He died in action over occupied France (ES Feb 26 2007 p16p of a plaque erected in St Mathias, Hanford).

Schools *Best dressed Reception Class in the North Midlands 1998.* Reception class at Sutherland Primary School, Beaconfield Drive, Blurton (ES Nov 15 2008 p27). *The Trentham 10* were ten members of Save Trentham High (School) Action Group who started to walk to the Houses of Parliament to hand in a petition to save the school from closure, on May 9 2008 (ES May 10 2008 p6). The school was later reprieved.

Smith, Frank *The 'Potteries' Poet.* (1901-61). Born Longton. Worked as an electrician at a local colliery. Resided Trentham. Wrote over 450 small-scale poems; his lengthier ones are called 'The Trentham Narratives'. A collection entitled 'The 'Potteries' Poet 70 and more poems' edited by John A. Harvey, appeared in 1971.

Sport See Football, Golf, Horse racing, Powerlifting, Squash, Swimming.

Squash *'one of the best laid-out and equipped squash courts in the Midlands'* 1950. At Trentham Golf Club, built 1939, also described as 'two of the most modern in the country' (SCP Nov 1950 p28. Dec 1950 p32).

Sutherland, Elizabeth *Greatest of British heiresses.* (1765-1839). Daughter of William, 17th Earl of Sutherland; the peerage of the earldom of Sutherland, according to traditional details of some Scottish writers, is the *'most ancient in North Britain, and gives way to few, if any, in all Europe beside'.* She succeeded as suo jure Countess of Sutherland in 1766, contested but proved in her favour by the House of Lords in 1771. She married George Granville Leveson-Gower, 2nd Marquis of

Stafford of Trentham Hall in 1785. The Sutherland's right to carry the sceptre before a British monarch was established in 1822. The first claim was made by Pevsner in Buildings of England: Staffordshire (1974) p284; the second claim was made in Burke's Peerage (1871).

Sutherland-Leveson-Gower, George Granville William *UK's greatest-ever private landowner to 1995*. (1828-92). Of Trentham Hall. 3rd Duke of Sutherland, who owned 1.4 million acres in 1883 (GBR 1995 p163).

Sutherland-Leveson-Gower, Harriet Elizabeth Georgiana *A 'great Whig lady'*. (1806-1868), 3rd daughter of George Howard, 6th Earl of Carlisle. Married George Granville Leveson-Gower (later Sutherland-Leveson-Gower) (d1861) of Trentham Hall. She made Stafford House (the Sutherland's London residence), an important centre of society. Mistress of the Robes to Queen Victoria; it was the demand on the Queen to get rid of her and other Whig Ladies that led to the 'Bedchamber Plot' and the restoration of Lord Melbourne and the Whigs to office; principle consoler to the Queen in her bereavement 1860; entertained Garibaldi at Trentham Hall April 1864; her letters were published by her son Lord Ronald Gower (DNB) (TTH p87) (SHC 1933 p39).

Sutherland-Leveson-Gower, Millicent Fanny *'Meddlesome Millie'*. (1867-1955). (nee) St Clair-Erskine, daughter of 4th Earl of Rosslyn. Married (1884) Cromartie Sutherland-Leveson-Gower, 4th Duke of Sutherland (d1913) of Trentham Hall. She was known as such during her Trentham years, having acquired a reputation as a social reformer in local politics. She founded of a holiday home for poor Potteries children at Hanchurch 1898; helped found the Potteries and Newcastle Cripples' Guild (or North Staffs Cripples' Aid Society, or Cripples' Aid Society, or Potteries' Cripples' Guild) 1901, which had a convalescent home firstly at Hanchurch, latterly at Longfield Cottage; Arnold Bennett

Millicent Fanny Sutherland-Leveson-Gower dressed for a ball in her halcyon days as a society.

caricatured her in several of his novels as 'Interfering Iris, the Countess of Chell'.

Sweets *Staffordshire's earliest-known documentation of oakcakes*. In the account book of Mrs Frances Sherrington, housekeeper at Trentham Hall, recording the purchase of oatcakes in the week 12th to the 19th March, 1679/80, 6d for oatcakes (SRO, D593/R/1/6/4) (The Staffordshire Oakcake, a history. Pamela Sambrook. 2009. p68p of the accounts, with additional info from the author).

Staffordshire's largest gooseberry to 1798. Perhaps that grown at Trentham Aug 1798 weighing 20 dwts. 9 grs, and measuring 5 inches in circumference (SA Aug 11 1798). *Trentham Tart* was a desert cake like a Bakewell Tart only containing raspberry, not strawberry (info Pam Sambrook).

Swimming *National Youth Champion 100m backstroke (15-16 age group) 2008, World School Games 2009 Gold 200m backstroke*. David Gregory of Trentham, born Ascot, c1993. The first was achieved at Sheffield, where he set a new British record with 58.21 seconds; the second was achieved at Qatar setting a new meeting record of 2.02.20 seconds. In 2010 he was ranked Britain No. 1 for his age in 100m, 200m and 400m backstroke (ES Aug 1 2008 p44pc. April 1 2010 Olympic hopeful supplement pVIII).

Taylor, Matthew *Youngest ever kidney transplant patient at Birmingham Hospital*. When aged 5, of Blurton, Feb 1982 (ES Your Week Feb 17 2007 p6).

Trentham Gardens *First country house gardens in Staffordshire open to the public*. Trentham Gardens were partially opened to the public in 1835 (TTH p95). *Second oldest cast iron bridge ever built*. Crossed the Trent opposite the orangery, built by Thomas Farnolls in 1794, and existed to 1931 (TTH p97). *First ban-*

The perfect setting for a fun day out

Where else could you raise the family for a full day's enjoyment for less than £2.00 per person? At Trentham Gardens you can have fun on the lake, enjoy a host of exciting new rides or...drive as you want, or just relax in the beautiful surroundings and soak up the atmosphere. Children enjoy the zoo, the roundabout the angelic...

TRENTHAM GARDENS
Trentham Gardens Limited. Stoke-on-Trent. Staffordshire. Telephone (0782)

From an early 1980s advert for Trentham Gardens.

dleader at Trentham Gardens ballroom was Al Berlin, nephew of Irving Berlin, 1932 (ES Your Week May 27 2006 p11). *Last North Staffordshire appearance of The Beatles* was at Trentham Gardens ballroom, Oct 1963 (ES Your Week March 25 2006 p12p). *Britain's first bare foot walk.* 'Barfuss' in the Italian Garden, 2008. Could it be the originators of this walk were aware Trentham Gardens had a previous association with bare foot practices, in that it had hosted what amounted to the unofficial European Barefoot Water Ski Championships between at least 1972-75. The Championship was organised by Stoke-on-Trent Water Ski Club on Trentham Lake. Skiers glided on the water using no skis. The winner was awarded the 'Oliver Rix Gargares European Barefoot Trophy', but the event was unrecognised as a championship by the British Water Ski Federation (UtNews Aug 20 1975 p1p).

Trentham Hall *Third longest house entry in Pevsner's 'Staffordshire' (perhaps his longest in any volume to a demolished house).* Trentham Hall at 89 lines (BOE pp283-5). *Strange but true!* When the family were resident at the Hall it was customary for relief to be given to all poor travellers passing on the road. It was established for labourers going and returning at harvest time, but for many years prior to 1820 had been given to all who apply, except soldiers, in parties. The provision - given at a Lodge, discretely hidden from the road - was a piece of good bread, weighing fourteen ounces, and a pint of good table beer. The average number calling in c1820 was between 50 and 100 daily. In August 1819 as many as 3,480 men, 530 women, and 356 children called for relief (SA March 25 1820. March 27 1920 p5 col 1).

Trentham Hall estate *First enclosure of a footpath* was through the Trentham Hall estate, after the passing of an Act of Parliament in mid 1770s. The Act stipulated that with an enclosure of a footpath an alternative footpath be created; the Leveson-Gowers merely substituted the Trentham-Stone road as the alternative path (Andrew Dobraszczyc, 2008). *Only Department of Environment Grade Two Star listing in Stoke-on-Trent.* Trentham Mausoleum, 1807-8, rare example in UK of Boullee-Ledoux inspired architecture. *Last annual training ground of the Imperial Staffordshire Yeomanry.* Trentham Park in 1907. In 1908 the Staffordshire Yeomanry be-

came a unit of the new Territorial Army, and the title 'Imperial' was dropped (The Uniforms of the British Yeomanry Force 1794-1914. No. 15. p19). *First to swim a length at Trentham Park swimming pool* was Norman Wainwright, Olympic swimmer, 1935 (ES Your Week Sept 9 2006 p9). *UK's only monkey forest.* Trentham Park, where in woodland a colony of Barbary Macaques have been bred since 2005 (Staffordshire Breaks 2006. Staffordshire Tourism). *'A Flagship Project for Archives', largest family collection of documents in Staffordshire Record Office.* The Sutherland Collection of papers purchased from the Sutherland family by Staffordshire Archive Service in March 2006 for £2,011,000, covering two thirds of a mile of shelving. The acquisition and presentation to the general public of it was an example to other archival services. The first scholar to use the collection for a published history was Prof Eric Richards in his 'The Leviathan of Wealth: The Sutherland Fortune in the Industrial Revolution' (1972) (info Chris Latimer, 2008).

War memorial *Staffordshire's only WW1 memorial gifted by women.* Trentham War Memorial situated by the Mausoleum. It was unveiled Oct 1921 by Sir Hill Child. An inscription on one side reads 'The Gift Of The Women Of Trentham'. The memorial was paid for by the trustees of the late Duke of Sutherland, but women at a public meeting in Trentham voted for a cross to crown the monument to commemorate their hard work in the War (Staffs Weekly Sentinel Oct 8 1921 pp5,10ps).

Warren, Richard Gordon *Founded a wild hybrid moth unknown to science.* (1912-99). Bank clerk, Lepidoptera authority, champion of Staffordshire wildlife habitats; of 32 Whitmore Road, Trentham; North Staffordshire Field Club Spanton Medalist 1950, Garner Medalist 1958. The moth was a wild hybrid between the Spring Usher and the Dotted Border Agriopis leucophaearia x marginaria (NSFCT 1999 pp20-21) (The Larger Moths of Staffordshire. DW Emly and RG Warren. 2001).

Willingham, Sarah *One of the '35 most successful women under 35' 2008.* Born 1974, brought up on The Westlands, catering businesswoman, former Newcastle High School pupil, rose to national fame as a consultant on BBC 2's 'The Restaurant' programme in 2007 and 2008, starring top chef Raymond Blanc. The claim was made by Management Today (ES Oct

30 2008 p14pc).

Tunstall See Wolstanton.

Tyrley Tyrley was Staffordshire's 38th largest parish (actually it was a quarter - a rating district made up of townships (Hales, Almington and Blore) - in the Shropshire parish of Drayton-in-Hales, covering Market Drayton), consisting of 6,589 acres; 79th closest parish to the county town, 12.3m NW; extremist length 3.2m; extremist width 4.5m. The chief settlements Hales, Almington and Blore, are all small villages. The district is famous having the site of the battle of Blore Heath.

Altitudes The highest point is 710 feet in Burnt Wood. The lowest point is 244 feet by the Tern by Walkmill Bridge.

Blore Heath Battle *One of the bloodiest battles in the Wars of the Roses.* Blore Heath, 1459; reputedly 2,400 Lancastrians and 60 Yorkists were slain (Staffordshire Breaks 2006. Staffordshire Tourism).

Church St Mary, at Hales, is one of 23 such

Preparing for the battle of Blore Heath in the Wars of the Roses, 1459. In the distance is Mucklestone church.

county dedications (most common dedication in the county); 13th last AP county church built 1856 (if Tyrley is accepted as an original parish!).

Farming *First importer of Friesian cattle from Holland into England.* Ernest Hall of Hales Hall, founder of the British Friesian Society.

Folklore *Tyrley's best.* There is a local tra-

dition three mermaids appear in Hempmill Brook on the anniversary of the battle of Blore Heath (1459); three mermaids appear in the arms of the Warburton family, a member of which fought in the battle (info Bruce Braithwaite). Only a mermaid with comb and mirror appears in the crest of the Warburton's of Ireland, formerly of Garryhinch (Burke's General Armoury).

Gardening *Chelsea Flower Show garden winner 1993.* 'The Woodland Garden' designed by Kate Chambers of Hales WI.

Geology Hales village and SW-SE half is Permian; Almington village, Pellwall, and NW-NE half is Bunter.

Place-name Tyrley first appears in Domesday Book, 1086, and means 'the leah on the river Tern' or perhaps 'the dry leah' (PNSZ p550).

Population Tyrley was 85th most-populated Staffordshire parish entity in 1801 with 581 people; 85th= in 1811 with 607; 84th in 1821 with 726; 85th in 1831 with 737; 88th in 1841 with 750; 88th in 1851 with 784; 88th in 1861 with 814; 84th in 1871 with 800; 87th in 1881 with 766; 87th in 1891 with 721; 88th in 1901 with 689. Tyrley could be ranked 72nd worst affected Staffordshire parish entity for loss of men in WW1, with 19 lives lost.

Quote *Choicest.* Vivian Bird in his Staffordshire, 1973, 'Prehistory and history have left their mark in this corner of Staffordshire which presses to within ten miles of Wales.'

Soane, Sir John *His last country house built.* The architect's last house was Pellwall 1822-28 (SGS p102) (OVH p32). *Soane at his weirdest.* The lodge at Pellwall (BOE p31).

Woods *Last wolf in England killed* was according to legend in Burnt Wood (NSFCT 1930 p163). *'one of the loneliest, prettiest woods I know'.* Jessie Edwards (pen name Frederick) (1893-1987), a nature and farming freelance writer of Park Springs Farm, on 'Badgers' Rough', believed to be Badger Wood (First edition, 1 inch OS map) at SJ 741331 (A Staffordshire Country Life. Jessie Frederick).

W-Z

Walton See Eccleshall.
Walton See Stone.

Whitmore Whitmore was Staffordshire's 118th largest parish, consisting of 2,015 acres; 77th closest parish to the county town, 12.1m NNW; extremist length 2.5m; extremist width 2.3m. The parish's chief settlement is Whitmore, a fairly small estate village, now surpassed in size by the affluent residential areas of Whitmore Heath and Baldwin's Gate. The parish is famous for the old county family of Mainwaring, their Whitmore Hall and its pretty timber-framed church.

The view of Whitmore church with Whitmore Hall in the distance is one of the best church-in-relation-to-hall vistas's in Staffordshire.

Altitudes The highest point is Whitmore Heath at 597 feet. The lowest point is 328 feet at the confluence of Meece and Acton Brooks on the south boundary.

Ball, Rev John *'the Presbyterian's Champion',* Whitmore's most famous old worthy. (1585-1640). Writer of religious treatises, minister of Whitmore 1610-39. He would not sign the Thirty-Nine Articles and was known as such in scorn. Throughout his incumbency he lived with the Mainwarings at Whitmore Hall; died on October 20th and is buried at Whitmore (SMC p174) (S&W p251) (TTTD p229). In 1952 the parish purchased a copy of his A Friendly Triall of the Grounds Tending to Separation etc. 1640, and The Power of Godliness etc. 1657, both are kept at the county record office.

Cheadle, Mr JW Whitmore's blacksmith poet. It was for him Major Cavenagh Mainwaring laid on an open-air concert in his honour in the grounds of Whitmore Hall in 1929. It was attended by Sir Joseph Lamb, MP for Stone Division, and more than 4,000 people, chiefly from the Potteries, who made the pilgrimage to the village on foot. The procession was organised by the Potteries Workers' Society. The concert included songs, all written by JW Cheadle, such as 'A Summer Reverie', 'Oh, Happy Years', 'The First Snowdrop', and 'Life's Eventide'

(SA July 20 1929 p9 col 4).

Church St Mary and All Saints in Whitmore is one of 3 such duel dedications in the county (for AP churches); 23rd= oldest county church dating from the C12 or roughly 1150. *'one of the most attractive (churches) in the archdeaconry of Stoke-on-Trent, being one of only two remaining half-timbered churches in Staffordshire'* St Mary & All Saints (SA July 17 1953 p4 col 4). Lichfield Diocese Best Kept Churchyard winner 2002.

Farming *Staffordshire's 67th and last enclosure by Private Act of land not including some open field arable.* Whitmore; 140 acres awarded 1846 by Act of 1841 (A Domesday of English enclosure acts and awards. WE Tate. 1978). *First potato riddling machine.* The Griffin Potato Riddler, named after its inventor Albert Henry Griffin (1877-1928) of Ivy House, Whitmore; from this machine Albert gained much fame and financial benefit.

Albert Henry Griffin, with the Griffin Potato Riddling machine.

Folklore *Whitmore's best.* Whitmore Hall stables are reputedly haunted by the ghost of a groom, buried in Whitmore churchyard, apparently trapped upstairs and died when the building caught fire in the 1780s or 1790s. Today no horse ever enters (Whitmore Hall visitor leaflet, 2006) (The North Staffs Magazine. April 2008 pp8,11pc of sleigh).

Geology Whitmore village and the south of the parish is Bunter; the north is Upper Coal Measures.

Howell, Thomas *Whitmore's longest serving vicar.* He served for 60 years, 1533-93.

Mainwaring, Edward *'one of the most devoted adherents of Cromwell'.* The Puritan squire (SA March 5 1954 p2 col 5). It is hard to say whether this was Edward Mainwaring (1577-1647), MP for Newcastle 1601, 1625 and a Commissioner for Staffordshire for the Scandalous Ministers Act 1642, or his son Edward Mainwaring (1602~3-75), 'pillar of the Roundhead cause in Staffordshire' who was ordered to demolish Heighley Castle 1645.

Mainwaring Arms Inn *One of the AA's*

1001 Great Family Pubs. The Mainwaring Arms, an old 'creeper-clad inn on the Mainwaring family estate' (book of the above title, 2005). *Where it was decided 'The Staffordshire Atlas' book should cover the pre-1974 county*. During a 2-hour boozy discussion between commissioning editor Prof Tony Phillips (Geography, Keele University) and colleagues at the Mainwaring Arms in c2005. Alternatively, the confines for this academic demographic atlas, due for publication in 2009, was to stay within the post-1974 administrative county.

Manorial business *The manor with no change in lordship since 1086*. Whitmore, allowing for inheritance in the female line, which occurred only four times, 1195, 1385, 1573, 1920 (VB p125). *Most (legitimate) sons of a lord in proportion to his overall issue*. Probably Rowland Mainwaring (1783-1862), the Rear Admiral, who fathered 15 sons and one daughter.

Place-name Whitmore first appears in Domesday Book, 1086, and means 'white moor' (PNSZ p574).

Poorest At Whitmore 'the Clays House' 1803, 'the Clay' 1808, 'the Clays' 1810, 1833, 'Clays house' 1819, 1821, 1824, 1828 must be the workhouse. Presumably, it lay in 'Clays lane' 1806 (D3332/6/1). In March 1835 the vestry planned to take over existing buildings for a workhouse. By Aug/ Sept 1835 they considered erecting a workhouse (D3332/6/3). After 1838 Whitmore poor, unable to support themselves, went to Newcastle Union workhouse on the south side of Keele Road, Thistleberry.

Population Whitmore was 131st most populated Staffordshire parish in 1801 with 234 people; 124th in 1811 with 291; 126th in 1821 with 302; 128th in 1831 with 281; 121st in 1841 with 367; 121st in 1851 with 377; 123rd in 1861 with 345; 124th in 1871 with 332; 126th in 1881 with 311; 121st in 1891 with 318; 120th in 1901 with 308. Whitmore could be ranked 135th= worst affected Staffordshire parish for loss of men in WW1, with one life lost.

Railways *World's first railway canteen* was probably that one reportedly set up 'during the severe weather, the company provide the driver and fireman with a cup of hot coffee at Whitmore' (there being no protection from the weather for enginemen and the footplates of the early locomotives), after the opening of the GJR, in 1837. It was the duty of the day porter to take the coffee to the engines, but at night firemen went to the station office for it (SA Feb 1 1952 p5 col 8). *Last passenger train to stop at Whitmore station* was on Feb 4 1952, by when only three such trains in each direction stopped at the station a day (SA Feb 1952 p5 col 7).

Smith,   Sampson *Staffordshire's longest serving choir-member (perhaps).*   (1841-1930). Of Whitmore, who, when 80, had been a member of Whitmore church choir for 72 years (newspaper cutting in Mainwaring Arms Inn).

Sampson Smith.

Stone, Samuel J *His best-known hymn.* 'The Church's One Foundation'. He was born at Whitmore Rectory on April 25 1839.

Whitmore Hall *Extremely rare example of a late Elizabethan stable block, and one of the oldest in the country*. At Whitmore Hall (Whitmore Hall visitor leaflet). *Unique Twyford bath*. Installed at Whitmore Hall, during the tenancy of Thomas Twyford, the sanitaryware pioneer, 1891-1921 (ES Sept 13 1996 p3). *Retriever Champion Cup winner 1920*. 'Tag of Whitmore' owned by TW Twyford (ES Dec 4 1998 p13). *Very rare bird in the UK* The Hoopoe (Epupa, Epops, Linn) a migrant from Egypt was seen and shot dead in the grounds of Whitmore Hall by a gamekeeper of the Mainwarings (SA Oct 20 1832) (Broughton's Scrapbook p455).

Willoughbridge (Dorothy Clive Garden) See Maer.

Wolstanton Wolstanton was Staffordshire's 12th largest parish, consisting of 10,816 acres; 63rd= farthest parish away from the Stafford, 15m NNW; extremist length 6.9m, making it 10th longest parish in Staffordshire; extremist width 4.8m. The chief settlement is Tunstall, one of the five town's of The Potteries. The parish is famous for the birth of Primitive Methodism, Harecastle Tunnel, mining.

Altitudes The highest point is Mow Cop at 1,099 feet. The lowest point is 390 feet by Lyme Brook near Knutton.

Apedale Colliery *Deepest mine in Britain by 1830s*. Apedale Colliery at 2000 feet (IANS p34). *Pioneer of the modern form of retreat mining in Staffordshire*. Apedale Colliery (ES July 15 2006 p12).

Holder of weekly productivity record. Apedale Colliery producing 161.9 cwt per manshift in May 1968; during the year ending March 1969 it became one of the few British mines to average over 5 tons a manshift over a year (ES July 15 2006 p12).

Athletics *National junior cross-country champion 1960.* Tony Walker of Kidsgrove, when aged 19 (ES July 4 2009 p28). *UK's No. 2 female road runner 2009.* Michelle Ross-Cope of Waterhayes, after setting a new course record (32 mins, 45 secs) when she won the Trafford 10k road race 2009, as well as clipping more than 5 minutes off the record for the Sub4 Stafford 20-mile road race 2009. Top of the UK ranking list was Mara Yamauchi of Harrow (ES March 18 2009 p48pc). *World Youth Triple Jump Champion 2009.* Ben Williams, aged 17, of Porthill at the World Youth Athletics Championships, Bressanone, Italy, with a jump of 15.91 metres (his personal best) (ES July 13 2009 pp40, 48pc).

Barker, Arthur *The 'drugless healer'.* Born 1886. Of Tunstall, who styled himself as a 'professional hypnotist and drugless healer', sentenced in Feb 1920 to four months in prison, on a charge of causing the death of one of his patients, Frances Annie Sharples on Sept 30 1919. But he had rendered such good services to the poor, friends and sympathizers marched on March 6 1920 from Biddulph through Brindley Ford, Packmoor and Newchapel to Tunstall where they demonstrated. A petition to have him released with 120,000 signatures was presented to the Home Secretary. Col Wedgwood, M.P. for Newcastle actually brought his name up in a question in the House of Commons. It was alleged Mrs Sharples was in any event in the advance stages of cancer (SA Feb 21 1920 p9 col 1. March 13 1920 p5 col 3. March 20 1920 p7 col 2. April 3 1920 p3 col 4).

Barlow, Charles *Wolstanton's villain.* Of New House, Red Street. He has been identified as the murderer of Sarah Smith (1742-63). Her gravestone in St Margaret's churchyard, Wolstanton, implies she was murdered. The inscription reads

'It was C____s B____w
That brought me to my end.
Dear parents, mourn not for me
For God will be my friend.
With half a pint of poyson
He came to visit me.
Write this on my grave
That all that read it may see.'

He was the father of her illegitimate child (ES Jan 1 2005 p2p). (NSFCT 1941 p39) (SLM June 1952 p15) (POP p171) (WWT p21) (COS p26p).

Beech, Jack *'Mr Kidsgrove'.* (c1915-97). Councillor for Kidsgrove for 45 years, former mayor of Newcastle borough, on Kidsgrove Town councillor for 25 years, Staffordshire County councillor for 20 years. It was planned that a garden to his memory be built opposite Kidsgrove Town Hall in 1998 (ES March 17 1998 photo).

Bennett, John *Wolstanton's unluckiest.* When aged 53, labourer, of Bath Street, Wolstanton, he was hit and killed by a golf ball whilst crossing Wolstanton Golf Links on March 17 1934 (SA April 7 1934 p10 col 4).

Beresford, Mrs Maureen *First female head of Wolstanton Grammar School.* A clinical psychologist, on its merger with Watlands Secondary School in Sept 1977 (ES Nov 4 1976).

Birchendale Colliery *'finest and most important (coke refinery) works in the country' c1912.* That at Birchenwood Colliery, consisting of 84 coke ovens and a by-product plant erected in 1908-9, and 72 more coke ovens and a benzol rectification plant erected in 1912 (SA Feb 27 1932 p10 col 5).

Bourne, John *Wolstanton's person with the earliest-surviving will.* It is dated 1522.

Bowls *English singles short-mat bowls champion 2003, English doubles short-mat bowls champion 2009.* Gareth Stanway, of Mow Cop; the doubles was with Nick Tideswell of Smallthorne Pioneer WMC (ES April 11 2009 p55pc).

Breeze, Mark *First person in Newcastle borough to be fined for fly-tipping.* When aged 37, of Leech Ave, Chesterton, in June 2006 (ES July 13 2006 p13).

Brick making *Largest brick and tile works in the country* was stated as being within Newcastle borough boundary (Staffordshire County Handbook c1958 p119).

Brindley, James *Wolstanton's most famous old worthy.* (1716-72). Canal engineer. Born at Thornsett, Derby-

Brindley - Wolstanton's most famous old worthy.

shire. He was a millwright's apprentice, then had a wheelwright's business in Leek. He constructed many canals; his Harecastle Tunnel is a great engineering feat on the Trent and Mersey through Wolstanton parish. He married Anne Henshall in Wolstanton church on 8th December 1765. By then he was certainly living at the hall, Turnhurst, in the parish. There he died on 27th September, and is buried at Newchapel.

Business/ industrial parks *'largest derelict land reclamation scheme of its kind in the country' 1990*. The new Parkhouse Industrial Estate 132 acres astriding the A34, near Chesterton. Perhaps what made it distinctive was it was jointly developed by a council, Newcastle MB, and a private company, WA Blackburn Ltd of Coventry (ES Feb 28 1990). *'one of the greenest business parks in the world'*. To be built at Blue Planet Chatterley Valley by Gazeley UK, costing £50m, and proposed being so environmentally friendly that it will actually be 'carbon positive' - with an on-site biofuel plant providing enough extra heat and energy for 650 local homes (The Birmingham Post Nov 9 2007 p7). *Lymedale Business Park's first factory unit opened*. CLS Wiring Systems in the Small Firms Centre in July 1998, on former site of Holditch Colliery (ES July 18 1998). *National home of Recreation Managers' Association of Great Britain (RMA, 1956)*. Kidsgrove, in 2008.

Cadman, John *Institution of Mining and Metallurgy Gold Medal winner 1933, founder of world's first school of Petroleum Technology, one of the few Englishmen awarded the ancient title of Pasha (first class)*. (1877-1941). Born at the Villas, Silverdale; he was also awarded the first County Mining Scholarship by Staffordshire to study mining and geology at Armstrong College, part of Durham College of Science. The Petroleum Technology school was founded in 1908. In 1912 he set up the first degree course in Petroleum Technology (SA March 25 1933 p6 col 3) (ES Dec 22 2006 p14. Jan 16 2010 p25p).

Cartlidge, Holly *Knutton's 'Little Angel', unluckiest*. She was accidentally run over by a relation on the driveway of her home in Hazel Road, Chesterton, aged 4, 2005 (ES July 22 2006 p18).

Cheeseman, Peter *Longest-serving theatre director of an English provincial theatre in modern times*. Died 2010. When he retired from the New Victoria Theatre,

Basford, in 1988.

CHURCHES St Margaret at Wolstanton is one of 4 such county dedications (of AP churches); 98th= oldest AP county church dating from 1390. *Note* the tomb of Sir William Sneyd (d1571) under a modern arch in the north east corner with the recumbent effigies of Sir William and his wife, Anne (nee Barrowe) of Flickersbrooke, Cheshire. Round the sides of the tomb are the figures of their 15 children. The effigy of Anne has been mutilated, but local legend has it she was carved without hands as she had lived without them for many years. She was very proud and haughty, but also idle and did not dress herself; since her hands were of no use her husband had them cut off (GNHS p123)(LGS p256) (NUL pp49p,50) (JME part ii pp26-27) (POP p171) (CHMS p57) (SLM June 1952 p14) (WWT p facing 29, p30). *Note also* the cartouche tablet to William Sneyd (d1689), which Sidney A Jeavons in his The Monumental Effigies of Staffordshire survey rates as 'outstanding' and most probably from the Stanton workshop (JME part iv pp57-58 pl 9) (CHMS p57). *Largest grant awarded by the Staffordshire Environmental Fund to 2009*. £200,000 for the restoration of the 6.5 acre churchyard and burial ground, over three years from early 1999 to 2002 (info Staffs Environmental Fund, created 1997). *In the churchyard*. The grave of Sarah Smith - see Charles Barlow; the earthenware grave of Samuel Willshaw (d1755). It was once one of many manufactured by potters as late as the 1760s. The names and the epitaphs of the deceased were painted in raised 'slip'. Some of these are in Liverpool Museum (WWT p22).

St Thomas at Mop Cop was built in 1841-2. *In the churchyard* is the grave of Hannah Dale (see).

Cinema *First Tunstall (and Potteries) cinema*. Barber's Palace, which stood on the south side of The Boulevard (formerly Station Road), 1909 (POTP p29). *The venue for Saturday Northern soul allnighters 1972-?* The Golden Torch, alias The Torch, Tunstall. Earlier, and from the 1940s, it was the Little Regent Cinema (earlier a church, then ice rink), which was converted 1965 into a mod nightclub by Christopher Burton, a contemporary of Ivor Abadi, founder of the Twisted Wheel club, Manchester. After that club's closure in 1971, the Torch, became *the* new venue for Saturday northern soul all-nighters, holdings its first on March 11 1972 (Wikipedia, 2009).

Cliff, Clarice *'the most-discussed pottery designer of the 20th century'*. (1899-1972). Born Meir St, Tunstall, employed at AJ Wilkinson's Newport Pottery, Middleport; its managing director, Colley Shorter, became her lover, and later husband. Her jazzy range of Art Deco pottery - most notably her Bizarre ware - not only thrilled a generation but has enjoyed a vogue among collectors since her death. Her own team of paintresses, were known as the 'Bizarre Girls'. The claim was made by The Sentinel (POTP p62) (ES Sept 17 2005 p11).

Clarice Cliff with examples of her Bizarre Ware cups and saucers.

Climbing First rock climbing ascent of the Old Man of Mow. K Maskery by the Spiral Route, pre-1960 (Staffordshire Gritstone. British Mountaineering Council. 1989. p286).

Coal mining *Unusually rich variety of coal seams*. North Staffordshire, ranging from the lower qualities suitable for power station fuels to high grade metallurgical coals (Staffordshire Handbook c1966 p73). *'North West Frontier'*. Colloquial way of referring to the north west side of the North Staffordshire Coalfield containing the collieries at Silverdale, Apedale and Kidsgrove (info Geoff Mould, North Staffordshire Mining History Group, 2008). *Earliest documentation of coal mining in North Staffordshire*. Tunstall 1282 (HOS 1998 p15). See also Walter Sylvester, and Collieries - Apedale, Birchendale, Holditch, Silverdale, Wolstanton.

Combat sports *Britain's first women's amateur boxing match* was to be staged at Kay's Club, Chell, in 1997 until 13 year-old contestant Emma Brammer of Stanfields withdrew (ES Your Week Spet 29 2007 p7).

Competitions *National Pub Quiz Competition winners 2006*. The Clayheads, based at the Oxford Arms, May Bank. The competition is run by Punch Taverns (ES Jan 7 2008 p12pc). *BBC Midlands Today School of Rock winners 2007*. My Sergeant Mask, a rock group formed by pupils at James Brindley High School, Westcliffe.

Cook, Joseph *Treaty of Versailles signatory, 'father of the Australian navy'*. Australian Prime Minster 1913-14, born Silverdale Dec 7 1860. Died 1947 (ES Dec 22 2006 p14).

Cricket *Junior League who provided seven players for England*. Kidsgrove Junior League. They were:- Bob Taylor, David Steele, Ken Higgs, John Morris, Robert Bailey, Kim Barnett and Dominic Cork (ES May 24 2008 p31).

Cumberbatch, IW *Pioneer into research into remedies for dangers arising from dust, first mining engineer to adopt wet cutting*. CBE, of Silverdale (SLM Spring 1955 p8p).

Dale, Hannah *The 'Child of Wonder', the 'Mow Cop Giantess'*. (1881-92). Of Dales Green. She weighed in excess of 32 stone; on her 10th birthday she stood 4ft 11ins, chest 55 inches, thigh 3 ft 1 inch, and calf 23 inches. A medical expert described her as 'one of the greatest wonders of the day'. She was exhibited at carnivals etc. The inscription on her grave in St Thomas' church, Mow Cop, reads

Mow Cop's 'Child of Wonder' - Hannah Dale who died aged just eleven.

> "Here lies my dust, - the child of wonder
> I bid farewell, to all behind
> and now I dwell just over yonder
> in heaven with God - so Good and Kind"

(Leek Commonplace Book p242) (TB May 1995 p1p).

Darts *'Greatest flinger of tungsten that ever drew breathe'*, *'greatest player in the sport's history'* (ES Oct 12 2009 p44), *'Stoke's answer to William Tell'* (Daily Telegraph Sport Jan 5 2010 pS20), *World darts champion 1990, 1992, 1995-2002, 2004-6, 2009-2010 'most World Championship titles' by 2008, World Matchplay champion 1995, 1997, 2000-04, 2006, 2009 - 'most World Matchplay titles' by 2008, World Grand Prix champion 1998-*

Phil 'The Power' Taylor of May Bank, phenomenonal world darts champion.

2000, 2002-03, 2005-06, 2008, 'most World Grand Prix titles won by an individual player' by 2008, Midland Sports Personality 2006. Phil 'The Power' Taylor (b1960), of May Bank (ES Aug 29 2006 p18. Oct 30 2006 p40. Jan 6 2009 p6pcs) (BBC Midlands Today Dec 4 2006) (GBR 2008 p250). In addition, Taylor is Party-Poker.net Las Vegas Desert Classic (Darts) Champion 2002, 2004, 2006, 2008, 2009 and PartyPoker.com Grand Slam of Darts Champion 2008 (this is a contest of the best players of Professional Darts Corporation and British Darts Organisation). In addition, Taylor holds the record for the highest average in a televised event with the 116.01 thrown against John Part in the Whyte & Mackay Premier League, achieved in April 2009. With his victory in the Skybet World Grand Prix 2009 he held all five major knockout trophies on the PDC circuit - Ladbrokes.com world championship, Blue Square Open, Stan James World Matchplay and the Las Vegas Desert Classic. With his win of the Professional Darts Corporation World Title 2010 he emulates John Lowe by winning world titles in three separate decades (ES July 7 2008 p42pc. Oct 13 2008 p48pc. Nov 24 2008 p42. July 27 2009 p44pc. Oct 12 2009 p44).

Deakin, Fanny *North Staffordshire's only Communist councillor, 'Red Fanny'*. (1883-1968). Advocate of child and maternal welfare issues. Born Silverdale into a large and poor family. Motivated by the poverty she observed around her, she entered politics and was the first woman to be elected onto Wolstanton

Fanny Deakinn, 'Red Fanny' of Silverdale, social welfare campaigner.

Council as a Labour member in 1923; Communist from 1927. Nicknamed 'Red Fanny' after her visits to the Soviet Union in 1927, and 1930. County Councillor 1934-46; first communist appointed alderman in Newcastle-under-Lyme Borough 1941-. The Fanny Deakin Maternity Home, Chesterton, 1947-70, was subsumed into the Maternity department of the City General Hospital. 'Go See Fanny Deakin!' Joyce Holliday's play appeared in 1991 (ES Your Week Sept 9 2006 p9) (Wikipedia, 2009).

Ecology *First carbon positive warehouse in the country, 'most sustainable distribution centre in the world' 2009*. The Blue Planet warehouse at Chatterley Valley business park, a joint venture between Advantage West Midlands, North Staffordshire. The warehouse, with a floorspace of 500,000 sq ft and whose total energy and heat is generated from renewable sources, won the first North Staffordshire Urban Design Awards, which were held in 2009. The building is also the first development in the world to receive an outstanding rating from the Building Research Establishment Environmental Assessment Method (ES Sept 15 2009 p15pc).

Engineering *Site of Britain's first jet engine production*. The Derwent jet was produced by Rolls-Royce between Oct 1944 and Dec 1945 at 'Factory 81', Milehouse (ES Nov 14 1994 p8p. Your Week Aug 19 2006 p9). *Management Today European Quality Award winner 1994*. D2D electronics, West Ave, Kidsgrove, a subsidiary of ICL, founded 1992, who also won Management Today awards for best electronics factory in UK, and best factory in Midlands (ES Nov 11 1994).

Farming *Staffordshire's 14th and last enclosure of land by Provisional Order confirmed in pursuance of annual general Act 1845 and 1848*. Wolstanton Marsh; 70 acres Awarded by Act of 1898 (A Domesday of English enclosure acts and awards. WE Tate. 1978).

Faulds, Dr Henry *Pioneer of Dactylography (science of identification by finger prints), first to forecast that fingerprints would be useful in the detection of crime, first to win a conviction using fingerprints.* (c1844-1910). A Scotsman, sometime of James Street, Wolstanton. Sir William J Herschel had independently reached a similar conclusion about fingerprints at a somewhat earlier date in India, but it was Faulds who published first - 'Skin Furrows of the Hand' in 'Nature' magazine 1880. After returning from Japan, where he had lived 1874-85, he spent a few years in London, before coming to Fenton as assistant to Dr Dawes. Whilst there he was police surgeon for about eight years. Afterwards he practised in Hanley for many years. The first claims are from SA March 22 1930 p7; the third claim is from ES Sept 16 2006 p12.

Fitchford, William *'one of the oldest bellringers in the country' 1953*. When aged 79 in 1953, of Wolstanton, bellringer at St Margaret's since 1886, captain since 1904 (SA July 31 1953 p2 col 6).

Folklore *Kidsgrove's best.* A spot at the north end of one of the Harecastle Tunnels is believed to have been where Christina Collins was murdered by bargees and gives rise to stories of a headless ghost at Kidsgrove. But she was, in fact, murdered near Rugeley. The same or another lady ghost called Kit Crewbucket haunts Telford's Tunnel; the name may be just a play on the old pronunciation of Kidsgrove. These apparitions, are the same as, or have been confused with, a black dog ghost or boggart at Kidsgrove which foretells a mining disaster. *Newchapel's best.* That George Frederick Handel (1685-1759) reputedly composed the 'Harmonious Blacksmith' whilst on a visit to Turnhurst Hall. He is supposed to have been inspired by the clanking of a smith in the neighbourhood. *Wolstanton's best.* The tradition that Wolstanton took its name from Wolstan, and that St Wolstan, or his ancestors were born at Dimsdale near Wolstanton (NSFCT 1886 p53).

It is said George Frederick Handel composed the 'Harmonious Blacksmith' after hearing the clanking of a smith near Turnhurst Hall.

Football *Record for an international against Scotland.* The England 7-2 victory at Wembley 1955, four of the goals were scored by Dennis Wilshaw (1926-2004), born Packmoor. He was the first player to score four goals in an international match at Wembley; Wolverhampton Wanderers 1944-57. He ended his career at Stoke City in 1961 (ES Sept 27 2008 p30). *Big winners!* Six men from Kidsgrove win a pools syndicate of £103,525.28 on a stake of £4 (ES Your Week March 17 2007 p6. Jan 30 2010 p32. Feb 6 2010 p36p).

Fox, W. Terry *Cheshire poet laureate 2008.* Of Whitehall, Kidsgrove, his collections of poetry include 'Dance of Fools' and 'Village Verse'. Cheshire CC appoint a new poet for their county each year (ES Feb 2 2008 p21).

Geology The townships of Chell, Oldcott, and Wedgwood are Middle Coal Measures: Chatterley, Chesterton, Knutton Ransliffe, Tunstall and Wolstanton townships are Upper Coal Measures; Brierley Hurst is Millstone Grit (Mow Cop hill), Middle Coal Measures (rest). Stadmorslow is Upper Coal Measures. *'superior to any other in the Kingdom, for the purpose of mealing'.* Mow Cop grit stone; the best for grinding corn meal, according to an advert in The Staffordshire Advertiser, April 1 1826 (info Andrew Dobraszczyc).

Golf *North Staffordshire's first Professional Golf Championship* was held at Wolstanton Golf Course in 1950, won by Fred Middleton of Greenway Hall Golf Club (SLM May 1950 p125p).

Harpur, Rev T *Brindley Ford's hero.* Formerly of Brindley Ford, awarded the M.C. for distinguished service in the field as a chaplain, for fearlessness and coolness as leader of a party of stretcher-bearers in helping to clear away wounded under heavy machine gun and shell fire, during the Hindenburg System at St Quentin, Nov 1918 (SA Nov 30 1918 p7 col 7).

Harecastle Tunnel *'our Eighth Wonder of the world - the subterraneous Navigation which is cutting by the great Mr Brindley who handles Rocks as easily as you would Plum Pies'* The tunnel according to a contemporary of Brindley (SL p236). *Largest civil engineering project ever carried out in Britain to 1777* (IANS pp20-21); *World's first straight and level transport canal tunnel of more than 2600 meters* (NSJFS 1978 p33); *First transport tunnel in England and in its day the longest* (IAS p171) James Brindley's Harecastle Tunnel.

Health and well being *'one of the cleanest hospitals in the country'.* Bradwell Hospital, rated excellent by Patient Environment Action Teams, 2006 (ES Aug 12 2006 p16). *First purpose-built occupation centre for training mentally handicapped children in the country (probably in the world)* was that which was built in Milehouse Lane, 1937-38 (SA Jan 13 1959 p10 col 4). *3rd purpose-built home in Britain for dementia sufferers.* The Claybourne

Centre, opened by Methodist Homes next to Westcliffe Hospital in 1997 (ES June 17 1999 p17p) (info Annmarie Walton).

Henshall, Rich. *Earliest person recorded in Wolstanton parish register.* Alias Aston. For his burial on March 30 1624.

Holditch Colliery *Last surviving survivor of the Holditch pit disaster 1937.* Fred Taylor, a 31-year-old fireman at the pit, who had just finished his shift when fire broke out at the end of the coal face just before 6am on July 2 1937; 30 men died in the disaster; he was still living in 1997 (ES July 3 1997 photo). *Britain's safest pit 1976.* Holditch Colliery, after reducing the number of workdays lost compared with 100,000 manshifts worked by a massive 53% (ES June 24 1976).

Hoon, G W *Last chairman of Wolstanton Urban District.* Born 1895; the District was taken into Newcastle MB in 1932. Mr Hoon was living at Bradwell Grange, Bradwell, in 1975 (ES Oct 31 1975).

Hooper, Miss Carol *Midlands area Coal Queen 1971.* Income tax officer, aged 19, of Uplands Ave, Westcliffe, Chell (SA & Chron Aug 26 1971 p1p).

Housing *Oldest council houses in Britain 1976.* Possibly two C15 dwellings in Church Lane, Wolstanton. They had been just bought by Newcastle Borough for conversation into habitable modern accommodation. The properties were listed (ES Aug 13 1976). *Strange but true! In 2006* 31 inter-related people lived in Gort Rd, Cross Heath; they were four generations of the Ghaewski, Davies, Everill, Trigg and Clewes families (ES Sept 21 2006 pp1,6-7).

Iron working *Earliest blast or oldest coke-fired furnace in North Staffordshire.* Partridge Nest or Throstles' Nest Furnace, Springwood Road, Chesterton, dated at c1760 or 1768 (NSJFS 1964 p116. 1965 p91).

Johnson, Kevin *Longest-serving one-pub licensee in Stoke-on-Trent (probably).* At The Talisman Inn, Furlong Road, Tunstall, built 1961, since 1987 (ES March 31 2008 p18pc).

Joines, Helena *World's first kidney removal day patient.* Of Bradwell, 38, Jan 24 2006 at University Hospital of North Staffordshire by Dr Anurag Golash (ES March 29 2006 pp1,6p).

Law *Staffordshire's first prosecution under (Section 1) Public Meeting Act, 1908.* When William Ball, grocer's manager, High Street, Kidsgrove, was charged with being disorderly at a political meeting during the 1910 General Election campaign at the Victoria Hall, Kidsgrove, with the intent of preventing the meeting occurring. Daniel Boulton, a member of the committee of the Kidsgrove Conservative Association, brought the case before Kidsgrove County Police Court on Feb 24 1910. The case was adjourned (SA Feb 26 1910 p5 col 6).

Lidgett, Rev J Scott *The 'Grand Old Man of Methodism', 'Archbishop of Methodism'.* (1854-1953). Methodist minister and local politician, born Lewisham, who started his career at Tunstall, 1876. President of the Methodist Conference 1908 (DNB). The first quote is a re-quote from SA June 19 1953 p4 col 7. The second is from ES Sept 13 2008 p31.

Machin, Emma *Miss Staffordshire 2009, Miss Port Vale 2009/10.* Born c1990. Former magician's assistant, of Shrewsbury Drive, Chesterton (ES June 2 2009 p5pc. April 16 2010 p6pc).

Marchant, Samantha and **Amanda** *Big Brother 8 runners-up, first twins on Big Brother.* Of Cotswold Ave, Knutton, 18; they were also the first contestants to appear in the Channel 4 2007 show (ES May 31 2007 pp19, 24pc).

Martial Arts *She won 66 trophies in just 19 competitions, with 52 first-place finishes.* Charlie Maddock, kickboxer, aged 14, of Packmoor, in 2009. These trophies included three golds at the Judgement Day International, and nine medals in total across three national martial arts competitions. In the martial arts super league, she won four grand champion titles and was voted competitor of the year for all ages and genders after going throughout the year unbeaten. In the 14 events in which she did not come first she achieved either second or third place (ES Dec 22 2009 p40pc). *World record for snapping chopsticks against throat 2010.* Peter Love of Tunstall, 49, a martial arts instructor, specialising in Shaolin Kung Fu, with 30 beating the previous record of 12 at NEC Arena, Birmingham (ES May 27 2010

Peter Love setting the world record for snapping chopsticks, 2010.

p13pcs).

Mason, Brewster *Bancroft Gold medalist.* Born Kidsgrove, awarded 1948 by

RADA where he was studying to become an actor (ES Oct 13 2007 staying in p13).

Military defence *First meeting of the Tunstall Rifle Volunteers* took place on Nov 18 1859; the first meeting for the Kidsgrove company took place on Nov 29 1859 (SA Jan 14 1860 p5 col 4).

Millins, Matthew *Earliest person recorded in Newchapel parish register.* For his burial on Aug 6 1724. He was the son of James and Eliz Millins.

Natural history *First sighting of a Lanthorn fly (flying glow worm) in England.* 1678, by Ralph Sneyd at Bradwell; preceding the first official noting of one by two years, and the first official noting of one by the Royal Society by six years (NHS p236).

Neilson, Donald *Kidsgrove's villain, 'the Black Panther'.* Serial killer. Born 1936. On Jan 14 1975 he kidnapped Lesley Whittle, a 20-year old heiress of Highley, Shrops, and hid her at the bottom of a shaft in Boathouse Lane, Bath Pool Valley. He intended to ransom her for £50,000, but either by accident or design she died and was found in the shaft in March 1975. Neilson was captured in Mansfield, Notts, in Dec 1975, tried and sentenced in July 1976 (The Capture of the Black Panther: Casebook of a killer. H Hawkes. 1978) (MCGM pp114-115) (ES March 8 1995 pp10-11ps) (KAIW p21).

Payne, Leif *Child model in the Cooperative's biggest ever promotion.* Born 2000. Of Harriseahead, pupil at Thursfield Primary School, starring on billboards in a multi-million advertising campaign for the company nationwide in 2009 (ES Feb 14 2009 p10pc).

Place-names Wolstanton first appears in Domesday Book, 1086, and means 'Wulfstan's tun'. The first appearance of other places are:- Chesterton (1201) 'ancient fortification, city tun'; Kidsgrove (c1596) 'the place of the stall or fold of the calves'; Knutton (1086) 'Cnut's tun' or 'the tun at the hillock'; Tunstall (1162) 'site of the farmstead' (PNSZ).

Political agitation *First gathering to agitate for trade unionism in North Staffordshire* was held on Wolstanton Marsh led by John Doherty, 1830 (info Bob Fyson).

Poorest Wolstanton workhouse, said to have been originally a number of small cottages bought by the parish authorities, was at the NE end of the Marsh. In 1814 it housed 102 inmates (WITP p11). From 1838 the whole parish entered Wolstanton

Poor Law Union. Its workhouse was built in Turnhurst Road, near Chell in 1841, and was known as Chell Workhouse and later Westcliffe Institution. It closed in 1922 (with the merger of the union with that of Stoke inmates moved to Stoke) and was demolished in 1993. It could be claimed probably as *Staffordshire's union workhouse with the most famous alumni*, child inmates including: Charles Shaw (1832-1906), minister of religion (Methodist New Connexion), Tunstall, who had to enter the workhouse in 1842 after his father lost his job; Shaw chronicles his time there in 'When I was a Child' (1903; subsequently much in demand and reprinted): George Herbert Barber (1860-1946), 'The Cinema King' of Tunstall, who entered the workhouse in 1867, motherless and with an infirm father. In later life he published 'From Small Beginnings' and 'From Workhouse to Lord Mayor' (POTP pp28-29, 189).

Population Wolstanton was 13th most populated Staffordshire parish in 1801 with 4,679 people; 10th in 1811 with 6,990; 10th in 1821 with 8,572; 9th in 1821 with 10,853; 8th in 1841 with 16,575; 8th in 1851 with 22,191; 7th in 1861 with 32,029; 5th in 1871 with 41,824; 5th in 1881 with 47,216; 5th in 1891 with 50,885; 6th in 1901 with 57,994. Wolstanton & Kidsgrove (excludes Tunstall) could be ranked 9th worst affected Staffordshire parish entity for loss of men in WW1, with 636 lives lost.

Pottery *UK's leading ceramic tile manufacturer 2008.* Johnson Tiles (H & R Johnson Ltd), formed 1901. Based at Highgate Pottery, S end of Harewood St, Tunstall (ES April 17 2008 p14).

Powerlifting *World's Strongest Man* competitor. Carl Broomfield from Chell (ES May 10 2006 p12).

Pubs and hotels *One of the best B&Bs in Britain.* The Gables, 570-572 Etruria Rd, Basford (The Good Bed and Breakfast Guide: Over 1000 of the best B&Bs in Britain. 1990. p314). *One of the first pubs saved by the Potteries Pub Preservation Group.* The Archer Inn, Wolstanton, which closed 1998; reopened as the New Smithy Inn 2001 (ES May 8 2006 p12).

Railways *Fancy that!* Mow Cop is mentioned in the Flanders and Swann song 'Slow Train' written 1963, lamenting the loss of British stations and railway lines cut in the early 1960s due to the Beeching reforms; the station, along with Scholar Green, was actually in Cheshire.

Relgious non conformity *First wedding in the Wesleyan Chapel, Chell* was between Mr JT Darn of Acres Nook, Goldenhill and Miss Florence Furnival of Waterlow Road, Burslem, in April 1931, although the chapel was erected in 1874 (SA April 18 1931 p10 col 6). *One of the earliest Primitive Methodist preachers.* James Nixon, born Goldenhill, 1785 (BS p330) (OTP p12). *Last sermon of Hugh Bourne (founder of Primitive Methodism)* was perhaps at Newchapel Wesleyan Methodist Chapel, Sunday Jan 18 1852 (SVB p130).

Rhodes, John Harold *Packmoor's hero, V.C., Croix de Guerre medalist.* (1891-1917). Of Mellor St, Packmoor, who stormed an enemy pillbox and captured 9 Germans single-handedly (MR2 p230).

Richardson, Albert Goodwin *One of the founders of the Ceramic Society.* Of Lydon, Dawn Street, Tunstall, principal of AG Richardson & Co. Ltd of Tunstall. Died 1954 (SA Nov 19 1954 p4 col 7).

Roads *First tramcar at Chesterton.* The village was connected to the tram system on July 25 1900 (SA July 28 1900 p4 col 7).

Roman Catholic *The church built by unemployed men.* Sacred Heart RC, Queen's Ave, Tunstall, 1925-30 (ES Your Week Nov 18 2006 p9), founded by Father Patrick Ryan (d1952). *North Staffordshire's first Catholic bishop.* Humphrey Bright, priest in charge at Sacred Heart 1952-; later ranked number two in the hierarchy of the Birmingham Archdiocese (TWWW Nov 1 2008 p3p).

Sailing *First to circumnavigate Britain and Ireland non-stop, single-handed, with no human intervention, fastest to do this, fastest to circumnavigate Ireland.* Peter Keig (b1954), yachtsman, formerly of Wolstanton, residing Belfast by 2008. He achieved the first record in 2000 in 18 days; but his time was beat by Michel Kleinjans with 12 days in 2002. His second record was achieved in 2001 (ES May 31 2008 p33).

Scott, Terry *Last resident of Longbridge Hayes.* Builder of Peel Street (since 1942), the sole operator at a public inquiry in 1990 into whether Newcastle MB council could compulsorily purchase land and property in his street (ES March 3 1990).

Silverdale Colliery *NCB Western Area production record for coal from one face.* Silverdale Colliery in 1976 by producing 21,519 tons; the previous best in the pit was 16,215 tons in March 1973; while the previous record output from a face at any pit was 21,013 tons produced by miners at Lea Hall Colliery, Rugeley, in 1970. In 1976 NCB Chief Sir Derek Ezra proclaimed Silverdale one of Europe's most successful collieries (ES March 4 1976. Oct 19 1976). *Last coal mined at Silverdale Colliery* was mined on Dec 24 1998; it was on show in Silverdale church in 2008.

Smith, David and **Stella** *Family who quit their council house for a tent.* He and she aged 31 and 26 respectively, and their four (or six?) children, who left Wilmot Drive, on the Lower Milehouse estate, because of intimidation and vandalism to their home in summer 1990. The council refused to rehouse them as they had effectively made themselves homeless. Rather than return to the estate the family intended to camp at Trentham Gardens (ES Aug 16 1990).

Sneyd, Edward *Wolstanton's longest-serving vicar.* He served 40 years, 1756-96.

Sport see Athletics, Bowls, Climbing, Cricket, Darts, Football, Golf, Martial Arts, Powerlifting, Sailing, Tennis.

Tennis *'the greatest day in the history of lawn tennis in Staffordshire'.* When top tennis players played an exhibition match at Basford Tennis Club on Monday May 11 1936, in aid of the North Staffordshire Royal Infirmary, according in to Mr J Fielding Taylor, chairman of the Staffordshire Lawn Tennis Association. There was Fred J Perry and HW Austin, Britain's first men's couple. In addition, Miss Kathleen Stammers (Britain's No. 1 woman player along with Miss Dorothy Round), Miss Freda James, Mrs HW Austin, Miss Nancy Lyle, a member of the Wightman Cup team, Mr HH Dickin, and Mr CM Jones, a Kent county player (SA May 16 1936 p3 col 5).

Tunstall *'the pleasantest village' in the Potteries.* Tunstall, according to J Aikin in The Country Around Manchester (1795). *Strange but true!* Tunstall received food parcels from Australia in 1948 after being adopted by a place there called Heidelberg (ES Aug 9 2008 p27).

Tunstall Park *'the finest work in wrought iron in the district - always excepting the magnificent Trentham Hall gates'.* Tunstall Park Gates, officially

A jubilant Linda Whalley after becoming Slimming World's Greatest Loser 2005.

opened June 18 1908. They were made by local ironsmith William Durose, given in memory of Thomas Peake by his children (SA June 20 1908 p8 col 6).

Whalley, Linda *Slimming World's Greatest Loser 2005.* Born 1950/1. Of Whitehouse Rd, Milehouse, losing 20 stone in 4 years

(ES Aug 29 2006 p23p).

Windsor, Miss Delia *Barnsley Music Festival Mezzo-soprano class 1st prize 1928, 1929.* When aged in her 20s, formerly of Goldenhill, later of Fizinghall, Bradford (Staffordshire Weekly Sentinel March 30 1929 p8p).

Wolstanton Colliery *Deepest colliery shaft in England by mid 1960s.* No. 2 shaft of Wolstanton Colliery at 3,432 feet (GBR 1965 p185. 1966) (POP p171) (NUL p176 at 1045 yards); or deepest coal mining shaft in Western Europe and became known as the 'Superpit' of North Staffordshire (Staffordshire Past Track 2006). *National Coal Board national pit safety winner 1981.* Wolstanton Colliery (ES Your Week Aug 12 2006 p6).

Some key abbreviations

A Audley - An Out of the Way, Quiet Place. R Speake. 1974

AAD Ashbourne and the Dove. Published by Dawson & Abbson. 1839

ABUD A History and Guide to St Mary's Parish Church, Uttoxeter. Alan Smith.

AGT A Grand Tour. Neville Malkin. 1976

AHJ Audley Historian. 1995 -

AOPP Audley in Old Picture Postcards. Robert Speake. 1984

APB Archaeological Papers (reprinted from SA). SAH Burne

AVH Alstonefield: A Village History. Jeni Edwards. 1985

BAST Birmingham Archaeology Society Transactions. 1870-

BIOPP2 Biddulph 'Images of England' volume 2. Derek J Wheelhouse. 2005

BOb Burton Observer

BPS Bye-Paths of Staffordshire. Rev Weston E Vernon Yonge. 1911

BS Bibliotheca Staffordiensis. Rupert Simms. 1894

BVC Betley A Village of Contrasts. Robert Speake. 1980

CCSHO Capital Crimes Staffs Hanging Offences. Ros Prince. 1994

CHMS The Old Parish Churches of Staffordshire and the West Midlands County. Mike Salter. 1989

CL Country Life. 1897 -

COS Curiosities of Staffordshire. Ros Prince. 1992

CVH Cheddleton, a Village History. Robert Milner. 1983

D44/A/PO/33 or similar accession record in Staffordshire Record Office

DNB Dictionary of National Biography.

DP Myths and Legends of East Cheshire and the Moors. Doug Pickford. 1991

DPMM Magic Myths and Memories in and around the Peak District. Doug Pickford. 1993

E The Old Road to Endon. Robert Speake. 1974

E&S Express and Star (Wolverhampton newspaper)

ECC Eccleshall. Peter & Margaret Spufford. 1964

EGH England's Ghostly Heritage. Terence Whitaker. 1989

EH The Copper and Lead Mines of Ecton Hill. John A Robey & Lindsey Porter. 1972

ELSONSS Honours & Awards: The Prince of Wales's (North Staffordshire Regiment) 1914-1919. JCJ Elson. 2004

ES Evening Sentinel, since retitled The Sentinel

FLJ Folklore Journal. 1883-1991

FOS Folklore of Staffordshire. Jon Raven. 1978

FS Forgotten Shrines. Dom Bede Camm. 1910

FWNS Famous Women of North Staffordshire. Patricia Pilling. 1999

GBR Guinness Book of Records. 1955 -

GLS Ghosts & Legends of Staffordshire & Black Country. David Bell. 1994

GNHS. Natural History of Staffordshire. Robert Garner. 1844

GNHSS. Natural History of Staffordshire (Supplement). Robert Garner. 1844 HAF

HAOE The Hermits and Anchorites of England. Rotha Mary Clay. 1914

HOC History of Cheadle. R Plant. 1881

HOE History of Etruria. E J D Warrillow. 1952

HOKHistory of Keele. Christopher Harrison. 1986

HOLF A History of Leekfrith (Meerbrook and its Locality). Mary Breeze. 1995

HOLS History of Leek. John Sleigh. 1862. 1883

HOS History of Staffordshire. MW Greenslade and DG Stuart. 1st ed 1965. 3rd ed 1998

HOU History of Uttoxeter. F Redfern. 1865 1886

HPG The Haunted Pub Guide. Guy Lyon Playfair. 1985

IANS Industrial Archaeology of North Staffordshire. WJ Thompson. 1976

IOM Inns of the Midlands. Norman Tiptaft. 1951

IRIM Ipstones Revealed in Memories. The Ipstones Reminiscence Group. 2004

JME This relates to a survey of church memorials by Jeavons, appearing in BAST

JSPS Jottings of a Staffordshire Parson's Son - dedicated to the people of Ilam, Blore Ray and Okeover. John Graves 1998?

KES Kings England Staffordshire. A Mee. 1937

L Longnor, St Bartholomew's Church. 1980

LFYA Leek Fifty Years Ago. Compiled by MH Miller. 1887

LGS Little Guide to Staffordshire or 'Staffordshire.' C Masefield. (1910) 1919 (1923) 1930

LHSB G30 Local History Source Books. Staffs County Council.

LiMe Lichfield Mercury

LMV Most Valiant of Men. Fred Leigh. 1993

LQCL The Limestone Quarries of Caldon Low. Basil Jeuda. 2000

M Madeley. R Nicholls

MCS Staffordshire & The Black Country Murder Casebook. David Bell. 1996

MJW Maer. A Guide to the Village and Church. John Wild. 1987. 1989

MMM Murders, Myths and Monuments of North Staffordshire. WM Jamieson. 1979

MOM Memories of Mayfield. Mayfield Heritage Group. 1993

MR2 A guide to Staffordshire & The Black Country The Potteries & The Peak. Michael Raven. 2004

NCSS Non-Conformist Chapels and Meetinghouses in Staffordshire and Shropshire. The Historical Monuments of England. 1986

NHS Natural History of Staffordshire. Robert

Lightning Source UK Ltd.
Milton Keynes UK
24 July 2010

157430UK00001B/30/P